英譯廣東口語詞典

A Dictionary of Cantonese Colloquialisms In English

關傑才 著

商務印書館

英譯廣東口語詞典

作　者	……	關傑才
責任編輯	……	劉秀英
出　版	……	商務印書館（香港）有限公司
		香港鰂魚涌芬尼街2號D僑英大廈
印　刷	……	美雅印刷製本有限公司
		九龍官塘榮業街6號海濱工業大廈4樓B1
版　次	……	1990年1月第1版
		1995年2月第3次印刷
		© 1990　商務印書館（香港）有限公司
		ISBN 962 07 0131 3　（平裝）
		ISBN 962 07 0109 7　（精裝）

Printed in Hong Kong

目　錄

序言 ･････････････････････････････････････ 關傑才　　i
Preface ･･･････････････････････････ Kwan Kit Choi　　ii
說明 ･･ iv
粵語九聲示意圖 ････････････････････････････････ vi
詞典正文 ･･･････････････････････････････････ 1—254
補遺 ･････････････････････････････････････ 256—316
條目筆劃索引 ･･･････････････････････････ 317—342
條目拼音索引 ･･･････････････････････････ 343—376
編後記 ･････････････････････････････････････ 377

序

　　學習一種外國語較易，但學習一種地方方言則難。因地方方言有地方色彩、傳統習慣等語音問題，此等問題，在廣州話，更爲顯著。

　　廣州話是由古代漢語蛻變而來，因此在日常口語中，仍保留古詞古語，所異者爲音變而已。此外，廣州又爲歷代對外交通通道和貿易商埠，在交接之間，滲入外來語，亦屬自然。這是廣州話詞滙複雜及豐富的原因。

　　余爲廣東人，雖南人北相，但確生於禪而長於穗，且對我廣東俚語，知之不少。猶記於四十年代末，常爲數來穗習粵語之外邦人士，解答彼等偶有所聞而從未有所學之俗諺。彼等更促余擇其常要者，編成講義，藉助彼等學之未逮。余對此提議，唯莞爾而却，蓋爲避嫌，免使彼等教師誤會。

　　由於內地推行普通話，年靑廣東人皆能講普通話，反而對於粵語俗諺，多不理解，遑論泰西外人乎。有見於粵語有其本身歷史因素，且在內在外的溝通上仍不失其效用，遂亦邯鄲學步，進行編寫。況環視書肆中，缺粵諺英譯者。廼於癸亥（一九八三年）因眼疾息景後，着手整理多年所積素材，除英譯外，並盡所知，加以普通話相應詞，使成爲普通話，廣東話，英語三位一體。三年獨耕，卒底於成。

丙寅重九
關傑才序於蓼莪書齋

PREFACE

It is comparatively easy to study a foreign language but it is not so to study a local dialect. This is because local dialects have their own local colours, their own traditional habits and their own pronunciations and these problems are outstanding in Cantonese dialect.

There is no doubt that Cantonese dialect derived from ancient Chinese language and so it still reserves more or less some old sayings and archaic expressions, which we can see in our famous writings, poetries, stories and legends or even fictions. In addition to this, as Canton has become one of the main passages to and from foreign countries for hundreds of years, it is natural that some loanwords have come into the dialect and thus made it rather complicate and rich with words, phrases and glossaries.

Although I am sometimes taken for a northerner or even Japanese, I am a hundred percent Cantonese born at Fatshan (Fushan) in Kwongtung province and brought up in Canton, and have taken interest in my 'mother tongue', especially the colloquial expressions each of which can convey a whole complicated thought in only a simple phrase or sentence.

I can now remember that when I worked as dean of studies for Canton YMCA Middle School, I used to have a chat with some of the foreigners who came to Canton to study Cantonese and they also used to ask me the meanings of the colloquial expressions which they occasionally heard about and which they hadn't been taught in their lessons. This is, of course, not an easy job because I had to choose the most suitable English equivalents to what they were ignorant of. They could converse with Cantonese people but they were far from understanding the slangs, especially those of which only the first parts are given and the second parts are unstated, leaving the puns to the hearer to get what they are actually involved. This kind of slangs, I daresay, still puzzle most of the younger Cantonese people of to-day, not to speak of foreigners.

In view of this, I began to sort out and rectify the materials I had collected for years and set my hand to the work to translate them into English in 1983, only a few weeks after my retirement. Fortunately, the reference books in my possession helped me a lot. Except for those to which I could find no equivalents and had to adopt free translation, I did my best to match as many as possible with homologous English expressions. I, however, sincerely hope that your advices will be given should there be mistakes.

At last, I must add that this book consists of only 2002 entries, but it includes the most common and important ones in our daily conversation.

Kwan Kit Choi

説　明

一、　本書只收錄廣東人日常口頭俚語及歇後語，其中過份粗鄙的，則不在收錄範圍內。除詞意可以望文生義外，盡可能都在每條條目下，加以註譯普通話對應詞及該俚語的來源或背景，倘條目和條目之間有相關意義的，更註明參閱編號，藉作參考。

二、　每條條目，均用音譯、直譯及對譯或意譯。音譯以 "translit."（Transliteration）標明，直譯以 "lit."（literlization）標明。
　　　音譯是根據中華書局出版的"中華新字典"粵語注音方案。在注音（國際音標）右上角的數目字為聲調。"1"代表"高平"；"2"代表"高上"；"3"代表"高去"；"4"代表"低平"；"5"代表"低上"；"6"代表"低去"；"7"代表"高入"；"8"代表"中入"及"9"代表"低入"等粵語九聲聲調（見附"粵語九聲示意圖"）。倘有些為廣東人口語音而非正讀字音時，則按九聲聲調原則而加以變化，務使為口語化，但正讀字音，亦併標明。
　　　直譯是按字譯出。此為最易也最難的一環。尤其是在雙音叠字的條目中，更難兼顧文法及字義。如拘泥於文法，則失諸原意，如拘泥於字義，又失諸文法或語法上的結構。處此兩難情形下，寧取"似通不通，不通似通"的直譯原則了。
　　　對譯是以英語相應詞或稱同義詞而達到信達雅的譯法。因此在翻譯時便極力採用這種方法，且在可能範圍內多譯幾句，以便比較。但粵語有它本身獨有辭藻或表達方式，在英語詞句中，未必有恰當的對應詞，只好以相近意義的或逕以意譯譯出了。

三、　廣東話不少是有音無字，或有字有音而該字（正字）早已廢棄，不復為人所識。為此每條條目所用的字，皆為俗字或近音字。如果間有正字而人所共知時，則在俗字後以"〈 〉"符號一併列出，表示"〈 〉"內的字爲正字。如"鬼鼠"的"鼠"字，實爲"祟"字的粵音，故條目中則寫成"鬼鼠〈祟〉"。又如遇一音兩字時，則以"/"（斜綫）符號表示"或者"的意思。如"鬼揞眼"中的"揞"有作"搇"時，則寫作"鬼揞/搇眼"。

四、　本書所採用的查閱方法，是先根據條目的首字的筆劃數目（多以俗寫筆劃計算），然後再根據該首字的起筆（即我們習慣書寫時的第一筆）在索引中按次翻查。

　　起筆次序爲"一"起（木，扭，去，及平等字屬之），"ノ"起（手，今，年及多等字屬之），"、"起（江，羊，安，放及高等字屬之），"｜"起（睇，啱，口，量，臨及過等字屬之），"㇆"起（陪，蛋，也，門及發等字屬之）及"ㄴ"起（將，嫌，縮及收等字屬之）。例如"冤字"條目中的"冤"字爲十劃，起筆爲"、"，在索引先查出十劃，再找"、"起，當能查出該條條目編號爲11953了。

五、　鑒於不少廣東俚語寫法並沒正統，如在"刁眼角"條目中的"刁"字，有人寫"刁"或"丟"。"刁"和"丟"不但筆劃不同，而起筆亦異，因此本書又提供條目首字音查索引（用一般英文拼音）。例如"刁"和"丟"的拼音都是"diu"，按字母次序翻查，即可查出。

六、　本書所用符號有：
1.　／　號表示"或者"。即／號前後的字或句子，都可替換使用。
2.　〈　〉號表示該符號內的字爲正字。
3.　[　]　號表示該符號內的字，可有可無。
4.　「　」號表示該符號內的字爲諧音字。
5.　(　)　號表示該符號內的字或句子爲解釋或補充。
6.　〔　〕　號表示註釋。
7.　──　號表示該符號後面的字或句爲前句的歇後語。

粵語九聲示意圖

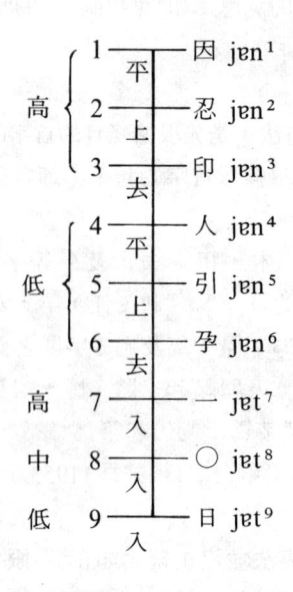

```
      ┌ 1 ─平── 因 jɐn¹
   高 ┤ 2 ─上── 忍 jɐn²
      └ 3 ─去── 印 jɐn³

      ┌ 4 ─平── 人 jɐn⁴
   低 ┤ 5 ─上── 引 jɐn⁵
      └ 6 ─去── 孕 jɐn⁶

   高   7 ─入── 一 jɐt⁷
   中   8 ─入── ○ jɐt⁸
   低   9 ─入── 日 jɐt⁹
```

註：○為有音無字，音在一與日之間。

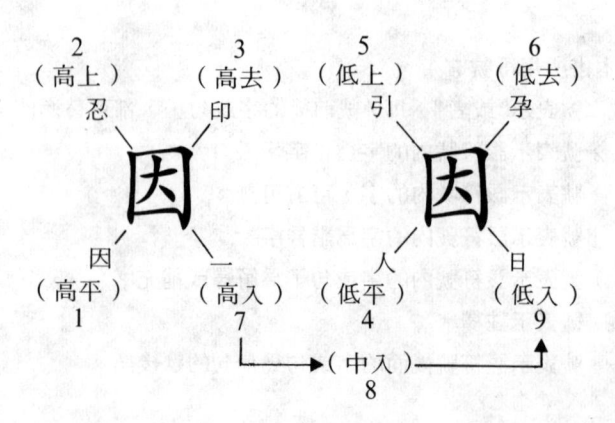

```
      2              3              5              6
    （高上）       （高去）       （低上）       （低去）
      忍             印             引             孕

           因                            因

      因             一             人             日
    （高平）       （高入）       （低平）       （低入）
      1              7              4              9
                         →（中入）←
                             8
```

一 畫

0001 一人計短，二人計長
jɐt⁷ jɐn⁴ gɐi³ dyn², ji⁶ jɐn⁴ gɐi³ tsœŋ⁴ (translit.)
One man's device is short, two men's is long. (lit.)
Two heads are better than one.
Four eyes see more than one.
〔註〕相當"三個臭皮匠合成一個諸葛亮"。

0002 一人做事一人當
jɐt⁷ jɐn⁴ dzou⁶ si⁶ jɐt⁷ jɐn⁴ dɔŋ¹ (translit.)
A man does, a man undertakes. (lit.)
One must bear the consequences of one's own act.

0003 一人得道，雞犬升天
jɐt⁷ jɐn⁴ dɐk⁷ dou⁶, gei¹ hyn² siŋ¹ tin¹ (translit.)
When a man becomes immortal, all his hens and dogs ascend to heaven. (lit.)
When a man gets to the top, all his friends and relatives get there with him.

0004 一了百了
jɐt⁷ liu⁵ bak⁸ liu⁵ (translit.)
One finished and a hundred also finished. (lit.)
Death pays all debts.
Do away with the main trouble and the others will end with it.

0005 一刀兩斷
jɐt⁷ dou¹ lœŋ⁵ dyn⁶ (translit.)
One knife cuts it into two. (lit.)
Make a clean break with somebody.
Cut the connection with somebody.
Have done with somebody.

0006 一山不能藏二虎
jɐt⁷ san³ bɐt⁷ nɐŋ⁴ tsɔŋ⁴ ji⁶ fu² (translit.)
A mountain cannot hide two tigers. (lit.)
At daggers drawn.
Have an exclusive attitude.

0007 一口咬定/實
jɐt⁷ hau² ŋau⁵ diŋ⁶/sɐt⁹ (translit.)
One bite, it is fixed. (lit.)
Speak in an assertive tone.
To insist on saying.

0008 一子錯，滿盤皆落索
jɐt⁷ dzi² tsɔ³, mun⁵ pun⁴ gɐi¹ lɔk⁹ sɔk⁸ (translit.)
One careless move makes the whole game of chess get confused. (lit.)
One careless move loses the whole game.
A wrong step causes a masty tumble.
〔註〕相當於"一着不慎，滿盤皆輸"。

0009 一弓射兩箭
jɐt⁷ guŋ¹ sɛ⁶ lœŋ⁵ dzin³ (translit.)
A bow shoots two arrows. (lit.)
Kill two birds with one stone.
〔註〕相當於"一箭雙雕"。

0010 一不做，二不休
jɐt⁷ bɐt⁷ dzou⁶, ji⁶ bɐt⁷ jɐu¹ (translit.)
The first doesn't do it, the second doesn't stop it. (lit.)
In for a penny, in for a pound.
As well be hanged for a sheep as for a lamb.

0011 一手一脚
jɐt⁷ sɐu² jɐt⁷ gœk⁸ (translit.)
One hand and one foot. (lit.)
Go on with something all by oneself.

0012 一天光晒
jɐt⁷ tin¹ gwɔŋ¹ sai³ (translit.)
The sky becomes bright. (lit.)
Be happy to see the clouds roll by.
Be happy to see the silver lining of the cloud.
〔註〕形容霧霾盡散，重睹光明。參閱"守得雲開見月明"（0657）條。

0013 一生兒女債，半世老婆奴
jɐt⁷ san¹ (sɐŋ¹) ji⁴ nœy⁵ dzai³, bun³ sɐi³ lou⁵ pɔ⁴ nou⁴ (translit.)
The whole life is full of sons' and daughters' debts; half a life is a slave for wife. (lit.)
A man husbands his family.
a wife and children are a man's burdens.
〔註〕指男子要負起家庭重擔。

0014 一件還一件
jɐt⁷ gin⁶ wan⁴ jɐt⁷ gin⁶ (translit.)
One piece is still one piece. (lit.)
This is this and that is that.
These two cases should be handled respectively.
〔註〕指事情不能混淆，應分別處理。參閱"一筆還一筆"（0050）條。

0015 一死了之
jɐt⁷ sei² liu⁵ dzi¹ (translit.)
A death finishes all. (lit.)
Death pays all debts.
Death quits all scores.

0016 一次生，兩次熟
jɐt⁷ tsi³ saŋ¹, lœŋ⁵ tsi³ suk⁹ (translit.)
Strangers the first time, but friends the second time. (lit.)
Soon get to know each other.
Strangers at first, friends later on.
Be clumsy at first but skilful later on.

0017 一字咁淺
jɐt⁷ dzi⁶ gɐm³ tsin² (trans-

lit.)
As simple as the character '一
(one)'. (lit.)
Be as easy as ABC.
〔註〕形容事情非常簡單。

0018 一竹篙打死一船人
jɐt⁷ dzuk¹ gou¹ da² sei³ jɐt⁷
syn⁴ jɐn⁴. (translit.)
Beat a whole boat's people to
death with a bamboo pole.
(lit.)
Take one for all.
Completely negate all with a word.
Knock all down at one stroke.
〔註〕表示"一棍子統統打死"或"以一概全"的意思，但通常用作否定語式來表示不能輕率推論或不可以一概全。
One swallow does not make a summer.
Can't take a bad one for all.

0019 一言爲定
jɐt⁷ jin⁴ wei⁴ diŋ⁶ (translit.)
One word fixes it.
A bargain is a bargain.
That's a deal.
You've got a deal.

0020 一言難盡
jɐt⁷ jin⁴ nan⁴ dzœn⁶ (translit.)
One word can't say all. (lit.)
It's a long story.
Can't put all in a word.

0021 一身蟻
jɐt⁷ sɐn¹ ŋai⁵ (translit.)

The whole body is covered with
ants. (lit.)
Subject oneself to annoyance.
Get into trouble.
〔註〕形容招惹了不少麻煩。

0022 一沉百踩
jɐt⁷ tsɐm⁴ bak⁸ tsɐi² (translit.)
One man sinks and a hundred
men will trample him. (lit.)
Everyone hits a man who is down.
Once one meets with a crushing defeat, everybody joins to condemn him.
〔註〕比喻當一個人一旦失敗，便受歧視。相當於"牆倒衆人推"。

0023 一波三折
jɐt⁷ bɔ¹ sam¹ dzit⁸ (translit.)
One wave with three curves. (lit.)
Meet with difficulties one after the other.
Strike one snag after another.

0024 一波未平，一波又起
jɐt⁷ bɔ¹ mei⁶ piŋ⁴, jɐt⁷ bɔ¹
jɐu⁶ hei² (translit.)
Before a wave comes down,
another arises. (lit.)
Troubles come one after another.

0025 一物治一物，糯米治木蝨
jɐt⁷ mɐt⁹ dzi⁶ jɐt⁷ mɐt⁹, nɔ⁶
mɐi⁵ dzi⁶ muk⁹ sɐt⁷
(translit.)

One thing controls another thing; glutinous rice controls bed-bugs. (lit.)
Everything has its vanquisher.
〔註〕相當於一物降一物。

0026　一枝公
jɐt⁷ dzi¹ guŋ¹　(translit.)
Only one man.　(lit.)
Be all aone.
By oneself.
〔註〕一個人（詼諧説法，指男性），相當於"光棍兒一個"。

0027　一面屁
jɐt⁷ min⁶ pei³　(translit.)
A faceful of wind from bowels. (lit.)
Feel ashamed of (having been abused).
〔註〕表示一鼻子灰或被人罵得滿面羞慚的意思。

0028　一哥
jɐt⁷ gɔ¹　(translit.)
Elder brother the first.　(lit.)
A man of men.
The leader.
A man of mark.
A man who seeks to do others down.
〔註〕指男性的第一把手或爭強好勝的人。

0029　一隻乙噉
jɐt⁷ dzɛk⁸ jyt⁹ gɐm²　(translit.)
Be like a duckling.　(lit.)
Be tired like a dog.
Be out of spirits.

〔註〕形容人在工作後累得很的樣子。

0030　一隻手掌拍唔響
jɐt⁷ dzɛk⁸ sɐu² dzœŋ² pak⁸ m⁴ hœn²　(translit.)
One palm can not clap a sound. (lit.)
It needs two to make a quarrel.
〔註〕相當於"一個巴掌拍不響"。

0031　一隻屐噉
jɐt⁷ dzɛk⁸ kɛk⁹ gɐm²　(translit.)
Be like one of clogs.　(lit.)
Be crestfallen.
〔註〕形容人垂頭喪氣的樣子。

0032　一陣間
jɐt⁷ dzɐn⁶ gan¹　(translit.)
A moment.　(lit.)
A little while.
In a moment.
One moment
〔註〕即一會兒。

0033　一理通，百理明
jɐt⁷ lei⁵ tuŋ¹, bak⁸ lei⁵ miŋ⁴ (translit.)
One reason is understood and a hundred reasons are also understood.　(lit.)
Have a profound grasp of the basic principle and everything is within one's grasp.

0034　一動不如一靜
jɐt⁷ duŋ⁶ bɐt⁷ jy⁴ jɐt⁷ dziŋ⁶ (translit.)
A movement is not so good as a repose.　(lit.)

You may go farther and fare worse.
It would be better not to move about.

0035 一戚都冇
jɐt⁷ duŋ⁶ dou¹ mou⁵ (translit.)
Have not even a pile. (lit.)
Have no cards to play.
Be at one's wit's end.
Be not a penny worth.
〔註〕表示沒有辦法或一文不值。

0036 一清二楚
jɐt⁷ tsiŋ¹ ji⁶ tsɔ² (translit.)
One cleaning and two distictions. (lit.)
Be as plain as noonday.
Be as clear as day.

0037 一時一樣
jɐt⁷ si⁴ jɐt⁷ jœŋ⁶ (translit.)
One time one shape. (lit.)
Change one's mind as time goes on.
Have an unstable temperament.
Be unsteady in mind.
〔註〕參閱"五時花，六時變"條（0304）。

0038 一家皮宜，兩家着數
jɐt⁷ ga¹ pei⁴ ji⁴, lœŋ⁵ ga¹ dzœk⁶ sou³ (translit.)
Advantage to one family and to two families as well. (lit.)
Not only does it profit oneself but both sides.
〔註〕形容做一件事對兩方面都有好處。

0039 一家唔知一家事
jɐt⁷ ga¹ m⁴ dzi¹ jɐt⁷ ga¹ si⁶ (translit.)
Our family does not know another family's affairs. (lit.)
No one knows what the other side of the world looks like.
〔註〕即一家不知一家事。參閱"唔同床唔知被爛"條（1219）。

0040 一個做好，一個做醜
jɐt⁷ gɔ³ dzou⁶ hou², jɐt⁷ gɔ³ dzou⁶ tsɐu² (translit.)
One does good and another does bad. (lit.)
One puts out an iron hand and another, a velet glove.
〔註〕相當於"一個唱紅臉，一個唱白臉"。

0041 一個够本，兩個有利
jɐt⁷ gɔ³ gɐu³ bun², lœn⁵ gɔ³ jɐu⁵ lei⁶ (translit.)
One is enough for the capital and two make profit. (lit.)
Sell one's life dearly.

0042 一個餅印噉
jɐt⁷ gɔ³ bɐŋ² jɐn³ gɐm² (translit.)
Be out of the same cake-mould. (lit.)
Be as like as two peas.
Be the spitting image of...
〔註〕形容兩個人或物十分相像。

0043 一啖砂糖一啖屎
jɐt⁷ dam⁶ sa¹ tɔŋ⁴ jɐt⁷ dam⁶ si² (translit.)
A swallow of sugar and a

swallow of dung. (lit.)
With an iron hand in velvet glove.
Temper justice with mercy.
〔註〕形容"恩威並施"的態度。

0044 一部通書睇到老
jɐt⁷ bou⁶ tuŋ¹ sy¹ tai² dou³ lou⁵ (translit.)
Read only an almanac through life. (lit.)
Follow the beaten track.
Go on in the same old rut.
Stick in the mud.
〔註〕指做人不識變通。

0045 一條鎖匙唔聞聲，兩條鎖匙冷冷響。
jɐt⁷ tiu⁴ so² si⁴ m⁴ mɐn⁴ sɛŋ¹, lœŋ⁵ tiu⁴ so² si⁴ laŋ¹ laŋ¹ hœn² (translit.)
One key makes no sound, but two keys sound loudly. (lit.)
A bell without striker never rings by itself.
Two women mating with a man are great quarrellers.
〔註〕比喻夫婦之間不容第三者，否則難免齟齬頻生了。

0046 一眼關七
jɐt⁷ ŋan⁵ gwan¹ tsɐt⁷ (translit.)
An eye watches seven. (lit.)
Be all eyes.
Keep one's eyes open.
Keep one's eyes polished.
〔註〕相當於"眼觀六路"。

0047 一場歡喜一場空
jɐt⁷ tsœŋ⁴ fun¹ hei² jɐt⁷ tsœn⁴ hung¹ (translit.)
Once of happiness and once of emptiness. (lit.)
Draw water with a sieve.

0048 一朝天子一朝臣
jɐt⁷ tsiu⁴ tin¹ dzi² jɐt⁷ tsiu⁴ sɛn⁴ (translit.)
Every new emperor has his own new courtiers. (lit.)
A new chief brings in his own trusted followers.
A new nail drives out another.

0049 一筆勾銷
jɐt⁷ bɐt⁷ ŋɐu¹ siu¹ (translit.)
One stroke of the pen cancels all. (lit.)
Write off at a stroke.
Annul all.

0050 一筆還一筆
jɐt⁷ bɐt⁷ wan⁴ jɐt⁷ bɐt⁷ (translit.)
One pen is still one pen. (lit.)
This is this and that is that; both should not get tangled.
These two sums/terms should be managed respectively.
〔註〕基本上和"一件還一件"相同，但這較着重於金錢方面，而"一件還一件"則着重於事情方面。參閱該條（0014）。

0051 一傳十，十傳百
jɐt⁷ tsyn⁴ sɐp⁹, sɐp⁹ tsyn⁴ bak⁸ (translit.)

One person spreads to ten and ten persons spread to a hundred. (lit.)
Spread from mouth to mouth.

0052　一網打盡
jɐt⁷ mɔŋ⁵ da² dzɐn⁶　(translit.)
One net gets all. (lit.)
Sweep everything into one's net.
Make a clean sweep.

0053　一腳牛屎
jɐt⁷ gœk⁸ nɐu⁴ si²　(translit.)
One foot is full of cow's dung. (lit.)
Be country-born.
A country cousin.
〔註〕諷刺別人土氣。

0054　一腳踢
jɐt⁷ gœk⁸ tɛk⁸　(translit.)
Kick with one foot. (lit.)
Do everything alone.
Do all jobs without an assistant.
〔註〕指獨自做某事，或"全包了"的意思。

0055　一腳踏兩船
jɐt⁷ gœk⁸ dap⁶ lœŋ⁵ syn⁴ (translit.)
One foot stands on two boats. (lit.)
Play both ends against the middle.
Seek favour with opposing parties.
Attempt to make profit in two ways.

0056　一模一樣
jɐt⁷ mou⁴ jɐt⁷ jœŋ⁶　(translit.)
One mould and one shape. (lit.)
Be as like as two peas.
Be exactly alike.
〔註〕參閱"一個餅印噉"條（0042）。

0057　一轆木噉
jɐt⁷ luk¹ muk⁶ gɐm²　(translit.)
Be like a log. (lit.)
Be awkward in one's movement.
〔註〕比喻呆板，不靈活，木頭人似的。

0058　一樣米養百樣人
jɐt⁷ jœŋ⁶ mɐi⁵ jœŋ⁵ bak⁸ jœŋ⁶ jɐn⁴　(translit.)
One kind of rice feeds hundred kinds of men. (lit.)
Brothers born of the same mother differ from each other in characters.
Many men, many minds.

0059　一輪嘴
jɐt⁷ lœn² dzœy²　(translit.)
A wheel of mouths. (lit.)
Wag one's tongue.
〔註〕形容人説話滔滔不絶。

0060　一磚豆腐想升仙
jɐt⁷ dzyn¹ dɐu⁶ fu⁶ sœŋ² siŋ¹ sin¹　(translit.)
After eating a cake of beancurd, one wants to ascend to heaven to become a supernatural being. (lit.)

Be eager to attain the highest position in one step.
Be anxious to accomplish one's purpose in one move.
〔註〕指某些人妄想求成功捷徑，相當於"妄想一步登天"。

0061　一擔擔
jɐt⁷ dam³ dam¹　(translit.)
A carrying pole with two loads on it.　(lit.)
Two of a kind come together.
There is not much to choose between the two.
Six of one and half-a-dozen of the other.
〔註〕表示同一類，半斤八兩，或臭味相投的意思，多含貶義。

0062　一頭霧水
jɐt⁷ tɐu⁴ mou⁶ sœy²　(translit.)
A headful of dews.　(lit.)
Make neither head nor tail of something.
Be lost in a fog.
Be buried at sea.
Smile in a mist of tears.
〔註〕相當於"糊裏糊塗"或"摸不着頭腦"。

0063　一講曹操，曹操就到
jɐt⁷ gɔŋ² tsou⁴ tsou¹, tsou⁴ tsou¹ dzɐu⁶ dou³　(translit.)
At the mention of Tsou Tsou*, Tsou Tsou arrives.　(lit.)
(*Tsou Tsou was the Prime Minister of the state of Wei (魏) in the period of Three Kingdoms 220-265 A.D.)
Talk of the devil and he will appear.
〔註〕參閱"日頭唔好講人，夜晚唔好講神"條（0366）。

0064　一蟹不如一蟹
jɐt⁷ hai⁵ bɐt⁷ jy⁴ jɐt⁷ hai⁵　(translit.)
Each crab is worse than the one before.　(lit.)
Go from bad to worse.
From the smoke into the smother.
Each one is worse than the last.
〔註〕相當於"每況愈下"。

0065　一嚿飯噉
jɐt⁷ gɐu⁶ fan⁶ gɐm²　(translit.)
Be like a clump of cooked-rice.　(lit.)
Be as stupid as an owl.
Be fat witted.
〔註〕形容人笨拙無能或不機靈；相當於"飯桶"。

0066　一鑊泡
jɐt⁷ wɔk⁹ pou⁵　(translit.)
A frying-pan of foam.　(lit.)
Be irremediable.
Be unmanageable.
〔註〕比喻事情糟到不可收拾。

0067　一鑊撟起
jɐt⁷ wɔk⁹ kiu⁵ hei²　(translit.)
Scratch up with a frying-pan.　(lit.)

Fall to the ground.
Be forced to declare bankcruptcy.
〔註〕表示徹底失敗或被迫破產。

0068　一鑊熟
jɐt⁷ wɔk⁹ suk⁹　(translit.)
Be well-done in one frying-pan. (lit.)
Not a single one survives.
Be destroyed lock, stock and barrel.
Make a clean sweep of...
〔註〕形容一伙人中無一倖免。

二　畫

0069　二一添作五
ji⁶ jɐt⁷ tim¹ dzɔk⁸ ŋ⁵　(translit.)
Divide ten by two to get five. (lit.)
Go fifty-fifty.
Go halves with somebody.
〔註〕表示均分兩份的意思。

0070　二口六面
ji⁶ hɐu² luk⁶ min⁶　(translit.)
Two mouths and six faces. (lit.)
Talk face to face.
Have a face-to-face talk.
〔註〕指面對面地談。也有人說"三口六面"。

0071　二仔底 —— 死跟
ji⁶ dzɐi² dɐi²—sei² gɐn¹ (translit.)
The bottom card is '2',— following to die. (lit.)
Stick like a limpet.
〔註〕"二仔底"原指人沒有什麼真本領，所以別人做什麼，他也做什麼。

0072　二世祖
ji⁶ sɐi³ dzou²　(translit.)
An ancestral inheritor of the second generation. (lit.)
A fop.
〔註〕指不務正業，揮霍祖業的敗家子。

0073　二叔公割禾 —— 望下撅
ji⁶ suk⁷ guŋ¹ gɔt⁸ wɔ⁴—mɔŋ⁶ ha⁶ kyt⁹　(translit.)
Great Uncle II cuts paddies.— He hopes for the second half part. (lit.)
Hope for the future.
Hope for the coming profit.
〔註〕意即希望將來。

0074　十人生九品
sɐp⁹ jɐn⁴ sɐn¹ gɐu² bɐn²　(translit.)
Ten men have nine characters. (lit.)
Brothers born of the same mother differ from each other in characters.
Many men, many minds.
〔註〕形容每個人的性格和想法都不一樣。參閱"一樣米養百樣人"條（0058）。

0075 十三點
sɐp⁹ sam¹ dim² (translit.)
Thirteen o'clock. (lit.)
Be more deranged than normal.

0076 十月芥菜 —— 起心
sɐp⁹ jyt⁹ gai³ tsɔi³—hei² sɐm¹ (translit.)
Tenth month's mustard plant — the heart grows. (lit.)
Begin to be fond of love affairs.
Hope to get married in haste.
Begin to know love affair.
〔註〕相當於"臘月的白菜 ——凍（動）了心"，意指少男少女已懂男女間的事。

0077 十五個銅錢分兩份——七又唔係，八又唔係
sɐp⁹ ŋ⁵ gɔ³ tuŋ⁴ tsin⁴ fɐn¹ lœn⁵ fɐn⁶—tsɐt⁷ jɐu⁶ m⁴ hɐi⁶, bat⁸ jɐu⁶ m⁴ hɐi⁶ (translit.)
Divide fifteen copper cashes into two equal parts,—it is neither seven nor eight. (lit.)
Cannot make up one's mind.
One's mind goes pit-a-pat.
Be greatly upset.
〔註〕指"拿不定主意"。參閱"三心兩意"（0139），"心多多"（0345）及"寡母婆咁多心"（1719）各條。

0078 十年唔逢一閏
sɐp⁹ nin⁴ ŋ⁴ fuŋ⁴ jɐt⁷ jœn⁶ (translit.)
Not to meet a leap year in ten years. (lit.)
Once in a blue moon.
It is a chance of lifetime.
〔註〕形容稀有或罕見。

0079 十年唔耕，九年唔種
sɐp⁹ nin⁴ ŋ⁴ gaŋ¹, gɐu² nin⁴ ŋ⁴ dzuŋ³ (translit.)
Have neither ploughed for ten years nor planted for nine years. (lit.)
Be out of practice [on something].
Seldom or never make a practice [of something].
〔註〕指久不練習或"荒疏"。參閱"丟生晒"（0622）及"丟疏咗"（0624）各條。

0080 十指孖埋
sɐp⁹ dzi² ma¹ mai⁴ (translit.)
Ten fingers stick together. (lit.)
One's fingers are all thumbs.
〔註〕形容笨手笨腳的樣子。

0081 十拿九穩
sɐp⁹ na⁴ gɐu² wɐn² (translit.)
Grasp ten and assure nine. (lit.)
With an ace of success.
Hold the cards in one's hand.
Only one out of ten would be missed.
Safe bind, safe found.
It's dollars to buttons.

0082 十隻手指有長短
sɐp⁹ dzɛk⁸ sɐu² dzi² jɐu⁵

tsœn⁴ dyn² (translit.)
Among ten fingers, there are long ones and short ones. (lit.)
Every bean has its black.
No rose without a thorn.
Not all roses.
〔註〕形容人或物難免有缺點。

0083 十個甕缸九個蓋
sɐp⁹ gɔ³ uŋ³ gɔŋ¹ gɐu² gɔ³ gɔi³ (translit.)
Ten big earthen water-jars with nine lids. (lit.)
Fail to make both ends meet.
Run into debt to repay debts.
〔註〕比喻收支無法相抵或過着借債還債的生活。相當於"挖東牆補西牆"。

0084 十畫都未有一撇
sɐp⁹ wak⁹ dou¹ mei⁶ jɐu⁵ jɐt⁷ pit⁸ (translit.)
There is not a left-falling stroke in ten strokes yet. (lit.)
Even the slightest sign of the commencement of something is still unseen.
〔註〕相當於"八字還沒一撇兒"。

0085 丁文食件
diŋ¹ mɐn¹ sik⁹ gin⁶ (translit.)
Buy one and eat one. (lit.)
Pay for one first and then another.
Pay by the piece.
〔註〕表示論件付值或付酬的意思。

0086 七七八八
tsɐt⁷ tsɐt⁷ bat⁸ bat⁸ (translit.)
Seventy and eighty percent. (lit.)
The great majority of something.

0087 七老八十
tsɐt⁷ lou⁵ bat⁸ sɐp⁹ (translit.)
Seventy or eighty years old. (lit.)
Live to a great age.
〔註〕指人上了年紀。

0088 七國咁亂
tsɐt⁷ gwɔk⁸ gɐm³ lyn⁶ (translit.)
Be as disorderly as the seven warring states. (lit.)
Be in a disorderly situation.
〔註〕形容地方亂得一塌糊塗。

0089 七零八落
tsɐt⁷ liŋ⁴ bat⁸ lɔk⁹ (translit.)
Seven pieces and eight drops. (lit.)
Go to rack and manger.
Scattered here and there.
In disorder.

0090 七嘴八舌
tsɐt⁷ dzœy² bat⁸ sit⁹ (translit.)
Seven mouths and eight tongues. (lit.)
All are talking at once.
Cause a hot discussion with each other at the same time.

0091 七竅生煙
tsɐt⁷ hiu³ (kiu³) saŋ¹ jin¹ (translit.)
The seven cavitiess are spurting smoke. (lit.)
Fly into a rage.
Bluster oneself into anger.
See red.

0092 人一世，物一世
jɐn⁴ jɐt⁷ sɐi³, mɐt⁹ jɐt⁷ sɐi³ (translit.)
The whole life of a man and the whole life of a thing. (lit.)
Seldom or never in life is it to exist with such a thing.
Can hardly meet with such a wonderwork in life.
〔註〕形容遇上人生難見的事物或難得一見的奇觀等等時，須抓緊時機去看，去嘗試。

0093 人山人海
jɐn⁴ san¹ jɐn⁴ hoi² (translit.)
People mountain people sea. (lit.)
A sea of faces.
Huge crowd of people.

0094 人比人，比死人
jɐn⁴ bei² jɐn⁴, bei² sei² jɐn⁴ (translit.)
When a man compares himself with another person, the comparision will cause death. (lit.)
Comparisions are odious.
〔註〕表示不能拿自己較劣處境跟別人的較優境遇相比。

0095 人心不足蛇吞象
jɐn⁴ sɐm¹ bɐt⁷ dzuk⁷ sɛ⁴ tɐn¹ dzœŋ⁶ (translit.)
A man with a discontented heart is like the snake which wants to swallow up an elephant. (lit.)
No man is contented with his own possessions.
Man is greedy for gains.
Millionaires always think they ought to be billionaires.
〔註〕即貪得無饜。

0096 人心肉做
jɐn⁴ sɐm¹ juk⁹ dzou⁶ (translit.)
A man's heart is made of flesh. (lit.)
Have a good conscience.
Be conscientious.
〔註〕表示憑著良心的意思。

0097 人心隔肚皮
jɐn⁴ sɐm¹ gak⁸ tou⁵ pei⁴ (translit.)
A person's heart is separated by the skin of belly. (lit.)
No one can read the mind of another person.
〔註〕即人心難測。

0098 人生路不熟
jɐn⁴ saŋ¹ lou⁶ bɐt⁷ suk⁹ (translit.)
The man is new and the road is unknown. (lit.)
Be a complete stranger.

〔註〕相當於"人地生疏"。

0099 人在人情在
jɐn⁴ dzɔi⁶ jɐn⁴ tsiŋ⁴ dzɔi⁶ (translit.)
While a man exists, his sensibilities also exist. (lit.)
While a man lives, his favours are remembered.

0100 人有三衰六旺
jɐn⁴ jɐu⁵ sam¹ sœy¹ luk⁹ wɔŋ⁶ (translit.)
A man has three decling fortunes and six prosperities. (lit.)
Man sometimes suffers misfortunes and sometimes has strokes of good fortune.
〔註〕表示人生有不如意之時,也有得意的日子。

0101 人有三急
jɐn⁴ jɐu⁵ sam¹ gɐp¹ (translit.)
A man has three emergencies. (lit.)
Have one's needs to do.
〔註〕這是表示要上廁所去的委婉語。

0102 人有失手,馬有失蹄
jɐn⁴ jɐu⁵ sɐt⁷ sɐu² , ma⁵ jɐu⁵ sɐt⁷ tɐi⁴ (translit.)
A man may have a slip of hand, a horse may have a slip of hoof. (lit.)
Even a sharp shooter may miss the target.
There is always many a slip-up in a man's job.

0103 人同此心,心同此理
jɐn⁴ tuŋ⁴ dzi² sɐm¹ , sɐm¹ tuŋ⁴ dzi² lei⁵ (translit.)
Every man has the same mind and every mind has the same reason. (lit.)
Everybody feels the same.

0104 人多手腳亂
jɐn⁴ dɔ¹ sɐu² gœk⁸ lyn⁶ (translit.)
More men make hands and feet confused. (lit.)
Too many cooks spoil the broth.

0105 人多好做作
jɐn⁴ dɔ¹ hou² dzou⁶ dzɔk⁸ (translit.)
More men can do better. (lit.)
Many hands make light work.

0106 人老心不老
jɐn⁴ lou⁵ sɐm¹ bɐt⁷ lou⁵ (translit.)
Old but young in the heart. (lit.)
Be young in spirit for one's old age.
An old demon of lust.
〔註〕形容人不因上了年紀而感衰老。

0107 人老精,鬼老靈
jɐn⁴ lou⁵ dzɛiŋ¹ , gwɐi² lou⁵ lɛŋ⁴ (translit.)
An old man is wise and an old ghost is efficacious. (lit.)

Experience teaches.
Old birds are not so easily caught with chaff.
A fall into the pit, a gain in your wit.
〔註〕相當於"薑是老的辣"。參閱"大一歲，長一智"條（0158）。

0108 人爭一口氣，佛爭一爐香
jɐn⁴ dzɐŋ¹ jɐt⁷ hɐu² hei³, fɐt⁹ dzɐŋ¹ jɐt⁷ lou⁴ hœŋ¹ (translit.)
A man strives for a mouthful of air; Buddha strives for a pot of incense-sticks. (lit.)
Make a good show of oneself.
Try to win credit for...
Try to bring credit to...

0109 人怕出名豬怕壯
jɐn⁴ pa³ tsœt⁷ mɛŋ⁴ dzy¹ pa³ dzɔŋ³ (translit.)
Man is afraid to be well-known and pigs are afraid to become fat. (lit.)
Fame brings trouble.

0110 人要衣裝，佛要金裝
jɐn⁴ jiu³ ji¹ dzɔŋ¹, fɐt⁹ jiu³ gɐm¹ dzɔŋ¹ (translit.)
A man needs clothes to look nicer; Buddha needs gold-foil to look more magnificent. (lit.)
Fine feathers make fine birds.
The tailor makes the man.

0111 人急智生
jɐn⁴ gɐp⁷ dzi³ saŋ¹ (translit.)

The wisdom comes out when a man worries. (lit.)
Have quick wits in an emergency.

0112 人面獸心
jɐn⁴ min⁶ sɐu³ sɐm¹ (translit.)
A man's face with a beast heart. (lit.)
A wolf in lamb's skin.

0113 人情世故
jɐn⁴ tsiŋ⁴ sɐi³ gu³ (translit.)
Human feelings and the world affairs. (lit.)
The ways of the world.
Worldly wisdom.
〔註〕泛指做人的道理。

0114 人情物理
jɐn⁴ tsiŋ⁴ mɐt⁹ lei⁵ (translit.)
Human feelings and the reasons of things. (lit.)
Gifts in general.
〔註〕指禮物。

0115 人細鬼大
jɐn⁴ sɐi³ gwɐi² dai⁶ (translit.)
A small boy has the nature of a big ghost. (lit.)
Be young but tricksy.
Be young but mature.
〔註〕比喻小孩子年紀雖輕但已成熟或詭計多端。

0116 人望高處，水往低流
jɐn⁴ mɔŋ⁶ gou¹ tsy³, sœy² mɔŋ⁶ dai¹ lɐu⁴ (translit.)

Men hope for the heights; water flows downwards. (lit.)
Everybody hopes to climax himself.
No priestling, small thought he may be, but wishes someday Pope to be.
It is everybody's hope to be promoted.
〔註〕比喻人總要往上爬。

0117　人渣
jɐn⁴ dza¹　(translit.)
Dregs of men. (lit.)
A scum of a community.
A black sheep.
One of the dregs of society.
〔註〕指社會渣滓，敗類。

0118　人無千日好
jɐn⁴ mou⁴ tsin¹ jɐt⁹ hou²　(translit.)
A man has not a thousand good days. (lit.)
No man is fortunate forever and ever.
A man cannot tempt his own fate.
No man can always have fortune on his side.

0119　人算不如天算
jɐn⁴ syn³ bɐt⁷ jy⁴ tin¹ syn³　(translit.)
A man's calculation is not so good as that of heaven. (lit.)
Man proposes, God disposes.
An ounce of luck is better than a pound of wisdom.
The Fates decide all.

0120　人窮志不窮
jɐn⁴ kun⁴ ji³ bɐt⁷ kun⁴　(translit.)
The man is poor but his aspiration is high.
Be poor but ambitious.

0121　人窮志短
jɐn⁴ kun⁴ ji³ dyn²　(translit.)
The man is poor and so his ambition is short. (lit.)
Humble oneself for being poor.

0122　人講你又講
jɐn⁴ gɔŋ² nei⁵ jɐu⁶ gɔŋ²　(translit.)
You say what other people have said. (lit.)
Echo the statement of others.
You are a parrot.

0123　入境問禁
jɐp⁹ giŋ² mɐn⁴ gɐm³　(translit.)
Entering a country, one has to ask the prohibitions of the country. (lit.)
Do in Rome as the Romans do.

0124　入鄉隨俗，出水隨灣
jɐp⁹ hœŋ¹ tsœy⁴ dzuk⁹; tsœt⁷ sœy² tsœy⁴ wan¹　(translit.)
Entering a village, one should follow the traditional habits of the village; coming out of the river, one should follow the curves of the bay. (lit.)

二畫

Do in Rome as The Romans do.

0125　八十歲番頭嫁 ── 攞路行
bat⁸ sɐp⁶ sœy³ fan¹ tɐu⁴ ga³ ── lɔ² lou⁶ haŋ⁴ (translit.)
Remarry at the age of eighty — look for roads to walk. (lit.)
Make a rod for one's own back.
〔註〕比喻自尋煩惱。

0126　八卦
bat⁸ gwa³ (translit.)
The eight diagrams. (lit.)
Put one's finger in another's pie.
Have an oar in every man's boat.
Make fetushes abd superstition.
〔註〕形容人愛管閒事或某些迷信的人的舉動。

0127　八婆
bat⁸ pɔ⁴ (translit.)
An eight diagrams woman. (lit.)
A Nosy Parker.
A shrewish woman.
A woman with supersitious disposition.
〔註〕指好管閒事的女人，潑婦或迷信婦女。

0128　刁/丟眼角
diu¹ ŋan⁵ gɔk⁸ (translit.)
Cast eye corners. (lit.)
Cast sheep's eyes at somebody.
Make eyes at somebody.
〔註〕表示送秋波或使眼色的意思。

0129　刁/丟僑扭擰
diu¹ kiu⁴ nɐu² liŋ⁶ (translit.)
Create difficulties and be bashful. (lit.)
Strike attitudes.
Put on affected manners.
〔註〕形容女孩子調皮，不聽話，難以對付。

0130　刁/丟蠻
diu¹ mɛn⁴ (translit.)
Be rude and unreasonable. (lit.)
Be impervious to reason.
〔註〕表示蠻橫，不講理。

0131　乜都〔係〕假
mɛt¹ dou¹ [hɐi⁶] ga² (translit.)
All is false. (lit.)
Pledge not to give up.
It can't be helped.
〔註〕常表示誓不罷休的意思，但亦表示無能爲力之意。

0132　又姣又怕痛，見人生仔又眼紅
jɐu⁶ hau² jɐu⁶ pa³ tuŋ³, gin³ jɐn⁴ saŋ¹ dzai² jɐu⁶ ŋan⁵ huŋ⁴ (translit.)
Be both coquettish and afraid of aching, but jealous of seeing someone give birth to a baby. (lit.)
Be not ambitious but jealous of other's achievement.
〔註〕含貶義，指人自己不肯做，但

又嫉妒別人的成就。

0133　又試
jɐu⁶ si³　*(translit.)*
Again.　*(lit.)*
Once again.
〔註〕即再次。

三　畫

0134　三十六度板斧都出齊/埋
sam¹ sɐp⁶ luk⁹ dou⁶ ban² fu²
dou¹　tsœt⁷　tsai⁴/mai⁴
(translit.)
Exercise up all one's thirty-six movements of the broad axe.　(lit.)
Be at the end of one's wits.
〔註〕表示想盡辦法或智窮才盡。

0135　三十六着，走爲上着
sam¹ sɐp⁶ luk⁹ dzœk⁹, dzɐu²
wɐi⁴　sœŋ⁶　dzœk⁹　*(translit.)*
Of thirty-six ways, running away is the best.　(lit.)
It is best to seek safety in flight.
It is best to take to one's heels.
The best thing to do is to run away as fast as one's legs could carry one.

0136　三九兩丁七
sam¹ gɐu² lœŋ⁵ diŋ¹ tsɐt⁷
(translit.)
Three nines become two persons and seven-tenths.　(lit.)

Only a few people.
There are only ones and twos.
〔註〕指人數不多，只有三兩人而已。

0137　三〔九〕唔識七
sam¹ [gɐu²] m⁴ sik¹ tsɐt⁷
(translit.)
Know not seven out of three [and nine] men.　(lit.)
Be strange to each other.
Nobody knows one another.
〔註〕表示誰也不認識誰。

0138　三口兩脷
sam¹ hau² lœŋ⁵ lei⁶　*(translit.)*
Three mouths and two tongues.　(lit.)
Show an unstable temperament.
Play fast and loose.
Eat one's words.
〔註〕比喻言而無信。

0139　三心兩意
sam¹ sɐm¹ lœŋ⁵ ji³　*(translit.)*
Three minds and two ideas.　(lit.)
Cannot make up one's mind.
Shilly-shally.
Be in two minds about...
Show a manner of instability.
Be in minds about...
〔註〕參閱"心多多"（0345），"十五個銅錢分兩份"（0077）及"寡母婆咁多心"（1719）各條。

0140　三不管

sam¹ bɐt⁷ gun² (translit.)
Three sides do not administer. (lit.)
Be under nobody's jurisdiction.
Be nobody's business.

0141 三水佬睇走馬燈——陸續有來
sam¹ sœy² lou² tai² dzɐu² ma⁵ dɐŋ¹—luk⁹ dzuk⁹ jɐu⁵ lɔi⁴ (translit.)
A native of Sam Sœy watches a lantern with paper horse running around and around,— they come one after another. (lit.)
Come in succession.
Come one after another.
〔註〕表示人或事件接踵而來的意思。

0142 三分顏色當大紅
sam¹ fɐn¹ ŋan⁴ sik⁷ dɔŋ³ dai⁶ huŋ⁴ (translit.)
Hope for big red(scarlet) after gaining three Chinese grams of colour. (lit.)
Get an inch and then an ell.
Be a little favoured and then hope for much more.
〔註〕形容人稍獲別人青睞，便囂張起來。亦有得寸進尺的意思。參閱該條（1325）。

0143 三句不離本行
sam¹ gœy³ bɐt⁷ lei⁴ bun² hɔŋ² (translit.)
Three sentences are not beyond one's own business. (lit.)
Talk shop.
Can hardly speak without a shop talk.

0144 三扒兩撥
sam¹ pa⁴ lœn⁵ but⁹ (translit.)
Rake thrice and poke twice. (lit.)
Hurriedly.
Promptly.
Hurry through.
With the utmost promptitude.
〔註〕表示急急忙忙的意思。

0145 三更窮，四更富
sam¹ gaŋ¹ kuŋ⁴, sei² gaŋ¹ fu³ (translit.)
Be poor at the third beating of the watchman's drum, but rich at the fourth beating. (lit.)
One's poverty or wealth is inconstant.
〔註〕形容一個人貧富不定。

0146 三長兩短
sam¹ tsœŋ⁴ lœn⁵ dyn² (translit.)
Three lengths and two shortnesses. (lit.)
An unexpected misfortune.
Something unfortunate, especially death.
〔註〕常指不幸事故，尤指死。

0147 三枝桅
sam¹ dzi¹ wɐi² (translit.)

A fishing junk with three masts. (lit.)
A re-married widow.
〔註〕含貶義，指再婚婦女。

0148　三姑六婆
sam¹ gu¹ luk⁹ pɔ⁴　(translit.)
Three maidens and six old women. (lit.)
A bevy of shrewish women.
〔註〕Three maidens（三姑）:
1. Buddhist nun（尼姑），
2. Taoist nun（道姑），
3. Fortune telling woman（卦姑）。

Six old women（六婆）:
1. Procuress（牙婆），
2. Marriage go-between（媒婆），
3. Medium（師婆，巫婆），
4. Villianess（虔婆，鴇母），
5. Female quack（藥婆），
6. Midwife（穩婆）。

0149　三隻手
sam¹ dzɛk⁸ sɐu²　(translit.)
Three-handed. (lit.)
A pickpocket.

0150　三羣五隊
sam¹ kwɐn⁴ ŋ⁵ dœy⁶　(translit.)
Three crowds and five teams. (lit.)
In groups.
In small parties.

0151　三腳櫈
sam¹ gœk⁸ dɐŋ³　(translit.)
Three-legged stool. (lit.)
An unreliable person or thing.
Be unreliable.
〔註〕比喻不可靠的人或靠不住的東西。

0152　三歲定八十
sam¹ sœy³ diŋ⁶ bat⁸ sɐp⁹　(translit.)
Age of three decides on the age of eighty. (lit.)
The child is father of the man.
〔註〕相當於"三歲看大，七歲看老"。

0153　三頭六臂
sam¹ tɐu⁴ luk⁹ bei³　(translit.)
Three heads and six arms. (lit.)
Be superman-like.
An extraordinarily able person.

0154　工多藝熟
guŋ¹ dɔ¹ ŋai⁶ suk⁹　(translit.)
More practice makes craftsmanship become mature. (lit.)
Constant practice makes perfect.

0155　下扒輕輕
ha⁶ pa⁴ hɛŋ¹ hɛŋ¹　(translit.)
The chin is light. (lit.)
Talk at random.
Only cackle without laying an egg.

Talk through one's hat.
With one's tongue in one's cheek.
〔註〕比喻人説得出，做不到或不顧後果，胡説八道。

0156 下馬威
ha⁶ ma⁵ wɐi¹ (translit.)
Show power while getting down from a horse. (lit.)
Display one's authority soon after one comes into power.
Deal somebody a head-on blow at first sight.

0157 下欄
ha⁶ lan⁴ (translit.)
Inferior income. (lit.)
Tips.
Additional income.
Service charge.
〔註〕指外快或小賬。

0158 大一歲，長一智
dai⁶ jɐt⁷ sœy³, dzœŋ² jɐt⁷ dzi³ (translit.)
Being one more year older, one gets one more wit. (lit.)
Experience teaches.
A fall into the pit, a gain in one's wit.
〔註〕參閱"人老精，鬼老靈"條（0107）。

0159 大人物
dai⁶ jɐn⁴ mɐt²ᐟ⁹ (translit.)
A big man. (lit.)
A somebody.
A great man.

0160 大小通吃
dai⁶ siu² tuŋ¹ hɛk⁸ (translit.)
Big and small ones are all eaten. (lit.)
Sweep everything into one's net.
Sweep all before one.

0161 大大話話
dai⁶ dai⁶ wa⁶ wa²ᐟ⁶ (translit.)
Tell a big lie. (lit.)
Estimate approximately.
Inflatedly speaking.
〔註〕表示粗略估計或誇張地説的意思。

0162 大方
dai⁶ fɔŋ¹ (translit.)
Be generous. (lit.)
Be liberal.
Be generous with one's money.
Have a dignified bearing.
Be graceful and poised.

0163 大王眼
dai⁶ wɔŋ⁴ ŋan² (translit.)
Big ruler's eyes. (lit.)
A glutton for gains.
〔註〕比喻人貪心，胃口很大。

0164 大石責死蟹
dai⁶ sɛk⁹ dzak⁸ sei² hai⁵ (translit.)
A big rock suppresses a crab to death. (lit.)
Bring pressure to bear on somebody.
Pressure somebody into doing

something.

〔註〕比喻用強硬手段來壓服別人。

0165 大好沉香當爛柴
dai⁶ hou² tsɐm⁴ hœŋ¹ dɔŋ³ lan⁶ tsai⁴ (translit.)
The best lign aloe is regarded as decayed firewood. (lit.)
Pure gold is regarded as copper.
Waste one's talent on a petty job.
Be unable to tell good and bad apart.
Be sold like refuse.

〔註〕比喻不知人善用或把高檔貨作低檔貨賤價出售等。

0166 大好鮮花插在牛屎裏
dai⁶ hou² sin¹ fa¹ tsap⁸ dzɔi⁶ ŋɐu⁴ si² lœy⁵ (translit.)
Transplant a very good fresh flower in a lump of cow's manure. (lit.)
Cast pearls before a swine.
Come into bloom under night.

〔註〕即"一朵鮮花插在牛糞上"。

0167 大行其道
dai⁶ hɐŋ⁴ kei⁴ dou⁶ (translit.)
Be popular. (lit.)
Be in the trend.
Prevail throughout.

0168 大光燈
dai⁶ gwɔŋ¹ dɐŋ¹ (translit.)
Gasificational lamp. (lit.)
A person panting with rage.

A person who has a big mouth.
A loud mouth.

〔註〕原指汽燈，煤氣燈（打氣煤油燈）。這種燈燃點時，發出很大的"噓噓聲"。後來有人用此語比喻怒氣冲冲或大聲說話的人。

0169 大耳窿
dai⁶ ji⁵ luŋ¹ (translit.)
A big aperture of ear. (lit.)
A loan-shark.

〔註〕即高利貸者。

0170 大泡和
dai⁶ pau¹ wɔ⁵ (translit.)
Dai Pau Wɔ. (a nickname of a certain man) (lit.)
Be muddleheaded.

〔註〕從前有人渾名爲"大泡和"的，做事糊裏糊塗。後人便以此名比喻人糊塗或無能，笨拙。

0171 大枝嘢
dai⁶ dzi¹ jɛ⁵ (translit.)
A big piece. (lit.)
Be as proud as Punch.
Be puffed up with pride.

〔註〕表示驕傲，傲慢的意思。

0172 大事化小，小事化無
dai⁶ si⁶ fa³ siu², siu² si⁶ fa³ mou⁴ (translit.)
Turn big affairs into small ones and small ones into none. (lit.)
Bring the problem to naught.

0173 大花面搋眼淚——離行離捺
dai⁶ fa¹ min² giu² ŋan⁵ lœy⁶—lei⁴ hɔŋ⁴ lei⁴ lat⁹

(translit.)
An actor with painted face wipes tears — separate by a space. (lit.)
Be out of the place.
Go beyond what is proper.
Have no relation with...
〔註〕表示不合規格或距離甚遠的意思，也可轉喻指和某人（物）扯不上關係。

0174　大花筒
dai⁶ fa¹ tuŋ⁴　(translit.)
A big kaleidoscope.　(lit.)
An extravagant spender.
〔註〕比喻大手大腳亂花錢的人。

0175　大食唔窮倒算窮
dai⁶ sik⁹ m⁴ kuŋ⁴ dou²/³ syn³ kuŋ⁴　(translit.)
Big eater will not become poor but reverse calculation causes poverty.　(lit.)
Lose a ship for a halfpenny worth of tar.
Go for wool and come home shorn.
〔註〕比喻因小失大。

0176　大食細
dai⁶ sik⁹ sɐi³　(translit.)
The big eat the small.　(lit.)
Small fish are always the best food of big ones.

0177　大炮友
dai⁶ pau³ jɐu²　(translit.)
A cannon-friend.　(lit.)
A teller of tall stories.
A man who fonds of talk big.

〔註〕指愛吹牛皮的人。

0178　大限難逃
dai⁶ han⁶ nan⁴ tou⁴　(translit.)
Be unable to run away from the big limitation.　(lit.)
Meet one's fate.
Pay one's debt to Nature.
What is worried about is sure to occur.

0179　大家心照
dai⁶ ga¹ sɐm¹ dziu³　(translit.)
Understand each other without saying.　(lit.)
Have a tacit understanding.
〔註〕表示不言而喻的意思。

0180　大陣仗
dai⁶ dzɐn⁶ dzœŋ⁶　(translit.)
A big formation.　(lit.)
Go in for an ostentation.
Break a butterfly on the wheel.
〔註〕表示排場大或小題大做的意思。

0181　大海撈針
dai⁶ hɔi² ŋau⁴ dzɐm¹　(translit.)
Dredge a needle in a big sea.　(lit.)
Look for a needle in a bottle of hay.
Fish a needle out of the ocean.

0182　大隻騾騾
dai⁶ dzɛk⁸ lœy⁵ lœy⁵　(translit.)
A man of strong build.　(lit.)

As big as a mule.
Be as stout as a horse.
〔註〕形容人個子高大，含貶義。

0183　大粒佬
dai⁶ lɐp⁷ lou²　(translit.)
A big cubic one.　(lit.)
A man of mark.
A man of men.
〔註〕大人物的謔稱。

0184　大喊十
dai⁶ ham³ sɐp⁶　(translit.)
A big shouter.　(lit.)
A person who shouts out for trifles.
A loud mouth.
〔註〕比喻嗓門兒大，常爲小事便大喊大叫的人。

0185　大番薯
dai⁶ fan¹ sy⁴′⁵　(translit.)
A big sweet potato.　(lit.)
A fool.
〔註〕比喻愚笨的人。

0186　大喉腩
dai⁶ hɐu⁴ nam⁵　(translit.)
Have a big throat and a big belly.　(lit.)
A rapacious person.
A person who has a very good appetite.
〔註〕形容人胃口大，貪多，貪心。

0187　大諗頭
dai⁶ lɐm² tɐu⁴　(translit.)
A big thought.　(lit.)
Be too ambitious for...
Hot oneself up with ambition
Hitch one's waggon to a star.
〔註〕形容人抱負過高的意思。

0188　大模屍樣
dai⁶ mou⁴ si¹ jœŋ⁶　(translit.)
A big mould like a corpse.　(lit.)
Be haughty.
Be in ostentatious manner.
〔註〕比喻人神氣十足的樣子，含貶義。

0189　大禍臨頭
dai⁶ wɔ⁶ lɐm⁴ tɐu⁴　(translit.)
Big calamity comes onto the head.　(lit.)
The black ox has trod on one's foot.

0190　大搖大擺
dai⁶ jiu⁴ dai⁶ bai⁴　(translit.)
Big shake and big display.　(lit.)
Swagger about.

0191　大話夾好彩
dai⁶ wa⁶ gap⁸ hou² tsɔi²　(translit.)
Big lies with good luck.　(lit.)
All by good luck.
〔註〕表示幸虧或僥倖的意思。

0192　大覺瞓
dai⁶ gau³ fɐn³　(translit.)
Have a big sleep.　(lit.)
Sleep on both ears.
Be carefree.
Not to care a pin.
〔註〕比喻睡大覺，安心，或無憂無慮。

0193 大雞唔食細米
dai⁶ gɐi¹ m⁴ sik⁹ sɐi³ mɐi⁵ (translit.)
A big hen does not eat small rice. (lit.)
Care naught for trifles.
〔註〕比喻不屑於幹小事或做賺錢少的生意。

0194 大碌藕
dai⁶ luk⁷ ŋɐu⁵ (translit.)
Big lotus root. (Dai Luk ŋɐu was a nickname of a certain person) (lit.)
An extravagant spender.
A debauchee.
〔註〕比喻亂花錢的人。"大碌藕"是一個人的渾名。往昔佛山每年均有"秋色"舉行，而且需要很多人抬"色"。該名"大碌藕"的人年年均往抬"色"。他抬"色"時姿態別具一格，把"色"左搖右擺。這種動作廣東人稱爲"抌"（fiŋ⁶音）。而"抌"中又有亂花錢的意思。所以借"大碌藕"抬色——亂抌來比喻"亂花錢的人"。

0195 大懵
dai⁶ muŋ² (translit.)
A big muddler. (lit.)
A blunder head.
Be muddle-headed.
〔註〕指頭腦糊塗。

0196 大驚小怪
dai⁶ giŋ¹ siu² gwai³ (translit.)
Great terror and small pecularity. (lit.)

A storm in the tea cup.
Make a fuss.

0197 大纜絞唔埋
dai⁶ lam⁶ gau² m⁴ mai⁴ (translit.)
Cannot twist together with a rope. (lit.)
Make a world of difference.
It is far from the argument each sticks to.
There is some difference to something.
Cannot meet somebody half-way.
〔註〕指人們各持己見，不能互相遷就。

0198 士（事）急馬行田
si⁶ gɐp⁷ ma⁵ haŋ⁴ tin⁴ (translit.)
When a soldier is in emergency, he lets the horse walk across the field. (lit.)
By hook or crook.
By fair means or foul.
Act according to the circumstances.
〔註〕中國象棋有士，馬及象等。馬走"日"字形的對角線，而象則走"田"字的對角線，兩者不能混亂。"士"和"事"同音。這句話的意思是說當"士"（暗喻"事情"）告急時，便要不擇手段或隨機應變了。

0199 土鯪魚
tou² lɛŋ⁴ jy⁴ (translit.)
Local dace. (lit.)

〔註〕土鯪魚是一種廣東特有的人工養殖淡水魚。

0200 千年道行一朝喪
tsin¹ nin⁴ dou⁶ hɐŋ⁶ jɐt⁷ dziu¹ sɔŋ³ (translit.)
A thousand years' high moral attainment losee in one morning. (lit.)
All the good deeds're spoilt by only an ill doing.

0201 千里送鵝毛，物輕情意重
tsin¹ lei⁵ suŋ³ ŋɔ⁴ mou⁴, mɐp⁹ hiŋ¹ tsiŋ⁴ ji⁶ dzuŋ⁶ (translit.)
The goose feather is sent from a thousand li away; it is light, but it is full of affection. (lit.)
The trifling gift sent from afar conveys deep affection.

0202 千金小姐當作丫鬟賣
tsin¹ gam¹ siu² dzɛ² dɔŋ³ dzɔk⁸ a¹ wan⁴ mai⁶ (translit.)
A young lady of high birth is sold as a slave girl. (lit.)
Pure gold is regarded as copper.
Waste one's talent on a petty job.
Be unable to tell good and bad apart.
Be sold like refuse.
〔註〕參閱"大好沉香當爛柴"條（0165）。

0203 千真萬確
tsin¹ dzɐn¹ man⁶ kɔk⁸ (translit.)
One thousand of truth and ten thousand of accuracy. (lit.)
Be as sure as fate.
The truth, the whole truth, and nothing but the truth.

0204 千揀萬揀，揀着個爛燈盞
tsin¹ gan² man⁶ gan², gan² dzœk⁹ gɔ³ lan⁶ dɐŋ¹ dzan² (translit.)
Having made a thousand and even ten thousand choices, one eventually chose a broken shallow cup for oil. (lit.)
The most careful choice is often the worst choice.
〔註〕表示儘管精挑細選，仍然有可能選擇錯誤。

0205 小心駛/使得萬年船
siu² sɐm¹ sɐi² dɐk⁷ man⁶ nin⁴ syn⁴ (translit.)
Care can drive a ship for ten thousand years. (lit.)
Take care and care will prevail.

0206 小鬼唔見得大神
siu² gwɐi² m⁴ gin³ dɐk⁷ dai⁶ sɐn⁴ (translit.)
A small ghost does not dare to see a big god. (lit.)
Be not natural and liberal enough.
Humble oneself too much to rub elbows with upper-crusts.
〔註〕形容人不夠自然大方，或指人過份自卑而不敢和上流社會交

三畫

往。

0207 小財唔出，大財唔入
siu² tsɔi⁴ m⁴ tsœt⁷, dai⁶ tsɔi⁴ ŋ⁴ jɐp⁹ (translit.)
If no small money is given out, no big money will come in. (lit.)
An empty hand is no lure for a hawk.
A hook without a small fish makes no big fish jump at the bait.
〔註〕形容在商業上，如果不花少量的錢去做廣告或搞其他足以吸引顧客的活動，則無法賺到大錢。

0208 小氣
siu² hei³ (translit.)
Small air. (lit.)
Be narrow-minded.
Be small-minded.
〔註〕表示心胸狹窄或小心眼兒的意思。

0209 小家種
siu² ga¹ dzuŋ² (translit.)
The clan of mean persons. (lit.)
Act in a mean-spirited manner.
A mean-spirited person.
〔註〕指卑鄙而吝嗇的人。

0210 小意思
siu² ji³ si¹ (translit.)
A little meaning. (lit.)
A slight token of regard.
Nothing important.
〔註〕常用於對自己所送出的禮物的謙稱，但亦指事情並不嚴重。

0211 山人自有妙計
san¹ jɐn⁴ dzi⁶ jɐu⁵ miu⁶ gɐi³ (translit.)
A mountain dweller naturally has a good plan. (lit.)
I have hit an idea.
I have had an inspiration.

0212 山大斬埋有柴
san¹ dai⁶ dzam² mai⁴ jɐu⁵ tsai⁴ (translit.)
One can gather a lot of firewood to cut sticks in a big mountain. (lit.)
Many a pickle makes a mickle.
Drip-drops become a river.
〔註〕相當於"積少能成多"。參閱該條（1838）。

0213 山高水低
san¹ gou¹ sœy² dɐi¹ (translit.)
The mountain is high and the river is low. (lit.)
An unexpected misfortune.
Something unfortunate.
〔註〕比喻不幸事情或意外，參閱"有乜冬瓜豆腐"條（0535）。

0214 山窮水盡
san¹ kuŋ⁴ sœy² dzœn⁶ (translit.)
The mountain impoverishes and the river ends. (lit.)
Beat the end of one's rope.
Be up the creek.
Live with one's bottom dollar.
〔註〕比喻身處絕境或走投無路。

0215 口不對心

hɐu² bɐt¹ dœy³ sɐm¹ (translit.)
The mouth is not compatible with the heart. (lit.)
Carry fire in one hand and water in the other.
Speak with one's tongue in one's cheek.
〔註〕參閱"口是心非"條（0220）。

0216 口水多過茶
hɐu² sœy² dɔ¹ gwɔ³ tsa⁴ (translit.)
Mouth water is more than tea. (lit.)
Talk the hind leg off a dog.
Have a loose tongue.
Wag one's tongue.
Shoot off one's mouth.
〔註〕形容人説話太多，含貶義。

0217 口多多
hɐu² dɔ¹ dɔ¹ (translit.)
Many-mouthed. (lit.)
Be loose-tongued.
Shoot off one's mouth.
〔註〕形容人多嘴多舌。

0218 口垃濕
hɐu² lɐp⁹ sɐp⁷ (translit.)
The odds and ends for the mouth. (lit.)
Between-meal nibbles.
Snacks.
〔註〕指零吃兒，零食。

0219 口花花
hɐu² fa¹ fa¹ (translit.)
Have a flowery mouth. (lit.)
Talk frivolously.
Speak frivolity.
〔註〕形容人輕浮，能說會道（尤指男人對女人）。

0220 口是心非
hɐu² si⁶ sɐm¹ fei¹ (translit.)
The mouth says 'yes', but the heart says 'no'. (lit.)
Carry fire in one hand and water in the other.
Speak with one's tongue in one's cheek.
〔註〕參閱"口不對心"條（0215）。

0221 口甜舌滑
hɐu² tim⁴ sit⁹ wat⁹ (translit.)
The mouth is sweet and the tongue is smooth. (lit.)
Be honey tipped.
Oil one's tongue.

0222 口爽荷包垃
hɐu² sɔŋ² hɔ⁴ bau¹ lɐp⁹ (translit.)
Mouth is brisk but purse is stickly. (lit.)
Words pay no debts.
Words come out fast, money goes out slow.
〔註〕比喻表面慷慨，實則吝嗇。亦即所謂口惠而實不至。

0223 口窒窒
hɐu² dzɐt⁹ dzɐt⁹ (translit.)
The mouth obstructs. (lit.)
Stammer out.
Stutter out.
Hum and ha.
〔註〕表示結結巴巴地說話或欲言又

止。

0224 口疏疏
hɐu² sɔ¹ sɔ¹ (translit.)
The mouth slips. (lit.)
Make no secret of anything.
Be loose-lipped.
〔註〕形容人嘴快,沒法保守秘密。

0225 口輕輕
hɐu² hɛŋ¹ hɛŋ¹ (translit.)
The mouth is light. (lit.)
Make easy promises.
〔註〕表示輕諾的意思。參閱"下扒輕輕"(0155)及"托塔都應承"條(0599)。

0226 上天無路,入地無門
sœŋ⁵ tin¹ mou⁴ lou⁶, jɐp⁹ dei⁶ mou⁴ mun⁴ (translit.)
There is neither a road to heaven nor a door to hell. (lit.)
Be in desperate straits.
Be in a quandary.
Be in a devil of a hole.

0227 上氣唔接下氣
sœŋ⁶ hei³ m⁴ dzip⁸ ha⁶ hei³ (translit.)
The upper air cannot connect with the lower air. (lit.)
Be out of breath.
Be panting.
〔註〕形容人呼吸急促,氣喘吁吁。

0228 上得山多終遇虎
sœŋ⁵ dɐk⁷ san¹ dɔ¹ dzuŋ¹ jy⁶ fu² (translit.)
The one who goes up mountains too often will one day meet a tiger. (lit.)
The fish which nibbles at every bait will be caught.

0229 上當
sœŋ⁵ dɔŋ³ (translit.)
Be taken in. (lit.)
Be fooled
Be caught with chaff.
Be duped.
Can be put in pledge.
Have a hocking value.
〔註〕意爲受騙,但有時又用於表示東西有典當的價值。

0230 上樑唔正下樑歪
sœŋ⁶ lœŋ⁴ m⁴ dzɛŋ³ ha⁶ lœŋ⁴ mɛ² (translit.)
If the upper beam is crooked, the lower one will be out of plumb. (lit.)
Those below will follow the bad example set by those above.
〔註〕即"上樑不正下樑歪"。

0231 也文也武
ja⁶ mɐn⁴ ja⁶ mou⁵ (translit.)
Be well-versed in polite letters and martial arts. (lit.)
Make a show of power.
Swagger about.
〔註〕形容人耀武揚威,橫行霸道。

四畫

0232　不了了之
bɐt⁷ liu⁵ liu⁵ dzi¹　(translit.)
Let the unfinished thing finish itself. (lit.)
Let it take its own course.
End up with nothing definite.

0233　不打不相識
bɐt⁷ da² bɐt⁷ sœŋ¹ sik⁷ (translit.)
No fighting, no friends are made. (lit.)
No discord, no concord.
Build up friendship after an exchange of blows.

0234　不打自招
bɐt⁷ da² dzi⁶ jiu¹　(translit.)
Self confess without being beaten. (lit.)
Make a confession without duress.

0235　不是冤家不聚頭
bɐt⁷ si⁶ jyn¹ ga¹ bɐt⁷ dzœy⁶ tɐu⁴ (translit.)
If they were not opponents, they would not meet together. (lit.)
Dogs and cats are sure to meet.
Enemies are bound to meet in the same place.

0236　不到黃河心不死
bɐt⁷ dou³ wɔŋ⁴ hɔ⁴ sɐm¹ bɐt⁷ si²/sei² (translit.)
The heart will not die until reaching the Yellow River. (lit.)
Go to all lengths to do something.
Hang on.
Refuse to give up until all hope is gone.

0237　不理三七二十一
bɐt⁷ lei⁵ sam¹ tsɐt⁷ ji⁶ sɐp⁹ jɐt⁷　(translit.)
Not to care if three times seven is twenty-one. (lit.)
Rain or shine.
Fling caution to the winds.
Be regardless of the consequences.
Chance the duck.
〔註〕即不顧一切，無論如何或不管怎樣的意思。

0238　天下烏鴉一樣黑
tin¹ ha⁶ wu¹ a¹ jɐt⁷ jœŋ⁶ hɐk⁷　(translit.)
All crows in the world are equally black. (lit.)
Devils everywhere are devils of the same kind.
There is nothing different under the sun.

0239　天無絕人之路
tin¹ mou⁴ dzyt⁹ jɐn⁴ dzi¹ lou⁶ (translit.)
Heaven never puts a man in a dead end. (lit.)
It is a long lane that has no turning.
God always tempers the wind to the shorn lamb.

0240　天堂有路你不走，地獄無門闖進來

四畫

tin¹ tɔŋ⁴ jɐu⁵ lou⁶ nei⁵ bɐt⁷ dzɐu², dei⁶ juk⁹ mou⁴ mun⁴ tsɔŋ² dzœŋ³ lɔi⁴ *(translit.)*
You do not take the road to heaven, but push yourself to hell where there is not a door. *(lit.)*
You cut your own throat.
You go to your doom.
You bring yourself to ruin.

0241 天跌落嚟當被冚
tin¹ dit³ lɔk⁶ lɐi⁴ dɔŋ³ pei⁵ kam² *(translit.)*
If the sky falls down, use it as a quilt. *(lit.)*
Take it easy.
Be unconcerned with one's present situation.
〔註〕表示對目前處境處之泰然。

0242 天網恢恢，疏而不漏
tin¹ mɔŋ⁵ fui¹ fui¹, sɔ¹ ji⁴ bɐt⁷ lɐu⁶ *(translit.)*
The heaven's net is vast; it never leaks though it is thin. *(lit.)*
Justice has long arms.
Heaven's vengeance is slow but sure.

0243 木口木面
muk⁹ hɐu² muk⁹ min⁶ *(translit.)*
Wooden mouth and wooden face. *(lit.)*
Be wooden-faced.
Be slow in reacting.
Be wooden-headed.

〔註〕無表情；遲鈍，比較"木獨"條（0245）。

0244 木匠擔枷 —— 自作自受
muk⁹ dzœŋ⁶ dam¹ ga¹ — dzi⁶ dzɔk⁸ dzi⁶ sɐu⁶ *(translit.)*
A carpenter carries a wooden-collar — suffering from his own work. *(lit.)*
As one brews, so one must drink.
Fry in one's own grease.

0245 木獨
muk⁹ duk⁹ *(translit.)*
Wooden-faced. *(lit.)*
Be as wooden as a dummy.
Be unsocial.
Not to have a social nature.
〔註〕形容人不大好講話或不善交際。比較"木口木面"條（0243）。

0246 冇口齒
mou⁵ hau² tsi² *(translit.)*
Have no mouth and teeth. *(lit.)*
Break one's promise.
Break one's words.
〔註〕形容人不講信用。

0247 冇天裝
mou⁵ tin¹ dzɔŋ¹ *(translit.)*
No place in the sky to hold. *(lit.)*
An evil-doer.
〔註〕指連上天也不容的作惡份子。

0248 冇牙老虎
mou⁵ ŋa⁴ lou⁵ fu² *(translit.)*
A toothless tiger. *(lit.)*

Fire.

〔註〕比喻火災。

0249　冇癮

mou⁵ yen⁵　(translit.)

No addiction.　(lit.)

Bored.

Senseless.

Feel no interest in something.

〔註〕無聊，沒意思，沒趣或對（某事）不感興趣。

0250　冇手尾

mou⁵ sɐu² mei⁵　(translit.)

No hands and tails.　(lit.)

Leave things about.

〔註〕形容人做事有頭無尾，或者做完一件事，不收拾東西。

0251　冇心肝

mou⁵ sɐm¹ gɔn¹　(translit.)

Have no heart and liver.　(lit.)

Pay no attention to...

Be inattentive.

Be unconcerned with...

〔註〕形容人對什麼事情都不在意。

0252　冇心機

mou⁵ sɐm¹ gei¹　(translit.)

Have no heart.　(lit.)

Be in no mood.

Be impatient.

〔註〕指沒有心情或沒有耐性。

0253　冇收（修）

mou⁵ sɐu¹　(translit.)

Have no close.　(lit.)

Be at loose ends.

Fail to make an end of the trouble.

Be unable to bring things to a satisfactory conclusion.

Be at one's wit's end.

〔註〕表示難以收拾或毫無辦法的意思。

0254　冇衣食

mou⁵ ji¹ sik⁹　(translit.)

Have neither clothes to wear nor food to eat.　(lit.)

Disregard one's morality and righteousness.

Be guilty of bad faith.

Break faith with somebody.

〔註〕指不顧道義或對人背信。語出粵劇伶人輩，但已成為一般人的口語了。

0255　冇耳性

mou⁵ ji⁶ siŋ³　(translit.)

Without nature of ears.　(lit.)

Have a memory like a sieve.

Have bad memory.

Be forgetful.

〔註〕表示健忘的意思，含貶義。

0256　冇尾飛鉈

mou⁵ mei⁵ fei¹ tɔ⁴　(translit.)

A flying plummet without tail.　(lit.)

A person without any trace.

〔註〕相當於"斷線風箏"，指難於尋找他踪跡的人。

0257　冇走盞

mou⁵ dzɐu² dzan²　(translit.)

Without any extent.　(lit.)

Leave no margin of ... (time/space/money)

四畫

Leave no space for something.
Be in the bag.
〔註〕指沒有餘地，但也表示有把握，十拿九穩的意思。參閱"冇走雞"（0258）條。

0258 冇走雞
mou⁵ dzɐu² gɐi¹ (translit.)
No hens to run away. (lit.)
Be in the bag.
Be well in hand.
〔註〕相當於"十拿九穩"。參閱該條（0081）。

0259 冇兩句
mou⁵ lœn⁵ gœy³ (translit.)
Without two sentences. (lit.)
Be too intimate with somebody to have anything to argue.
〔註〕形容與人相處融洽，沒有爭執。

0260 冇呢枝歌仔唱
mou⁵ ni¹ (nei)¹ dzi¹ gɔ¹ tsɐi² tsɔŋ³ (translit.)
There is no such a song to sing. (lit.)
The times are different.
Such an opportunity is no longer seen.
Sing another song.
〔註〕相當於"過了這村，沒有這個店"。暗示時代不同了或再沒有這個機會了。

0261 冇咁大隻蛤乸隨街跳
mou⁵ gɐm³ dai⁶ dzɛk⁸ gɐp⁸ na² tsœy⁴ gai¹ tiu³ (translit.)
There is no such a big frog hopping about in the street. (lit.)
Greed often causes loss.
Go for wool and come back shorn.
〔註〕告誡別人貪心反招損失。

0262 冇咁大隻鴿就唔好喊咁大聲
mou⁵ gɐm³ dai⁶ dzɛk⁸ gɐp³ dzɐu⁴ m⁴ hou² ham³ gɐm³ dai⁶ sɛŋ¹. (translit.)
If the pigeon is not so big, it should not cry so loudly. (lit.)
Do not throw straws against the wind.
One should not swim beyond one's depth.
Cut one's coat according to one's cloth.
Spend no more than one can afford.
Undertake what one can do.
〔註〕比喻做事應量力而為。

0263 冇咁大個頭就唔好戴咁大頂帽
mou⁵ gɐm³ dai⁶ gɔ³ tɐu⁴ dzɐu⁶ m⁴ hou² dai³ gɐm³ dai⁶ dɛŋ² mou². (translit.)
If one has not such a big head, one should not put on such a big hat. (lit.)
〔註〕同"冇咁大隻鴿就唔好喊咁大聲"（0262）。

0264 冇咁大隻鴿，就唔會喊咁大聲

mou⁵ gɐm³ dai⁶ dzɛk⁸ gɐp³,
dzɐu⁴ m⁴ wui⁵ ham³ gɐm³
dai⁶ sɛŋ¹   *(translit.)*
If the pigeon were not so big, it would not cry so loudly. (lit.)
Within one's power.
Be fully competent for...
Be fully able to...
One can spend as much as one can afford.
〔註〕暗示有這麼的勢力或財力才能夠……。

0265 冇咁大個頭，就唔會戴咁大頂帽
mou⁵ gɐm³ dai⁶ gɔ³ tɐu⁴
dzɐu⁴ m⁴ wui⁵ dai³ gɐm³
dai⁶ dɛŋ² mou⁴ *(translit.)*
If one had not such a big head, one would not put on such a big hat. (lit.)
〔註〕同"冇咁大隻鴿，就唔會喊咁大聲"（0264）

0266 冇咁衰講到咁衰
mou⁵ gɐm³ sœy¹ gɔŋ² dou³
gɐm³ sœy¹   *(translit.)*
Be not so bad but be said to be so bad. (lit.)
Paint somebody/something in dark colour.
Put false colour upon somebody/something.
〔註〕表示把人或物描得更黑。

0267 冇料
mou⁵ liu²   *(translit.)*
Have no materials. (lit.)
Be ill-educated.
Be low-level in knowledge/technique.
〔註〕形容人沒有學問或知識，技術水平低。

0268 冇家教
mou⁵ ga¹ gau³   *(translit.)*
Have no family teaching. (lit.)
Lack home education.
Be not cultured.
〔註〕泛指缺乏家庭教育，尤指小孩不懂禮貌。參閱"有爺生冇乸教"（0563）條。

0269 冇晒符
mou⁵ sai³ fu⁴   *(translit.)*
Have not any Taosit magic incantations. (lit.)
Be at one's wit's end.
Be at the end of one's tether.
〔註〕表示智窮才盡，完全沒了辦法。

0270 冇晒符弗〈法〉
mou⁵ sai³ fu⁵ fit¹   *(translit.)*
None of charms and amulets can do. (lit.)
〔註〕同"冇晒符"（0269）。

0271 冇相干
mou⁵ sœŋ¹ gɔn¹   *(translit.)*
Have no concern. (lit.)
Nothing serious.
It does't matter.
Never mind.
It's nothing.
It's all right.
〔註〕即沒關係，不要緊。

0272 冇紋路
mou⁵ mɐn⁴ lou⁶　(translit.)
Be like the wood without any grain.　(lit.)
Have no sense of propriety.
Do not act on principle.
Be careless and casual.
〔註〕形容人做事沒分寸，無原則，沒譜兒，或漫不經心。

0273 冇根兜
mou⁵ gɐn¹ dɐu¹　(translit.)
Have no roots.　(lit.)
Have no sense of propriety.
Do not act on principle.
Be careless and casual.
〔註〕同"冇紋路"（0272）。

0274 冇眼屎乾淨盲
mou⁵ ŋan⁶ si² gon¹ dzɛŋ⁶ maŋ⁴　(translit.)
Become cleanly blind without any gum in the eyes.　(lit.)
Out of sight, out of mind.
Let the loss be loss.
Cut the loss.
〔註〕表示眼不見，心不煩或趕緊脫手，免多受損失等意思。

0275 冇眼睇
mou⁵ ŋan⁶ tɐi²　(translit.)
Have no eyes to see.　(lit.)
Turn a blind eye to...
Throw in one's hand.
〔註〕表示撒手不管的意思。

0276 冇得斟
mou⁵ dɐk⁷ dzɐm¹　(translit.)
Have no more discussion.　(lit.)
Leave something out of consideration.
Make no concession to...
Be at one's wit's end.
〔註〕表示沒商量，不加考慮或不作讓步等意思。

0277 冇得諗
mou⁵ dɐk⁷ ŋɐm²　(translit.)
Be not worth thinking.　(lit.)
Leave something out of consideration.
〔註〕表示無法加以考慮的意思。

0278 冇幾何
mou⁵ gei² hɔ²　(translit.)
Not many times.　(lit.)
Not ...so often.
Seldom.
Seldom or never.
〔註〕表示不經常；不常的意思。

0279 冇揸拿
mou⁵ dza¹ na⁴　(translit.)
Have nothing to get hold of.　(lit.)
Gain no guarantee against loss.
〔註〕即沒有保證的意思。

0280 冇腰骨
mou⁵ jiu¹ gwɐt⁷　(translit.)
Have no spinebone.　(lit.)
Be not reliable.
Be untrustworthy.
Be undependable.
〔註〕指人沒骨氣；靠不住。

0281 冇哪更
mou⁵ na¹ gaŋ¹　(translit.)
Have no connection.　(lit.)
Not to the point.

Be wide of the mark.
Have not a bit relation with...
〔註〕即不沾邊兒的意思。參閱"冇
哪唲"條（0282）。

0282　冇哪唲
mou⁵ ŋa¹ nɐŋ¹　(translit.)
Be not related to.　(lit.)
Have nothing to do with...
Do not get entangled with...
Establish no relations with...
〔註〕表示沒聯繫或沒關係的意思。
參閱"冇哪更"條（0281）。

0283　冇話好講
mou⁵ wa⁶ hou² gɔŋ²　(translit.)
Have not any words to say.　(lit.)
Can find nothing to say.
Be stuck for an answer.
〔註〕即無話可說。

0284　冇解
mou⁵ gai²　(translit.)
Have no explanation.　(lit.)
It is unreasonable (that...)
〔註〕意爲"不像話"，多作引語。

0285　冇掩雞籠 —— 自出自入
mou⁵ jim² gɐi¹ luŋ⁴—dzi⁶ tsœt⁷ dzi⁶ jɐp⁹　(translit.)
A chicks' bamboo—cage without door—everyone goes out and comes in freely.　(lit.)
The place where everybody can cine and go at random.
〔註〕指可以隨意來去的地方。

0286　冇樣叻
mou⁵ jœŋ⁶ lɐk⁷　(translit.)
Nothing good.　(lit.)
Be good for nothing.
Be good for naught.
〔註〕形容人一無所長。

0287　冇趙雙
mou⁵ tɔŋ³ sœŋ¹　(translit.)
There is not another row.　(lit.)
Not to double-cross somebody at all.
It is not a fish story.
There is no... more than this.
Be absolutely genuine.
Be as true as a die.
〔註〕表示不騙人，確實如此的意思。

0288　冇頭烏蠅
mou⁵ tɐu⁴ wu¹ jiŋ¹　(translit.)
A headless fly.　(lit.)
Act/Run helter-skelter.
Do not act in a planned way.
〔註〕形容人亂闖亂撞或做事無計劃。

0289　冇聲氣
mou⁵ sɛŋ¹ hei²　(translit.)
Have no sound and air.　(lit.)
Have got no information.
Beyond hope.
〔註〕表示沒有消息或沒有希望的意思。

0290　冇檳榔唔嗍得出汁
mou⁵ bɐn¹ lɔŋ⁴ m⁴ dziu⁴ dɐk⁷ tsœt⁷ dzɐp⁷　(translit.)
Without betel-nuts, no juice can

be chewed out. (lit.)
Every why has its wherefore.
There is no smoke without fire.
Nothing is stolen without hands.
〔註〕表示事出有因的意思。參閱"無風不起浪"條（1491）。

0291 冇聲正經
mou^5 lei^4 dzin^3 gin^1 (translit.)
Have not a bit of seriousness. (lit.)
Be not so decent as one should be.
〔註〕表示不夠嚴肅或不夠正派的意思。

0292 冇聲搭霎
mou^5 lei^4 dap^8 sap^8 (translit.)
Have not a bit of care. (lit.)
〔註〕同"冇紋路"（0272）。

0293 冇譜
mou^5 pou^2 (translit.)
Have no musical notes. (lit.)
Be incoherent.
Be unreasonable.
Break the routine.
〔註〕即"離譜，沒準兒"。也指某些狀態達到令人不能忍受的程度。

0294 牙尖嘴利
ŋa^4 dzim^1 dzœy^2 lei^6 (translit.)
The teeth are pointed and the mouth is sharp. (lit.)
Be flannel-mouthed.
Be eloquent.

0295 牙烟
ŋa^4 jin^1 (translit.)
The teeth are smoky. (lit.)
Be dangerous.
Be unsteady.
Be horrible.
〔註〕表示危險的，不穩固的，恐怖的，難看的。

0296 牙斬斬
ŋa^4 dzam^2 dzam^2 (translit.)
The teeth are chopping and chopping. (lit.)
Chop in.
Shoot one's mouth.
Wag one's tongue.
Tend to speak about oneself.
Be talky.
〔註〕形容人好滔滔不絕地講話來表現自己。

0297 牙齒痕
ŋa^4 tsi^2 hɐn$^{2/6}$ (translit.)
The scar caused by teeth. (lit.)
The offence given to somebody.
An old score.
〔註〕指對別人的冒犯或宿怨。

0298 牙齒當金使
ŋa^4 tsi^2 dɔn^3 gam^1 sɐi^2 (translit.)
Teeth are used as gold. (lit.)
Be as good as one's words.
Keep one's promise.
Keep one's words.
〔註〕表示一諾千金或說話算數的意思。

0299 牙擦擦

ŋa⁴ tsat⁸ tsat⁸ (translit.)
The teeth keep on brushing. (lit.)
Be talky.
Wag one's tongue.
Boast too much of oneself.
〔註〕形容人誇誇其談，驕傲自大。

0300 扎實
dzat⁸ sɐt⁸ (translit.)
Be sound enough. (lit.)
Be sturdy enough.
Be firm enough.
Be strong enough.
〔註〕形容物品堅固或人健碩。

0301 支質
dzi¹ dzɐt⁷ (translit.)
Variety. (lit.)
Item.
Be long-winded.
Be too wordy.
Push and pull.
〔註〕作名詞用時，意爲"名堂"或"項目"。作形容詞用時，意爲"囉唆"。作動詞用時，意爲"把禮物推來推去"，亦有人説"支支質質"。

0302 支整
dzi¹ dziŋ² (translit.)
Dress up. (lit.)
Be fond of making/dressing oneself up like a peacock.
Care much about dresses.
Like to be affected.
〔註〕形容人過份講究打扮。

0303 五行欠金
ŋ⁵ hɐŋ⁴ him³ gɐm¹ (trans-lit.)
There lacks gold in the five primary elements*. (lit.)
Be in low water.
Be penniless.
Be broke.
〔註〕比喻沒有錢的意思。
The five primary elements are : metal (金), wood (木), water (水), fire (火) and earth (土).

0304 五時花六時變
ŋ⁵ si⁴ fa¹ luk⁹ si⁴ bin³ (translit.)
The flower comes into bloom at 5 o'clock and changes at 6. (lit.)
Have an unstable temperament.
Change one's mind as time goes on.
Be unsteady in mind.
〔註〕表示拿不定主意的意思。參閲 "一時一樣"條（0037）。

0305 切肉不離皮
tsit³ juk⁹ bɐt⁷ lei⁴ pei⁴ (translit.)
The flesh cut still sticks to the skin. (lit.)
Blood is thicker than water.
Nothing is as affectionate as flesh and blood.
〔註〕表示親情難捨的意思。

0306 手瓜硬
sɐu² gwa¹ ŋaŋ⁶ (translit.)
The muscle of arms is hard. (lit.)
Have real power.

四畫

Be in a position of strength.
〔註〕比喻有實力或有勢力。

0307 手多多
sɐu² dɔ¹ dɔ¹ (translit.)
Have many hands. (lit.)
Touch anything that one sees.
〔註〕形容多手多腳，愛亂摸亂弄。

0308 手忙腳亂
sɐu² mɔŋ⁴ gœk⁸ lyn⁶ (translit.)
Hands busy and feet confused. (lit.)
Be all in a hustle of excitements.

0309 手板係肉；手背又係肉
sɐu² ban² hɐi⁶ juk⁹; sɐu² bui³ jɐu⁶ hɐi⁶ juk⁹ (translit.)
The palms of hands are flesh and the backs of them are also flesh. (lit.)
Have friendly relation with both parties.
Can not treat either side with partiality.
〔註〕表示和雙方都有友情關係故很難偏袒哪一方的意思。

0310 手急眼快
sɐu² gɐp¹ ŋan⁵ fai³ (translit.)
Deft hands and quick eyes. (lit.)
Save the tide.
Seize the right time.
Be quick of eye and deft of hand.

0311 手氣

sɐu² hei³ (translit.)
The air of hands. (lit.)
Luck at gambling.

0312 手指拗出唔拗入
sɐu² dzi² au² tsœt⁷ m⁴ au² jɐp⁹ (translit.)
Fingers are bent out but not bent in. (lit.)
Help and protect outsiders.
〔註〕指自己人不幫自己人却去幫助外人的行爲。

0313 手痕痕
sɐu² hɐn⁴ hɐn⁴ (translit.)
The hand itches. (lit.)
Be eager to try.
〔註〕即手癢；躍躍欲試的意思。

0314 手搵口食
sɐu² wɐn² hau² sik⁹ (translit.)
Hands gain and mouth eats. (lit.)
Live from hand to mouth.
〔註〕形容收入不多，沒積蓄，僅能糊口。

0315 手緊
sɐu² gɐn² (translit.)
The hand is tight. (lit.)
Be short of cash.
Be in low water.
One's money is tight.
Be out at elbows.
〔註〕表示缺乏現金或拮据。

0316 牛皮燈籠 —— 點極都唔明
nɐu⁴ pei⁴ dɐŋ¹ luŋ⁴—dim² gik⁹ dou¹ m⁴ miŋ⁴ (trans-

lit.)
A lantern mounted with hide—
not transparent—no matter
how it is lit. (lit.)
Not understand what one is taught.
Be poor at understanding what somebody says.
Be thick-headed.
〔註〕歇後語，"點"（燃點，指點）和"明"（光明，明白）都是雙關詞。

0317　牛死送牛喪
nɐu⁴ sei² suŋ³ nɐu⁴ sɔŋ¹ (translit.)
Attend a funeral procession of a cow when it is dead. (lit.)
Flog a dead horse.
Feed a dead horse with nice hay.
Work for a dead horse.
Throw good money after bad.
Throw helve after the hatchet.
〔註〕比喻明知絕望還花功夫去幹或想補償損失，反而損失更大。

0318　牛唔飲水，唔揿得牛頭低
nɐu⁴ m⁴ jɐm² soey², m⁴ gɐm⁶ dɐk⁷ nɐu⁴ tɐu⁴ dai¹ (translit.)
If a cow does not want to drink water, no one can push its head down. (lit.)
You may take a horse to the water, but you can not make him drink.

Of one's own will.
Of one's own accord.
〔註〕指任何事不能強迫人去幹，一切必須自願。

0319　牛高馬大
nɐu⁴ go¹ ma⁵ dai⁶ (translit.)
As tall as an ox and big as a horse. (lit.)
Stand like a giant.
〔註〕形容人生得又高又大，但常用於貶義句子中。

0320　牛噍牡丹——唔知花定草
ŋɐu⁴ dziu⁴ mau⁵ dan¹—ŋ⁴ dzi¹ fa¹ diŋ⁶ tsou² (translit.)
An ox chews peony.—It does not know whether it is flower or grass. (lit.)
Not know chalk from cheese.
Cast pearls before swine.
〔註〕比喻不識好歹。

0321　牛頭唔對馬嘴
ŋɐu⁴ tɐu⁴ m⁴ dœy³ ma⁵ dzœy² (translit.)
A cow's head does not match with a horse's mouth. (lit.)
The answer is incongruous with the question.
Fly off at a tangent.
Lose the thread of one's discourse.
Beside the point.
Be irrelevent to...

〔註〕即"牛頭不對馬嘴"。

0322 公死有肉食,婆死有肉食
guŋ¹ sei² jɐu⁵ juk⁹ sik,⁹ pɔ⁴ sei² jɐu⁵ juk⁹ sik⁹ (translit.)
There is flesh to eat no matter whether the husband or the wife dies. (lit.)
Effortlessly gain profit/cash in on others' efforts/conflict.
Take advantage of a conflicting situation to profit oneself.
〔註〕表示坐收漁人之利的意思。

0323 公説公有理;婆説婆有理
guŋ¹ syt⁸ guŋ¹ jɐu⁵ lei⁵, pɔ⁴ syt⁸ pɔ⁴ jɐu⁵ lei⁵ (translit.)
Husband says he has reason; wife says she also has reason. (lit.)
There is much to be said on both sides.
Everything has two sides.
Each clings to his own view.
Both parties claim to be in the right.

0324 今時唔同往日,一個酸梅兩個核
gam¹ si⁴ m⁴ tuŋ⁴ wɔŋ⁵ jɐt⁹, jɐt⁷ gɔ³ syn¹ mui⁴ lœŋ⁵ gɔ³ wɐt⁶ (translit.)
The present time is different from the past days, a sour plum has two stones. (lit.)
The two cannot be mentioned in the same breath.
There have been the vicissitudes of life.
One's present situation is different from the past one.
〔註〕意即今非昔比。

0325 反口覆舌
fan² hɐu² fuk¹ sit⁹ (translit.)
Turn over the mouth and tongue. (lit.)
Not to keep one's words.
Break one's promise.
Deny one's words.
〔註〕意即不履行諾言,言而無信。

0326 反斗
fan² dɐu² (translit.)
Overturn a peck of trouble. (lit.)
Be naughty/mischievous.
〔註〕形容小孩子坐不住,淘氣調皮。

0327 反骨
fan² gwɐt⁷ (translit.)
Over-turned bones. (lit.)
Have a rebellious disposition.
〔註〕形容人忘恩負義,翻臉無情。

0328 反骨仔
fan² gwɐt⁷ dzɐi² (translit.)
A person with over-turned bones. (lit.)
A betrayer.
A rebel.
〔註〕參閱"反骨"(0327)。

0329 反面

fan² min² (translit.)
Turn over the face. (lit.)
Suddenly turn out to be hostile to one's...
〔註〕即翻臉。

0330 反轉豬肚就係屎
fan² dzyn³ dzy¹ tou⁶ dzɐu⁴ hɐi⁶ si² (translit.)
Turn a pig's stomach inside out and there manure appears. (lit.)
Turn friendship into hostility.
Change friendship into anger.
Suddenly turn out to be hostile to one's friend.
〔註〕意即瞬即翻臉無情。

0331 分甘同味
fɐn¹ gɐm¹ tuŋ⁴ mei⁶ (translit.)
Share the sweet to have the same taste. (lit.)
Enjoy the diet together.
Share and share alike.

0332 火上加油
fɔ² sœŋ⁶ ga¹ jɐu⁴ (translit.)
Add oil on the fire. (lit.)
Pour oil on fire.

0333 火遮眼
fɔ² dzɛ¹ ŋan⁵ (translit.)
The fire covers the eyes. (lit.)
Be too angry to see anything/anybody.
〔註〕形容人極度憤怒的樣子。

0334 火頸
fɔ² gɛŋ² (translit.)
Firy neck. (lit.)
Be irritable.
Be irascible.
〔註〕意指脾氣暴燥或容易激動。

0335 火腿繩
fɔ² tœy² siŋ⁴ (translit.)
The rope used to tie a ham. (lit.)
The person who puts himself under the patronage of somebody.
The person who depends on somebody's status for his position.
〔註〕諷刺倚仗有權勢的人抬高自己的身價或攀龍附鳳的人。我國火腿價值昂貴，奸商取巧，綁以粗大麻繩上秤，如此則麻繩的重量和價值，便和火腿相等。

0336 火燒棺材 —— 大炭（歎）
fɔ² siu¹ gun¹ tsɔi⁴—dai⁶ tan³ (translit.)
The fire burns a coffin — big charcoal (enjoyment). (lit.)
Live high.
Live like pigs in clover.
Lie on a bed of flowers.
〔註〕比喻過着享受的生活，養尊處優。

0337 火燒旗竿 —— 長炭（歎）
fɔ² siu¹ kei⁴ gɔn¹—tsœŋ⁴ tan³ (translit.)
The fire burns the flag staff — long charcoal (enjoyment). (lit.)

四畫

Live in clover as long as life lasts.
〔註〕比喻人一生能養尊處優。

0338 火燒燈芯 —— 有炭（歎）
fo² siu¹ dɐŋ¹ sɐm¹—mou⁵ tan³ (translit.)
The fire burns a wick — on charcoal (enjoyment). (lit.)
Lead a dog's life.
Bear hardship.
〔註〕比喻過着貧困的生活或境況堪悲。

0339 火麒麟 —— 週身引（癮）
fo² kei⁴ lœn²ᐟ⁴—dzɐu¹ sɐn¹ jɐn⁵ (translit.)
A firy Chinese unicorn (Kylin) — the whole body is full of fuses (addiction). (lit.)
The person who is addicted to all kinds of lusts.
〔註〕比喻嗜好多的人。

0340 心大心細
sɐm¹ dai⁶ sɐm¹ sɐi³ (translit.)
The heart is either big or small. (lit.)
Feel come hesitation in doing something.
Hesitate to do something.
〔註〕形容猶疑不決，拿不定主意。

0341 心中有屎
sɐm¹ dzuŋ¹ jɐu⁵ si² (translit.)
There is manure in the heart. (lit.)
Have a guilty conscience.
〔註〕相當於作賊心虛或心中有鬼。

0342 心中有數
sɐm¹ dzuŋ¹ jɐu⁵ sou³ (translit.)
There is a sum in the heart. (lit.)
Know what is what.
Know fairly well.
Have a pretty good idea of...

0343 心不在焉
sɐm¹ bɐt¹ dzɔi⁴ jin⁴ (translit.)
The heart is out. (lit.)
Be absent-minded.
Listen inattentively.

0344 心甘命抵
sɐm¹ gɐm¹ mɐŋ⁶ dɐi² (translit.)
The heart is will and the fate deserves it. (lit.)
On a voluntary basis.
Of one's own accord.
On one's own initiative.
〔註〕表示自願或主動的意思。

0345 心多多
sɐm¹ dɔ¹ dɔ¹ (translit.)
Have many minds. (lit.)
Cannot make up one's mind.
Shilly-shally.
Be in two minds about...
Show a manner of instability.
Be in minds about...
〔註〕表示三心二意，拿不定主意。
參閱"十五個銅錢分兩份"

（0077），"三心兩意"（0139）及"寡母婆咁多心"（1719）各條。

0346　心安理得
sɐm¹ ɔn¹ lei⁵ dɐk⁷　(translit.)
The heart is void of offence. (lit.)
Feel at ease and justified.
Have a clear conscience.

0347　心灰意冷
sɐm¹ fui¹ ji³ laŋ⁵　(translit.)
The heart is ashy and the will is cold. (lit.)
Feel disheartened.
Be downhearted.
Lose interest in...

0348　心足
sɐm¹ dzuk¹　(translit.)
The heart contents itself. (lit.)
To one's heart's content.
Express one's satisfaction.

0349　心肝椗
sɐm¹ gɔn¹ diŋ³　(translit.)
The footstalk of heart and liver. (lit.)
One's darling.
One's dear heart.
Hold somebody/something dear.
Somebody/something nearest one's heart.
〔註〕即心肝寶貝兒。

0350　心服口服
sɐm¹ fuk⁹ hɐu² fuk⁹　(translit.)
Both the heart and the mouth are subordinate to. (lit.)
Be sincerely convinced.

0351　心急
sɐm¹ gɐp⁷　(translit.)
The heart hurries up. (lit.)
Be short-tempered.
Be impatient.
In a hurry.

0352　心思思
sɐm¹ si¹ si¹　(translit.)
With a thought in the mind. (lit.)
Have a mind to do something.
Ponder over...
Be spoiling for...
〔註〕即老是想着或惦記着的意思。

0353　心神恍惚
sɐm¹ sɐn⁴ fɔŋ² fɐt⁷　(translit.)
The heart becomes blurred and indistinct. (lit.)
Lose one's presence of mind.
Have a bee in one's bonnet.
Suffer from fidgets.

0354　心淡
sɐm¹ tam⁵　(translit.)
The heart becomes insipid. (lit.)
Be discouraged.
Show indifference towards...
Lose heart.
Lose confidence in...
〔註〕表示心灰意冷，失去信心或不感興趣。參閱"心灰意冷"條

（0347）。

0355 心都凉晒
sɐm¹ dou¹ lœŋ⁴ sai³　(translit.)
The heart feels cool.　(lit.)
Gloat over one's enemy's misfortune.
〔註〕表示幸災樂禍的心態。

0356 心郁郁
sɐm¹ juk¹ juk¹　(translit.)
The heart moves about.　(lit.)
Find it in one's heart to do something.
Would like very much to do something.
〔註〕表示動了心想做……的意思。

0357 心煩
sɐm¹ fan⁴　(translit.)
The heart is troubled.　(lit.)
Vex oneself.
Be vexed.
〔註〕表示獨自煩惱的意思，參閱"腌悶"條（1479）。

0358 心照不宣
sɐm¹ jiu³ bɐt⁷ syn¹　(translit.)
The heart understands without mentioning.　(lit.)
Have a tacit understanding.

0359 心嗰句，口嗰句
sɐm¹ gɔ² gœy³, hɐu² gɔ² gœy³　(translit.)
The heart says so and the mouth also says so.　(lit.)
Say what one thinks about.
The tongue speaks what the heart thinks.
Say from the bottom of one's heart.
Be outspoken in the expression of one's opinions.
〔註〕即心中想什麼，嘴上說什麼。

0360 心領
sɐm¹ liŋ⁵　(translit.)
The heart accepts it.　(lit.)
No, thank you.
I appreciate your kindness but I must decline the offer.
〔註〕用於婉言謝絕對方禮物或好意的客氣話。

0361 心酸
sɐm¹ syn¹　(translit.)
The heart feel sour.　(lit.)
Be deeply grieved.
Nurse a grievance.
Feel sad.

0362 心亂如麻
sɐm¹ lyn⁶ jy⁴ ma⁴　(translit.)
The heart is as confused as tangled hemp.　(lit.)
One's mind is in a tangle.
Be utterly confused and disconcerted.
Be completely upset.

0363 六耳不同謀
luk⁹ ji⁵ bɐt⁷ tuŋ⁴ mɐu⁴　(translit.)
Six ears cannot plot together.　(lit.)
Two's company, three's none.
〔註〕表示三人共同做事，意見多，難於一致的意思。

0364 六神無主
luk⁹ sɐn⁴ mou⁴ dzy² (translit.)
The six vital organs lose their function. (lit.)
Be covered with confusion.
Be thrown into confusion.

0365 六親不認
luk⁹ tsɐn¹ bɐt⁷ jiŋ⁶ (translit.)
Not to recognize six relations. (lit.)
Turn one's back upon all one's relations.

0366 日頭唔好講人，夜晚唔好講神
jɐt⁹ tɐu² m⁴ hou² gɔn² jɐn⁴, jɛ⁶ man⁵ m⁴ hou² gɔn² sɐn⁴ (translit.)
Don't speak of men by day and of gods by night.
Talk of the devil and he will appear.
〔註〕相當於一説曹操，曹操就到。

0367 日慳夜慳，唔够老公一舖攤
jɐt⁹ han¹ jɛ⁴ han¹, m⁴ gou³ lou⁵ guŋ¹ jɐt⁷ pou¹ tan¹ (translit.)
What is spared day and night is not enough for a husband to gamble 'Fantan' for once. ('Fantan' is a form of gambling.) (lit.)
All is lost on an occasion.
All goes down the drain at once.

Penny wise and pound foolish.
〔註〕比喻小處精明，大處浪費。

0368 少件膶
siu² gin⁶ jœn² (translit.)
Lack of a piece of liver. (lit.)
Be flighty.
Be more abnormal than normal.
〔註〕形容人心理不正常。廣東人稱"肝"爲"膶"。

0369 少數怕長計
siu² sou³ pa³ tsœŋ⁴ gɐi³ (translit.)
A little quantity fears to be counted for long. (lit.)
Many a little makes a mickle.
〔註〕指儘管每次算起來都微不足道，但長期計算也就很可觀了。

0370 水上扒龍船，岸上人有眼
sœy² sœŋ⁶ pa⁴ luŋ⁴ syn⁴, ŋɔn⁶ sœŋ⁶ jɐn⁴ jɐu⁵ ŋan⁵ (translit.)
Row dragon boats on the water, the people on both banks have eyes. (lit.)
Lookers-on see better.
Lookers-on see more than the players.
On-lookers see most of the game.
〔註〕比喻旁觀者清。

0371 水上扒龍船，岸上夾死仔
sœy² sœŋ⁶ pa⁴ luŋ⁴ syn⁴, ŋɔn⁶ sœŋ⁶ gap⁸ sei² dzɐi² (translit.)
Others row dragon boats on the water but people on the bank

squeeze child to death. (lit.)
Key oneself up over other's business.
Feel both anxious and nervous at other's business.
〔註〕原義指在龍舟競渡中，岸上人看得緊張時，連小兒也夾死。因此轉喻指替別人着急。

0372　水瓜打狗——唔見咗一撅
sœy² gwa¹ da² gɐu²—m⁴ gin³ dzɔ² jɐt⁷ kyt⁹ (translit.)
Beat a dog with a cucumber — one half of it is lost. (lit.)
Half of something is lost.
〔註〕表示失去一半的意思。

0373　水汪汪
sœy² wɔŋ¹ wɔŋ¹ (translit.)
Be watery. (lit.)
Have only a forlorn hope.
Come to nothing.
Be below the standard.
〔註〕表希望不大，渺茫，及不上要求等。

0374　水浸眼眉
sœy² dzɐm³ ŋan⁶ mei⁴ (translit.)
The water floods eyebrows. (lit.)
The black ox has trod on one's foot.
Be at death's door.
〔註〕意指災害已降臨到頭上。

0375　水鬼升城隍
sœy² gwai² siŋ¹ siŋ⁴ wɔŋ⁴ (translit.)
A water ghost is promoted to being City God. (lit.)
Set a beggar on horse back and he will ride to the devil.
〔註〕現多含貶義，表示小人得志的意思。

0376　水過鴨背
sœy² gwɔ³ ap⁸ bui³ (translit.)
The water flows over the back of a duck. (lit.)
Be like water off duck's back.
Be forgetful of...
〔註〕比喻聽說話，唸書等不在意，轉眼便忘得一乾二淨。

0377　水落石出
sœy² lɔk⁹ sɛk⁹ tsœt⁷ (translit.)
When the water goes down, the rock comes out. (lit.)
Come out in the wash.

0378　水溝油
sœy² kɐu¹ jɐu⁴ (translit.)
Mix water with oil. (lit.)
Cannot get along with each other.
Feel hostility towards each other.
〔註〕"溝"即"混合"，水與油是無法混合的，故此語表示合不來的意思。

0379　水靜河飛
sœy² dziŋ⁴ hɔ⁴ fei¹ (translit.)
The water is still and the river is flying. (lit.)

There is nobody everywhere.
There is not anybody here and there.
Silence reigns in the place.
The market is dull.
〔註〕表示到處無人或市場清淡。（按"水靜河飛"實爲"水靜（淨）鵝飛"的音誤，而且和本意也不同。）

0380 巴結
ba¹ git⁸ (translit.)
Flatter. (lit.)
Play up to somebody.
Fawn upon somebody.
Toady somebody.
Tickle somebody's ears.

0381 巴結有錢佬好過拜靈菩薩
ba¹ git⁸ jɐu⁵ tzin² lou² hou²
gɔ³ bai³ ŋɐn⁴ pou⁴ sat⁸
(translit.)
It is better to toady rich men than it is to worship efficacious gods. (lit.)
It is much more advantageous to rub elbows with the rich.
〔註〕"佬"即人，"好過"即勝過。

0382 巴閉
ba¹ bɐi³ (translit.)
Noisy. (lit.)
Make a noise about something.
Be bustling with noise and excitement.
Be in a bustle.
Speak in excitement.
Make a noise in the world.
Be great in strength and impetus.
Of great celebrity.
Win popularity.
A great occasion.
〔註〕形容人做事緊張忙亂，喧囂，或者形容人在社會上了不起，勢力大，亦可以形容場面隆重，排場大。

0383 巴渣
ba¹ dza¹ (translit.)
Make a noise. (lit.)
Long-tongued.
Gossipy.
Nosy.
〔註〕形容人多嘴，好管閒事。

0384 引狼入屋拉鷄仔
jɐn⁵ lɔŋ⁴ jɐp⁹ uk⁷ lai¹ gɐi¹
dzɐi² (translit.)
Invite a wolf into the house to drag chickens. (lit.)
Bring disaster upon oneself.
Invite loss for oneself.
Invite a wolf to watch chickens.
〔註〕即"引狼入室"。

五畫

0385 正一陳顯南
dziŋ³ jɐt⁷ tsɐn⁴ hin² nam²/⁴
(translit.)
Be really the man by the name of Tsɐn Hin Nam. (lit.)
Be verbose.
Make repetition to a tiresome

extent.

〔註〕指喜歡反反覆覆地說同一件事的人。

0386 正斗/正嘢

dzɛn³ dɐu²/dzɛŋ³ jɛ⁵ (translit.)

Be legitimated. (lit.)

Certified product.

Be genuine.

Be excellent.

〔註〕表示好貨色或真貨色的意思。

0387 平生不作虧心事，半夜敲門也不驚

piŋ⁴ saŋ¹ bɐt⁷ dzɔk⁸ kwɐi¹ sɐm¹ si⁶, bun³ jɛ⁶ hau¹ mun⁴ ja⁵ bɐt⁷ giŋ¹ (translit.)

Nothing against the conscience is done in the ordinary life, there is no fear to knock on the door at midnight. (lit.)

A long roll of thunder frightens no man with a clear conscience.

0388 左耳入，右耳出

dzɔ² ji⁵ jɐp⁹, jɐu⁶ ji⁵ tsœt⁷ (translit.)

Come into the left ear and out of the right ear. (lit.)

In at one ear and out at the other.

0389 左手嚟，右手去

dzɔ² sɐu² lɐi⁴, jɐu⁶ sɐu² hœy³ (translit.)

Come to the left hand and go from the right. (lit.)

In at one hand and out at the other.

〔註〕比喻金錢來的容易去的快。

0390 左右做人難

dzɔ² jɐu⁶ dzou⁴ jɐn⁴ nan⁴ (translit.)

It is difficult to be a human on either the left or the right. (lit.)

Be in a quandary about...

Be between Scylla and Charybdis.

Be a friend with a saint and a devil.

0391 本地薑唔辣

bun² dei⁶ gœŋ¹ m⁴ lat⁹ (translit.)

Local gingers are never hot. (lit.)

Grass is always greener on the other side of the fence.

〔註〕指本地培養的人材不及外來者，含貶義。

0392 本事

bun² si⁶ (translit.)

The originality. (lit.)

Be capable.

Ability.

0393 甘心咯！

gɐm¹ sɐm¹ lɔk⁸ (translit.)

How sweet my heart is! (lit.)

How pleased I am to see it!

〔註〕在幸災樂禍的時候所說的話，意即"我的心很涼啊！"。

0394 未見官先打三十大板

mei⁶ gin³ gun¹ sin¹ da² sam¹

sɐp⁹ dai⁶ ban² (translit.)
Be put to torture with a plank for thirty times before seeing the county Magistrate. (lit.)
Suffer a loss before the gain.
Visible disadvantage comes before the invisible advantage.
〔註〕相當於"未見其利，先見其害"。

0395 未見其利先見其害
mei⁶ gin³ kei⁴ lei⁶ sin¹ gin³ kei⁴ hɔ⁶ (translit.)
See the injury before seeing the profit. (lit.)
Visible disadvantage comes before the invible advantage.
Suffer a loss before an uncertain gain.

0396 未知心腹事，先聽口中言
mei⁶ dzi¹ sɐm¹ fuk⁷ si⁶, sin¹ tiŋ³ hɐu² dzuŋ¹ jin⁴ (translit.)
Listen to the words by mouth before knowing the affairs in the heart. (lit.)
Words out of the mouth are the words indeed.
A straw shows which way the wind blows.

0397 未登天子位，先置殺人刀
mei⁶ dɐŋ¹ tin¹ dzi² wɐi⁶, sin¹ dzi³ sat⁹ jɐn⁴ dou¹ (translit.)
Buy a knife to kill people before coming to the throne. (lit.)
Exercise one's power before filling the position.
Be puffed up with pride before becoming rich.
Begin to do something that one is incompetent to do before one is qualified to do it.

0398 未學行先學走
mei⁶ hɔk⁶ haŋ⁴ sin¹ hɔk⁶ dzɐu² (translit.)
Begin to run before learning to walk. (lit.)
Learn to run before learning to walk.
〔註〕即不會走就想跑。

0399 未觀其人，先觀其友
mei⁶ gun¹ kei⁴ jɐn⁴, sin¹ gun¹ kei⁴ jɐu⁵ (translit.)
See his friends before seeing the man. (lit.)
You can judge a man by the friends he keeps.

0400 石地堂鐵掃把——硬打硬——
sɛk⁹ dei⁶ tɔŋ⁴ tit⁸ so³ ba², —— ŋaŋ⁶ da² ŋaŋ⁶ (translit.)
Stone threshing floor and iron broom—hardness against hardness. (lit.)
A Roland for an Oliver.
Nip and tuck.
When Greek meets Greek, then comes the tug of war.
〔註〕即"勢均力敵"。參閱"半斤八両"（0504）條。

0401 石灰籮
sɛk⁹ fui¹ lɔ⁴ (translit.)
A bamboo basket used for holding lime. (lit.)
A person who is hated wherever he goes.
〔註〕比喻到處幹壞事，到處留有污點穢迹的人，到處都不受歡迎的人。

0402 石沉大海
sɛk⁹ tsɐm⁴ dai⁶ hɔi² (translit.)
A rock sinks into a big sea. (lit.)
Disappear forever.
Be obliterated from one's memory.

0403 石罅米——雞啄
sɛk⁹ la³ mɐi⁵—gɐi¹ dœŋ¹ (translit.)
The rice in the cleft of the rock — to be picked by hens. (lit.)
A man who is generous only in giving money to ladies.
〔註〕諷刺只肯在女人身上花錢的男人，在廣東話裏，"雞"常指妓女。

0404 世界仔
sɐi³ gai³ dzɐi² (translit.)
The guy of the world. (lit.)
A lickspittle.
A worldly-wise person.
A person who knows the ways of the world.
〔註〕指善於逢迎拍馬，八面玲瓏的人。

0405 世界輪流轉
sɐi³ gai³ lœn⁴ lɐu⁴ dzyn² (translit.)
The world goes around and around. (lit.)
Everybody has the turn of the wheel.
Everybody meets with the Fortune's wheel.
By turns does the Fortune's wheel go around.
〔註〕表示人的命運如車輪般轉動（變）。參閱"風水輪流轉"（1036）條。

0406 去揾周公
hœy³ wɐn² dzɐu¹ guŋ¹ (translit.)
Go to look for Duke Dzɐu. (lit.)
Go to bed.
Go to sleep.
〔註〕這是把孔子說過"久矣乎不夢見周公"的話來比喻去睡覺。

0407 古老石山
gu² lou⁵ sɛk⁹ san¹ (translit.)
Ancient potted rocky mountain. (lit.)
An old fogy.
〔註〕指頑固保守的人。

0408 古老當時興
gu² lou⁵ dɔŋ³ si⁴ hiŋ¹ (translit.)
Old fashion is thought as a new trend. (lit.)
Take an old style as the vogue

of the day.

0409　古/蠱惑
gu² wak⁹　(translit.)
Be sly.　(lit.)
Be tricksy.
Be as crafty as a fox.
Know a trick or two.
〔註〕表示詭計多端或狡猾的意思。

0410　古縮
gu² suk⁷　(translit.)
Old and shrinkable.　(lit.)
Be quiet and unsocial.
Shrink into oneself.
〔註〕形容人沉默寡言，性情不合羣，不愛交際。

0411　瓦風領 —— 包頂頸
ŋa⁵ fuŋ¹ nɛŋ⁵—bau¹ diŋ² gɛŋ²　(translit.)
An earthen wind-collar—be sure to support the neck. (lit.)
Be sure to argue to the contrary.
The person who likes to bicker.
〔註〕指專和人擡槓的人。

0412　扒灰
pa⁴ fui¹　(translit.)
Rake ashes.　(lit.)
Incest with one's daughter-in-law.
〔註〕指公公和媳婦有亂倫關係。

0413　扒逆水
pa⁴ ŋak⁹ sœy²　(translit.)
Row against the current. (lit.)
Deal with something in con-trary manner.
〔註〕相當於"反其道而行之"。

0414　打理
da² lei⁵　(translit.)
Take care of.　(lit.)
Manage.
Run.
〔註〕料理，管理。

0415　打牙祭
da² ŋa⁴ dzɐi³　(translit.)
Beat teeth ceremony.　(lit.)
Eat one's fill.
Gorge oneself with a tuck-in.
〔註〕即大吃一頓。

0416　打牙鉸
da² ŋa⁴ gau³　(translit.)
Beat the jawbones.　(lit.)
Have a chat with somebody.
〔註〕表示和人閒談，閒聊。

0417　打尖
da² dzim¹　(translit.)
Jump into the middle of a queue. (lit.)
Push oneself into a queue out of the turn.
Jump the queue.
〔註〕即加塞兒。

0418　打同通
da² tuŋ⁴ tuŋ¹　(translit.)
Have a mutual communication. (lit.)
Act in collusion with each other.
Be in collaboration with each other.
〔註〕意即串通，互相勾結。

0419 打[大]赤肋
da² [dai⁶] tsik⁸/tsɛk⁸ lɐk⁹
(translit.)
Bare oneself. (lit.)
Strip oneself to the waist.
〔註〕打赤膊的意思。

0420 打死不離親兄弟
da² sei² bɐt⁷ lei⁴ tsɐn¹ hiŋ¹ dɐi⁶ (translit.)
It is full brothers who can fight to death together to defend each other. (lit.)
Blood is thicker than water.

0421 打死狗講價
da² sei² gɐu² gɔn² ga³
(translit.)
Drive a hard bargain over the dog which was beaten to death. (lit.)
Fish in trouble water.
Take advantage of somebody's fault to practise an extortion.
〔註〕指既成事實後再談條件或講價錢,一方可慢天要價,另一方處於不利地位。

0422 打如意算盤
da² jy⁴ ji³ syn³ pun⁴
(translit.)
Reckon on the abacus of wishful thinking. (lit.)
Wish to have one's own will.
Work out a plan advantageous to oneself.
Have one's smug calculations.

0423 打地舖
da² dei⁶ pou¹ (translit.)
Sleep on the ground. (lit.)
Make up a bed on the ground.
〔註〕把被褥等舖在地上睡覺。

0424 打法功夫還鬼願
da² fat⁸ guŋ¹ fu¹ wan⁴ gwɐi² jyn⁶ (translit.)
The work to expound the teachings of Buddhism is to fulfil the vow of ghosts. (lit.)
Work in a perfunctory manner.
Lie down on the job.
〔註〕指敷衍塞責,磨洋工。

0425 打完齋唔要和尚
da² jyn⁴ dzai¹ m⁴ jiu³ wɔ⁴ sœŋ¹ (translit.)
After the Buddhist fasts, Buddhist monks are no longer needed. (lit.)
Kick down the ladder.
Once on shore, pray no more.
〔註〕相當於"過河拆橋"。參閱"過橋抽板"條(1648)。

0426 打劫紅毛鬼,進貢佛蘭西
da² gip³ huŋ⁴ mou⁴ gwɐi², dzœn³ guŋ³ fɐt⁹ lan¹ sɐi¹
(translit.)
Rob red-haired ghost of something and offer it to France. (Red-haired ghost a nickname standing for Englishman.) (lit.)
Rob Peter to pay Paul.
〔註〕比喻取之於甲而予之於乙。

0427 打斧頭

da² fu² tɐu⁴　(translit.)
Beat the head of an axe.　(lit.)
Cook up an expence account to line one's pockets.
Do not give the whole story.
〔註〕即揩油（常指代買東西或代辦事從中佔點兒小便宜），亦轉喻表示講述一件事時作了些隱瞞。

0428　打個白鴿轉
da² gɔ³ bak⁹ gɐp⁸ dzyn³ᐟ⁶
(translit.)
Make a pigeon round.　(lit.)
Turn around.
Walk around.
〔註〕表示打一個轉或到附近走走的意思。

0429　打到褪
da² dou³ tɐn³　(translit.)
Go backward.　(lit.)
Be retrogressive.
Be out of luck.
Be down on one's luck.
〔註〕表示倒退，後退或倒運的意思。如意爲"倒運"時，廣東人又說成"行路都打倒褪"。

0430　打特
da² dɐk⁹　(translit.)
Be stunned.　(lit.)
Be astounded.
Be startled.
〔註〕表示事情來得很突然，使自己暗暗吃驚的意思。又作"打突兀"。

0431　打敗仗
da² bai⁶ dzœŋ³　(translit.)

Be defeated.　(lit.)
Fall sick.
Take sick.
Be taken ill.
〔註〕即"病倒了"，在口語上和戰爭沒有什麼關係。

0432　打真軍
da² dzɐn¹ gwɐn¹　(translit.)
Fight with real weapons. (lit.)
Work in real earnest.
Do the business with special capital.
〔註〕意即認真地幹或以實際資本做生意。

0433　打退堂鼓
da² tœy³ tɔŋ⁴ gu²　(translit.)
Beat the drum to dismiss the court.　(lit.)
Back out one's promise.
Beat a retreat.
〔註〕指人收回承諾的意思。

0434　打草驚蛇
da² tsou² giŋ¹ sɛ⁴　(translit.)
Beat the grass and frighten the snake.　(lit.)
Wake a sleeping dog.
Cause undesired agitation.

0435　打荷包
da² hɔ⁴ bau¹　(translit.)
Beat the purse.　(lit.)
Pick a pocket.
〔註〕小偷或扒手掏錢包。

0436　打得更多夜又長
da² dɐk⁷ gɐŋ¹ dɔ¹ jɛ²ᐟ⁶ jɐu⁶

tsœŋ⁴ (translit.)
The more the night-watching drum is beaten, the longer the night becomes. (lit.)
It wastes time only to talk.
Fine words butter no parsnips.
Actions speak louder than words.
〔註〕表示空言無益，行動勝於空言的意思。

0437 打蛇隨棍上
da² sɛ⁴ tsœy⁴ gwɐn³ sœŋ⁵ (translit.)
Beat a snake and it creeps up along the stick. (lit.)
Take advantage of the tide.
Seize occasion by the forelock.
At the bare idea of...
〔註〕表示順著情勢，乘機提出自己的想法或要求。

0438 打單
da² dan¹ (translit.)
Type an invoice. (lit.)
Blackmail somebody.
Practise extortion.
Extort money from somebody.
〔註〕匪徒給人寫恐嚇信，勒索錢財。

0439 打單泡
da² dan¹ pou¹ (translit.)
Do business single-handed. (lit.)
A travelling trader working all by himself.
Take independent action.
〔註〕跑單幫的人或表示單獨行動的

意思。

0440 打腳骨
da² gœk³ gwɐt⁷ (translit.)
Beat the bone of the leg. (lit.)
Fleece somebody of his money.
Hold up.
〔註〕表示攔路搶劫或敲竹槓。

0441 打橫嚟
da² waŋ⁴ nɐi⁴ (translit.)
Lay crosswise. (lit.)
Be impervious to all reasons.
〔註〕意即不講道理。

0442 打輸數
da² sy¹ sou³ (translit.)
Be thought as a loss. (lit.)
Give up for loss.
〔註〕表示已作爲損失計。

0443 打邊爐同打屎窟
da² bin¹ lou⁴ tuŋ⁴ da² si² fɐt¹ (translit.)
Beat chafing dish and beat the buttocks. (lit.)
Out of all comparison.
Cannot be in comparison with...
As different as chalk from cheese.
〔註〕比喻兩者不能相比。

0444 打頭陣
da² tɐu⁴ dzɐn⁶ (translit.)
Fight in the van. (lit.)
Take the lead.
〔註〕表示領頭的意思。

0445 打鐵趁熱
da² tit³ tsɐn³ jit⁶ (translit.)
Strike the iron while it is hot. (lit.)

Strike the iron while it is hot.
Take advantage of the opportunity.
At the first opportunity.

0446 打錯主意
da² tsɔ³ dzy² ji³　(translit.)
Beat out a wrong idea.　(lit.)
Get a wrong idea into one's head.
Get down from the wrong side of the wall.

0447 打錯算盤
da² tsɔ³ syn³ pun⁴　(translit.)
Wrongly reckon on the abacus.　(lit.)
Form a wrong estimation.
Make a wrong decision.
Be out in one's reckoning.

0448 打瀉茶
da² sɛ² tsa²/⁴　(translit.)
Over-turned tea.　(lit.)
A widowed maiden. (a maiden whose fiancé died before wedding.)
〔註〕指訂了婚而未出嫁便喪未婚夫的女人。

0449 打齋鶴
da² dzai¹ hɔk⁶　(translit.)
The crane which does penace for the crime of the dead.　(lit.)
A steerer.
A person who seduces somebody to live the life of Riley.
A person who leads somebody astray.
〔註〕引誘人墮落的人。

0450 打雜
da² dzɐp⁹　(translit.)
Do all jobs.　(lit.)
Do odd jobs.
A person of all work.
〔註〕即雜工。

0451 打醒十二個精神
da² siŋ² sɐp⁹ ji⁶ gɔ³ dziŋ¹ sɐn⁴　(translit.)
Wake twelve spirits.　(lit.)
Raise one's spirits.
Arouse one's spirits.
Cheer up.
Prick up one's ears.
〔註〕表示提起精神，當心，"提高警惕"的意思。

0452 打爛砂盆問到篤
da² lan⁶ sa¹ pun⁴ mɐn⁶ dou³ duk⁷　(translit.)
Breaking an earthen rice-washing basin, one asks to the bottom.　(lit.)
Get to the bottom of the matter.
Search into a matter.
Seek after truth.
〔註〕即"打破沙鍋問到底"。

0453 打爛齋砵
da² lan⁶ dzai¹ but⁸　(translit.)
Break the bowl for holding vegetarian diet.　(lit.)
Break one's fast.
Break abstinence.

Break oneself of a habit.
Return to laity.
〔註〕比喻破戒或還俗。

0454 打響頭炮
da² hœŋ² tɐu⁴ pou³ (translit.)
Fire the first cannon. (lit.)
Meet with a first success.
〔註〕表示旗開得勝的意思。

0455 仔大仔世界
dzɐi² dɐi⁶ dzɐi² sɐi³ gai³ (translit.)
It is the son's world since he is grown up. (lit.)
Let one's adult son take the responsibility for a decision.
〔註〕表示兒子大了，由他自己作主的意思。

0456 生人勿近
saŋ¹ jɐn⁴ mɐt⁹ gɐn⁶ (translit.)
A person no living man can get near. (lit.)
A person whom one finds it hard to get along with.
〔註〕形容一個難以相處的人。

0457 生人唔生膽
saŋ¹ jɐn⁴ m⁴ saŋ¹ dam² (translit.)
Born without a gall. (lit.)
Be as timid as a hare.
〔註〕比喻膽小。

0458 生人霸死定
saŋ¹ jɐn⁴ ba³ sei² dɐŋ⁶ (translit.)
A living man occupies the place for his death. (lit.)
Act like a dog in the manger.
〔註〕相當於"佔着茅坑不拉屎"。

0459 生勾勾
saŋ¹ ŋɐu¹ ŋɐu¹ (translit.)
Be raw. (lit.)
Be undone.
Be still alive.
〔註〕指未煮熟的或仍然活着的。

0460 生仔唔知仔心肝
saŋ¹ dzɐi² m⁴ dzi¹ dzɐi² sɐm¹ gɔn¹ (translit.)
Give birth to a son but know nothing about his heart and liver. (lit.)
It is hard to know people's hidden intention.
〔註〕相當於"人心難測"。

0461 生白果——腥夾悶
saŋ¹ bak⁶ gwɔ²—sɛŋ¹ gap³ mun⁶ (translit.)
Raw ginkoes—they smell evil frowsy and sulky. (lit.)
Be fastidious.
Be hypercritical.
〔註〕形容人難以討好的性格或好吹毛求疵。

0462 生安白造
saŋ¹ ɔn¹ bak⁶ dzou⁶ (translit.)
Make believe. (lit.)
Tell the tale.
Invent a story.
Make up an out-and-out fabrication.
〔註〕表示虛構，編造的意思。

0463 生骨大頭菜 —— 種「縱」壞
saŋ¹ gwɐt⁷ dai⁶ tɐu⁴ tsɔi³ —— dzuŋ³ wai⁴ *(translit.)*
Bony turnips — ill planted (spoiled). (lit.)
Be ill spoiled.
〔註〕"種"和"縱"同音，借諧音來喻"被寵壞"的意思。

0464 生雞精
saŋ¹ gɐi¹ dziŋ¹ *(translit.)*
The spirit of a cock. (lit.)
A luster.
〔註〕比喻好色的人。

0465 生死有定
saŋ¹ si² (sei)² jɐu⁵ diŋ⁶ *(translit.)*
Life and death are destined. (lit.)
Every bullet has its billet.

0466 生蝦咁跳
saŋ¹ ha¹ gɐm³ tiu³ *(translit.)*
Hop like a living shrimp. (lit.)
Be hot under the collar.
Be like a cat on hot bricks.
Have ants in one's pants.
〔註〕表示因氣憤而坐立不安。

0467 生蟣貓入眼
saŋ¹ dzi¹ mɐu¹ jɐp⁹ ŋan⁵ *(translit.)*
A cat with ringworms coming into its eyes. (lit.)
Feast one's eyes on somebody/something.

Love at first sight.
Take to somebody/something at sight.
〔註〕比喻一見便喜歡而瞇着眼睛盯着的神態，即"一見鍾情"的意思。

0468 生蟲拐杖
saŋ¹ tsuŋ⁴ gwai² dzœŋ² *(translit.)*
A worm-eaten walking stick. (lit.)
A person lacking responsibility.
A person who can't be relied upon for help.
A broken reed.
〔註〕比喻不可靠的人。

0469 白手興家
bak⁶ sɐu² hiŋ¹ ga¹ *(translit.)*
Start a family with empty hands. (lit.)
Start from scratch.

0470 白食
bak⁹ sik⁹ *(translit.)*
Eat without paying. (lit.)
Have a free meal.
Have the run of one's teeth.
〔註〕意即免費吃一頓

0471 白斬雞
bak⁹ dzam² gɐi¹ *(translit.)*
A steamed hen chopped into pieces. (lit.)
A steamed hen.
〔註〕即"白切雞"，爲粵菜之一。

0472 白鼻哥
bak⁹ bei⁶ gɔ¹ *(translit.)*

A white nose. (lit.)
A failure as a candidate.
〔註〕常指考試落第的人。

0473　白撞
bak⁹ dzɔŋ⁶　(translit.)
Seek after a chance. (lit.)
Pass oneself off as somebody's friend to deceive.
Be on the loaf, inventing a lame excuse to cheat somebody.
〔註〕形容人藉詞或藉着關係來騙人。

0474　白撞雨 —— 濆「讚」壞
bak⁶ dzɔŋ⁶ jy⁵—dzan³ wai⁶ (translit.)
Shower—be badly spatted (praised). (lit.)
Be spoiled by being praised.
Spoil somebody by praising too much.
〔註〕"白撞雨"即"驟雨","濆"即"濺落"。"濆"和"讚"同音,因此借指"被人讚壞了"。

0475　白霍
bak¹ fɔk³　(translit.)
Have a look at nobody. (lit.)
With colours flying and band playing.
Faint oneself in bright colours.
Make a boast of oneself.
Take pride in oneself.
〔註〕形容人態度輕浮。常和"沙塵"連用,組成"沙塵白霍"一語。參閱"沙塵"(0798)條。

0476　白鴿眼
bak⁹ gɐp³ ŋan⁵　(translit.)

White pigeon's eyes. (lit.)
Be snobbish.
Look upon somebody with disdain.
〔註〕即"勢利眼"。

0477　白蟮上沙灘 —— 唔死一身潺
bak⁹ sin⁶ sœŋ⁵ sa¹ tan¹—m⁴ sei² jɐt⁷ sɐn¹ san⁴ (translit.)
A white eel gets on to the sand—thoug it may not be dead, its body gets full of synovia. (lit.)
Get out of disatress but into trouble.
When fatality goes out of the door, trouble comes in at the rear window.
〔註〕表示縱能逃過死亡,但也麻煩很多的意思。

0478　瓜老襯
gwa¹ lou⁵ tsɐn³　(translit.)
Old enough to collapse while it is time. (lit.)
Meet with one's death.
Meet one's fate.
Die a death.
〔註〕死亡的俗稱。

0479　瓜直
gwa¹ dzik⁶　(translit.)
Collapse straight. (lit.)
Fall flat.
Meet with one's death.
Meet one's fate.
〔註〕表示完全失敗或死亡的意思。

參閱"瓜老襯"（0478）及"瓜得"（0481）條。

0480 瓜柴
gwa¹ tsai⁴　(translit.)
Collapse like a piece of firewood.　(lit.)
〔註〕同"瓜老襯"（0478）。

0481 瓜得
gwa¹ dɐk⁷　(translit.)
Collapse.　(lit.)
Be done for.
Meet with one's death.
Meet one's fate.
Fall flat.
〔註〕"瓜老襯"和"瓜柴"着重死亡的意思。但"瓜直"及"瓜得"則着重於"一切完蛋"這方面的意義。

0482 他他條條
ta¹ ta¹ tiu⁴ tiu⁴　(translit.)
Have a comfortable life.　(lit.)
Go easy.
Lead a happy-go-lucky life.
Be as snug as a bug in a rug.
Calmly.
〔註〕表示生活舒適，工作清閒的意思。但當作副詞用時，則有隱重，沉着之意。

0483 甩身
lɐt¹ sɐn⁷　(translit.)
Get off the body.　(lit.)
Get away from...
Extricate oneself from...
Slip one's pursuer.
Lay down one's responsibility.
Put the blame on others.
〔註〕表示脫身或把責任或過失委於他人的意思。

0484 甩拖
lɐt¹ tɔ¹　(translit.)
Separate the trailer.　(lit.)
Break off friendly relation with one's lover.
Break one's appointment.
〔註〕常指和愛人分手。參閱"掟煲"（1303）條。但亦表示失約。參閱"甩底"（0485）條。

0485 甩底
lɐt⁷ dɐi²　(translit.)
The bottom comes off.　(lit.)
Break one's appointment.
〔註〕表示失約的意思。

0486 甩繩馬騮
lɐt⁷ siŋ⁴ ma⁵ lɐu¹　(translit.)
A monkey on the loose.　(lit.)
Be on the loose.
A person who kicks over the trace.
Be like a dog on the loose.
〔註〕比喻難駕馭，難以約束的人。

0487 甩鬚
lɐt⁷ sou¹　(translit.)
Whiskers come off.　(lit.)
Be unbecoming.
Lose face.
Make a fool of oneself.
Bring disgrace upon oneself.
〔註〕即丟臉或出醜。

0488 包尾大番
bau¹ mei⁵ dai⁶ fan¹　(translit.)
The band at the end of a procession.　(lit.)

Close the rear.
Come out last.
The last of the successful candidates.
〔註〕廣東各地每有酧神巡遊時，例有一隊樂隊殿後，這樂隊稱爲"大番"。現轉喻指壓尾或壓尾的人。

0489 包拗頸
bɐu¹ au³ gɛŋ² (translit.)
Be sure to band a neck. (lit.)
Be sure to argue to the contrary.
Ram an argument home.
〔註〕表示專門跟人擡槓的意思。

0490 包撞板
bau¹ dzɔŋ⁶ ban² (translit.)
Be sure to knock against the board. (lit.)
Always make a mistake.
Be sure to go wrong.
Be sure to make trouble.
〔註〕表示專出岔子的意思。

0491 失失慌
sɐt⁷ sɐt⁷ fɔŋ¹ (translit.)
Get frightened. (lit.)
Be all in a fluster.
Be in a flurried manner.
〔註〕慌慌張張。參閱"慌失失"條（1638）。

0492 失匙夾萬
sɐt⁷ si⁴ gap⁸ man⁶ (translit.)
The safe without key. (lit.)
A guy who can hardly obtain money from his rich father.
〔註〕指無法從父親處要到錢的富家子。

0493 失威
sɐt⁷ wɐi¹ (translit.)
Lose power. (lit.)
Lose face./Humiliate oneself.
Be thrown into the shade./Commit a breach of etiquette.
Be completely discredited.
〔註〕指丟臉或出醜。

0494 失魂魚
sɐt⁷ wɐn⁴ jy² (translit.)
The fish losing its soul. (lit.)
An absent-minded person.
A rash person.
A person who is scared out of his wits.
〔註〕泛指心不在焉，莽撞，或驚慌失措的人。

0495 失魂落魄
sɐt⁷ wɐn⁴ lɔk⁹ pak⁸ (translit.)
Lose one's soul and drop one's spirit. (lit.)
Stand aghast.
Be like a duck in a thunderstorm.
Have a bee in one's head.
Suffer from the fidgets.
〔註〕形容人精神恍惚，驚慌失措，坐立不安或受驚的樣子。

0496 失驚無神
sɐt⁷ giŋ¹/gɛŋ¹ mou⁴ sɐn⁴ (translit.)
Suddenly get frightened. (lit.)
Be seized with a panic.

0497　禾桿冚珍珠
wɔ⁴ gɔn² kɐm² dzɐn¹ dzy¹
(translit.)
Rice-straws cover pearls. (lit.)
Put on rags over glad rags.
Feign oneself to live in poverty.
〔註〕比喻裝窮相。又指把珍貴的東西用平凡的東西掩蓋着。

0498　皮鞋筋——一扯到口
pei⁴ hai⁴ gɐn¹—jɐt⁷ tsɛ²
dou³ hɐu² (translit.)
The string used to make shoes,—one pull reaches the mouth. (lit.)
Be impatient of waiting for...
Be short-tempered.
An impetuous person.
Be impetuous.
〔註〕指性急的人。

0499　立心不良
lap⁹ sɐm¹ bɐt⁷ lœŋ⁴ (translit.)
Set a wicked heart. (lit.)
Be ill-disposed.

0500　立立亂
lap⁹′⁴ lap⁹′² lyn⁶ (translit.)
Disordered. (lit.)
Be all in a muddle.
Be topsy-turvy.
Be at sixes and sevens.
Be in a mess.

Be caught unawares.
Be taken by surprise.
〔註〕形容人受驚嚇以後神色變異的樣子。

0501　立實心腸
lap⁹ sɐt⁹ sɐm¹ tsœŋ⁴ (translit.)
Fix the heart and intestines firmly. (lit.)
Make up one's mind.
Make a definite decision.
〔註〕即下定決心。

0502　立糯
nɐp⁹ nɔ⁶ (translit.)
Sticky and slow. (lit.)
Slow-motioned.
Be slow in action.
Be snail-paced.
〔註〕表示慢吞吞的意思。

0503　冚席瞓石
kɐm² dzɛk⁹ fɐn³ sɛk⁹
(translit.)
Cover the body with a mat and sleep on the rock. (lit.)
Lead a beggar's life.
Sleep in the open.
〔註〕比喻過着乞丐般的生活。但有時作露宿街頭的該諧語。

0504　半斤八両
bun³ gɐn¹ bat⁸ lœŋ² (translit.)
Half a catty and eight taels. (16 taels = a catty) (lit.)
Six of one and half a dozen of the other.
Draw level with...

五畫

When Greek meets Greek, then comes the tug of war.
Tweedledum and tweedledee.
Be even with...
Break even.
There is not much to choose between the two.
〔註〕參閱"石地堂，鐵掃把"（0400）和"你有張良計，我有過牆梯"（0771）。

0505 半天吊
bun³ tin¹ diu³ *(translit.)*
Hang half way to the sky. *(lit.)*
Be neither willing to stoop to conquer nor able to stand on tiptoe to obtain.
Hang in the balance.
〔註〕比喻高不成，低不就或安危或成敗未定。參閱"高不成，低不就"條（1201）。

0506 半吞半吐
bun³ tɐn¹ bun³ tou³ *(translit.)*
Half swallow and half vomit. *(lit.)*
Hums and ha's.
Hesitate in speaking.

0507 半夜三更
bun³ jɛ⁶ sam¹ gaŋ¹ *(translit.)*
Half night and the third beating of a watchman's drum. *(lit.)*
In the depth of night.
Late at night.

0508 半夜食黃瓜 —— 不知頭定尾
bun³ jɛ⁶ sik⁹ wɔŋ⁴ gwa¹ — bɐt⁷ ji¹ tɐu⁴ diŋ⁶ mei⁵ *(translit.)*
Eat cucumber at midnight — not knowing if it is head or tail. *(lit.)*
Not know the whole story.
Be ignorant of the beginning and the end of...
Make neither head nor tail of...
〔註〕比喻對事情摸不着頭腦。

0509 半信半疑
bun³ sœn³ bun³ ji⁴ *(translit.)*
Half believe; half doubt. *(lit.)*
Be not quite convinced.
Be somewhat suspicious of...

0510 半途出家
bun³ tou⁴ tsœt⁷ ga¹ *(translit.)*
Become a Buddhist monk or nun late in life. *(lit.)*
Switch to a job one hasn't been trained before.

0511 半桶水
bun³ tuŋ² sœy² *(translit.)*
Half a pail of water. *(lit.)*
A smatterer.
〔註〕相當於"半瓶醋"。比喻知識膚淺，對事物一知半解的人。

0512 市橋蠟燭 —— 假細芯「心」
si⁵ kiu⁴ lap⁹ dzuk⁷ — ga² sɐi³ sɐm¹ *(translit.)*

The candle-sticks made in Si Kiu (the name of a small town near Canton) — they pretend to be small wick (heart). (lit.)

With one's tongue in one's cheek.
Show hypocritic loving concern for somebody.
Make a false display of affection.

〔註〕借"芯"字的諧音作"心"用，意指"假情假義"。市橋為廣州附近的一小市鎮。過去當地的製蠟燭商人，為了減低成本，增加利潤，把燭芯做得特別粗大，但露出燭外的燃點部分則特細，使人錯覺以為燭芯也一樣細。

0513　田雞東
tin⁴ gɐi¹ duŋ¹　(translit.)
Frog hosts. (lit.)
Each pays his share for a meal.
Go Dutch.
Club together.
〔註〕指幾個人湊錢或分攤費用吃東西的意思。

0514　田雞過河 —— 各有各蹽
tin⁴ gɐi¹ gwo³ hɔ⁴—gɔk⁸ jɐu⁵ gɔk⁸ jaŋ³　(translit.)
Frogs swim across the river — each stretches its legs for its own way. (lit.)
Need makes the old wife trot.
Make the best of one's own way.
Everyone puts his best leg forward.
Each takes to his legs.
〔註〕即各走各的路。

0515　四方木 —— 踢一踢，郁一郁
sei³ fɔŋ¹ muk⁶—tɛk⁹ jɐt⁷ tɛk⁹, juk⁷ jɐt⁷ juk⁷
(translit.)
A square log — kick it once and it moves once. (lit.)
A slow coach.
A lazybones.
〔註〕形容遲鈍的人。又用以指懶人。

0516　四方辮頂
sei³ fɔŋ¹ bin¹ dɛn²　(translit.)
Square head with a pigtail. (lit.)
A person who spends money on the lady who doesn't really love him.
〔註〕指把金錢花在不是真心愛自己的女人身上的人。

0517　加鹽加醋
ga¹ jim⁴ ga¹ tsou³　(translit.)
Add both salt and vinegar. (lit.)
Lay on thicker colours.
Pain somebody/something with thicker colours.
Lend colour to...
Give an exaggerated report.

0518　奶媽湊/抱仔 —— 人家物
nai⁵ ma¹ tsɐu³ / pou⁵ dzɐi² —

五畫

jɐn⁴ ga¹ mat⁹ (translit.)
A wet-nurse carries a baby in her arms,— It belongs to the others. (lit.)
Belong to another person.
〔註〕形容東西是人家的。

0519 出人頭地
tsœt⁷ yɐn⁴ tɐu⁴ dei⁶ (translit.)
Above other's heads. (lit.)
Come out first.
Be beyond all others.
Be out of the ordinary.

0520 出手低
tsœt⁷ sɐu² dɐi¹ (translit.)
Put out the hand low. (lit.)
Be not so generous with one's money.
Be mean over money matters.
Be too mean to loosen one's purse strings a little longer.
Offer as low as possible.

0521 出名
tsœt⁷ mɛŋ² (translit.)
The name is well-known. (lit.)
Come to fame.
Be famous.

0522 出息
tsœt⁷ sik⁷ (translit.)
Get the interest out. (lit.)
Promising/Be promising.
High-spirited/Be above the average.
High-minded.
High-toned.

〔註〕作形容詞用，意爲有前途的，品格高尚的或優秀的。和"出色"有別，參閱B084該條。

0523 出車
tsœt⁷ tsɛ¹ (translit.)
Take out the car. (lit.)
Work as a streetwalker.
Make easy money. (a lady)
〔註〕即當妓女。

0524 出面
tsœt⁷ min² (translit.)
Show off face. (lit.)
Act as a mediator.

0525 出風頭
tsœt⁷ fuŋ¹ tɐu⁴ (translit.)
Let the wind head come out. (lit.)
Cut a dash.
Make a fine figure of oneself.
Be fond of the limelight.
Be in the limelight.

0526 出氣
tsœt⁷ hei³ (translit.)
Let out the air. (lit.)
Vent one's disgust on somebody/something.

0527 出術
tsœt⁷ sœt⁹ (translit.)
Make a trick. (lit.)
Work out a practical scheme.
Device means.
〔註〕表示打鬼主意的意思。

0528 出符弗〈法〉。
tsœt⁷ fu⁴ fit¹ (translit.)
Let out incantations. (lit.)
Plot a conspiracy.

〔註〕即打鬼主意。參閱"出鶉哥"條（0533）。

0529 出處不如聚處
tsœt⁷ tsy³ bɐt⁷ jy⁴ dzœy⁶ tsy³ (translit.)
The original place is not like the gathering place. (lit.)
Exported articles are better and more than they are in the place where they are produced.
〔註〕指產品在產地不如在外地市場質量好，數量多。

0530 出頭
tsœt⁷ tɐu⁴ (translit.)
Show up the head. (lit.)
Take the lead.
Bear responsibility.
Show one's talent and the talent shows itself.

0531 出貓
tsœt⁷ mau¹ (translit.)
Take out a cat. (lit.)
Exercise fraud in an examination.
Take a written examination by unfair means.
〔註〕指考試時作弊。

0532 出醜
tsœt⁷ tsɐu² (translit.)
Show off ugliness. (lit.)
Be in disgrace.
Incur disgrace.

0533 出鶉哥
tsœt⁷ liu¹ gɔ¹ (translit.)
Let out a mynah. (lit.)

Plot a conspiracy.
〔註〕即打鬼主意。參閱"出符弗"條（0528）。

六　畫

0534 有一利必有一害
jɐu⁵ jɐt⁷ lei⁶ bit⁷ jɐu⁵ jɐt⁷ hɔi⁶ (translit.)
Where is an advantage, there is a disadvantage. (lit.)
No rose without a thorn.
Fire can make our houses warm but it can also burn them down.
There is no fire without smoke.

0535 有乜冬瓜豆腐
jɐu⁵ mɐt⁷ duŋ¹ gwa¹ dɐu⁶ fu⁶ (translit.)
In case of hard-skinned cucumber and bean curd. (lit.)
If worst comes to worst.
In case of misfortune.
〔註〕表示萬一不幸的意思。

0536 有人辭官歸故里，有人漏夜趕科場
jɐu⁵ jɐn⁴ tsi⁴ gun¹ gwɐi¹ gu³ lei⁵, jɐu⁵ jɐn⁴ lɐu⁶ jɛ⁶ gɔn² fɔ¹ tsœŋ⁴ (translit.)
Some resign from their official posts and return to their own native places, but others rush to the Examination Hall at night. (lit.)
Some go up the steps but others

come down.
Some people are willing to take over what others give up.

0537 有口無心
jɐu⁵ hɐu² mou⁴ sɐm¹ (translit.)
Having mouth but having no heart. (lit.)
Not really mean what one says.
Be sharp-tongued but not malicious.

0538 有口難言
jɐu⁵ hau² nan⁴ jin⁴ (translit.)
Having mouth but hard to say. (lit.)
Find it hard or embarrasing to say.

0539 有仇不報非君子
jɐu⁵ tsɐu⁴ bɐt⁷ bou³ fei¹ gwɐn¹ dzi² (translit.)
He who does not revenge himself on enmity is not a gentleman. (lit.)
Demand blood for blood.

0540 有分有寸
jɐu⁵ fɐn¹ jɐu⁵ tsyn³ (translit.)
Have fractions and inches. (lit.)
Know one's distance.
Know what to do.

0541 有分數
jɐu⁵ fɐn¹ sou³ (translit.)
Have graduation. (lit.)
Know what to do and what not to do.
Have a good sense of propriety.
〔註〕即有主意；心中有數。

0542 有心唔怕遲，十月都係拜年時
jɐu⁵ sɐm¹ m⁴ pa³ tsi⁴, sɐp⁹ jyt⁹ dou¹ hɐi⁶ bai³ nin⁴ si⁴ (translit.)
An intention is never late; the tenth month is also the time to pay a lunar new year call. (lit.)
Better late than never.

0543 有心無力
jɐu⁵ sɐm¹ mou⁴ lik⁹ (translit.)
Have heart but have no strength. (lit.)
Have a good mind but lack ability to...
Be unable to do what one wants very much to...

0544 有心裝冇心人
jɐu⁵ sɐm¹ dzɔŋ¹ mou⁵ sɐm¹ jɐn⁴ (translit.)
Deliberately watch somebody that does something unintentionally. (lit.)
Find fault with somebody with cherished desire.
Have intention to seek fault done without intention.
Set a trap for somebody.
〔註〕指故意找無心之失或設圈套陷害人。

0545 有皮宜唔使使頸

jɐu⁵ pei⁴ ji⁴ m⁴ sɐi² ies² gɛŋ²
(translit.)
Whenever there are small gains, there is no need to make use of the neck. (lit.)
Be all out for small advantages in spite of reluctance.
〔註〕表示有便宜便要做的意思。

0546 有奶便是娘
jɐu⁵ nai⁵ bin⁶ si⁶ nœŋ⁴
(translit.)
Any woman that can give the breast is mother. (lit.)
He that serves God for money will serve the devil for better wages.

0547 有自唔在，攞苦嚟辛
jɐu⁵ dzi⁶ m⁴ dzɔi⁶, lɔ² fu² lɐi⁴ sɐn¹ (translit.)
Not to get free and easy but endure hardship and toil. (lit.)
Make a rod for one's own back.
〔註〕表示自找麻煩的意思。

0548 有名無實
jɐu⁵ miŋ⁴ mou⁴ sɐt⁹ (translit.)
Have name but no reality. (lit.)
In name but not in deed.
Exist in name only.
Not worthy of the name.

0549 有屁就放
jɐu⁵ pei³ dzɐu⁶ fɔŋ³ (translit.)
Break your wind! (lit.)

Say away!
Say it out!
〔註〕即有話便說。

0550 有咗
jɐu⁵ dzɔ² (translit.)
Have had it. (lit.)
Be heavy with child.
Conceive a child.
Be pregnant.
〔註〕(指女人) 有喜或懷孕。

0551 有兩下散手
jɐu⁵ lœŋ⁵ ha⁵ san² sɐu²
(translit.)
Having two tactics. (lit.)
Have real skill.
Know one's stuff.
〔註〕即確有一手。

0552 有事鍾無艷，無事夏迎春
jɐu⁵ si⁶ dzuŋ¹ mou⁴ jim⁶, mou⁴ si⁶ ha⁶ jiŋ⁴ tsœn¹
(translit.)
Call for Dzuŋ Mou Jim when there is trouble, but as soon as the trouble has gone, go on the spree with Ha Jiŋ Tsœn. (lit.)
Dzuŋ Mou Jim — the lawful wife of Emperor Syn of Tsɐi (齊).
Ha Jiŋ Tsœn — Emperor Syn's royal concubine.
Pray God for help while drowning, but once go on shore, pray no more.
Once out of danger, cast the deliverer behind one's back.

六畫

〔註〕參閱"打完齋唔要和尚"(0425)及"過橋抽板"(1648)條。

0553 有其父必有其子
jɐu⁵ kei⁴ fu⁶ bit⁷ jɐu⁵ kei⁴ dzi² (translit.)
Such a father has such a son. (lit.)
Like father, like son.
Like begets like.
〔註〕含褒貶兩義。褒義參閱"虎父無犬子"條(0974)。貶義表示其父不仁，其子亦不仁的意思。

0554 有招架之功，無還手之力
jɐu⁵ dziu¹ ga³ dzi¹ guŋ¹, mou⁵ wan⁴ sɐu² dzi¹ lik⁹ (translit.)
Can resist but cannot return a blow. (lit.)
Can only ward off blows.
Fail to return a like for like.

0555 有咁啱得咁蹺
jɐu⁵ gɐm³ ŋam¹ dɐk⁷ gɐm³ kiu² (translit.)
Things happen at the same time. (lit.)
By a curious coincidence.
What a happy coincidence!
As luck would have it.
〔註〕表示巧合的意思。

0556 有風駛盡𢃇
jɐu⁵ fuŋ¹ sɐi² dzœn⁶ lei⁵ (translit.)
When there is wind, set up all sails. (lit.)
Pack all sails before the wind.
Take advantage of opportunity to the full extent.
〔註〕表示盡量利用機會的意思。

0557 有眼不識泰山
jɐu⁵ ŋan⁵ bɐt⁷ sik¹ tai³ san¹ (translit.)
Having eyes but not knowing Tai San. (lit.)
Be too blind to recognize the sun.

0558 有眼無珠
jɐu⁵ ŋan⁵ mou⁴ dzy¹ (translit.)
Having eyes without pupils. (lit.)
Be as blind as a bat.
Wrongly exercise one's judgement.
Misvalue somebody.
〔註〕參閱"走眼"(0713)，"睇差一皮"(1548)及"跌眼鏡"(1556)各條。

0559 有酒有肉多兄弟
jɐu⁵ dzɐu² jɐu⁵ juk⁹ dɔ¹ hiŋ¹ dɐi⁶ (translit.)
When one has wine and meat, many friends come together. (lit.)
A heavy purse makes friends come.
The one that holds the purse holds friends.

0560 有得震冇得瞓
jɐu⁵ dɐk⁷ dzɐn³ mou⁵ dɐk⁷ fɐn³ (translit.)
Tremble without sleep. (lit.)
Tremble with fear.

Be terror-stricken.
Strike terror into one's heart.
〔註〕暗喻膽戰心驚的心態。

0561　有得諗
jɐu⁵ dɐk⁷ ŋɐm² 　(translit.)
Have something to think about. (lit.)
Be worth a consideration.
〔註〕表示值得考慮的意思。

0562　有景轟
jɐu⁵ giŋ² gwɐŋ² 　(translit.)
Have something behind. (lit.)
There must be an inside story.
There must be a sinister design.
〔註〕即"內有乾坤"。

0563　有爺生冇乸教
jɐu⁵ jɛ⁴ saŋ¹ mou⁵ na² gau³ (translit.)
Have father to breed but have no mother to teach. (lit.)
Be not cultured at home.
Lack home education.
〔註〕參閱"冇家教"（0268）條。

0564　有意栽花花不發，無心插柳柳成蔭
jɐu⁵ ji³ dzɔi¹ fa¹ fa¹ bɐt⁷ fat⁸, mou⁴ sɐm¹ tsap⁸ lɐu⁵ lɐu⁵ siŋ⁴ jɐm¹ (translit.)
Plant flowers intentionally, but they never come into bloom; transplant willow slips unintentionally, but they grow to be a shade. (lit.)
Deliberation causes failure but incuriosity brings forth success.

0565　有福同享，有禍同當
jɐu⁵ fuk⁷ tuŋ⁴ hœŋ², jɐu⁵ wɔ⁶ tuŋ⁴ dɔŋ¹ 　(translit.)
Have bliss to share and calamity to face together. (lit.)
Cast in one's lot with somebody.
Stand together through thick and thin.
For better or worse, friendship exists.

0566　有碗話碗，有碟話碟
jɐu⁵ wun² wa⁶ wun², jɐu⁵ dip⁹ wa⁶ dip⁹ 　(translit.)
Say bowls when there are bowls; say dishes when there are dishes. (lit.)
Tell the whole story.
Tell it as it is.
Tell the truth, the whole truth, and nothing but the truth.
〔註〕指老老實實地説。

0567　有錢使得鬼推磨
jɐu⁵ tsin² sɐi² dɐk⁷ gwɐi² tœy¹ mɔ⁶ 　(translit.)
Money can make a ghost push a grinder. (lit.)
Where there are wages, there are pages.
Money makes the mare go.
〔註〕參閱"財可通神"條（1213）。

0568　有錢佬話事
jɐu⁵ tsin² lou² wa⁶ si⁶ (translit.)
Rich men master all. (lit.)
Money talks.

0569 有錢就身痕
jɐu⁵ tsin² dzɐu⁶ sɐn¹ hɐn⁴
(translit.)
Whenever one has money, his body feels itching. (lit.)
Money burns a hole in one's pocket.
〔註〕表示一有錢便要花光的意思。

0570 有頭毛冇人想生鬎鬁
jɐu⁵ tɐu⁴ mou⁴ mou⁵ jɐn⁴ sœŋ² saŋ¹ lat⁸ lei¹ (translit.)
If the head were full of hair, no one would prefer to have favus of the scalp on it. (lit.)
Have no alternative but to make such an unwise decision.
Be driven to such a stupid move.
〔註〕隱喻迫於無奈，才出此下策。

0571 有頭有面
jɐu⁵ tɐu⁴ jɐu⁵ min⁶ (translit.)
Have head and face. (lit.)
Be famed for one's post.
Be well-known and titled.
〔註〕表示在社會上有地位的意思。

0572 有頭威，冇尾陣
jɐu⁵ tɐu⁴ wɐi¹ mou⁵ mei⁵ dzɐn⁶ (translit.)
Having heading power and influence but no ending formation. (lit.)
A brave beginning but a poor ending.

Fine start, poor finish.
Do something by halves.
Leave one's work half done.
〔註〕參閱"虎頭蛇尾"條（0976）。

0573 有麝自然香
jɐu⁵ sɛ⁶ dzi⁶ jin⁴ hœŋ¹
(translit.)
Musk has its natural fragrance. (lit.)
Good wine needs no bush.
〔註〕相當於"好酒客自來，不必自我吹噓"。

0574 有鷄仔唔管管牙「麻」鷹
jɐu⁵ gɐi¹ dzɐi² m⁴ gun² gun² ŋa³ ma⁴ jiŋ¹ (translit.)
Not to restrain one's own chicks, but restrain eagles. (lit.)
Lay the blame on the wrong shoulder.
Put the shoe on the wrong foot.
〔註〕表示責備不該責備的人的意思。

0575 西南二伯父
sɐi¹ nam⁴ ji⁶ bak⁸ fu²
(translit.)
Second uncle of Si Nam. (lit.)
An indulgent senior.
〔註〕從前西南（沿廣三鐵路的一小市鎮）有醬園東主，人尊稱之為二伯父。他對懶散伙計，從不嚴加管束，反而任其所為，甚至給予錢財揮霍，及至不可救藥時，才把他解僱，使他在醬園行業中無法立足。比喻：指見到青少年

幹壞事，採取袖手旁觀，縱容甚至慫恿的老年人。

0577 死人尋舊路
sei² jɐn⁴ tsɐm⁴ gɐu⁶ lou⁶ (translit.)
A dead man looks for his old way. (lit.)
Follow one's own old tracks.
Do something in the usual way.
〔註〕本意指依照行過的路徑走，但引伸喻按老方法做。

0577 死人燈籠——報大數
sei² jɐn⁴ dɐŋ¹ luŋ⁴—bou³ dai⁶ sou³ (translit.)
A dead man's lentern,-reporting a bigger sum. (lit.)
Make a mountain out of a molehill.
Pull the long bow.
Cook up an exaggerative report.
〔註〕比喻小題大做，吹牛或虛構誇大報告等。俗例在成年人死後，家人例在門外懸掛燈籠。籠上用藍色寫上死者年歲，但必按死者實際年齡加多三歲。

0578 死口咬實
sei² hɐu² ŋɐu⁵ sɐt⁹ (translit.)
Dead mouth bites firmly. (lit.)
Stand by one's guns.
Stick to what one says.
〔註〕表示堅持所說的意思。

0579 死心不息
sei² sɐm¹ bɐt⁷ sik⁷ (translit.)

Death would make no stop. (lit.)
Insist on not giving up.
Have a one-track mind.
Be as obstinate as a mule.
〔註〕相當於"死心眼兒"。

0580 死心塌地
sei² sɐm¹ tap⁸ dei⁶ (translit.)
The heart is bent to. (lit.)
Be hell-bent on somebody.

0581 死牛一便頸
sei² ŋɐu⁴ jɐt⁷ bin⁶ gɛŋ² (translit.)
A dead cow turns its head on one side. (lit.)
Take the laws into one's own hand.
Insist on going one's own way.
Be hell-bent on having one's own way.
Be as stubborn as a mule.
Be stiff-necked.
Stick to one's guns.
〔註〕比喻形容人固執，堅持己見，不聽勸告。

0582 死死地氣
sei² sei² dei⁶ hei³ (translit.)
Do with dead air. (lit.)
Be reluctant but have no alternative but to...
〔註〕指無可奈何地幹。

0583 死有餘辜
sei² jɐu⁵ jy⁴ gu¹ (translit.)
Death would be too good. (lit.)

六畫

Death would not expiate all one's crimes.
〔註〕表示雖死亦不足蔽其罪的意思。

0584 死估估
sei² gu⁶ gu⁶ (translit.)
Quite dead. (lit.)
Be dull.
Be poor-witted.
Be inactive.
Be inflexible.
〔註〕表示呆板不識變通或不夠活躍的意思。

0585 死性不改
sei² sin³ bɐt⁷ gɔi² (translit.)
The dead nature does not change. (lit.)
Be as stubborn as a mule.
All ill nature never turns.

0586 死咗條心
sei² dzɔ² tiu⁴ sɐm¹ (translit.)
The heart dies. (lit.)
Better give up the idea altogether.
Drop the idea foever.
Have no more illusions about the matter.
〔註〕表示不再作幻想。

0587 死唔眼閉
sei² m⁴ ŋan⁵ bɐi³ (translit.)
Died with eyes open./Not close one's eyes when one dies. (lit.)
Nurse a grievance even when one dies.
Die with an everlasting regret.

0588 死冤
sei² jyn¹ (translit.)
Tangle to death. (lit.)
Stick like a limpet.
Pester somebody endlessly for something.
〔註〕參閱"二仔底"（0071），"吊靴鬼"（0672）及"死纏爛打"（0592）各條。

0589 死蛇爛鱔
sei² sɛ⁴ lan⁶ sin⁵ (translit.)
A dead snake and rotten eel. (lit.)
Be too lazy to stir a finger.
Be too tired to move.
〔註〕形容人懶得不想動或疲倦得動也不想動。

0590 死慳死抵
sei² han¹ sei² dɐi² (translit.)
Deadly save and deadly sustain. (lit.)
Pinch and screw.
Tighten one's belt.

0591 死雞撐飯蓋
sei² gɐi¹ tsaŋ³ fan⁶ gɔi³ (translit.)
A dead hen still props up the lid of a rice-cooker. (lit.)
Be the devil's advocate.
Show reluctance to eat crow.
Be shabby-genteel.
〔註〕暗喻理虧也嘴硬，仍要強辯，或擺窮架子。

0592 死纏爛打
sei² tsin⁴ lan⁶ da² (trans-

lit.)
Annoy with death and beat badly. *(lit.)*
Pester somebody endlessly for something.
〔註〕相當於"死氣白賴"或"胡纏"。參閱"二仔底"（0071），"死冤"（0588）及"吊靴鬼"（0672）各條。

0593　耳邊風
ji⁵ bin¹ fuŋ¹　*(translit.)*
A puff of wind at the ear. *(lit.)*
An unheeded advice.
〔註〕指不被人接受的忠告。

0594　百足咁多爪
bak⁸ (bat⁸) dzuk⁷ gɐm³ dɔ¹ dzɐu²　*(translit.)*
Have as many legs as a centipede. *(lit.)*
Cover up one's track.
Put nobody on one's track.
Go everywhere one likes.
〔註〕比喻行踪飄忽。

0595　百忍成金
bak⁸ jɐn² siŋ⁴ gɐm¹　*(translit.)*
A hundred pieces of patience will become gold. *(lit.)*
Patience is a plaster for all sores.

0596　托大腳
tɔk⁸ dai⁶ gœk⁸　*(translit.)*
Support a big leg on one's shoulder. *(lit.)*
Lick the boots of somebody.
Eat somebody's toads.
Butter up somebody with fine words.
〔註〕相當於"拍馬屁"或"抱粗腿"。

0597　托水龍
tɔk⁸ sœy² luŋ⁴　*(translit.)*
Support a water dragon. *(lit.)*
Embezzle somebody's money.
〔註〕表示盜用別人的款項的意思。

0598　托手踭
tɔk⁸ sɐu² dzaŋ¹　*(translit.)*
Support an elbow. *(lit.)*
Give somebody a flat refusal.
Refuse somebody's request.
〔註〕表示拒絕的意思。

0599　托塔都應承
tɔk⁸ tap⁸ dou¹ jiŋ¹ siŋ⁴　*(translit.)*
Promise even to hold a pagoda on the palm of a hand. *(lit.)*
Give promise easily.
〔註〕相當於"上刀山也答應"。但實在指輕諾而已。

0600　朽樛
lau² gau⁶　*(translit.)*
Be tangled. *(lit.)*
At sixes and sevens.
Be in a mess.
Have a tangled relation with one another.
Build up a carnal relationship.
〔註〕形容亂七八糟，又指不正常的男女關係。

0601　地膽/地頭蟲
dei⁶ dam²/dei⁶ tɐu⁴ tsuŋ⁴

(translit.)
The gall of land. (lit.)
A cock on his own dunghill.
Local villain (或 bully).
The man on the spot.
〔註〕指土生土長的人或地痞的頭子，後者相當於"地頭蛇"。

0602　而依哦哦
ji⁴ ji¹ ŋɔ⁴ ŋɔ⁴　(translit.)
Hesitate to say. (lit.)
Feel some hesitation in doing/ saying something.
Be shilly-shally.
Hum and haw.
〔註〕形容猶豫不決或支吾其詞。

0603　老行（音肯）
lou⁵ hɐŋ²　(translit.)
Old popular man. (lit.)
A person in luck.
A person who is winning popularity.
A man of the moment.
A man of mark.
〔註〕指當紅的人或走運的人。

0604　老人成嫩仔
lou⁵ jɐn⁴ siŋ⁴ nyn⁶ dzɐi²
(translit.)
An old person becomes a child. (lit.)
Once a man and twice a child.

0605　老人精
lou⁵ jɐn⁴ dzin¹　(translit.)
The spirit of an old man. (lit.)
A young child of prudence.
An old head on young shoul-

ders.
〔註〕形容小孩子年紀雖小，但行為老練，參看"年少老成"（0638）及"老積"（B106）條。

0606　老友記
lou⁵ yeo⁵ gei³　(translit.)
Old friend. (lit.)
An old acquaintance.
An old friend.
〔註〕老相識；老朋友。

0607　老行尊
lou⁵ hɔŋ⁴ dzyn¹　(translit.)
An old hand in the trade. (lit.)
An old timer in the line.
〔註〕指本行的老手或老行家。

0608　老定
lou⁵ diŋ⁶　(translit.)
Be calm. (lit.)
Not stir an eyelid.
Calm oneself.
Remain calm in face of...
Keep one's head.
〔註〕即鎮定；冷靜。

0609　老虎唔發威當病貓
lou⁵ fu² m⁴ fat⁸ wɐi¹ dɔŋ³ bɐŋ⁶ mau¹　(translit.)
A tiger exercising no power is thought as sick cat. (lit.)
Take/Mistake a sleeping wolf for a dead dog.
Regard a warrior with gentle looks as a coward.
〔註〕這口語用以警告對方，不可以為自己可欺。

0610　老虎頭上釘虱（蝨）乸

lou⁵ fu² tɐu⁴ sœŋ⁶ dɛŋ¹ sɐt⁷ ŋa² （translit.）
Spike lice on a tiger's head. （lit.）
Beard the lion in his den.
Dare to pull the tail of a fierce dog.
〔註〕"耗子舔貓鼻子——找死"或"太歲頭上動土"。

0611 老虎乸
lou⁵ fu² ŋa² （translit.）
A tigress. （lit.）
One's shrewish wife.
One's wife.
〔註〕謔稱悍妻或自己的妻子。

0612 老契
lou⁵ kɐi³ （translit.）
Close friend. （lit.）
A blossom friend.
A swearing friend.
An adulterer/adulteress.
A paramour.
〔註〕本指結誼關係的互稱。由於廣東人稱情夫爲"契家佬"及情婦爲"契家婆"的緣故，又轉爲情夫或情婦的謔稱。

0613 老番睇榜
lou⁵ fan¹ tɐi² bɔŋ² （translit.）
A foreigner has a look at the list of successful candidates. （lit.）
Bring up the rear.
The first from the bottom.
〔註〕爲名列榜尾的幽默說法。

0614 老鼠拉龜——冇埞埋手
lou⁵ sy² lai¹ gwɐi¹——mou⁵ dɛn⁶ mai⁴ sɐu² （translit.）
A rat drags a tortoise,—no place to put a hand on. （lit.）
Get no access to...
Be at one's wit's end.
〔註〕相當於"狗咬刺蝟——下不得嘴"。

0615 老鼠跌落天平——自己秤自己
lou⁵ sy² dit⁸ lɔk⁹ tin¹ piŋ⁴——dzi⁶ gei² tziŋ³ dzi⁶ gei² （translit.）
A rat falls down on to the scales—it weighs (praises) itself. （lit.）
Sing one's own praise.
Plume oneself on...
〔註〕借"秤"字的諧音來挖苦別人自己稱讚自己。

0616 老鼠貨
lou⁵ sy² fɔ³ （translit.）
Mouse goods. （lit.）
The stolen good sold at a bargain price.
〔註〕指以低價出售的賊贓。

0617 老貓燒鬚
lou⁵ mau¹ siu¹ sou¹ （translit.）
An old cat burns its beard. （lit.）
An experienced marker misses the target.
〔註〕相當於"老馬失蹄"。

0618 老奸巨猾

lou⁵ gan¹ gœy⁶ wat⁹ *(translit.)*
Old cunningness and big hypocrite. *(lit.)*
Be as cunning as an old fox.

0619 老糠搾出油
lou⁵ hɔŋ¹ dza³ tsœt⁷ jɐu⁴ *(translit.)*
Squeeze oil out of old chaffs. *(lit.)*
Get oil out of rocks.
Put a squeeze on poor people.
〔註〕即在窮人身上壓搾的意思。

0620 老竇/豆都要多
lou³ dɐu⁶ dou¹ jiu³ dɔ¹ *(translit.)*
Have a desire for more fathers. *(lit.)*
Be greedy for gains.
Be covetous to grasp all.
〔註〕形容一個人貪得無厭。

0621 老襯
lou⁵ tsɐn³ *(translit.)*
An old fool. *(lit.)*
A sucker.
A relation by marriage.
〔註〕指容易被騙的人。後來因姻親的"親"字廣東人讀成"襯"音，所以又謔稱"親家"爲老襯。

0622 丟生晒
diu¹ saŋ¹ sai³ *(translit.)*
Give all up. *(lit.)*
Be out of practice.
Show neglect of one's skill.
〔註〕即荒疏。

0623 丟架
diu¹ ga² *(translit.)*
Throw away the airs of greatness. *(lit.)*
Lose face.
Be disgraced.
Make an ass of oneself.
Make a sorry spectacle of oneself.
Commit a breach of etiquette.
〔註〕本指"丟臉"或"出洋相"，參閱"出醜"（0532）條。這口語又作失禮的意思，參閱"抬棺材甩褲"（0886）條。

0624 丟疏咗
diu¹ sɔ¹ dzɔ² *(translit.)*
Without practice. *(lit.)*
Be out of practice.
Show neglect of one's skill.
〔註〕同"丟生晒"（0622）

0625 行行企企
hɐŋ⁴ hɐŋ⁴ kei⁵ kei⁵ *(translit.)*
Walk and stand. *(lit.)*
Lounge away.
Be of assistance to somebody.
〔註〕指無所事事，但又相當於"幫閒"。

0626 行行出狀元
hɔŋ⁴ hɔŋ⁴ tsœt⁷ dzɔŋ⁶ jyn⁴ *(translit.)*
Every trade has its own 'dzɔn jyn'. (a title conferred on the scholar who came first in the Highest Imperial Examination) *(lit.)*
There is always an outstanding

master in every trade.
Everyone can come to fame in his own trade.

0627 行船好過灣
haŋ⁴ syn⁴ hou² gwɔ³ wan¹ (translit.)
Sailing is better than anchoring a boat. (lit.)
It is better to have a little to do than it is to do none.
〔註〕相當於"不怕慢，只怕站"。

0628 行船爭解纜
haŋ⁴ syn⁴ dzɐŋ¹ gai² lam⁶ (translit.)
Fight to untie the cable (cast off) while beginning to set sail. (lit.)
Take the lead.
〔註〕指領先行動。

0629 行得正，企得正
hɐŋ⁴ dɐk⁷ dzɛŋ³ (dziŋ³), kei⁵ dɐk⁷ dzɛŋ³ (dziŋ³) (translit.)
Both walk and stand in the right way. (lit.)
Be on one's best behaviours.
Play fair and square.
〔註〕行爲正直的意思。

0630 伊捞七
ji¹ lou¹ tsɐt⁷ (translit.)
Generally. (lit.)
Generally speaking...
〔註〕這是插入式的口頭語，意爲一般來説。

0631 先入爲主
sin¹ jɐp⁷ wɐi⁴ dzy² (translit.)
The first impression is the master. (lit.)
First impressions are unchangeable.
Have a prejudice against...
Preconceived ideas keep a strong hold.

0632 先小人後君子
sin¹ siu² jɐn⁴ hɐu⁶ gwɐn¹ dzi² (translit.)
Be a narrow-minded person first and then a gentleman. (lit.)
Make sure of every trifling matter before generosity.
Be narrow-minded before being generous.
〔註〕指當雙方進行一項交易或合作時，應該先講好利益的分配，以免日後因財失義。至於彼此將來是否計較，此乃日後的事。

0633 先下手爲強
sin¹ ha⁶ sɐu² wɐi⁴ kœŋ⁴ (translit.)
It is stronger to attack first. (lit.)
Catch the ball before the bound.
It is more advantageous to shoot the first arrow.
Steal somebody's thunder.
Take the wind out of somebody's sails.

0634 先使未來錢
sin¹ sɐi² mei⁶ lɔi⁴ tsin⁴ (translit.)

Spend the future money in advance. (lit.)
Anticipate one's wages/income.
Have one's corn in the blade.
〔註〕參閱"寅食卯糧"條（1348）。

0635 先敬羅衣後敬人
sin¹ giŋ³ lɔ⁴ ji¹ hɐu⁶ giŋ³ jɐn⁴ (translit.)
Respect silky clothes first and then the man. (lit.)
Fine clothes are in preference to man.
People usually open doors to fine clothes.

0636 先禮後兵
sin¹ lɐi⁵ hɐu⁶ biŋ¹ (translit.)
Politeness first and war later. (lit.)
A dog often barks before it bites.
Try peaceful means before force.

0637 年三十晚謝竈 —— 好做唔做
nin⁴ sam¹ sɐp⁹ man⁵ dzɛ⁶ dzou³—hou² dzou⁶ m⁴ dzou⁶ (translit.)
Thank the god of kitchen at the lunar new year's eve — what should be done is undone. (lit.)
Do not do what one should do.
Did not do what one should have done.
〔註〕前人多在年尾祭竈，以示謝意。在封建時代，有所謂官三民四蛋家五之説，意即階級分明，官方在農曆十二月廿三，民間在十二月廿四而蛋家則在十二月廿五日舉行，不容混亂，如果在除夕時舉行謝竈，則該做而不做了。

0638 年少老成
nin⁴ siu³ lou⁵ siŋ⁴ (translit.)
Young but mature. (lit.)
An old head on young shoulders.

0639 年晚煎堆 —— 人有我有
nin⁴ man⁵ dzin¹ dœy¹—jɐn⁴ jɐu⁵ ŋɔ⁵ jɐu⁵ (translit.)
Deep oil fried pop-grain balls at the close of the year — others have and I have. (lit.)
Possess oneself of the same as others do.
〔註〕廣東習俗無論貧富，在年晚時，例有煎堆（一種球形的油炸食物，中實以爆穀，外蓋芝麻），以取來年富有之意。

0640 朱義盛 —— 不變色
dzy¹ ji⁶ siŋ² — bat⁷ bin³ sik⁷ (translit.)
Dzy Ji Siŋ — never change the colour. (lit.)
Be just as of old.
As before.
Be just the same.
Be the very person.
〔註〕喻依然故我。在二三十年代，廣州市狀元坊有一朱義盛金飾店，專做鍍金首飾，以永不變色

作號召，遂引致無人不知"不變
色"，成爲俚語。

0641　多個香爐多隻鬼
dɔ¹ gɔ³ hœŋ¹ lou⁴ dɔ¹ dzɛk⁸
gwɐi² 　(translit.)
One more censer, one more
ghost. (lit.)
The more the competitors, the
keener the competition.
The keener the competition is,
the narrower the margin of
profit will be.
〔註〕比喻多一同業，多一競爭或多
一同業，利潤相應減少。

0642　合晒心水
hɐp⁹ sai³ sɐm¹ sœy²　(translit.)
Agree with the state of mind.
(lit.)
After one's own heart.
To one's own liking.
〔註〕指合心意，參閱"合晒合尺"條
（0643）。

0643　合晒合尺
hɐp⁹ sai³ hɔ⁴ tsɛ¹　(translit.)
Correspond to 5 2 (the num-
bered musical notation).
(lit.)
Be after one's own heart.
To one's own liking.
Fit in with...
Be fit like a glove.
Tight fit.
〔註〕表示合心意的意思，參閱"合
晒心水"條（0642），但又表示
完全符合的意思。"合"（讀作
"荷"的去聲，"尺"則讀"扯"的
平聲。"合尺"爲粵樂的主音，相
當於 5 2 音階，粵曲界無論唱者
或玩樂器者，必先正線"合尺"音
爲較音標準，以免走音。普通話
相應詞爲"合心意"或"正對勁
兒"。

0644　自己工
dzi⁶ gei² guŋ¹　(translit.)
Self work. (lit.)
Piece work.
Reckon by piece.
〔註〕即計件工。

0645　自己身有屎
dzi⁶ gei² sɐn¹ jɐu⁵ si²
(translit.)
One's own body is covered with
manure. (lit.)
Be conscious of one's own fault/
guilt.
Feel qualms about one's own
action.
Feel compunction.
〔註〕指作賊心虛，心中有鬼或問心
有愧。參閱"心中有屎"條
（0341）。

0646　自打嘴巴
dzi⁶ da² dzœy² ba¹　(translit.)
Smack on one's own mouth.
(lit.)
Contradict oneself.
Be self-contradictory.
〔註〕即自相矛盾。

0647　自投羅網
dzi⁶ tɐu⁴ lɔ⁴ mɔŋ⁵　(trans-

lit.)
Fall into one's own trapping net on voluntary basis. (lit.)
Put one's own head in the noose.

0648 自掛自酌
dzi⁶ dzam¹ dzi⁶ dzœk⁸ (translit.)
Pour for oneself and drink all by oneself. (lit.)
Make an arbitrary decision and act peremptorily.
Be in the enjoyment of one's own life all by oneself.
〔註〕指獨斷獨行或獨自享受個人生活。

0649 竹紗
dzuk⁷ sa¹ (translit.)
Bamboo silk. (lit.)
Poplin.
〔註〕即府綢（一種細，薄布）。

0650 竹織鴨 —— 冇心肝
dzuk⁷ dzik⁷ ap⁸—mou⁵ sɐm¹ gɔn¹ (translit.)
A duck knitted with bamboo tapes — without heart and liver (lit.)
An absent-minded person.
Be absent-minded.
〔註〕參閱"心不在焉"條（0343）。

0651 各自爲政
gɔk⁸ dzi⁶ wɐi⁴ dziŋ³ (translit.)
Everyone governs in his own way. (lit.)
Each one minds his own business.
Each one cleaves his own opinion.
〔註〕指各自做自己的事或各持己見。

0652 各花落各眼
gɔk⁸ fa¹ lɔk⁹ gɔk⁸ ŋan⁵ (translit.)
Every flower falls to every man's eyes. (lit.)
Beauty is but subjective.
Beauty exists in the eyes of the beholder.
Different people make different appraisals of beauty.
〔註〕比喻每個人對美的不同看法。

0653 各適其適
gɔk⁸ sik⁷ kei⁴ sik⁷ (translit.)
Each enjoys what he enjoys. (lit.)
Each takes what he needs.
Each does what he thinks is right.
Each takes what he likes to.
Each goes his own way.
〔註〕指各取所需，各行其是或各取所愛。

0654 江山易改，品性難移
gɔŋ¹ san¹ ji⁶ gɔi², bɐn² siŋ³ nan⁴ ji⁴ (translit.)
It is easy to alter rivers and mountains but difficult to change a person's character. (lit.)
It is difficult to change one's

skin.
The child is father to the man.
What is bred in the bone will come out in the flesh.
A leopard can not change his spots.

0655 江西佬舞/打死馬騮——有家歸不得

gɔŋ¹ sɐi¹ lou² mou⁵/da² sei² ma⁵ lɐu¹—jɐu⁵ ga¹ gwɐi¹ bɐt⁷ dɐk⁷ (translit.)

A native of Gɔŋ Sɐi makes his monkey dance/beats his monkey to death—having home but cannot go back. (lit.)

Be at the end of one's rope.
Be pushed to the wall.
Be beyond hope.

〔註〕比喻陷入困境或進退兩難。從前廣州和佛山兩地，常有人在街頭耍猴子戲，藉以乞取生活費用，這些舞猴者，多爲江西省人。假如他們賺錢的主角死了，他們便要淪落異鄉了。

0656 忙狼

mɔŋ⁴ lɔŋ⁴ (translit.)

As busy as a wolf. (lit.)

Be in a hurry.
Make haste.

〔註〕形容人忽忽忙忙的樣子。

0657 守得雲開見月明

sɐu² dɐk⁷ wɐn⁴ hɔi¹ gin³ jyt⁹ miŋ⁴ (translit.)

Await the clouds to open till the moon is seen. (lit.)

Wait till the clouds roll by.

0658 羊毛出在羊身上

jœŋ⁴ mou⁴ tsœt⁷ dzɔi⁶ jœŋ⁴ sɐn¹ sœŋ⁶ (translit.)

Wool comes from sheep's bodies. (lit.)

Whatever is given is paid for.
All charges are shifted on to consumers.

0659 羊牯

jœŋ⁴ gu² (translit.)

A ram. (lit.)

An outsider.
A layman.
An ignoramus.
A dupe.
A pigeon.

〔註〕從前粵劇演員，稱觀衆爲"羊牯"，蓋譏爲外行人，但後爲騙子們利用，作爲易受騙的笨人的代名詞。

0660 充大頭鬼

tsuŋ¹ dɐi⁶ tɐu⁴ gwɐi² (translit.)

Pretend to be a big-headed ghost. (lit.)

Put on the appearance of a man of wealth.
Be shabby—genteel.
Live in genteel poverty.

〔註〕指冒充闊氣或窮也要裝門面。

0661 交帶

gau¹ dai³ (translit.)

Undertake for the job. (lit.)

Be responsible.
Bear responsibility for...

〔註〕表示盡責或對……負責的意

0662 安份
ɔn¹ fɐn⁶ (translit.)
Keep one's obligation. (lit.)
Know one's distance.
Dare not tempt one's fate.
Live to one's heart's content.
Rest content with one's present situation.
Not to go beyond one's bounds.
〔註〕表示有自知之明不敢妄想或對目前境遇心滿意足的意思。

0663 安份守己
ɔn¹ fɐn⁶ sɐu² gei² (translit.)
Keep one's obligation and good behaviours. (lit.)
Abide by laws and behave oneself well.
〔註〕表示奉公守法，不作壞的勾當的意思。

0664 米已成炊
mɐi⁵ ji⁵ siŋ⁴ tsœy¹ (translit.)
The rice is well-cooked. (lit.)
The die is cast.
〔註〕指既成事實。

0665 同人唔同命，同遮唔同柄
tuŋ⁴ jɐn⁴ m⁴ tuŋ⁴ mɛŋ⁶, tuŋ⁴ dzɛ¹ m⁴ tuŋ⁴ bɛŋ³ (translit.)
Men are same but fate is different; umbrellas are same, but handles are different. (lit.)
Men were born with different fates.
No man has the same fortune.
〔註〕比喻人生際遇，各有不同。

0666 同行如敵國
tuŋ⁴ hɔŋ⁴ jy⁴ dik⁹ gwɔk⁸ (translit.)
The same trade is like a hostile nation. (lit.)
Two of a trade never agree.

0667 同撈同煲
tuŋ⁴ lou¹ tuŋ⁴ bou¹ (translit.)
Work and cook together. (lit.)
Share weal and woe with each other.
Live together through fair and foul.
〔註〕相當有福同享有禍同當。

0668 同檯食飯，各自修行
tuŋ⁴ tɔi⁴ sik⁹ fan⁶, gɔk⁸ dzi⁶ sɐu¹ haŋ⁴ (translit.)
Eating meal at the same table, everyone cultivates morality to become a Buddhist. (lit.)
Each does what he thinks is right.
Each cultivates his own virtue.
〔註〕表示各人有自己的道德修養標準的意思。

0669 吊吊扔
diu⁶ diu¹/² fiŋ³ (translit.)
Hang and let it sway. (lit.)
Swing this way and that way.
Not to reach a definite decision.
Be not assured.
〔註〕本意是晃來晃去。後引伸表示

事情未到決定階段或仍未獲得保證。

0670 吊砂煲
diu³ sa¹ bou¹　(translit.)
Hang up the earthen cooking-pot.　(lit.)
Be out of work.
Be too poor to have a meal.
Go hungry.
〔註〕比喻失業，但亦喻斷炊或沒得吃。

0671 吊起嚟賣
diu³ hei² lɐi⁴ mai⁶　(translit.)
Hang up for sale.　(lit.)
Hoard up for heigher price.
Sell at a price.
Raise the market upon something.
Play the market.
Form an unduly high estimation of oneself.
〔註〕表示奇貨可居或抬高身價的意思。

0672 吊靴鬼
diu³ hœ¹ gwɐi²　(translit.)
The ghost that sticks to boots.　(lit.)
A limpet.
The person who sticks somebody like a bur.
〔註〕表示胡纏的意思，參閱"二仔底"（0071）條。

0673 吊癮
diu² jɐn⁵　(translit.)
Hang up the addiction.　(lit.)

Not to satisfy the craving for the time being.
〔註〕相當於"沒勁"。

0674 早知今日，何必當初？
dzou² dzi¹ gɐm¹ jɐt⁹, hɔ⁴ bit⁷ dɔŋ¹ tsɔ¹　(translit.)
Had this day been known earlier, why must it have been done?　(lit.)
It is too late to ask oneself why one has gone astray when one knows the consequence to be so serious.
〔註〕指對過去的錯誤行為導致的後果，悔之已晚了。參閱"早知今日，悔不當初"條（0675）。

0675 早知今日，悔不當初
dzou² dzi¹ gɐm¹ jɐt⁹, fui³ bɐt⁷ dɔŋ¹ tsɔ¹　(translit.)
Had one known the consequence of today, one would not have gone astray/done so.　(lit.)
It is too late to repent for having gone astray/done so when one knows the consequence to be so serious.
〔註〕同"早知今日，何必當初？"（0674）。

0676 早知燈係火，唔使黑摸摸
dzou² dzi¹ dɐŋ¹ hɐi⁶ fɔ², m⁴ sɐi² hɐk⁷ mɔ² mɔ²　(translit.)
If a lamp had been known to be fire, there would have been no need to feel about in the dark.

六畫

(lit.)
It is too late to repent of one's previous ignorance.
It is too late to regret for having missed the opportunity to do something.
〔註〕指對過去無知或失去機會而不……時,悔之已晚了。

0677 光棍佬教仔 —— 便宜莫貪
gwɔŋ¹ gwɐn³ lou² gau³ dzɐi² — pin⁴ ji⁴ mɔk⁹ tam¹ (translit.)
A swindler teaches his son—not to be covetous of any advantage. (lit.)
Do not jump at any easy baits.
Don't try to get things on the cheap.

0678 光棍遇着冇皮柴
gwɔŋ¹ gwɐn³ jy⁶ dzœk⁹ mou⁵ pei⁴ tsai⁴ (translit.)
A bare stick(swindler) meets a bare firewood(swindler). (lit.)
A swindler takes in a swindler.
Diamond cut diamond.
A nip and tuck.
〔註〕"光棍"為廣東人對騙子的叫法,但句中的"光棍"本義是"光禿禿而沒皮的木棍"而"冇皮柴"也是光禿禿而沒皮的木棍,兩者既然同是一樣東西,廣東人便以這"光棍"喻騙子的"光棍",全句意思是說"大家不相上下"而成為騙中騙,用於貶義方面。

0679 因小失大
jɐn¹ siu² sɐt⁷ dai⁶ (translit.)
Lose the big because of the small. (lit.)
Spoil a ship for a halfpenny worth of tar.

0680 肉刺
juk⁹ tsɛk⁸ (translit.)
The flesh itches. (lit.)
Make one's heart ache.
Be loath to part with.../leave...
Be reluctant to spend/have spent so much on something.
〔註〕表示捨不得的意思。

0681 肉酸
juk⁹ syn¹ (translit.)
The flesh goes sour. (lit.)
Be ugly-looking.
Be creepy-crawly.
Make somebody's flesh creep.
Give somebody the creeps.
〔註〕表示醜陋,難看,但亦表示令人身上發癢。

0682 肉隨砧板上
juk⁹ tsœy⁴ dzɐm¹ ban² sœŋ⁶ (translit.)
The flesh is put on the chopping board. (lit.)
Be led by the nose.
Be bred at somebody's will.
Be laid by the heels.
〔註〕比喻任人宰割或任人支配。

0683 肉緊
juk⁹ gɐn² (translit.)
The flesh becomes tight. (lit.)
Be excited.

Feel anxious.
Be impatient.
〔註〕表示緊張，着急或不耐煩。

0684　奸賴
gan¹ lai³　(translit.)
Deny shamelessly.　(lit.)
Disavow.
Refuse to confess.
〔註〕表示抵賴不認帳；耍賴皮。

0685　好人事
hou² jɐn⁴ si²　(translit.)
Good man's kindness.　(lit.)
Be affable.
Be kindhearted.
〔註〕意爲心腸好，和靄。

0686　好人難做
hou² jɐn⁴ nan⁴ dzou⁶
(translit.)
To be a good man is difficult.
(lit.)
If you want to please everybody, you'll please nobody.
A sage is often regarded as a savage.
There are always those who are not satisfied with a good man.

0687　好女兩頭瞞
hou² nœy² lœn⁵ tɐu⁴ mun⁴
(translit.)
A good daughter deceives both sides (families).　(lit.)
Hide the truth of either of the two so as to please both.
Make the best of both worlds.
Sit on the hedge.
Cut both ways./ Bear two faces in one head.
〔註〕指把兩方任何一方的真相隱瞞以取悅雙方，但引伸成爲兩全其美，要兩面派或兩邊倒。

0688　好天揾埋落雨米
hou² tin¹ wɐn² mai⁴ lɔk⁹ jy⁵ mɐi⁵　(translit.)
While it is a fine day, look for rice for rainy days.　(lit.)
Gather hay against a rainy day.
Make hay while the sun shines.
〔註〕表示未雨綢繆的意思。

0689　好心唔怕做
hou² sɐm¹ m⁴ pa³ dzou⁶
(translit.)
Be not afraid to be good-hearted.　(lit.)
Have one's heart in the right place.
Have a heart.

0690　好心唔得好報
hou² sɐm¹ m⁴ dɐk⁷ hou² bou³　(translit.)
Good heart is not well-repaid.
(lit.)
Recompense good with evil.
Shoe the goose.

0691　好心着雷殛
hou² sɐm¹ dzœk⁹ lœy⁴ pɛk⁸
(translit.)
Good heart meets with the strike of thunder.　(lit.)
Bite the hand that feeds one.
Recompense good with evil.

0692　好水有幾多朝
hou² sœy² mou⁵ gei² dɔ¹

六畫

dziu¹ (translit.)
Good water won't come for many mornings. (lit.)
There is not much of such a good opportunity in one's life.
〔註〕比喻一生中好機會不多。

0693 好市
hou² si⁵ (translit.)
Good market. (lit.)
Sell well.
Sell like hot cakes.
Command a ready sale.
〔註〕指暢銷或賣得快

0694 好事不出門，壞事傳千里
hou² si⁶ bɐt⁷ tsœt⁷ mun⁴, wai⁶ si⁶ tsyn⁴ tsin¹ lei⁵ (translit.)
Good things do not go out of the door, ill things spread a thousand li. (lit.)
Good news goes on clutchers but ill news flies apace.

0695 好物沉歸底
hou² mɐt⁹ tsɐm⁴ gwɐi¹ dɐi² (translit.)
Good things sink to the bottom. (lit.)
The best fish swim near the bottom.

0696 好馬不食回頭草
hou² ma⁵ bɐt⁷ sik⁹ wui⁴ tɐu⁴ tsou² (translit.)
A good horse never comes back to eat the grass. (lit.)
Once quit, never back.
A bird flying away from the cage will never come back to be fed.
〔註〕比喻不再回頭受僱或一經放手，便再不回頭。

0697 好佬怕爛佬
hou² lou² pa³ lan⁶ lou² (translit.)
A good fellow fears a rascal. (lit.)
A pigeon makes no friends with a hawk.
A gentleman feels it beneath his dignity to argue with a rascal.
〔註〕表示好人或有教養的人不屑於和不講理的人或粗人爭吵或交往的意思。

0698 好眉好貌生沙蝨
hou² mei⁴ hou² mau⁶ saŋ¹ sa¹ sɐt⁷ (translit.)
Good looking but having sand hoppers. (lit.)
A fair face hides a foul heart.
Be nice in appearance but defective in quality.
〔註〕比喻人外表好但行爲劣或中看不中用。

0699 好啱偈
hou² ŋam¹ gɐi² (translit.)
Match well with. (lit.)
Be congenial to each other.
Get along well with each other.
〔註〕表示彼此志趣相投或彼此相處甚好的意思。

0700 好啱橋
hou² ŋam¹ kiu² (translit.)
Match well with. (lit.)

Be congenial to each other.
Get along well with each other.
〔註〕意思和"好啱偈"相同，參閱（0699）條。

0701　好食懶飛
hou³ sik⁹ lan⁵ fei¹　(translit.)
Be fond of eating but lazy to fly. (lit.)
Eat one's head off.
〔註〕即好吃懶做。

0702　好唱口
hou² tsœŋ³ hɐu²　(translit.)
A good singing mouth. (lit.)
Make irresponsible and sarcastic remarks.
Wag one's jaws.
〔註〕本義好嗓子。但引伸作會說風涼話，但又表示口若懸河的意思。

0703　好腳頭
hou² gœk⁹ tɐu⁴　(translit.)
Good foot-head. (lit.)
Be born with good luck to the family.
Come with good luck to somebody.
〔註〕指一出世或一到來便帶來幸運（指人或畜牲都可以）。

0704　好漢不吃眼前虧
hou² hon³ bɐt⁷ hɛk⁸ ŋan⁵ tsin⁴ kwɐi¹　(translit.)
A good fellow eats no loss immediately. (lit.)
It is better to show a clean pair of heels than it is to show a bare pair of hands.
It is better to avoid visible loss than it is to brave it out.

0705　好戲在後頭
hou² hei² dzɔi⁶ hɐu⁶ tɐu⁴　(translit.)
The good performance is at the later part of the entertainment. (lit.)
There will be something interesting to see a little later.
〔註〕暗喻還有事發生。

0706　好聲好氣
hou² sɛŋ¹ hou² hei³　(translit.)
Good sound and good air. (lit.)
Speak in kindly manner.
〔註〕形容心平氣和的說話態度。

0707　收手
sɐu¹ sɐu²　(translit.)
Put away the hands. (lit.)
Stay one's hand.
Throw in one's hands.
〔註〕表示住手不再幹或放棄的意思。

0708　收檔
sɐu¹ dɔŋ³　(translit.)
Shut up the stall. (lit.)
Declare bankruptcy.
Close the stall/shop for the night.
Stop wagging the tongue.
Not to do it any more.
〔註〕本義爲宣佈破產，關門休息。如果對人說時，則叫人不要再說或做下去。

六畫

0709 收科
sɐu¹ fɔ¹ (translit.)
Bring to an end. (lit.)
End up./Put an end to...
Wind up.
Make something reach a satisfactory settlement.
Wash one's hand of...
Stay one's hand.
〔註〕本爲粵劇"煞科"（收場）的術語，但轉義爲結束收手或使……圓滿解決。

七畫

0710 快刀斬亂麻
fai³ dou¹ dzam² lyn⁶ ma⁴ (translit.)
Quick knife cuts off tangled hemp. (lit.)
Cut the Gordian knot.
Take quick action.
Give a quick hand at something.
Cut the Gordian knot.
〔註〕表示乾脆利落，速戰速決的意思。

0711 走馬看花
dzɐu² ma⁵ hɔn³ fa¹ (translit.)
Ride a running horse to look at flowers. (lit.)
Take a scamper through something.
Gain a superficial understanding through cursory observation.
〔註〕指匆匆看過，未有深入了解。

0712 走唔過……嘅手指罅
dzɐu² m⁴ gɔ³……gɛ³ sɐu² dzi² la³ (translit.)
Cannot run away from the gaps of somebody's fingers. (lit.)
See through somebody's tricks.
Twist somebody round one's finger.
〔註〕表示洞悉某人的陰謀或可以左右某人的意思。

0713 走眼
dzɐu² ŋan⁵ (translit.)
The eyes run away. (lit.)
Slip from sight.
Be negligent in checking.
Misjudge somebody/something.
〔註〕表示看不到或判斷錯誤。參閱"有眼無珠"（0558），"睇差一皮"（1548）及"跌眼鏡"（1556）各條。

0714 走路
dzɐu² lou² (translit.)
Run away. (lit.)
Desert.
Show a clean pair of heels.
Take to one's legs.
Make away/Make away with...
Run away.
〔註〕即逃跑，逃亡或挾帶……而逃。參閱"趯更"條（1957）。

0715 走雞
dzɐu² gɐi¹ (translit.)
The hen runs away. (lit.)
Miss the opportunity.
Miss the bus.
Slip through one's fingers.
〔註〕表示失去機會的意思。

0716 走歸左

dzɐu² gwɐi¹ dzɔ² (translit.)
Run to the left. (lit.)
Go astray.
〔註〕比喻行差踏錯或入歧途。

0717 走寶
dzɐu² bou² (translit.)
The treasure runs away. (lit.)
Slip through one's fingers.
Incur a heavy loss.
Miss a chance.
Lose one's maid's chastity.
〔註〕比喻失之交臂或少女失貞。

0718 豆腐刀──兩便面
dɐu⁶ fu⁶ dou¹—lœŋ⁵ bin⁶ min² (translit.)
A knife used to cut beancurd—both sides are cutting blades. (lit.)
Sit on both sides of the hedge.
Cut both ways.
〔註〕即"要兩面派";"銅板切豆腐──兩面光"。

0719 車天車地
tsɛ¹ tin¹ tsɛ¹ dei⁶ (translit.)
Turn both the sky and earth. (lit.)
Have an idle talk with somebody.
Make an extravagant remark.
Make an extravagant boast of oneself.
〔註〕指和人瞎扯,吹牛或過分吹噓自己。

0720 求人不如求己
kɐu⁴ jɐn⁴ bɐt⁷ jy⁴ kɐu⁴ gei² (translit.)

Begging others is not like begging oneself. (lit.)
Turn one's own hand to do one's own business.
God help those who help themselves.

0721 求求其其
kɐu⁴ kɐu⁴ kei⁴ kei⁴ (translit.)
Casual. (lit.)
Slap together.
Huddle up.
In a slapdash manner.
Casually.
At random.
Anything/Anybody will do.
〔註〕表示隨便或馬馬虎虎的意思。在選擇方面而言,參閱"是是但但"(1083)條。

0722 夾份
gap⁸/gɐp⁸ fɐn² (translit.)
Crowd shares together. (lit.)
Club together.
Club shares.
Pool shares.
〔註〕表示湊份子,湊錢,合伙;分攤的意思。參閱"田雞東"條(0513)。

0723 弄巧反拙
luŋ⁶ hau² fan² dzyt⁸ (translit.)
Try to make good of something but end up with a blunder. (lit.)
Try to outsmart oneself but turn out to be foolish.

七畫

Ride one's horse to death.

0724 弄假成真
luŋ⁶ ga² siŋ⁴ dzɐn¹ *(translit.)*
Try to make believe but turn out to be reality. (lit.)
What was make-believe has become reality.

0725 夭嫋鬼命
ŋɐn¹ liu¹ gwɐi² mɛŋ⁶ *(translit.)*
As thin and brittle as ghost's life. (lit.)
Be in delicate health.
〔註〕形容人十分瘦弱的樣子。

0726 把屁
ba² pei³ *(translit.)*
Useless fart. (lit.)
Be of no use.
Be useless.
What is the use of...?
What is the use to do something?
〔註〕參閱"把鬼"（0727）條。此外作反問語時，表示有甚麼用處的意思。相當於"頂個屁用"。

0727 把鬼
ba² gwɐi² *(translit.)*
Muddle the ghost. (lit.)
Be of no use.
Be useless.
It wastes one's energy/time to...
〔註〕表示毫無用處的意思外，還含有白費氣力或時間的意思。

0728 抌氣
dɐn³ hei³ *(translit.)*

Complain with angry breath. (lit.)
Nurse a grievance.
〔註〕表示發洩怨氣，一肚子怨氣的意思。

0729 抌蝦籠
dɐn³ ha¹ luŋ² *(translit.)*
Yank the bamboo cage for holding shrimps. (lit.)
Pick somebody's pocket.
〔註〕比喻掏人的錢包。

0730 扮豬食老虎
ban⁶ dzy¹ sik⁹ lou⁵ fu² *(translit.)*
Feign to be a pig to eat a tiger. (lit.)
Play the fool.
Feign oneself to be foolish.
A wise man often acts the fool.
Feign ignorance.
〔註〕意即裝笨相。

0731 扮嘢
ban⁶ jɛ⁵ *(translit.)*
In disguise. (lit.)
Strike an attitute.
Make believe.
〔註〕表示裝腔作勢的意思。

0732 扮傻
ban⁶ sɔ⁴ *(translit.)*
Pretend to be mad. (lit.)
Play the fool.
Feign ignorance.
Pretend to be ignorant of...
〔註〕即"裝瘋賣傻"，"裝蒜"或對……詐作不知。

0733 扯皮條

tsɛ² pei⁴ tiu⁴′² *(translit.)*
Drag leather straps. *(lit.)*
Procure for prostitutes.
〔註〕指替娼妓介紹嫖客。

0734　扯風波
tsɛ² fuŋ¹ bɔ¹ *(translit.)*
Hoist a typhoon signal. *(lit.)*
Be heavy with child.
〔註〕懷胎的詼諧說法。

0735　扯貓尾
tsɛ² mau¹ mei⁵ *(translit.)*
Pull a cat's tail. *(lit.)*
Collaborate with each other to hide the truth from somebody.
Each of the two acts in collaboration to pull the wool over the eyes of somebody.
〔註〕指兩人串通，互相呼應來瞞騙第三者，有時有人說成"拉或搖貓尾"，相當於"唱雙簧"。

0736　拋生藕
pau¹ saŋ¹ ŋɐu⁵ *(translit.)*
Throw a raw lotus-root. *(lit.)*
Bewitch a man by means of coquetry.
Coquette with a man.
〔註〕指女人以甜言蜜語向男人賣弄風情。

0737　拋浪頭
pau¹ lɔŋ⁶ tɐu⁴ *(translit.)*
Toss the head of wave. *(lit.)*
Come the bully over somebody.
〔註〕表示虛張聲勢來嚇人的意思。

0738　拋頭露面
pau¹ tɐu⁴ lou⁶ min⁶ *(translit.)*
Toss the head and show the face. *(lit.)*
(of a woman in feudal society) show one's face in public.
Show oneself to make a living.
〔註〕原指婦女出現在大庭廣衆中（封建道德認爲是丟臉的事）。現一般指公開露面。

0739　扭六壬
nɐu² luk⁹ jɐm⁴ *(translit.)*
Wring out six points (the ninth of the ten heavenly stems). *(lit.)*
Rack one's brains.
Resort to manoeuvres.
〔註〕表示絞盡腦汁或玩弄花招的意思。

0740　扭屎窟花
nɐu² si² fɐt⁷ fa¹ *(translit.)*
Twist hips in the shape of a flower. *(lit.)*
Try some tricks.
〔註〕即"耍花招"。

0741　扭計
nɐu² gɐi² *(translit.)*
Wring out a plan. *(lit.)*
Naughty; mischievous.
Employ all kinds of base devices.
Resort to manoevres.
Scheme against each other.
〔註〕相當於淘氣；頑皮或出鬼點子難人；搞鬼；跟人勾心鬥角。

0742　扭紋柴
nɐu² mɐn⁴ tsai⁴ *(translit.)*
Cross-grained firewood. *(lit.)*

A regular mischief.
A little mischief.
〔註〕比喻小孩子脾氣蠻橫或淘氣。

0743 扭擰
nɐu² niŋ⁶ (translit.)
Twist around. (lit.)
Strike attitudes.
Put on poses.
〔註〕表示扭扭捏捏（即羞澀不大方的姿態）的意思。

0744 扰心口
dɐm² sɐm¹ hɐu² (translit.)
Knock the mouth of heart. (lit.)
Fleece somebody of his money.
Extort money from somebody.
Be repentant of something wrong.
Be heart-broken.
Nurse a grief.
〔註〕即敲搾，又喻作悔恨或傷心。

0745 折墮
dzit⁸ dɔ⁶ (translit.)
Break off and fall. (lit.)
Be reduced to poverty by God's denouncement.
Obtain one's deserts.
〔註〕表示因受天譴而墮落或得到應有的報應。

0746 杉木靈牌 —— 唔做得主
tsam³ muk⁹ lɛŋ⁴/liŋ⁴ pai⁴— m⁴ dzou⁶ dɐk⁷ dzy² (translit.)
An ancestral tablet made of pine, — it can not be used as a real ancestral tablet. (lit.)
Be not in a position to decide/to make a decision.
〔註〕廣東習俗在長輩死後，必爲他設置用栗木做的神主牌作供奉之用，（相傳原出於春秋時介之推在被晉文公焚山求他出仕時，抱栗木而死，文公爲着紀念他，砍那栗木作木屐穿着，後人遂用栗木做神主牌。）但在未"上高"前，用杉木作爲臨時靈牌，故有杉木靈牌唔做得主（神主牌）這一句話。相當於"丫鬟帶鑰匙—— 當家不作主"。

0747 朳失
ŋɐt⁷ sɐt⁷ (translit.)
Too miserly. (lit.)
Square accounts to the smallest details.
Haggle over every penny.
〔註〕指斤斤計較。

0748 均真
gwɐn¹ dzɐn¹ (translit.)
Equalize. (lit.)
Be fair-minded.
Be impartial to...
See fair.
〔註〕表示公平或公正的意思。

0749 含冤莫白
hɐm⁴ jyn¹ mɔk⁹ bak⁹ (translit.)
Hold a wrong and can't be righted. (lit.)
Suffer an unrighted wrong.

0750 含血噴人
hɐm⁴ hyt⁸ pɐn³ jɐn⁴ (translit.)

Hold in a mouthful of blood and spurt it at somebody. (lit.)
Smite with the tongue.
Make malicious remark upon somebody.
Make slanderous accusations.

0751 秀才遇着兵──有理講不清
sɐu³ tsɔi⁴ jy⁶ dzœk⁹ biŋ¹—jɐu⁵ lei⁵ gɔŋ² bɐt⁷ tsiŋ¹ (translit.)
A scholar meets a soldier, — having reason but unable to be understood. (lit.)
Be unable to persuade somebody with reason.
Fail to reason with somebody for/against...
〔註〕表示不可理喻的意思。

0752 秀才遇老虎──吟詩都吟唔甩
sɐu³ tsɔi⁴ jy⁶ lou⁵ fu²—jɐm⁴ si¹ dou¹ jɐm⁴ m⁴ lɐt⁷ (translit.)
A scholar meets a tiger, — he cannot get rid of it even though he chants. (lit.)
Fail to shirk.
There is no way to evade... (doing something.)
〔註〕比喻勢難逃避。

0753 秀才手巾──包書「輸」
sɐu³ tsɔi⁴ sɐu² gɐn¹—bau¹ sy¹ (translit.)
A scholar's handkerchief — wrap books with (surely to lose) (lit.)
Stand to lose.
〔註〕相當於"孔子搬家──淨書（輸）"。（按："書"和"輸"同音）

0754 佛都有火
fɐt⁹ dou¹ jɐu⁵ fɔ² (translit.)
Even Buddha could have fire (get angry). (lit.)
It would try the patience of a saint.
It would provoke God to anger.
〔註〕表示難以容忍的意思。

0755 低頭切肉，把眼看人
dɐi¹ tɐu⁴ tsit⁸ juk⁹, ba² ŋan⁵ hɔn³ jɐn⁴ (translit.)
Bow the head down to cut meat and judge the customer. (lit.)
Choose a pigeon to cheat.
Pluck a pigeon.
〔註〕比喻先看對方是否可欺，再作決定。所謂"知己知彼"，亦即此意。

0756 低庄/莊
dɐi¹ dzɔŋ¹ (translit.)
The amount of bank is low. (lit.)
Be regardless of one's own social status.
Put oneself to a step lower.
Be mean about money matters.
〔註〕表示不理個人社會地位，降低自己或吝嗇的意思。

0757 低低地蹭舖
dɐi¹ dɐi¹ dei² gwan³ pou¹ (translit.)

Stumble lowly for once. (lit.)
Put one's pride in one's pocket and yield oneself.
Say uncle to somebody.
Say 'sorry' to somebody.
Admit being defeated.
〔註〕表示承認失敗，向人道歉或認輸。

0758 低聲下氣
dɐi¹ siŋ¹ (sɛŋ¹) ha⁶ hei³ (translit.)
Lower one's voice and compress one's air. (lit.)
Put one's pride in one's pocket.
Bear and forbear.
Be meek and submissive.
〔註〕一忍再忍或逆來順受的意思。

0759 作嘔
dzɔk⁸ au² (translit.)
Feel like vomiting. (lit.)
Be filled with nausea at the sight of...
Make one feel sick.
〔註〕表示要嘔吐，令人噁心的意思。

0760 作怪
dzɔk⁸ gwɐi³ (translit.)
Do something queer. (lit.)
Make trouble.
Do mischief.
〔註〕即搞鬼。

0761 作狀。
dzɔk⁸ dzɔŋ⁶ (translit.)
Attitudinize. (lit.)
Strike a pose.
Put on an act.

Act in affected manners.
〔註〕即裝腔作勢或裝模作樣。參閱"扮嘢"條（0731）。

0762 作賤自己
dzɔk⁸ dzin⁶ dzi⁶ gei² (translit.)
Make onself cheap. (lit.)
Run oneself down.
Spoil oneself.

0763 作死
dzɔk⁸ sei² (translit.)
Want to die. (lit.)
Take the road to ruin oneself.
〔註〕表示自尋死路的意思。

0764 作威作福
dzɔk⁸ wɐi¹ dzɔk⁸ fuk⁷ (translit.)
Show power and blessing. (lit.)
Come the bully over somebody.
Play the bully.
Throw one's weight about.
〔註〕表示妄自尊大，濫用權勢，盛氣凌人的意思。

0765 作賊心虛
dzɔk⁸ tsak⁹ sɛm¹ hœy¹ (translit.)
Be timid at heart for being a thief. (lit.)
Have a guilty conscience.
A bully fears to face the law.
〔註〕參閱"心中有屎"（0341）及"自己身有屎"條（0645）。

0766 佔上風
dzim³ sœŋ⁶ fuŋ¹ (translit.)
Usurp the top wind. (lit.)

Take the wind out of somebody's sails.
Have the advantage of somebody.
〔註〕表示佔得別人的好處或比別人有利的意思。

0767 佔皮宜
dzim³ pei⁴ ji⁴ (translit.)
Usurp small gains. (lit.)
Gain extra advantage by unfair means.
Profit at other's expense.

0768 你有半斤，我有八両
nei⁵ jɐu⁵ bun³ gɐn¹, ŋɔ⁵ jɐu⁵ bat⁸ lœŋ² (translit.)
You have half a catty, I have eight taels. (lit.)
Six of one and half a dozen of the other.
Be much of a muchness.
〔註〕參閱"半斤八両"（0504），"石地堂，鐵掃把"（0400），"你有張良計，我有過牆梯"（0771）及"你有乾坤，我有日月"（0772）各條。

0769 你有張良計，我有過牆梯
nei⁵ jɐu⁵ dzœŋ¹ lœŋ⁴ gɐi³, ŋɔ⁵ jɐu⁵ gɔ³ tsœŋ⁴ tɐi¹ (translit.)
You have Dzœŋ Lœŋ's devise and I have a ladder long enough for me to climb over the wall. (lit.)
Be evenly matched.
Be six of one and half a dozen of the other.

〔註〕相當於"你有關門計，我有跳牆法"。參閱"半斤八両"（0504）；"石地堂，鐵掃把"（0400）；"你有乾坤，我有日月"（0772）各條。

0770 你有乾坤，我有日月
nei⁵ jɐu⁵ kin⁴ kwɐn¹, ŋɔ⁵ jɐu⁵ jɐt⁹ jyt⁹ (translit.)
You have 'kin kwɐn'; I have the sun and the moon. (lit.)
'kin' — the first of the eight diagramms, standing for 'heaven'.
'kwɐn' — the seventh of the eight diagramms, standing for 'earth'.
When Greek meets Greek, there is the tug of war.
Neck and neck.
Be well-matched.
Be on a par with...
〔註〕參閱"半斤八両"，（0504）；"石地堂，鐵掃把"（0400）；"你有張良計，我有過牆梯"（0771）各條。

0771 你唔嫌我籮疏，我唔嫌你米碎
nei⁵ m⁴ jim⁴ ŋɔ⁵ lɔ⁴ sɔ¹, ŋɔ⁵ m⁴ jim⁴ nei⁵ mɐi⁵ sœy³ (translit.)
You do not cold-shoulder my dispersive bamboo basket and neither do I detest your smashed rice. (lit.)
Neither of the two detests the weak points of either side.

七畫

Be two of a kind.
〔註〕比喻彼此互不嫌棄或臭味相投。

0772 你做初一，我做十五
nei⁵ dzou⁶ tsɔ¹ jɐt⁷, ŋɔ⁵ dzou⁶ sɐp¹ ŋ⁵ (translit.)
You do the first day of the month; I do the fifteenth. (lit.)
Tit for tat.
Eye for eye.
〔註〕表示以牙還牙或針鋒相對的意思。

0773 你敬我一尺，我敬你一丈
nei⁵ giŋ³ ŋɔ⁵ jɐt⁷ tsɛk⁸, ŋɔ⁵ giŋ³ nei⁵ jɐt⁷ dzœŋ⁶ (translit.)
You offer me one foot, I'll offer you ten feet in return. (lit.)
I'll give you an ell for an inch.
I'll show greater respect for you if you do a little to me.
〔註〕比喻互相尊重。

0774 你嗰樖嘢我都有得出賣
nei⁵ gɔ²ᐟ³ luŋ⁵ jɛ⁵ ŋɔ⁵ dou¹ jɐu⁵ dɐk⁷ tsœt⁷ mai⁶ (translit.)
I have the same thing as that in your trunk for sale. (lit.)
That is a game two people can play.
〔註〕即你這套詭計，大家都會。

0775 你走你嘅陽關路，我過我嘅獨木橋
nei⁵ dzɐu² nei⁵ gɛ³ jœŋ⁴ gwan¹ lou⁶; ŋɔ⁵ gwɔ³ ŋɔ⁵ gɛ³ duk⁹ muk⁹ kiu⁴ (translit.)
You walk your road to Jœŋ Gwan and I walk over my single-plank bridge. (lit.)
Each has his role to play.
Each goes his own way.
Each follows his bent.
〔註〕表示各行其是，各走各的路，互不侵犯的意思。

0776 吞吞吐吐
tɐn¹ tɐn¹ tou³ tou³ (translit.)
Swallowing and vomiting. (lit.)
Hum and haw.
Feel some hesitation in speaking.
Stick in one's throat.
〔註〕參閱"而依哦哦"條（0602）。

0777 吞口水養命
tɐn¹ hɐu² sœy² jœŋ⁵ mɛŋ⁶ (translit.)
Swallow a mouth of water to live on. (lit.)
Hope to linger out longer.
Linger on in a worsening condition.
〔註〕表示苟延殘命（喘）的意思。

0778 谷住度氣
guk⁷ dzy⁶ dou⁶ hei³ (translit.)
Hold one's temper. (lit.)
Eat the leek.
〔註〕表示被迫忍受的意思。

0779 谷起泡腮/顋

guk⁷ hei² pau¹ (pɐu¹) sɔi¹ (translit.)
Puff out the cheeks. (lit.)
Be displeased.
Be out of sorts.
〔註〕表示不滿的意思。

0780 利口便辭
lei⁶ hɐu² bin⁶ tsi⁴ (translit.)
Be eloquent. (lit.)
Have a ready or silver tongue.
〔註〕表示口才敏捷的意思。

0781 利口唔利腹
lei⁶ hɐu² m⁴ lei⁶ fuk⁷ (translit.)
Benefit the mouth but not the belly. (lit.)
Good for mouth but bad for health.
〔註〕表示好吃的東西會損害健康的意思。

0782 兵來將擋，水來土掩
biŋ¹ loi⁴ dzœŋ³ dɔŋ², tsœy² loi⁴ tou² jim² (translit.)
Soldiers coming will be turned away by a general; water coming will be covered with soil. (lit.)
A Roland for an Oliver.
Pay tit for tat.
〔註〕表示針鋒相對的意思；參閱"你做初一，我做十五"（0774）條。

0783 身在福中不知福
sɐn¹ dzoi⁶ fuk⁷ dzuŋ¹ bɐt⁷ dzi¹ fuk⁷ (translit.)
The one that lives in weal does not know the weal. (lit.)
Disregard the happy life one enjoys.
Not to appreciate the enjoyment of a happy life one is in.

0784 身當命抵
sɐn¹ dɔŋ¹ mɛŋ⁶ dɐi² (translit.)
The body undertakes and the life deserves. (lit.)
Have only onself to blame.
Lay the blame on onself.
〔註〕即自承其咎。

0785 我都冇你咁好氣
ŋɔ⁵ dou¹ mou⁵ nei⁵ gɐm³ hou² hei³ (translit.)
I have no such good air as yours. (lit.)
I am now at my ease.
I am carefree now.
I won't have to strive for...
I'll close my eyes to...
I'll snap my fingers at...
I'll talk no more.
I am not going to talk to you any more.
〔註〕表示自己生活優遊或已達要求目的，不必再和人競爭的意思。此外又有不屑一顧或不願再談下去的意義。

0786 肚皮打鼓
tou⁵ pei⁴ da² gu² (translit.)
The skin of the abdomen is like a drum being beaten. (lit.)
Be as hungry as a hunter.
〔註〕表示腹如雷鳴的意思。

0787　肚裏蟲
tou⁵ lœy⁵ tsuŋ⁴　(translit.)
The worm in the belly.　(lit.)
A mind reader.
〔註〕即明白別人心意的人。

0788　坐一望二
dzɔ⁶ jɐt⁷ mɔŋ⁶ ji⁶　(translit.)
Sit one and hope for two. (lit.)
Hope for another after gaining one.
〔註〕形容貪心不足。

0789　坐定粒六
dzɔ⁶ diŋ⁶ lɐp⁷ luk⁹　(translit.)
Fix al the dice to six.　(lit.)
Feel sure of oneself.
Consider oneself to be a sure fire winner.
Have full confidence.
〔註〕比喻很有把握，十拿九穩；穩拿。

0790　坐穩釣魚船
tsɔ⁵ wɐn² diu³ jy⁴ syn⁴ (translit.)
Sit firmly in a fishing boat. (lit.)
Be on firm ground.
Success is within one's grasp.
〔註〕表示成功在握的意思。

0791　坐食山崩
dzɔ⁶ sik⁹ san¹ bɐŋ¹　(translit.)
Sitting and eating will cause a mountain collapse.　(lit.)
Sit idle without work and the whole fortune will be at last used up.
〔註〕即"坐吃山空"。

0792　沙哩弄銃
sa⁴′⁶ li¹ luŋ³′⁶ tsuŋ³　(translit.)
Act in improper way.　(lit.)
Act rashly.
Take thoughtless action.
〔註〕表示魯莽輕率，莽撞的意思。

0793　沙沙滾
sa⁶ sa⁶ gwɐn²　(translit.)
Make hiss.　(lit.)
Play the field.
〔註〕表示不踏實，粗心大意或東搞西搞，不專一的意思。

0794　沙/砂煲刁眼角
sa¹ bou¹ diu¹ ŋan⁵ gɔk⁸ (translit.)
Earthen rice-cookers take side-long glances at each other. (lit.)
Go hungry.
Suffer from hunger.
〔註〕比喻斷炊，無米下鍋。參閱"吊沙煲"（0670）條。

0795　沙/砂煲兄弟
sa¹ bou¹ hiŋ¹ dɐi⁶　(translit.)
Brothers cook with the same earthen rice-cooker.　(lit.)
Friends under stress of weather.
Friends in the same boat.
〔註〕指結幫拜把的兄弟，又比喻患難與共的朋友。

0796　沙塵

sa¹ tsɐn⁴　(translit.)
Sandy dust.　(lit.)
With colours flying and band playing.
Make a boast of oneself.
Take pride in oneself.
〔註〕形容人輕浮，驕傲，目中無人，又有好出風頭，愛誇誇其談，炫耀自己的意思。參閱"白霍"（0475）條。

0797　沙灣燈籠——何府「苦」
sa¹ wan¹ dɐŋ¹ luŋ⁴—hɔ⁴ fu²　(translit.)
Sa Wan lanterns—Hɔ's houses (why so).　(lit.)
What needs?
Why so?
For what reason?
Why bother?
Is it worth the trouble?
〔註〕沙灣爲在廣州附近，離市橋不遠的一個鄉村，村中人絕大多數人爲何姓的，且多望族。富有者常在門外懸掛大燈籠一對，上書"何府"二字，"府"和"苦"同音，因此諧音作"爲了甚麼"或"爲甚麼要這樣"的意思。

0798　沐恩弟子——週身債
muk⁹ jɐn¹ dei⁶ dzi²—dzɐu¹ sɐn¹ dzai³　(translit.)
A disciple steeped in gods' bounties,—his whole body is covered with debts.　(lit.)
Be over head and ears in debt.
Run into debt.
〔註〕有的人迷信且信奉多神，每遇逆境，輒向諸神許以三牲酹謝爲條件，祈求所願，倘所願果真實現時，則稱爲沐恩弟子，必要履行諾言。但求神時不祇祈求一神，因而弄到滿身都是諾言債。廣東人便以此喻"債臺高築"的意思。

0799　諗鬼食豆腐
tɐm³ gwɐi² sik⁹ dɐu⁶ fu⁶　(translit.)
Deceive a ghost into eating beancurd.　(lit.)
Cheat somebody into the belief.
〔註〕表示用缺乏可信性的謊言，騙人相信的意思。

0800　冷手執個熱煎堆
laŋ⁵ sɐu² dzɐp⁷ gɔ³ jit⁹ dzin¹ dœy¹　(translit.)
Pick up a hot deep-fried pop-grain ball with a cold hand.　(lit.)
Gain an unexpected advantage.
Gain pennies from heaven.
〔註〕比喻得到意外的便宜。

0801　初哥
tsɔ¹ gɔ¹　(translit.)
Be initiative.　(lit.)
A beginner.
A new hand.
For the first time.
〔註〕指第一次做某種事的人；生手。

0802　初歸心抱（新婦），落地孩兒
tsɔ¹ gwɐi¹ sɐm¹ pou⁵ (sɐn¹ fu⁵), lɔk⁹ dei⁶ hai⁴ ji⁴

(translit.)
The newly-married daughter-in-law and the newly born baby. (lit.)
It is too late to teach an old dog new tricks.
Bend a tree while it is young.
Babyhood is the time when a baby is bred.
〔註〕暗喻小孩或新人應要及早教導。（按"心抱"實爲"新婦"的音誤。）

0803　見人講人話，見鬼講鬼話
gin³ jɐn⁴ gɔŋ² jɐn⁴ wa², gin³ gwɐi² gɔŋ² gwɐi² wa² (translit.)
Seeing a man, speak man's language; seeing a ghost, speak ghost words. (lit.)
Speak to a saint like a saint, to a devil like a devil.
Scratch somebody where he feels an itch.
〔註〕即說投人所好的話的意思。

0804　見山就拜
gin³ san¹ dzɐu⁶ bai³ (translit.)
Worship the grave as soon as one sees it. (lit.)
Wrongly make sure of somebody/something without getting to the bottom.
Take A for B without making sure.
〔註〕比喻不問究竟，一眼望去便誤認甲爲乙。

0805　見地不平擔鋤鏟
gin³ dei⁶ bɐt⁷ pin⁴ dam¹ bɔŋ¹ tsan² (translit.)
Take a hoe and shovel when seeing the uneven ground. (lit.)
Cry out against injustice.
Ready to take up the cudgels for somebody/something.
Stand up for the weak sister.
〔註〕即抱打不平。

0806　見步行步
gin³ bou⁶ hɐŋ⁴ bou⁶ (translit.)
See a step, walk with a step. (lit.)
Pick one's steps.
Meet the situation step by step.
〔註〕相當於"走一步，見一步"。

0807　見屎窟郁唔見米白
gin³ si² fɐt⁷ juk⁷ m⁴ gin³ mɐi⁵ bak⁹ (translit.)
See the hips moving but not see the rice turn white. (lit.)
Pretened to be hard at work without getting anything done.
〔註〕貌似積極幹，毫無實效。

0808　見高就拜，見低就踩
gin³ gou¹ dzɐu⁶ bai³, gin³ dɐi¹ dzɐu⁶ tsai² (jai²) (translit.)
Worship the high one and tread the low one. (lit.)
Be snobbish.
Look down on somebody below

one but fawn upon somebody
far superior to one.
〔註〕表示諂上欺下的意思。

0809　見過鬼就怕黑
gin³ gɔ³ gwɐi² dzɐu⁶ pa³
hɐk⁷　(translit.)
After seeing a ghost, one becomes afraid of darkness. (lit.)
A burnt child dreads the fire.
Onec bitten, twice shy.
〔註〕相當於"一朝被蛇咬，三年怕草繩"。

0810　步步爲營
bou⁶ bou⁶ wɐi⁴ jiŋ⁴　(translit.)
Take care pace by pace. (lit.)
Pick one's steps.
Do something by inches.
Be on the alert against...
〔註〕表示小心翼翼提高警覺的意思。

0811　吟詩都吟唔甩
jɐm⁴ si¹ dou¹ jɐm⁴ m⁴ lɐt⁷
(translit.)
Cannot get rid of it in spite of chanting. (lit.)
There is no way to evade... (doing something).
Fail to shirk.
〔註〕同"秀才遇老虎——吟詩都吟唔甩"（0752）。

0812　吼
hɐu¹　(translit.)
Have a look at. (lit.)
Watch.
Take notice of...
Buy/Patronize
Hope for.../Woo...
Pursue
Take a fancy to...
〔註〕廣東人用"吼"作動詞用。意爲看守，注意，光顧或買及向……（異性）追求等。

0813　吼斗
hɐu¹ dɐu²　(translit.)
Would like to have. (lit.)
Hope for...
Woo...
Take a fancy to...
Can do with...
〔註〕表示希望得到或想要。

0814　別緻
bit⁹ dzi³　(translit.)
Special and fine. (lit.)
Be new and unusual.
〔註〕即新奇而不尋常。

0815　吹鬚轆眼
tsœy¹ sou¹ luk⁷ ŋan⁵ (translit.)
Blow the beard and roll the pupils of eyes. (lit.)
Fall into a rage.
Tear one's hair.
〔註〕相當於"吹鬍子，瞪眼"。

0816　忍唔住
jɐn² m⁴ dzy⁶　(translit.)
Stand it no more. (lit.)
Be out of patience with...
Swallow a camel.
A worm will turn.
〔註〕參閱"忍無可忍"條（0819）。

0817 忍無可忍
jɐn² mou⁴ hɔ² jɐn² (translit.)
Can't stand it any more. (lit.)
Be out of patience with...
Swallow a camel.
A worn will turn.
〔註〕表示難於容忍的意思。

八畫

0818 亞斗官
a³ dɐu² gun¹ (translit.)
Master A Dau. (lit.)
A person/fop who spends money like water.
〔註〕比喻揮金如土的人或紈袴子弟。原句本爲"大良亞斗官"（大良爲順德縣一村）。

0819 亞昆洗鑊 —— 內外都咁乾淨
a³ kwan¹ sɐi² wɔk⁹—nɔi⁶ ŋɔi⁶ dou¹ gɐm³ gɔn¹ dzɐŋ⁶ (translit.)
A Kwan washes a frying pan — both inside and outside are so clean. (lit.)
Be out of pocket.
Be broke to the world.
Turn one's pockets inside out.
Lose all one's money in gambling.
〔註〕比喻一貧如洗或賭錢輸光。

0820 亞茂整餅 —— 冇個樣整個樣
a³ mɐu⁶ dziŋ² bɛn²—mou⁵ gɔ³ jœŋ⁶ dziŋ² gɔ³ jœŋ⁶ (translit.)
A Mau makes cakes — making new shapes out of none. (lit.)
Affect/Try to be different from others.
Display originality.
Blaze a new path.
Have a unique style.
Be in a class by oneself.
Strike an attitude.
〔註〕比喻與衆不同，獨出心裁，別具一格，別開生面，甚至裝腔作勢等。

0821 亞單睇榜 —— 一眼睇晒
a³ dan¹ tɐi² bɔŋ²—jɐt⁷ ŋan⁵ hɐi² sai³ (translit.)
A single-eyed man reads a list of successful candidates, — one eye sees all. (lit.)
See with half an eye.
See at a glance.
Be clear at a glance.
That's the all and the one one can see.
〔註〕比喻一目了然或全部見到。

0822 亞超着褲 —— 焗住
a³ tsiu¹ dzœk³ fu³—guk⁹ dzy⁶ (translit.)
A Tsiu wears trousers — being oppressed. (lit.)
Be forced to do something.
Be driven by stress of...
Need must when the devil

drives.

〔註〕比喻被迫。

0823 亞崩叫狗 —— 越叫越走
a³ buŋ¹ giu³ gɐu²—jyt⁹ giu³ jyt⁹ dzɐu² (translit.)
A man with hare-lip calls a dog — the more he calls, the farther it runs. (lit.)
Kick over the traces.
Run away without obedience.
Be unable to restrain somebody.

〔註〕比喻不服從或無法約束。

0824 亞崩養狗 —— 轉性
a³ bɐŋ¹ jœn⁵ gɐu²—dzyn³ siŋ³ (translit.)
A man with hare-lip rears a dog, — it changes its nature. (lit.)
Have a change of nature.
Change skin.

〔註〕比喻人的性格改變。

0825 亞崩劏羊 —— 咩（哶）都冇得咩（哶）
a³ bɐŋ¹ tɔŋ¹ jœŋ⁴—ŋɛ¹(mɛ¹) dou¹ mou⁵ dɐk⁷ ŋɛ¹(mɛ¹). (translit.)
A man with hare-lip slaughters a goat — it bleats no more. (lit.)
Have lost one's tongue.
Hold one's tongue.
Not a sound is uttered.
Be forced to keep silence.

〔註〕比喻啞口無言或被迫禁止發言。

0826 亞駝〈馱〉行路 —— 春「中中」地
a³ tɔ² haŋ⁴ lou⁶—dzuŋ¹ dzuŋ¹ dei² (translit.)
A hump-back walks, — bending down(strike the happy medium,). (lit.)
Strike the happy medium
Be in moderation.
Be medium
Take a mean course.
Be fair to middling.

〔註〕比喻採取中庸之道處理或形容人或物過得去（還算好的意思）。

0827 亞駝〈馱〉賣蝦米 —— 大家都唔掂
a³ tɔ² mai⁶ ha¹ mɐi⁵—dai⁶ ga¹ dou¹ m⁴ dim⁴ (translit.)
A hump-back sells dreied shrimps, — both are not stright (alright). (lit.)
All play in hard luck.
All (will) have a lot of trouble.

〔註〕比喻彼此都倒霉或大家都會有麻煩。至於"現在倒霉"抑或"將有麻煩"則以説話的情況或上下理而定。（按："掂"本意爲"直"，但轉義爲"沒有麻煩"，"唔掂"意即"不是沒有麻煩" —— 負負得正 ——）。

0828 亞蘭嫁亞瑞 —— 大家累鬥累
a³ lan⁴ ga³ a³ sœy⁶—dai⁶ ga¹ lœy⁶ dɐu³ lœy⁶ (translit.)

A Lan marries to A Sui — one implicates another. (lit.)
Be implicative of each other.
Drag in one another.
〔註〕比喻互相牽累。

0829 亞聾送殯——唔聽枝死人笛
a³ luŋ⁴ suŋ³ bɐn³—m⁴ tɛŋ¹ dzi¹ sei² jɐn⁴ dɛk⁹ (translit.)
A deaf man attends the funeral procession,— not to listen to the pipe blown for the dead man. (lit.)
Turn a deaf ear to somebody.
〔註〕比喻充耳不聞或不願聽。參閱"借咗聾陳隻耳"條（1142）。

0830 亞聾燒炮——散晒
a³ huŋ⁴ siu¹ pau³,—san² ṣai³ (translit.)
A deaf man fires a firecracker,— all scatter about. (lit.)
Be disbanded./Be dissolved.
Break off the friendly relation with somebody.
Fizzle out.
Meet with a failure.
〔註〕比喻散夥，解散，關係終止，事情告吹或甚至遭到失敗。

0831 直腸直肚
dzik⁹ tsœŋ⁴ dzik⁹ tou⁵ (translit.)
Have straight intestines and tripe. (lit.)

Speak straightforward.
Be outspoken in the expression of one's opinions.
〔註〕比喻坦率陳詞。

0832 直程
dzik⁹ tsiŋ⁴ (translit.)
Straight way. (lit.)
Keep straight on.
Directly.
Straightway.
Sure enough.
To be sure.
〔註〕表示直接，逕直或當然，肯定的意思。

0833 直頭
dzik⁹ tɐu⁴ (translit.)
Straight ahead. (lit.)
Straightway.
〔註〕表示一直，直接的意思。

0834 兩公婆扒艇——你有你事
lœŋ⁵ kuŋ¹ pɔ²′⁴ pa⁴ tɛŋ⁵,— nei⁵ jɐu⁵ nei⁵ si⁶ (translit.)
A husband and a wife row a sampan,— you have your own affairs.
Mind your own business.
〔註〕相當於"敲鑼賣糖"——各幹一行。

0835 兩公婆見鬼——唔係你就係我
lœŋ⁵ guŋ¹ pɔ⁴ gin³ gwɐi²— m⁴ hɐi⁶ nei⁵ dzɐi⁶ hɐi⁶ ŋɔ⁵ (translit.)

The husband and the wife saw a ghost, — either you or I. (lit.)
Either of the two.

0836 兩個和尚擔水食，三個和尚冇水食
lœŋ⁵ gɔ³ wɔ⁴ sœŋ² dam¹ sœy² sik⁹, sam¹ gɔ³ wɔ⁴ sœŋ² mou⁵ sœy² sik⁹ (translit.)
Two monks carry water to cook with; three monks have no water to cook with. (lit.)
Too many cooks make no broth.
Everybody's business is nobody's business.
〔註〕比喻衆人的事沒有人理。

0837 兩睇
lœŋ⁵ tɐi² (translit.)
See either this side or that one. (lit.)
Be either definite or indefinite.
Not make up one's mind yet.
Betwixt and between.
〔註〕表示兩可之間或尚未決定的意思。（有人説"兩開"，意思相同。）

0838 兩頭唔到岸
lœŋ⁵ tɐu⁴ m⁴ dou³ ŋɔn⁶ (translit.)
Fail to reach ashore at both sides. (lit.)
Neither sink nor swim in the middle of the sea.
Be on the horns of a dilemma.
Be in a dilemma.
〔註〕表示進退兩難的意思。

0839 兩頭唔受中間受
lœŋ⁵ tɐu⁴ m⁴ sɐu⁶ dzuŋ¹ gan¹ sɐu⁶ (translit.)
Both sides do not accept it but the middle does. (lit.)
Line one' pocket.
Feather one's nest.
Neither of both parties but the third one takes...
〔註〕指中飽私囊，但亦指雙方不要，由第三者接受。

0840 兩騎牛
lœŋ⁵ kɛ⁴ ŋɐu²/⁴ (translit.)
Ride on two bulls. (lit.)
Take an equivocal attitude.
Sit on the fence.
Be a double-dealer.
〔註〕指態度模稜兩可或騎牆派。

0841 來者不善，善者不來
lɔi⁴ dzɛ² bɐt⁷ sin⁶, sin⁶ dzɛ² bɐt⁷ lɔi⁴ (translit.)
The person who comes is not kind; the person who is kind does not come. (lit.)
No coward dares to come.
He who comes harbours ulterior motives.
He who comes harbours malicious intentions.
〔註〕表示膽小的就不來或既來就是不懷好意的意思。

0842 來説是非者，便是是非人
lɔi⁴ syt⁸ si⁶ fei¹ dzɛ², bin⁶ si⁶

八畫

si⁶ fei¹ jɐn⁴ *(translit.)*
The person coming to tell tales is a gossip monger. (lit.)
The person who speaks ill of others will speak ill of you.

0843　到家
dou³ ga¹ *(translit.)*
Reach home. (lit.)
Reach a very high level.
Be excellent in...
〔註〕表示達到很高水平或在……方面極爲傑出的意思。

0844　到處楊梅一樣花
dou³ tsy³ jœŋ⁴ mui⁴ jɐt⁷ jœŋ⁶ fa¹ *(translit.)*
Red bayberries in every place bring forth the same flowers. (lit.)
Same trees at all places bear same fruits.
All tarred with the same brush.
〔註〕表示任何地方情況也是一樣的意思，但亦引伸喻一路貨色。

0845　到喉唔到肺
dou³ hɐu⁴ m⁴ dou³ fɐi³ *(translit.)*
Reach to the throat not to the lungs. (lit.)
Not enough to satisfy one's appetite.
Not enough to one's heart's content.
〔註〕本指不滿足食慾，但引伸喻意猶未足。

0846　青磚沙梨
tsɛŋ¹ dzyn¹ sa¹ lei²ᐟ⁴ *(translit.)*
A russet pear made out of black brick. (lit.)
Not only a penny-pincher but also money snatcher.
〔註〕比喻視財如命而且在別人身上打算盤的人。

0847　青頭仔
tsɛŋ¹ tɐu⁴ dzɐi² *(translit.)*
A green-headed boy. (lit.)
A young man without sexual experience.
〔註〕指未有性經驗的青少年。

0848　幸災樂禍
hɐŋ⁶ dzɔi¹ lɔk⁹ wɔ⁶ *(translit.)*
Lucky to see other's calamity and happy over other's misfortune. (lit.)
Gloat upon other's misfortune.
Take pleasure in other's calamity.

0849　東家唔打打西家
duŋ¹ ga¹ m⁴ da² da² sɐi¹ ga¹ *(translit.)*
Be dismissed by the eastern shop but employed by the western one. (lit.)
Lose at sunrise and gain at sunset.
Make up on the roundabouts what one loses on the swings.
Lose employment in one but get a job in the other.
〔註〕表示在職業方面失之東隅收之桑隅的意思。

八畫

0850 事不關己，己不勞心
si⁶ bɐt⁷ gwan¹ gei², gei² bɐt⁷ lou⁴ sɐm¹ (translit.)
The matter that does not concern one is not worried about. (lit.)
Mind one's own business.
Never trouble trouble till trouble troubles you.
Saw wood.

0851 事在人爲
si⁶ dzɔi⁶ jɐn⁴ wɐi⁴ (translit.)
Things are done by men. (lit.)
Where there is a will, there is a way.
All depends on human effort.

0852 事後孔明
si⁶ hɐu⁶ huŋ² miŋ⁴ (translit.)
After the event, everyone can be the man named Huŋ Miŋ. (lit.)
Huŋ Miŋ was Military Councillor of Suk⁹ Hɔn³ in the period of Three Kingdoms-B.C.221-253-. He was said to be able to forsee everything.
Be wise after the event.
The wit after the event is the wit of everybody.

0853 拍心口
pak⁸ sɐm¹ hɐu² (translit.)
Slap the mouth of heart (chest). (lit.)
Readily promise to undertake responsibility.
Be ready to do one's best to help somebody.
〔註〕表示拍胸膛一口承擔的意思。

0854 拍成佢
pak⁸ sɛŋ⁴ kœy⁵ (translit.)
Cause it to succeed. (lit.)
Make two sides agree to a deal.
Go between with the hope of making a match.
〔註〕指促使雙方成功。

0855 拍烏蠅
pak⁸ wu¹ jiŋ¹ (translit.)
Slap flies. (lit.)
Have a dull market.
Have a slack business.
〔註〕暗喻生意清淡。

0856 拍硬檔
pak⁸ ŋaŋ⁶ dɔŋ³ (translit.)
Slap the stall hard. (lit.)
Set one's shoulder to the wheel.
Help each other to work on.
Come to one's assistance.
Assist somebody with something.
Pool together our efforts.
〔註〕表示緊密地合作，互相配合的意思。

0857 拍膊頭
pak⁸ bɔk⁸ tɐu⁴ (translit.)
Tap somebody's shoulder. (lit.)
Hope for somebody to set his shoulder to the wheel.
Cry on somebody's shoulder.

Intend to have great facilities for friend's sake.
〔註〕指希望別人給自己方便或企求別人的同情。

0858 拍薑咁拍
pak⁸ gœŋ¹ gɐm³ pak⁸ (translit.)
Slap somebody like flattening a piece of ginger with a kitchen chapper. (lit.)
Give somebody a hard smack.
Knock the tar out of somebody.
〔註〕指把人痛打一頓。

0859 拍檔
pak⁸ dɔŋ³ (translit.)
Slap the stall. (lit.)
A partner.
A companion who works together with somebody.
〔註〕即伙伴。

0860 拆穿西洋鏡
tsak⁸ tsyn¹ sɐi¹ jœŋ⁴ gɛŋ³ (translit.)
Unmask a weatern mirror. (lit.)
Become aware of the camouflage.
Expose the fraud.
Give the lie to something.
〔註〕表示洞悉欺騙或揭露某事的虛偽。相當"撕開畫皮"。

0861 拃亂戈柄
dza⁶ lyn⁶ gwɔ¹ bɛŋ³ (translit.)
Disturb the dagger-axes and their handles. (lit.)

Make an interruption.
Put sand in the wheels.
Cause a hindrance.
〔註〕表示打斷別人的話或防礙別人事情的意思。

0862 拼死無大害
pun² sei² mou⁴ dai⁶ hɔi⁴ (translit.)
There is no harm is spite of death. (lit.)
Do something at the risk of...
Risk everything on a single throw.
Run one's head against a wall.
〔註〕表示不惜冒險去做的意思。

0863 拼啤
pun² pɛ² (translit.)
Consider nothing. (lit.)
Act shamelessly.
Act for better or worse.
Disregard one's dignity.
Be perverse.
Leave oneself to sink or swim.
〔註〕相當於耍無賴或耍賴，撒野。

0864 拼爛
pun² lan² (translit.)
Disregard everything. (lit.)
〔註〕同"拼啤"（0863）。

0865 抽水
tsɐu¹ sœy² (translit.)
Draw water. (lit.)
Take a cut off the winnings in gambling.
〔註〕指在賭博時，抽贏家的一部分錢。

0866 抽佣

tsɐu¹ juŋ² （translit.）
Draw commission. （lit.）
Draw a commission on the sale.
〔註〕即抽取佣金的簡稱。

0867 抽後脚
tsɐu¹ hɐu⁶ gœk⁸ （translit.）
Draw a hind leg. （lit.）
Pull somebody's leg.
Capitalize upon somebody's vulnerable statement.
〔註〕指把人説過的話重複來嘲弄他。相當於"抓辮子"。

0868 抽秤/掅
tsɐu¹ tziŋ³ （translit.）
Pick and weigh. （lit.）
Find fault with somebody.
Pick holes in...
Do nit-picking.
〔註〕表示挑剔或找錯兒的意思。相當於"找碴兒"。

0869 抽絲剝繭
tsɐu¹ si¹ mɔk⁷ gan² （translit.）
Draw silk and strip cocoons. （lit.）
Trace a fox to its den.
Analyse a cace to find out the truth.
〔註〕表示逐步追查真相或找出原因的意思。

0870 招搖過市
dziu¹ jiu⁴ gwɔ³ si⁵ （translit.）
Faunting through the streets. （lit.）
Be fond of showing oneself in the streets.
Be fond of limelight.
〔註〕表示喜歡在公衆場合炫耀或出風頭的意思。

0871 招搖撞騙
dziu¹ jiu⁴ dzɔŋ⁴ pin³ （translit.）
Act ostentatiously and swindle. （lit.）
Put on a good bluff.
〔註〕即假借名義行騙。

0872 拉人裙冚自己脚
lai¹ jɐn⁴ kwɐn⁴ kɐm² dzi⁶ gei² gœk⁸ （translit.）
Drag another person's skirt to cover one's own legs. （lit.）
Dress oneself in borrowed plumes.
〔註〕表示靠別人的聲望來抬高自己的意思。

0873 拉牛上樹
lai¹ ŋɐu⁴ sœn⁵ sy⁶ （translit.）
Pull a bull up a tree. （lit.）
Have difficulty in teaching somebody.
〔註〕比喻某人不易教導。

0874 拉柴
lai¹ tsai⁴ （translit.）
Drag firewood. （lit.）
Meet one's fate.
Die a death.
〔註〕指死亡。參閱"瓜直"（0479），"瓜柴"（0480）及"瓜老襯"（0478）各條。

八畫

0875 拉埋天窗
lai¹ mai⁴ tin¹ tsœŋ¹ (translit.)
Pull close the skylight. (lit.)
Establish a family.
Get married.
〔註〕指男女結合，成婚。

0876 抵死
dɐi² sei² (translit.)
Deserve the death. (lit.)
It serves somebody right.
Deserve the punishment/death.
Carry a sting. (of speech or article)
〔註〕相當於該死，活該的意思。有時又表示別人的説話或文章有刺的意思。

0877 抵到爛
dɐi² dou³ lan⁶ (translit.)
Very cheap indeed. (lit.)
Get the best value for one's money.
〔註〕表示價錢很便宜的意思。

0878 抵得諗
dɐi² dɐk⁷ nɐm² (translit.)
Can bear hardship. (lit.)
Can bear the burden of work and complaint.
〔註〕表示能任勞任怨的意思。

0879 抵賴
dɐi² lai⁶ (translit.)
Have another to blame. (lit.)
Shift the blame on to other shoulders.
Lay the blame on the wrong shoulders.
Disavow.
Make a denial of something.
〔註〕表示推卸責任，或不承認的意思。

0880 拖泥帶水
tɔ¹ nɐi⁴ dai³ sœy² (translit.)
Drag through mud and water. (lit.)
Be sloppy in one's work.
〔註〕表示做事拖拉，不利落。

0881 扻/砍頭埋牆
hɐm² tɐu²ᐟ⁴ mai⁴ᐧ tsœŋ⁴ (translit.)
Knock the head against the wall. (lit.)
Show repentance for having been foolish/ignorant.
〔註〕表示曾因無知做錯事而事後悔恨的意思。

0882 拘執
kœy¹ dzɐp⁷ (translit.)
Be particular with. (lit.)
Bother oneself about small matters.
Be punctilious.
Stand on ceremony.
〔註〕指計較小節或拘禮。

0883 拐帶
gwai² dai³ (translit.)
A man who kidnaps children. (lit.)
Kidnap.
〔註〕即誘拐小孩。

0884 抬棺材甩褲 —— 失禮死
人

tɔi⁴ gun¹ tsɔi⁴ lɐt⁷ fu³ —sɐt⁷ lɐi⁵ sei² jɐn⁴ (translit.)

One's trousers come down while one is carrying a coffin, — be discourteous to the dead man. (lit.)

Cut a sorry figure.

Commit a breach of etiquette.

〔註〕不像樣子，不成體統；失禮。

0885 拗手瓜

ŋau² sɐu² gwa¹ (translit.)

Join arms in collusion. (lit.)

Measure one's strength or power with somebody.

Show power against another.

〔註〕比喻和人較量實力。

0886 拗頸

au³ gɐŋ² (translit.)

Twist the neck. (lit.)

Argue against somebody.

Have a debate with somebody.

〔註〕表示爭執或抬槓的意思。

0887 枉作小人

wɔŋ² dzɔk⁸ siu² jɐn⁴ (translit.)

It is a vain attempt to be a mean person. (lit.)

Play the villain, but fail to gain any profit.

〔註〕枉費心機。

0888 制得過

dzɐi³ dɐk⁷ gwɔ³ (translit.)

It is worth doing. (lit.)

It will pay to do something.

It is worth while doing something.

〔註〕相當於"划得來"或"值得做"。（廣東話"制"意爲"做"。）

0889 狗上瓦桁 —— 有條路

gɐu² sœŋ⁵ ŋa⁵ haŋ¹ —jɐu⁵ tiu⁴ lou⁶ (translit.)

A dog goes up to the roof, — there is a road. (lit.)

With ulterior motives.

Have an aim.

〔註〕表示"別有用心"的意思。相當於耗子鑽水溝——各有各的路。

0890 狗咬呂洞賓 —— 不識好人心

gɐu² ŋau⁵ lœy⁵ duŋ⁶ ban¹ — bɐt⁷ sik⁷ hou² jɐn⁴ sɐm¹ (translit.)

A dog bites Lœy Dun Ban (one of the eight immortals of Taoism), — not know the good man's heart. (lit.)

Not know chalk from cheese.

Not know the good from the bad.

0891 狗咬狗骨

gɐu² ŋau⁵ gɐu² gwɐt⁷ (translit.)

Dogs eat dogs' bones. (lit.)

Put up an internecine fight.

There is no love between them.

〔註〕比喻狗咬狗；互相勾心鬥爭。

0892 狗眼看人低

gɐu² ŋan⁵ hɔn³ jɐn⁴ dɐi¹

(translit.)
A dog's eyes look down on people. (lit.)
Hold somebody in contempt.
Put on airs with despise.
Look down on somebody like a snob.

0893　受人二分四
sɐu⁶ jɐn⁴ ji⁶ fɐn¹ sei³ (translit.)
Accept one-third of ten cents. (lit.)
Be in the employ of a boss.
〔註〕從前使用硬幣時代廣東的稱爲小洋，每個銀圓（值一圓）純銀重量爲七錢二分，二角的爲一錢四分四釐，一角的爲七分二釐。在當時一間大商號的在事或稱司理（即今日的經理職位）月薪亦不過十圓多些，普通職員不會多過十圓。因此受人二分四（即一角的三分一）是指"受僱於人"的意思。

0894　受人錢財，替人消災
sɐu⁶ jɐn⁴ tsin⁴ tsɔi⁴, tɐi³ jɐn⁴ siu¹ dzɔi¹ (translit.)
The payee should endure the calamity on place of the payer. (lit.)
Accept suffering as payment for a debt.
After being paid, one must take one's life in one's hand to do something for somebody.

0895　受硬唔受軟
sɐu⁶ ŋaŋ⁶ m⁴ sɐu⁶ jyn⁵

八畫

(translit.)
Bear hardness but not accept softness. (lit.)
Submit to somebody's pressure after first turning down his gentle manners.
Browbeat the weak but fear the strong.
〔註〕表示欺軟怕硬的意思。

0896　受軟唔受硬
sɐu⁶ jyn⁵ m⁴ sɐu⁶ ŋaŋ⁶ (translit.)
Bear softness but refuse hardness. (lit.)
Submit to gentle manners but refuse to submit bully ones.
Prefer to be coaxed rather than threatened.
〔註〕相當於"吃軟不吃硬"。

0897　受落
sɐu⁶ lɔk⁹ (translit.)
Accept. (lit.)
Accept something.
Feel greatly flattered by somebody's praise.
〔註〕表示接受或被人稱讚後感到榮幸的意思。

0898　受唔住
sɐu⁶ m⁴ dzy⁶ (translit.)
Can not accept it. (lit.)
Can't stand it.
Can't bear for somebody to do something.
〔註〕表示忍不住或不能容忍某人做（某事）。

0899　受氣

sɐu⁶ hei³　*(translit.)*
Accept the air.　(lit.)
Suffer wrong.
Take the rap.
〔註〕表示受虐待，受不公正待遇或挨罵。

0900　和味
wɔ⁴ mei⁶　*(translit.)*
Good taste.　(lit.)
Be delicious.
Taste wonderful.
Have a wide margin of profits.
A good sum of money.
〔註〕表示味美；利潤多及大筆款項的意思。

0901　和齧
wɔ⁴ gwɔ²　*(translit.)*
A draw.　(lit.)
A dead heat.
A drawn game.
Neither win nor lose.
〔註〕無勝無負的平局，和局。

0902　使銅銀夾大聲
sai² tuŋ⁴ ŋɐn⁴ gap⁸ dai⁶ sɛŋ¹　*(translit.)*
Use false silver coins with a loud voice.　(lit.)
Thunder threats at somebody.
Seize the catch before the hound.
Take the wind out of somebody's sails.
〔註〕喻理虧在先，還要兇。銅銀爲僞做硬幣。在當時政府尚未接納蘇聯經濟專家"李茲羅斯"建議將白銀收歸國有前，國人仍使用純銀硬幣。狡黠者以銅鍍上銀色亂真。因往時民風敦厚，如使銅銀者大聲夾惡，每易得逞。

0903　使頸
sai² gɛŋ²　*(translit.)*
Use the neck.　(lit.)
Harden the neck for one's will.
Fly into a temper.
Feel wronged and act rashly.
Take huff for dissatisfaction.
〔註〕相當於"使性子"，耍脾氣；賭氣。

0904　刮龍
gwat⁸ luŋ²　*(translit.)*
Scrape a dragon.　(lit.)
Coin money by unfair means.
Coin one's brains by illegal means.
Reap huge profit.
〔註〕指利用不法手段去弄錢或動腦筋謀取暴利的行爲，如貪污。

0905　物以罕爲貴
mɐt⁹ ji⁵ hɔn² wɐi⁴ gwɐi³　*(translit.)*
Rare things are more expensive.　(lit.)
Precious things are never found in heaps.
The rarer it is, the more it is worth.

0906　物以類聚
mɐt⁹ ji⁵ lœy⁶ dzœy⁶　*(translit.)*
Things of the same kind gather together.　(lit.)
Birds of a feather flock to-

gether.

0907 物輕情義重
mɐt⁹ hiŋ¹ tsiŋ⁴ ji⁶ dzuŋ⁶ (translit.)
The thing is light but the friendship is weighty. (lit.)
A gift of trifling value conveys affection.

0908 物離鄉貴，人離鄉賤
mɐt⁹ lei⁴ hœŋ¹ gwɐi³, jɐn⁴ lei⁴ hœŋ¹ dzin⁶ (translit.)
Things leaving home are expensive; men leaving their native land become cheap. (lit.)
Articles leaving home become precious, but men, demeaned.

0909 知人口面不知心
dzi¹ jɐn⁴ hɐu² min⁶ bɐt⁷ dzi¹ sɐm¹ (translit.)
Know a man's mouth and face but know not his heart. (lit.)
Be familiar with somebody but ignorant of his true nature.

0910 知子莫若父
dzi¹ dzi² mɔk⁹ jœk⁹ fu⁶ (translit.)
A father knows his son better. (lit.)
No one knows a boy better than his father.

0911 知己知彼
dzi¹ gei² dzi¹ bei² (translit.)
Know oneself and know others. (lit.)

Besides knowing itself, an old fox has to know a fox-hunter.
It needs to understand both oneself and others.

0912 知其一不知其二
dzi¹ kei⁴ jɐt⁷ bɐt⁷ dzi¹ kei⁴ ji⁶ (translit.)
Know only one aspect of something not two. (lit.)
Have only one-sided view.
Have a smattering of..
Be aware of one aspect but ignorant of the other.

0913 知無不言，言無不盡
dzi¹ mou⁴ bɐt⁷ jin⁴, jin⁴ mou⁴ bɐt⁷ dzœn⁶ (translit.)
Say what is known and say all. (lit.)
Say all what one knows.
Say all one knows without reserve.

0914 知情識趣
dzi¹ tsiŋ⁴ sik⁷ tsœy³ (translit.)
Know what somebody is feeling and interested in. (lit.)
Know how to behave oneself to cope with somebody's feeling and interest.
〔註〕表示善於體會別人的意圖。

0915 肥缺
fei¹ kyt⁸ (translit.)
A fat job. (lit.)
A gravy train.
An armchair job.

0916 肥肥白白

fei⁴ fei⁴ bag⁶ bag⁶ (translit.)

Fat and white. (lit.)

Fair and plump.

〔註〕即又白又胖；皮膚白嫩，豐滿。

0917 返去舊時嗰度

fan¹ hœy³ gɐu⁶ si⁴ gɔ² lou⁶ (translit.)

Go back to the old place. (lit.)

Be gathered to one's fathers.
Go west.

〔註〕暗喻死亡。

0918 近山不可燒枉柴，近河不可洗枉水

gɐn⁶ san¹ bɐt⁷ hɔ² siu¹ wɔŋ² tsai⁴, gɐn⁶ hɔ⁴ bɐt⁷ hɔ² sɐi² wɔŋ² sœy² (translit.)

Those living near a mountain do not waste firewood, and those living near a river do not waste water. (lit.)

Waste not, want not.

〔註〕比喻不浪費便不會缺乏。

0919 近水樓臺先得月

gɐn⁶ sœy² lɐu⁴ tɔi⁴ sin¹ dɐk⁷ jyt⁹ (translit.)

The avilion near the water gets the moonlight first. (lit.)

Be in a favourable situation.

〔註〕比喻得地利，參閱"近住城隍廟求炷好香"（0920）；"近官得力"（0921）及"近厨得食"（0922）各條。

0920 近住城隍廟求炷好香

gɐn⁶ dzy⁶ siŋ⁴ wɔŋ⁴ miu² kɐu⁴ dzy³ hou² hœŋ¹ (translit.)

Living near the temple of the City-god, one can ask for a good set of incense-sticks. (lit.)

Hope to curry favour with somebody.
Intend to be favoured with what one asks for.

〔註〕參閱"近水樓臺先得月"（0919），"近官得力"（0921）及"近厨得食"（0922）各條。

0921 近官得力

gɐn⁶ gun¹ dɐk⁷ lik⁹ (translit.)

Near officials, one can obtain power. (lit.)

It is much more convenient to have a friend in court.

〔註〕參閱"近水樓臺先得月"（0919），"近住城隍廟求炷好香"（0920）及"近厨得食"（0922）各條。

0922 近厨得食

gɐn⁶ tsœy⁴ dɐk⁷ sik⁹ (translit.)

Near the kitchen, one can get a lot to eat. (lit.)

Be in a favourable position to gain advantage.

〔註〕參閱"近水樓臺先得月"

(0919)，"近住城隍廟求炷好香"(0920)及"近官得力"(0921)各條。

0923　金盆洗手
gɐm¹ pun⁴ sɐi² sɐu² (translit.)
Wash hands in a gold basin. (lit.)
Wash one's hands of...
Hang up one's axe.
〔註〕指洗手不幹。

0924　金睛火眼
gɐm¹ dziŋ¹ fɔ² ŋan⁵ (translit.)
Gold pupils and firy eyes. (lit.)
Keep one's eyesd polished.
Be lynx-eyed.
Be up to one's eyes in work.
〔註〕本義表示提高警覺或留心者的意思，但引伸喻工作忙得不可開交。

0925　命根
mɛŋ⁶ gɐn¹ (translit.)
The root of life. (lit.)
One's life blood.
One's beloved.
One's favourite.
〔註〕指特別寵愛的人或物。相當於"命根子"。

0926　的起心肝
dik⁷ hei² sɐm¹ gɔn¹ (translit.)
Take up the heart and liver. (lit.)
Pull up one's socks.
Brace oneself up.
Bestir oneself.
Make up one's mind.
〔註〕表示鼓起勇氣，下定決心及振作精神的意思。

0927　依揖/依依揖揖
ji¹ jɐp⁷/ji¹ ji¹ jɐp⁷ jɐp⁷ (translit.)
Get in carnal touch. (lit.)
Have illicit intercourse.
Carry on a clandestine love affair.
〔註〕喻男女間的私通或偷情。

0928　波羅雞——靠黐
bɔ¹ lɔ⁴ gɐi¹—kau³ tsi¹ (translit.)
Paper-pasted hens made in Bɔ Lɔ—depending on stickiness. (lit.)
The person who always profits himself at other people's expense.
A grabber of petty advantages.
〔註〕比喻專揩油的人。波羅為廣州八景之一（波羅浴日）。該地有一波羅廟，每逢神誕，不少善男信女在拜神祈福後，購買"紙雞"返家，以取吉利。該種"紙雞"栩栩如生，但因紙製，必用槳糊黐黏，但廣東人把"黐"又作"沾"（揩油的意思）解，一義之轉便諧格了。

0929　盲公布袋——自開自解
maŋ⁴ guŋ¹ bou³ dɔi⁶—dzi⁶

hɔi¹ dzi⁶ gai² (translit.)
A blind man's cloth-bag — self opening and self tying. (lit.)
Give comfort to oneself.
Console oneself.
Seek consolation for oneself.
〔註〕表示自我安慰的意思。因廣東人把"開解"兩字作"安慰"解。

0930 盲佬貼符 —— 倒貼
maŋ⁴ lou² tip⁸ fu⁴—dou³ tip⁸ (translit.)
A blind man sticks a Toaist magic incantation — sticking it upside down. (lit.)
A female goes to the expense of a man.
〔註〕女人給男人錢用，或養着男人。（註：借"貼"字雙關而成爲"津貼"的"貼"字。）

0931 盲拳打死老師傅
maŋ⁴ kyn⁴ da² sei² lou⁵ si¹ fu² (translit.)
Blind fists hit the old master to death. (lit.)
A poor hand may put the old master to death.
〔註〕表示新手有時也會比老手強。

0932 盲眼
mang⁴ ngan⁵ (translit.)
Blind eye. (lit.)
Blind.
〔註〕即瞎，失明。

0933 盲婆喂奶 —— 亂塞
maŋ⁴ pɔ⁴ wɐi³ nai⁵,—lyn⁶ sak⁷ (translit.)

A blind woman gives her baby the breast — stuff at random. (lit.)
Force soembody to accept what is given out.
Stuff a box/bag...with something.
〔註〕表示強人接受物件或把物件胡亂地向盛器裏塞進去的意思。

0934 盲摸摸
maŋ⁴ mɔ² mɔ² (translit.)
Feel the way ·in the dark. (lit.)
Do something without a plan.
Go about one's job in a haphazard way.
Do one's job without experience.
〔註〕意指瞎幹或做事無經驗。

0935 盲頭烏蠅
maŋ⁴ tɐu⁴ wu¹ jiŋ¹ (translit.)
A blind-headed fly. (lit.)
A bull in a china shop.
A blind flying person.
An absent-minded professor.
〔註〕比喻魯莽的人，漫無目的或無知的人。

0936 放下心頭大石
fɔŋ³ ha⁶ sɐm¹ tɐu⁴ dai⁶ sɛk⁹ (translit.)
Lay down the stone of the heart. (lit.)
Be free from anxiety.
〔註〕表示消除憂慮的意思。

0937 放白鴿
fɔŋ³ bak⁹ gɐp⁸ (translit.)
Set a pigeon free. (lit.)
Play a confidence game/trick.
〔註〕二人串通行騙，尤指騙子夫婦串通，女的改嫁給別人後，把錢財席捲而逃的一種騙局。

0938 放屁
fɔŋ³ pei³ (translit.)
Break wind. (lit.)
Talk rot.
Stuff and nonsense.
〔註〕相當於「胡說八道」。

0939 放虎歸山
fɔŋ³ fu² gwɐi¹ san¹ (translit.)
Let the tiger go back to the mountain. (lit.)
Lay trouble for the future.
〔註〕比喻引來後患。

0940 放路溪錢 —— 引死人
fɔŋ³ lou⁶ kɐi¹ tsin⁴ —jɐn⁵ sei² jɐn⁴ (translit.)
The paper-money (used in idolatry) scattered along roads,— leading a dead man. (lit.)
Tease cocks.
Be very attractive.
Be very charming.
〔註〕在出殯行列前，例有人沿途散放紙錢（溪錢），取意是賄賂途中遊魂野鬼，讓其引導死者到他的安息地。"引死人"的"引"是"帶引"的意思，但相關語則作"吸引"的"引"，因此便借這相關

語來喻女子的美色吸引異性。

0941 放聲氣
fɔŋ³ sɛŋ¹ hei³ (translit.)
Send out the sound and air. (lit.)
Leak out some information.
Give a hint.
Spread information.
〔註〕表示放風聲，露口風的意思。

0942 定晒形
diŋ⁶ sai³ jiŋ⁴ (translit.)
Fix the figure. (lit.)
Be stupefied.
Trance oneself.
〔註〕表示發愣或發呆的意思。

0943 定過抬油
diŋ⁶ gwɔ³ tɔi⁴ jɐu⁴ (translit.)
Be calmer than carrying two pots of oil on the shoulder. (lit.)
Compose oneself.
Keep one's head.
Be unperturbed.
Be bound to succeed.
Have the game in one's hands.
Have the ball at one's feet.
〔註〕除表示鎮定外還有勝券在握的意思。

0944 河水不犯井水
hɔ⁴ sœy² bɐt⁷ fan⁶ dzɛŋ² sœy² (translit.)
River-water does not offend well-water. (lit.)
Have no conflict with each

other.
Each follows his bent.
Live and let live.
〔註〕指互不侵犯。參閱"你走你嘅陽關路，我過我嘅獨木橋"條（0775）。

0945 空口講白話
huŋ¹ hɐu² gɔŋ² bak⁹ wa⁶
(translit.)
Empty mouth says vain words. *(lit.)*
Words pay no debts.
Fine words butter no parsnips.
〔註〕表示空言無用或口惠而實不至的意思。參閱"口爽荷包立"條（0222）。

0946 空心老倌
huŋ¹ sɐm¹ lou⁵ gun¹ *(translit.)*
An actor with a hollow heart. *(lit.)*
A person without real ability and learning.
A phony rich man.
A person who lives in genteel poverty.
〔註〕"老倌"爲廣東人對粵劇演員的稱呼。"空心老倌"本指"徒有虛名的演員"，但後來引伸比喻沒有真才實學的人，空頭富翁或家境貧窮却虛擺場面的人。

0947 官仔骨骨
gun¹ dzɐi² gwɐt⁷ gwɐt⁷
(translit.)
Be like the son of high official. *(lit.)*
Be well-groomed and dressed in fine clothes.
〔註〕指打扮得俏俊的男子。

0948 官字兩個口
gun¹ dzi⁶ lœŋ⁵ gɔ³ hɐu²
(translit.)
The Chinese character "官" (official) has two mouths. *(lit.)*
Official jargon may mean this or that.
Speak in bureaucratese.
〔註〕借中國字的"官"字字形，喻從政者或當官的人打官腔。

0949 官官相衞
gun¹ gun¹ sœŋ¹ wɐi⁶ *(translit.)*
Officials protect officials. *(lit.)*
Devils help devils.
Officials scratch the back of one another.
Bureaucrats shield one another.

0950 泥水佬開門口 —— 過得自己過得人
nɐi⁴ sœy² lou² hɔi¹ mun⁴ hɐu² — gwɔ³ dɐk⁷ dzi⁶ gei² gwɔ³ dɐk⁷ jɐn⁴ *(translit.)*
A brick-layer cuts a door in the wall, — let oneself pass through and let others pass through. *(lit.)*
Live and let live.
The hand that gives gathers.

〔註〕意思是説爲自己設想，也要爲人設想或自己方便時也要給人方便。

0951 泥菩薩過江 —— 自身難保

nɐi⁴ pou⁴ sat⁸ gwɔ³ gɔŋ¹,— dzi⁶ sɐn¹ nan⁴ bou² *(translit.)*

A clay stature of god crosses the river,— it fails to protect itself. *(lit.)*

Cannot protect oneself.

Be unable even to fend for oneself.

Be too busy with one's own work to help anybody.

0952 沫水舂牆

mei⁶ sœy² dzuŋ¹ tsœŋ⁴ *(translit.)*

Dive and come into the wall. *(lit.)*

Go through fire and water.

〔註〕即赴湯蹈火。（"沫水"即爲"潛水"，"舂牆"即爲"撞牆"的意思。）

0953 炒冷飯

tsɐu² laŋ³ fan⁶ *(translit.)*

Fry cooked-rice which was left over night. *(lit.)*

Lift the conception out of other's writing.

Act as a plagiarist.

Serve a standing dish.

〔註〕比喻重復別人説過的話或做過的事，沒新內容。

0954 易過借火

ji⁶ gwɔ³ jɛ³ fɔ² *(translit.)*

It is easier than borrowing fire. *(lit.)*

Be as easy as pie.

Be as easy as my eye.

〔註〕表示易如反掌的意思。

0955 長痛不如短痛

tsœŋ⁴ tuŋ³ bɐt⁷ jy⁴ dyn² tuŋ³ *(translit.)*

Prefer to have a short ache than a long ache. *(lit.)*

Better a finger off than aye waging.

0956 明人不做暗事

miŋ⁴ jɐn⁴ bɐt⁷ dzou⁶ ɐm³ si⁶ *(translit.)*

A bright person never does invisible things. *(lit.)*

Make no secret of everything.

An open-hearted person often acts in open manner.

0957 明刀明槍

miŋ⁴ dou¹ miŋ⁴ tsœŋ¹ *(translit.)*

Visible knife and visible spear. *(lit.)*

Before somebody's very eyes.

Conduct an evil activity in the open.

Do something openly.

〔註〕指公開地行事。參閱"擺明車馬"條（1908）。

0958 明火打劫

miŋ⁴ fɔ² da² gip⁸ *(translit.)*

Rob in the bright fire. (lit.)
Rob in the light of day.

0959 明槍易擋，暗箭難防
min⁴ tsœŋ¹ ji⁶ dɔŋ², ɐm³ dzin³ nan⁴ fɔŋ⁴ (translit.)
It is easy to stop a visible spear but hard to guard against an invisible arrow. (lit.)
Better to suffer an attack by overt than by covert.

0960 花天酒地
fa¹ tin¹ dzɐu² dei⁶ (translit.)
Flowery sky and wine earth. (lit.)
Indulge oneself in dissipation.
Lead a life of debauchery.

0961 花心
fa¹ sɐm¹ (translit.)
Flowery heart. (lit.)
Be insatiable in love.
Not to give one's mind to one's lover.
Play the field.
〔註〕形容人愛情不專一。

0962 花心蘿蔔
fa¹ sɐm¹ lɔ⁴ bak⁹ (translit.)
Flowery-hearted radish. (lit.)
The person who is not constant in love.
The person who is not single-minded on his lover.
〔註〕比喻"愛情不專一的男人"。

0963 花弗（扶）
fa¹ fit⁷ (translit.)
Be flowery. (lit.)
Be flashy without substance.
Be gaudy like a peacock.
〔註〕表示愛打扮或趕時髦的意思。相當於"花俏"。

0964 花多眼亂
fa¹ dɔ¹ ŋan⁵ lyn⁶ (translit.)
Too many flowers make eyes become perturbed. (lit.)
There are too many to choose.
Cannot see the wood for the trees.
〔註〕表示多得無從選擇的意思。

0965 花言巧語
fa¹ jin⁴ hau² jy⁵ (translit.)
Flowery words and clever speech. (lit.)
Fine words.
Have a sweet tongue.
Be clever at blandishment.

0966 花花公子
fa¹ fa¹ guŋ¹ dzi² (translit.)
A play-boy. (lit.)
A dandy.
A coxcomb.
A fop.

0967 花花綠綠
fa¹ fa¹ luk⁹ luk⁹ (translit.)
Flowery and green. (lit.)
Be full of colours.
Be brightly coloured.
Money note.
Money paper.
〔註〕除表示色彩繽紛的意思外；還喻紙幣。

八畫

0968 花門
fa¹ mun² (translit.)
Slide out of the door. (lit.)
Slip away.
Sneak out of one's job at the last moment.
〔註〕粵劇演員稱同伴不告而別或在臨上演前一走了之爲"花門"，後被引用於口頭俚語來表上述同樣意義。

0969 花靚仔
fa¹ lɛŋ¹ dzɐi² (translit.)
Flowery handsome kid. (lit.)
A youngster.
A young boy as green as grass.
A play-boy.
A youngster of rascality.
〔註〕指沒經驗的青少年，但貶義則喻流里流氣的青少年。

0970 呷醋
hap⁸ tsou³ (translit.)
Sip vinegare. (lit.)
Be jealous of one's own rival in love.
Get angry out of envy.
〔註〕即吃醋（指男女關係上的忌妒）。

0971 叔姪縮窒
suk⁷ dzɐt⁹ suk⁷ dzɐt⁹
(translit.)
Both uncle and nephew; shrink and stop. (lit.)
Be happy over having retreated from having to open one's purse.

〔註〕廣東諺語難懂，不僅外省人，甚至廣東人也有同感。以這句而言，的確使人瞠目不知所云，"縮窒"爲"叔姪"的諧音，意爲本來非破鈔不可，但由於吝嗇而縮手，結果正因縮手，不費分文，事後深自欣慰。

0972 忠忠直直，終須乞食
dzuŋ¹ dzuŋ¹ dzik⁹ dzik⁹,
dzuŋ¹ sœy¹ hɐt⁷ sik⁹
(translit.)
The person who is honest and straight may beg for food in the end. (lit.)
The properer one's behaviours are, the less luckier one will be.

0973 虎父無犬子
fu² fu⁶ mou⁴ jyn² dzi²
(translit.)
A tiger father has not a dog son. (lit.)
Like fahter, like son.
Like begets like.

0974 虎落平陽被犬欺
fu² lɔk⁹ piŋ⁴ jæŋ⁴ bei⁶ jyn²/
hyn² hei¹ (translit.)
A tiger coming down to the plain is bullied by dogs. (lit.)
Out of one's sphere of influence, out of one's power.
〔註〕比喻一個人不在自己的勢力範圍內便沒有勢力。參閱"龍游淺水遭蝦戲"條（1855）。

0975 虎頭蛇尾
fu² tɐu⁴ sɛ⁴ mei⁵ (translit.)
Tiger's head with snake's tail. (lit.)
Do something by halves.
Leave one's work half-done.
A brave beginning but a weak ending.
In like a lion, but out like a lamb.
〔註〕參閱"有頭威，冇尾陣"條（0572）。喻做事有始無終。

0976 門當戶對
mun⁴ dɔŋ¹ wu⁶ dœy³ (translit.)
Doors should match with doors of the same rank. (lit.)
Let beggars match with beggars.

0977 陀衰家
tɔ⁴ sœy¹ ga¹ (translit.)
The calamity involves the family in trouble. (lit.)
A person of rough luck implicates others.
A person who brings his bad luck to somebody.
〔註〕指牽連別人的人。

0978 屈質
wɐt⁷ dzɐt⁷ (translit.)
Be confined. (lit.)
Be cramped.
Be confined and limited.
〔註〕指地方侷促或地方狹窄。

0979 牀下底破柴 —— 撞大板
tsɔŋ⁴ ha⁶ dɐi² pɔ³ tsai⁴ —
dzɔŋ⁶ dai⁶ ban² (translit.)
Split firewood under the bed, — knock against the big board. (lit.)
Meet with a rebuff.
Be rebuked.
Run into snags.
Make a mistake.
Do wrong.
〔註〕除相當於"半夜叫城門 —— 碰釘子"外，還表示做錯的意思。

0980 姐
dzɛ¹ᐟ² (translit.)
Elder sister. (lit.)
Sister.
A general term for addressing a woman of one's own age.
A term for maidservant.
〔註〕對平輩婦女的稱呼，一般跟在名字後邊，或對女傭人的稱呼（dʒɛ²）。

0981 姐手姐腳
dzɛ² sɐu² dzɛ² gœk⁸ (translit.)
Maid's hands and feet. (lit.)
Be as weak as a cat.
Be feeble like a lady.
Work with a light hand.
〔註〕形容人手足無力或做事太斯文。

0982 妹仔大過主人婆
mui¹ dzai² dai⁶ gwɔ³ dzy²
jɐn⁴ pɔ⁴ (translit.)

八畫

A waiting maid is bigger than a hostest. (lit.)
Put the trivial above the important.
Spend much more on the trivial than on the important.
The tail wags the dog.
Put the cart before the horse.
〔註〕比喻做事沒分寸，或輕重倒置。

九　畫

0983　耐不耐
nɔi⁶ bɐt⁷ nɔi² （translit.）
Sometimes. (lit.)
Once in a [long] while.
Occasionally.
〔註〕表示偶爾，有時或不經常的意思。

0984　耐中
nɔi⁶ dzuŋ¹ （translit.）
Sometimes. (lit.)
Once in a [long] while.
Occasionally.
〔註〕同"耐不耐"（0983）及"耐唔中"（0985）。

0985　耐唔中
nɔi⁶ m⁴ dzuŋ¹ （translit.）
Sometimes. (lit.)
Once in a [long] while.
Occasionally.
〔註〕同"耐不耐"條（0983）。

0986　查家宅
tsa⁴ ga¹ dzak⁹ （translit.）
Inspect somebody's family and house. (lit.)
Get to the bottom of somebody / something.
See the root stock.
〔註〕比喻向人查根問底。

0987　耍太極
sa² tai³ gik⁹ （translit.）
Play 'Taichi'. (lit.)
Decline tactfully with all sorts of lame excuse.
Give the runaround.
Give an equivocal replay.
Shirk one's duty with tactful tactics.
〔註〕比喻藉詞推搪的手段或模棱兩可的態度或方法。不過亦喻婉詞推卸責任。

0988　耍花槍
sa² fa¹ tsœŋ¹ （translit.）
Braudish spears in a showy way. (lit.)
Have a quarrel for fun.
Make a joke on each other of the couple.
〔註〕夫婦間的調情。

0989　要風得風，要雨得雨
jiu³ fuŋ¹ dɐk⁷ fuŋ¹, jiu³ jy⁵ dɐk⁷ jy⁵ （translit.）
Have wind when wind is needed; have rain when rain is needed. (lit.)
Be able to gain what is wanted.

Do as one list.
〔註〕隨心所欲。

0990 面左左
min⁶ dzɔ² dzɔ² (translit.)
Turn the face to the left. (lit.)
Turn one's back upon somebody.
There is no love lost between them.
Be at odds with one another.
Be at loggerhead with one another.
〔註〕比喻彼此不和。

0991 面皮厚
min⁶ pei⁴ hɐu⁵ (translit.)
Thick-skinned face. (lit.)
Have a thick skin.
Be shameless.
Be thick-skinned.

0992 面紅
min⁶ huŋ⁴ (translit.)
The face becomes red. (lit.)
Blush for shyness/shame.
Blush with anger.

0993 面紅面綠
min⁶ huŋ⁴ min⁶ luk⁹ (translit.)
The face becomes red and green. (lit.)
Be red with anger.
Blush for excitement.
〔註〕表示非常憤怒。

0994 面懵心精
min⁶ muŋ⁵ sɐm¹ dzɛŋ¹ (translit.)
Stupid on the face but clever in the heart. (lit.)
Play the fool.
Feign oneself to be foolish.
〔註〕參閱"扮豬食老虎"（0730）條。

0995 相見好，同住難
sœŋ¹ giŋ³ hou², tuŋ⁴ dzy⁶ nan⁴ (translit.)
It is good to see each other sometimes but difficult to live together constantly. (lit.)
Familiarity breeds contempt.

0996 柑咁大個鼻
gɐm¹ gɐm³ dai⁶ gɔ³ bei⁶ (translit.)
The nose is as large as a loose-skinned orange. (lit.)
Turn up one's nose at...
Look down one's nose at somebody.
〔註〕形容驕傲的樣子。

0997 挑蟲入屎窟
tiu¹ tsuŋ⁴ jɐp⁹ si² fɐt⁷ (translit.)
Pick a worm and lead it into the rectum. (lit.)
Prepare a rod for one's own back.
Fry in one's own grease.
Invite trouble for oneself.
〔註〕比喻自作自受或自找麻煩。

0998 指天篤地
dzi² tin¹ duk⁷ dei⁶ (translit.)

九畫

Point at the sky and pierce the earth. (lit.)
Talk nonsense.
Sheer rubbish.
Drivel.
〔註〕相當於"胡說八道"。

0999 指手劃脚
dzi² sɐu² wak⁹ gœk⁸ (translit.)
Point with fingers and draw with feet. (lit.)
Order somebody about.
Lord it over somebody.
Be a backseat driver.
Give dictates to somebody.
〔註〕形容人那副作威作福發施號令的神態。

1000 指住禿奴罵和尚
dzi² dzy⁶ tuk⁷ nou⁴ ma⁶ wɔ⁴ sœŋ² (translit.)
Point at a bald head to heap abuse on a Buddism monk. (lit.)
Talk at somebody.
Make an oblique accusation/ Make oblique accusations.
〔註〕即指桑罵槐。

1001 指擬
dzi² ji⁵ (translit.)
Depend on. (lit.)
Count on somebody.
Rely on somebody/something.
Look to somebody for something.
〔註〕指望或依賴他人。

1002 契家佬
kɐi³ ga¹ lou² (translit.)
A kept lover. (lit.)
An adulterer.
A male cohabitant.
〔註〕即情夫,姘頭。

1003 契家婆
kɐi³ ga¹ pɔ²/⁴/⁶ (translit.)
A kept mistress. (lit.)
An adulteress.
A female cohabitant.
〔註〕即情婦,姘頭。

1004 毒鬥毒
duk⁹ dɐu³ duk⁹ (translit.)
Poison for poison. (lit.)
Pay tit for tat.
Like for like.
Like cures like.
Use poison as an antidote to poison.
〔註〕除表示行爲上的針鋒相對外,還含有醫學上的"以毒攻毒"的意思。

1005 耷尾
dɐp⁷ mei⁵ (translit.)
Hang down the tail. (lit.)
With the tail between the legs.
Be crestfallen.
Lose courage.
Lose one's spirits.
Show a complete lack of reserve strength.
Have no staying power.
〔註〕利用打敗的狗那副神態來喻人灰溜溜地,垂頭喪氣或缺乏後

勁。

1006 耷頭佬
dɐp⁷ tɐu⁴ lou² (translit.)
A man with his head hanging down. (lit.)
A man full of schemes and tricks.
An artful villian.
〔註〕比喻詭計多端的人。（古老傳說，"男怕望地，女怕望天"，意謂這兩種人心術不正。）

1007 耷頭耷腦
dɐp⁷ tɐu⁴ dɐp⁷ nou⁵ (translit.)
Hang down the head and brains. (lit.)
Be crestfallen.
Lose one's spirits.
Be listless.
〔註〕垂頭喪氣，精神不振作或沒精打采的意思。

1008 南嘸佬遇鬼迷
nam⁴ mɔ⁴ lou² jy⁵ gwɐi² mɐi⁴ (translit.)
A Toaist priest is enchanted by ghost. (lit.)
An expert marksman misses the target.
An old horse loses its way.
〔註〕和"張天師遇鬼迷"同義，意為專家也會失手。參閱"老貓燒鬚"條（0617）。

1009 食七咁食
sik⁹ tsɐt⁷ gɐm³ sik⁹ (translit.)
Be like eating in a mourning feast taken place on every other seventh day after the death of a man. (lit.)
Gorge oneself.
Have a good stomach.
〔註〕比喻狼吞虎嚥的吃或大吃大喝。家有喪事時，例如死者死後的每個第七天設置飲食，招待前來拜祭的親朋，但有些根本和死者家人毫無關係的貪食者亦來大吃一頓。主人家明知此事，毫不禁止或驅逐，任由彼等吃個痛快。

1010 食人唔腬骨
sik⁹ jɐn⁴ m⁴ lœ¹ gwɐt⁷ (translit.)
Eat men without vomiting bones. (lit.)
Be insatiable of profits.
Be covetous of everything.
Be greedy for gain.
〔註〕貪得無厭的意思。

1011 食少啖多覺瞓
sik⁹ siu² dam⁶ dɔ¹ gau³ fɐn³ (translit.)
Eat less, sleep more. (lit.)
Play for safety.
Earn no danger money.
〔註〕表示為安全計，不做危險的事或賺不義之財。

1012 食生菜咁食
sik⁹ saŋ¹ tsɔi³ gɐm³ sik⁹ (translit.)
Eat like eating lettuce. (lit.)
It is as easy as rolling a log.

It is as easy as pie.
〔註〕比喻極其容易。參閱"易過借火"條（0954）。

1013　食西北風
sik⁹ sɐi¹ bɐk⁷ fuŋ¹　(translit.)
Eat the northwest wind.　(lit.)
Live in poverty.
Suffer from hunger.
Have nothing to eat.
〔註〕生活貧困，缺乏糧食或捱餓。

1014　食夾棍
sik⁹ gap⁸ gwɐn³　(translit.)
Eat torture instruments.　(lit.)
Jump a claim.
Make a grab at what somebody should gain.
Take the wind out of somebody's sails.
〔註〕指攫取或利用手段去奪他人所應得的利益。"食夾棍"本為賭場術語，意指如莊閒兩家也有同一手牌贏錢時，則莊家有優先贏錢的權利。

1015　食死貓
sik⁹ sei² mau¹　(translit.)
Eat a dead cat.　(lit.)
Be unjustly blamed.
Endure the calamity for others.
Be made a scapegoat.
〔註〕替人受過的意思。相當於"背黑鍋"。

1016　食咗人隻車
sik⁹ dzɔ² jɐn⁴ dzɛk⁸ gœy¹
(translit.)
Eat another's chariot.　(lit.)
Take the wind out of somebody's sails.
Be overcovetous of everything.
Intend to drive somebody to his death.
〔註〕本為中國象棋的術語，但引伸比喻先發制人而佔盡上風，妄圖佔有一切或要人老命。

1017　食咗火藥
sik⁹ dzɔ² fɔ² jœk⁶　(translit.)
Have eaten gun-powder.　(lit.)
Be hot with rage.
Be beside oneself with rage.
〔註〕比喻怒不可遏。

1018　食枉米
sik⁹ wɔŋ² mɐi⁵　(translit.)
Eat rice without purpose.　(lit.)
A person of no use.
An idler/an idle bread eater.
〔註〕指白吃飯的人，參閱"食塞米"條（1024）。

1019　食拖鞋飯
sik⁹ tɔ¹ hai² fan⁶　(translit.)
Eat cooked-rice of slippers.　(lit.)
Sponge upon one's wife/girlfriend.
〔註〕指靠自己的妻子或女友賣色相過活的人。參閱"食軟飯"（1033）條。

1020　食屎食着豆
sik⁹ si² sik⁹ dzœk⁶ dɐu²
(translit.)

One happens to find out beans to eat while eating ordure. (lit.)
Have a fault on the right side.
Get a piece of good luck out of misfortune.
〔註〕表示因禍得福的意思，參閱"錯有錯着"條（1839）。

1021 食砒霜杜狗
sik⁹ pei¹ (fei¹) sœŋ¹ dou⁶ gɐu² (translit.)
Eat arsenic to put an end to a dog. (lit.)
Be at disadvantage before gaining an advantage.
〔註〕暗喻自己先受其害。

1022 食得禾米多
sik⁹ dɐk⁷ wɔ⁴ mɐi⁵ dɔ¹ (translit.)
Have eaten plenty of unhulled rice. (lit.)
Have made lots of people fall into one's dupery.
〔註〕表示騙得人多的意思。

1023 食鹽多過食飯，行橋多過行路
sik⁹ jim⁴ dɔ¹ gwɔ³ sik⁹ fan⁶, haŋ⁴ kiu⁴ dɔ¹ gwɔ³ han⁴ lou⁶ (translit.)
Having eaten more salt than cooked-rice and walked over more bridges than on roads. (lit.)
Have seen more elephants.
Have been weather-beaten a lot more.
Experience does it.

1024 食塞米
sik⁹ sɐk⁷ (sɐt⁷) mɐi⁵ (translit.)
A person who eats and waste rice. (lit.)
A person of no use.
An idler.
〔註〕比喻白吃飯而沒用的人，有人說成"食枉米"（sik⁹ wɔŋ² mɐi⁵）。

1025 食過夜粥
sik⁹ gwɔ³ jɛ⁶ dzuk⁷ (translit.)
Have eaten night-congee. (lit.)
Know Chinese martial arts (kung fu).
Serve one's apprenticeship with a master.
〔註〕比喻懂得武術（功夫），但亦引伸意為經過學徒階段。

1026 食過翻尋味
sik⁹ gwɔ³ fan¹ tsɐm⁴ mei⁶ (translit.)
Look for the taste again after having eaten. (lit.)
Would like to try once again.
Go for more after being satisfied with the initial gain.

1027 食碗面，反碗底
sik⁹ wun² min² fan² wun² dɐi² (translit.)
Eat with the top of the bowl but

turn over the bottom of it. (lit.)
Go back upon somebody.
Play somebody false.
Betray a friend.
〔註〕比喻忘恩負義或背叛朋友。

1028 食葱送飯
sik⁹ tsuŋ¹ suŋ³ fan⁶ (translit.)
Eat cooked-rice with green onion. (lit.)
Stand to sense.
〔註〕即通情達理。

1029 食飽無憂米
sik⁹ bau² mou⁴ jɐu¹ mɐi⁵ (translit.)
Eat worriless rice to the full. (lit.)
Have nothing to worry about.
Lead a happy life.
Lead an idle life.
〔註〕指生活無憂無慮或毫無牽掛。

1030 食飽飯等屎疴
sik⁹ bau² fan⁶ dɐŋ² si² ɔ¹ (translit.)
Wait to ease manure after eating to the full. (lit.)
Have nothing to do.
Live like an idle wheel.
〔註〕表示無所事事。

1031 食豬血疴黑屎 ── 立刻見功
sik⁹ dzy¹ hyt⁸ ɔ¹ hɐk⁷ si²── lɐp⁹ hɐk⁷ gin³ guŋ¹ (translit.)

Ease black manure as soon as one eats pig-blood ── see the effect instantly. (lit.)
Get the instant results.
The effect comes out at once.
〔註〕表示立竿見影。

1032 食穀種
sik⁹ guk⁷ dzuŋ² (translit.)
Eat seed-corns. (lit.)
Live on one's fat.
〔註〕即吃老本。

1033 食軟飯
sik⁹ jyn⁵ fan⁶ (translit.)
Eat soft cooked-rice. (lit.)
Sponge upon one's wife/girl-friend.
〔註〕同"食拖鞋飯"（1019）條。

1034 食貓麵
sik⁹ mau¹ min⁶ (translit.)
Eat noodles with cat's flesh. (lit.)
Incur blame for something.
Get it in the neck.
Have a stomach full of somebody's abuse.
〔註〕挨罵，受申斥。

1035 風水佬呃你十年八年，唔呃得一世
fuŋ¹ sœy² lou² ɐk⁷ nei⁵ sɐp⁹ nin⁴ bat⁸ nin⁴, m⁴ ɐk⁷ dɐk⁷ jɐt⁷ sɐi³ (translit.)
A master of geomancy can fool you for eight or ten years, but he cannot fool you a whole life. (lit.)

Time can witness to a fact.
〔註〕暗喻"時間會證明一切"或"事實會證明"。

1036 風水輪流轉
fuŋ¹ sœy² lœn⁴ lɐu⁴ dzyn² (translit.)
The wind and water (geomancy) goes around like a wheel. (lit.)
Every dog has his day.
Every cloud has a silver lining.
〔註〕比喻每人都有得志日，大致上和"世界輪流轉"（0405）所表示的意思相同，但"風水輪流轉"則着重所見到的結果，而"世界輪流轉"則較着眼於人生命運的所謂因果循環。

1037 風吹芫荽——衰「垂」到貼地
fuŋ¹ tsœy¹ jyn⁴ sɐi¹—sœy¹ (sœy⁴) dou³ tip⁸ dei² (translit.)
The wind blows the coriander—it becomes on the wane (droops) to the ground. (lit.)
Fall upon very unlucky days.
Meet with very bad luck.
Be the end of one's rope.
Come to a sticky end.
〔註〕借"垂"字諧音作"衰"，意為倒霉透了。

1038 風吹雞蛋殼——財散人安樂
fuŋ¹ tsœy¹ gɐi¹ dan⁶ hɔk⁸—

tsɔi⁴ san³ jɐn⁴ ɔn¹ lɔk⁹ (translit.)
The wind blows the shells of eggs—the money is given out out for ease of mind. (lit.)
Pay a price for one's safety/security.
Pay a sum of money for being well/the recovery of health/the ease of mind.
〔註〕表示付出代價才獲得安全/復原（疾病）或安心的意思。

1039 風流
fuŋ¹ lɐu⁴ (translit.)
Dissolute; loose. (lit.)
Seek or be in the limelight.
Leisurely and carefree mood.
〔註〕即出風頭或閒情逸致。

1040 風頭火勢
fuŋ¹ tɐu⁴ fɔ² sɐi³ (translit.)
Be in the head of wind and the power of fire. (lit.)
Be in the state of full blast.
Be at the trend of an event.
Be at the tendency of a movement.
〔註〕比喻正在緊張或全盛的時期。

1041 風頭躉
fuŋ¹ tɐu⁴ dɐn² (translit.)
The bulk of wind head. (lit.)
The person who is fond of limelight.
〔註〕指好引人注目的人，愛出風頭的人。

1042 風擺柳

fuŋ¹ bai² lɐu⁵ (translit.)
The willow waved by the wind. (lit.)
A person who takes no firm resolution.
Be changeful in ideas.
Be undecided.
〔註〕比喻猶豫不定或隨形勢而改變主意的人。

1043 看牛不及打馬草
hɔn¹ ŋɐu⁴ bɐt⁷ gɐp⁹ da² ma⁵ tsou² (translit.)
Watching cows cannot be compared with gathering hay for horses. (lit.)
It wastes time for a busy man to have a chat with an idler.
〔註〕看牛是悠閒的工作，但打馬草是急不容緩的任務，所以這俚語便喻一個趕急的人和從容的人閒談是會浪費時間甚至誤事的。

1044 看風駛艃
hɔn³ fuŋ¹ sɐi² lei⁵ (translit.)
See the wind to set sails. (lit.)
Trim the sails.
Run before the wind.
Take advantage of...
〔註〕即見風使舵，把握時機。

1045 怨命
jyn³ mɛŋ⁶ (translit.)
Repine the lot of life. (lit.)
Murmur against one's own lot.
Submit to one's own destiny.
Admit to having been determined by fate.
Acknowledge oneself predestined.
〔註〕自怨命運不濟或認命的意思。

1046 缸瓦船打老虎 —— 盡地呢一煲（舖）
gɔŋ¹ ŋa⁵ syn⁴ da² lou⁵ fu² — dzœn⁶ dei² nei¹ jɐt⁷ bou¹ (pou¹) (translit.)
The man in the boat loaded with earthenwares beats a tiger — finishing with the last pot (game). (lit.)
Shoot one's last bolt.
Bet one's bottom dollar.
Put all one's eggs in one basket.
〔註〕表示孤注一擲的意思。

1047 急時抱佛脚
gɐp⁷ si⁴ pou⁵ fɐt⁹ gœk⁸ (translit.)
While urgency comes, hold Buddha's feet. (lit.)
Seek help at the last moment.
Ask God for mercy when danger comes.

1048 急驚風遇着慢郎中
gɐp⁷ giŋ¹ fuŋ¹ jy⁶ dzœk⁶ man⁶ lɔŋ⁴ dzuŋ¹ (translit.)
The child who is attacked by acute infantile convulsions meet with a slow-moving physician. (lit.)
Be too impatient to wait.
Be very impatient of somebody's phlegmatic tempera-

ment.

〔註〕表示對別人慢條斯理的個性極不耐煩的意思。

1049 皇天不負有/苦心人
wɔŋ⁴ tin¹ bɐt⁷ fu⁴ jɐu⁵/fu² sɐm¹ jɐn⁴ (translit.)
Heaven will not forget those who have minds. (those whose hearts are bitter). (lit.)
God tempers the wind to the shorn lamb.
God helps those who help themselves.

1050 皇帝唔急太監急
wɔŋ⁴ dɐi³ m⁴ gɐp⁷ tai³ gam³ gɐp⁷ (translit.)
The emperor does not feel worried but the eunuch does. (lit.)
Key oneself up over other's business.
Feel both anxious and nervous at other's business.

〔註〕即爲別人着急。參閱"水上扒龍船，岸上夾死仔"條（0371）。

1051 拜神唔見雞
bai³ sɐn⁴ m⁴ gin³ gɐi¹ (translit.)
Lose a hen (as a sacrifice) while worshiping an idol. (lit.)
Bustle in and out with a murmur.
Complain with a murmur.

Go on uttering.
〔註〕形容人口中唸唸有辭忙來忙去的樣子。

1052 俗骨
dzuk⁹ gwɐt⁷ (translit.)
Vulgar bones. (lit.)
Be vulgar.
Be in bad taste.
〔註〕即俗氣。

1053 係咁意
hɐi⁶ gɐm² ji² (translit.)
With such an idea. (lit.)
Do it is as a token.
It is but a symbol.
Be symbolized.
〔註〕表示稍表心意而已或象徵性的意思。

1054 係威係勢
hɐi⁶ wɐi¹ hɐi⁶ sɐi³ (translit.)
With awe-inspiring and power. (lit.)
Make a false show of being in sad earnest.
Have a good backing.
〔註〕指像煞有介事或大有來頭的樣子。

1055 神不知鬼不覺
sɐn⁴ bɐt⁷ dzi¹ gwɐi² bɐt⁷ gɔk⁸ (translit.)
Neither gods nor ghosts know it. (lit.)
In top secret.
Without anybody knowing it.
Nobody knows it.

1056 神推鬼擁

九畫

sɐn⁴ tœy¹ gwɐi² uŋ² (translit.)
Both god and ghost push. (lit.)
One can't help oneself.
In spite of oneself.
〔註〕表示不由自主或身不由己的意思。

1057 神臺貓屎 —— 神憎鬼厭
sɐn⁴ tɔi⁴ mau¹ si² —sɐn⁴ dzɐŋ¹ gwɐi² jim³ (translit.)
The cat's manure on the altar — gods hate and ghosts abominate. (lit.)
An accused target.
The person at whom everybody shake his finger.
Be abominated by everybody.
Be accusable.
Be accursed.
〔註〕喻受人憎惡或討人厭的人。

1058 神魂顛倒
sɐn⁴ wɐn⁴ din¹ dou² (translit.)
Spirit and soul get upside down. (lit.)
Be out of one's head.
Be infatuated with...

1059 神憎鬼厭
sɐn⁴ dzɐŋ¹ gwɐi² jim³ (translit.)
Gods hate and ghosts abominate. (lit.)
Be abominated by everybody.
Be accusable.
Be accursed.
An accused target.
The person at whom everybody shakes his finger.
〔註〕表示令人討厭的意思,參閱"神臺貓屎"條(1057)。

1060 神神化化
sɐn⁴ sɐn⁴ fa³ fa³ (translit.)
Divinitified. (lit.)
Be silly and curious.
Be elusive.
Be not quite right in the mind.
〔註〕表示神經不正常或行爲使人捉摸不定。

1061 神神地
sɐn⁴ sɐn⁴ dei² (translit.)
Deificationally. (lit.)
Be not right in the mind.
Be abnormal in the mind.
Not to work properly.
〔註〕形容人神經不正常或機械運行不正常。

1062 恃老賣老
tsi⁵ lou⁵ mai⁶ lou⁵ (translit.)
Rely upon old age and sell seniority. (lit.)
Act like a Dutch uncle.

1063 洗碗有相砍
sɐi² wun² jɐu⁵ sœŋ¹ hɐm² (translit.)
Bowls would run up against each other when they are being washed. (lit.)
Familiarity would sometimes have a brush.

Familiarity breeds contempt.
〔註〕喻大家相處日久，難免有矛盾或衝突。

1064 洗腳唔抹腳
sɐi² gœk⁸ m⁴ mut⁸ (mat⁸) gœk⁸ *(translit.)*
Wash feet without wiping them. (lit.)
Money burns a hole in one's pocket.
Splash one's money about.
Play ducks and drakes with one's money.
〔註〕喻揮霍。

1065 洗濕個頭
sɐi² sɐp⁷ gɔ³ tɐu⁴ *(translit.)*
Wet the head. (lit.)
Hold a wolf by the ears.
Needs must when the devil drives.
Have no way to back down.
〔註〕比喻勢成騎虎，勢在必行或騎虎難下。

1066 恨死隔籬
hɐn⁶ sei² gak⁸ lei⁴ *(translit.)*
Make neighbours envy to death. (lit.)
Become the envy of others.
〔註〕表示成爲他人羨慕的目標。

1067 姜太公釣魚 —— 願者上釣
gœŋ¹ tai³ guŋ¹ diu³ jy²—jyn⁶ dzɛ² sœŋ⁵ diu² *(translit.)*
Grand Duke Gœŋ fished — those who were willing jumped at the bait. (lit.)
Swallow the bait of one's own accord.
Put one's own head in the noose.
Take a voluntary action.
Do something on a voluntary basis.

1068 度住屎窟裁褲
dɔk⁹ dzy⁶ si² fɐt⁷ tsɔi⁴ fu³ *(translit.)*
Measure one's hips to cut trousers. (lit.)
Cut one's coat according to one's cloth.
Pinch pennies.
Make both ends meet.
〔註〕比喻量入爲出，參閱"睇餸食飯，睇燭南無"條（1552）。

1069 扁鼻佬戴眼鏡 —— 冇得頂
bin² bei⁶ lou⁵ dai³ ŋan⁵ gɛŋ²—mou⁴ dɐk⁷ diŋ² *(translit.)*
A flat-nosed man wears spectacles — nowhere to support. (lit.)
Be more than a match for somebody/something.
Without equal.
〔註〕"頂"的意思，在廣東人意爲"支撐"，但廣東人又把"頂"轉義爲"競爭"或"比較"，這句俚語的歇後，便取這個意思了。因此便表示無可競爭或好極了，無可比擬的意思。

1070 炮仗頸
pau³ dzœŋ² gɛŋ² (translit.)
A neck like firecrackers. (lit.)
Be short-tempered.
Be apt to fly into rage and calm down soon.
〔註〕比喻脾氣暴燥，但不久平靜無事。

1071 客家佔地主
hak⁸ ga¹ dzim³ dei⁶ dzy² (translit.)
A guest occupies the position of a host. (lit.)
Reverse the positions of the host and the guest.
It is presumptuous of somebody to usurp on the owner's right.
Be like the camel which kicked its master out of the tent.
〔註〕喧賓奪主的意思。

1072 客氣
hak⁸ hei³ (translit.)
A guest's politeness. (lit.)
Stand on ceremony.
Be too polite.
Be too modest.

1073 施恩莫望報
si¹ jɐn¹ mɔk⁹ mɔŋ⁶ bou³ (translit.)
Showing favour is not the purpose of being repaid. (lit.)
Throw one's bread upon the waters.

1074 前人種果後人收
tsin⁴ jɐn⁴ dzuŋ³ gwɔ² hɐu⁶ jɐn⁴ sɐu¹ (translit.)
Ancestors planted the fruit, descendants reap it. (lit.)
Descendants reap what their ancestors sowed.
The good deeds the forerunners did will go down to their posterity.

1075 前世唔修
tsin⁴ sɐi³ m⁴ sɐu¹ (translit.)
Did not cultivate moral characters in the previous life. (lit.)
Suffer retribution for all ill deeds done in the previous existence.
〔註〕這句話的意思是說由於前生不修身，所以今生受到應得的報應。

1076 前世撈亂骨頭
tsin⁴ sɐi³ lou¹ lyn⁶ gwɐt⁷ tɐu⁴ (translit.)
The bones of the dead in the previous life were turned upside down. (lit.)
Be hostile to each other.
Feel hostility towards each other.
〔註〕比喻彼此仇視。

1077 派/派頭
pai¹/pai¹ tɐu⁴ (translit.)
Fashionable/fashionable style. (lit.)
Stylish/Be well-dressed.
Put on quite a show./Live in grand style.

Extravagant and ostention display.

1078 派行水/派片
pai³ hɐŋ⁴ sœy²/pai³ pin² (translit.)
Give out walking water./Send away slices. (lit.)
Grease the palm of somebody.
Offer somebody levies of money.
〔註〕"派行水"爲二三十年代向盜賊給予保護費的一種行爲，亦即所謂"買通"或"行賄"的意思。至於"派片"爲近代廉政公署未成立前，向部分治安人員或黑社會份子交出所謂保護費的行爲，名稱雖異，作用實同。

1079 眈天望地
dam¹ tin¹ mɔŋ⁶ dei⁶ (translit.)
Look up at the sky and down at the ground. (lit.)
Glance this way and that way.
Pay no attention to...
Be inattentive.
〔註〕東張西望或毫不留心的意思。

1080 是非只爲多開口
si⁶ fei¹ dzi² wɐi⁶ dɔ¹ hɔi¹ hɐu² (translit.)
Too much talk leads to error. (lit.)
Loquacity leads to troubles.
〔註〕意即言多語失。

1081 是非皆因強出頭
si⁶ fei¹ gai¹ jɐn¹ kœŋ⁵ tsœt⁷ tɐu⁴ (translit.)
Trouble comes merely becuase of taking the lead. (lit.)
A busybody often invites troubles.
〔註〕好出頭露面，易招惹是非。

1082 是非鬼/啄
si⁶ fei¹ gwɐi²/dœŋ¹ (translit.)
The ghost who carries tales. (lit.)
A scandalmonger.
〔註〕相當於"是非簍子"。

1083 是是但但
si⁶ si⁶ dan⁶ dan⁶ (translit.)
At convenience. (lit.)
Slap together.
Huddle a job through.
Anything/Anybody will do.
〔註〕參閱"求求其其"（0721）條。

1084 苦口婆心
fu² hɐu² pɔ⁴ sɐm¹ (translit.)
Bitter mouth with old woman's heart. (lit.)
Bitter pills may have wholesome effects.
Words importunate but heart compassionate.

1085 苦過弟弟
fu² gɔ³ di⁴ di² (translit.)
Bitter than a duckling. (lit.)
Go through all kinds of hardships.
Sink into the abyss of misery.
Find oneself in a tight corner.
〔註〕指嘗盡苦楚，陷入苦海或身處困境的意思。

1086 若要人不知，除非己莫爲

jœk⁹ jiu³ jɐn⁴ bɐt⁷ dzi¹, tsœy⁴ fei¹ gei² mɔk⁹ wɐi⁴ (translit.)

If one does not want people to know, one must not do it. (lit.)

There are eyes even in the dark.

One cannot conceal what one has done.

What is done by night will appear by day.

1087 英雄重英雄

jiŋ¹ huŋ⁴ dzuŋ⁶ jiŋ¹ huŋ⁴ (translit.)

A hero respects a hero. (lit.)

Like knows like.

1088 英雄莫問出處

jiŋ¹ huŋ⁴ mɔk⁹ mɐn⁶ tsœt⁷ tsy³ (translit.)

Not to ask the source of a hero. (lit.)

Not every great man was born with a silver spoon in his mouth.

1089 咬耳仔

ŋau⁵ ji⁵ dzɐi² (translit.)

Bite ears. (lit.)

Have a word in one's ear.

Whisper to somebody.

〔註〕即附耳而語。

1090 咬實牙齦

ŋau⁵ sɐt⁹ ŋa⁴ gɐn¹ (translit.)

Bite the gums firemly. (lit.)

Have patience with...

Endure hardship.

Swallow the leek.

〔註〕指極度忍耐或忍受痛苦或屈辱等。

1091 跪跪西西

ŋɐi¹ ŋɐi¹ sɐi¹ sɐi¹ (translit.)

Beg and beg again. (lit.)

Keep on pleading with somebody.

Beg a favour of somebody.

〔註〕表示懇求的意思。

1092 跪契爺咁跪

ŋɐi¹ kɐi³ jɛ⁴ gɐm³ ŋɐi¹ (translit.)

Beg like begging an adoptive father. (lit.)

Keep on begging a favour of somebody in real earnest.

〔註〕表示不斷向人懇求的意思。

1093 咧啡

lɛ⁵ fɛ⁵ (translit.)

Be untidy. (lit.)

Be in one's shirt sleeve.

Be dressed in casual wear.

Be sloppy-dressed.

Sloppy Joe.

Slap dash.

Do a sloppy job.

〔註〕形容人衣冠不整，不修邊幅或工作馬虎，吊兒郎當。

1094 咪拘

mɐi⁵ kœy¹ (translit.)

Not to be bigoted. (lit.)

Don't trouble me, please.

No. Thank you. I won't take/accept it.

〔註〕用於推却時的口語。

1095 柴哇哇
tsai⁴ wa¹ wa¹　(translit.)
Mess up. (lit.)
Run wild.
Make a mess like sheep without a shepherd.
Play a joke.
Bustle with joy and excitement.
〔註〕表示隨隨便便，馬馬虎虎，鬧着玩兒或喧鬧一番的意思。

1096 柴臺
tsai⁴ tɔi⁴　(translit.)
Hooting. (lit.)
Give a Bronx cheer.
Give somebody the bird.
Make cat calls.
〔註〕喝倒采。

1097 省鏡
saŋ¹ gɛŋ³　(translit.)
Save a mirror. (lit.)
Be very beautiful.
Have a good-looking face.
〔註〕形容女性美麗。

1098 屎氹關刀──聞「文」唔得舞「武」唔得
si² tɐm⁵ gwan¹ dou¹—mɐn⁴ m⁴ dɐk⁷ mou⁵ m⁴ dɐk⁷　(translit.)
General Gwan's knife in the manure pool—be neither smelled nor played with (be good at neither polite letters nor martial arts). (lit.)
Be capable of neither mental nor manual labour.

〔註〕這俚語是利用歇後語的"聞"和"舞"兩字來諧音"文"和"武"比喻一個人的不能文也不能武。

1099 屎急開坑
si² gɐp⁷ hɔi¹ haŋ¹　(translit.)
Not dig a pit until one has to go to stool. (lit.)
Make no timely preparations.
Make a frantic last-minute effort.
Have a cloak made when it begins to rain.
〔註〕表示臨渴掘井的意思。

1100 屎橋
si² kiu²　(translit.)
Useless plot. (lit.)
A useless plan.
An impractical device.
〔註〕比喻不實用的計策或方法。

1101 屎窟生瘡──有眼睇
si² fɐt⁷ saŋ¹ tsɔŋ¹—mou⁵ ŋan⁵ tɐi²　(translit.)
Have a boil on one of the hips—have no eyes to see it. (lit.)
Close one's eyes to...
Bear no sight of...
〔註〕表示目不忍睹或不願看一眼的意思。

1102 屋漏更兼逢夜雨
uk⁷ lɐu⁶ gɐŋ³ gim¹ fuŋ⁴ jɛ⁶ jy⁵　(translit.)
Not only does the roof of the house leak but also the night rain pours. (lit.)
Misfortunes never come singly.
It never rains but pours.

〔註〕比喻禍不單行。參閱"越窮越見鬼，肚餓打瀉米"條(1444)。

1103 眉頭一皺，計上心頭
mei⁴ tɐu⁴ jɐt⁷. dzɐu³, gɐi³ sœŋ⁵ sɐm¹ lɔi⁴ (translit.)
As soon as eyebrows frown, an idea comes into the heart. (lit.)
Hit upon an idea.
Have a sudden inspiration.
〔註〕表示心生一計的意思。

1104 眉精眼企
mei⁴ dziŋ¹ ŋan⁵ kei⁵ (translit.)
Eyebrows are clever and eyes are upright. (lit.)
Know a trick or two.
Be as smart as a steel trap.
〔註〕形容人長得機靈，精明能幹。

1105 飛擒大咬
fei¹ kɐm⁴ dai⁶ ŋau⁵ (translit.)
Fly to catch and have a big bite. (lit.)
Show one's horn.
Extort money from somebody to excess.
Show one's lustful manner.
〔註〕表示露出兇相，過份敲搾或露出色相等意思。

1106 姣屍扽篤
hau⁴ si¹ dɐn⁴ duk⁷ (translit.)
Be coquettish. (lit.)
Coquette in a lustful manner.
〔註〕形容女人故作嬌媚姿態。

1107 姣婆遇着脂粉客
hau⁴ pɔ⁴ jy⁶ dzœk⁹ dzi¹ fɐn² hak⁸ (translit.)
A dissolute woman meets a luster. (lit.)
Be two of a kind.
People of a kind come together.
Two of promiscuous sexes love each other at first sight.
〔註〕廣義是表示臭味相投的意思，狹義是亂交的男女一見鍾情。

十　畫

1108 原封不動
jyn⁴ fuŋ¹ bɐt⁷ duŋ⁶ (translit.)
The original seal is kept unmoved. (lit.)
Be kept in its integrity.
Be kept intact.

1109 起尾注
hei² mei⁵ dzy³ (translit.)
Grab the end bet. (lit.)
Usurp somebody's gains.
〔註〕比喻吞沒別人的利潤。

1110 起眼
hei² ŋan⁵ (translit.)
Raise eyes. (lit.)
Be worthy of notice.
Draw attention.
〔註〕引人注意。

1111 起痰
hei² tam⁴ (translit.)

Cause phlegm. (lit.)
Lick one's chop.
Show greed for...
Have a strong desire for...
Cast greedy eyes on...
〔註〕表示起了不良的慾念，或對……饞涎欲滴的意思，參閱"流口水"條（1077）。

1112 馬死落地行
ma⁵ se² lɔk⁹ dei⁶ haŋ⁴ (translit.)
Begin to walk after the death of a horse. (lit.)
One should help oneself when there is no help for one.
Stand on one's legs if dependence vanishes into the void.
〔註〕比喻無所依賴時，便要自力更生。

1113 馬屎憑官勢
ma⁵ si² pɐŋ⁴ gun¹ sɐi³ (translit.)
The manure of a horse depends upon officials' power. (lit.)
Throw one's weight about.
Pull one's rank on...
〔註〕比喻仗勢欺人或利用職權。

1114 桐油埕
tuŋ⁴ jɐu⁴ tsiŋ⁴ (translit.)
The large jar for wood oil. (lit.)
A man sticking to his old job like a bur.
A man doing the same job without any change.
〔註〕比喻改變不了自己職業的人，

相當於"桐油罐子無二用"。

1115 桄榔樹──一條心
fɔŋ² lɔŋ⁴ sy⁶—jɐt⁷ tiu⁴ sɐm¹ (translit.)
A coir-palm tree — only one heart. (lit.)
Love somebody heart and soul.
Apply one's mind to the person one loves.
Be single-minded in love.
Be constant in love.
〔註〕表示愛情專一。

1116 核突
wɐt⁹ dɐt⁹ (translit.)
Creeply and disgusting. (lit.)
Give somebody the creeps.
Make somebody's flesh creep.
Creepy-crawly.
Be nauseating.
〔註〕令人肉麻的，令人作嘔（討厭）的，參閱"肉酸"條（0681）。

1117 捉用神
dzuk⁸ juŋ⁶ sɐn⁴ (translit.)
Catch the spirit. (lit.)
Guess at what somebody means/thinks/likes.
Make a guess at something.
〔註〕表示猜測別人的用意或所好。

1118 捉字虱/蝨
dzuk⁸ dzi⁶ sɐt⁷ (translit.)
Catch fleas in a word. (lit.)
Find fault with the meaning of a Chinese character or a word.
Pick hole in the meaning of a sentence or a word.
〔註〕相當於"摳字眼兒"或"挑字眼

兒"。

1119 捉到鹿都唔會脱角
dzuk⁸ dou² luk⁹′⁸ dou¹ m⁴ wui⁵ tyt⁸ gɔk⁸ *(translit.)*
Not to know how to take off its horns after catching a deer. (lit.)
Let the opportunity slip.
Miss the bus.
〔註〕比喻有機會都不會利用。

1120 捉豬問地腳
dzuk⁸ dzy¹ mɐn⁶ dei⁶ gœk⁸ *(translit.)*
Catch a pig to ask for the foundation. (lit.)
Seek out the negotiator/the agent handling the job.
〔註〕表示經手是問的意思。

1121 捉黃腳鷄
dzuk⁸ wɔŋ⁴ gœk⁸ gɐi¹ *(translit.)*
Catch a yellow-legged cock. (lit.)
Extort money from a man by setting a sex-trap.
〔註〕男子冒稱一女子的丈夫，進房捉拿並指控被此女子勾引的男子與其妻幽會或勾引其妻，如此那冒牌丈夫便乘機敲詐一筆金錢。

1122 挃坭
dɐu⁶ nɐi⁴ *(translit.)*
Earth-like. (lit.)
Look shabby.
Be shabby in dress.
Be inferior.
Be of poor quality.

〔註〕形容人衣着襤褸或物品質量低劣。

1123 埋牙
mai⁴ ŋa⁴ *(translit.)*
Near to teeth. (lit.)
Start fighting.
Come to blows.
Begin to exchange blows.
Be spoiling for a fight.
〔註〕表示動手打架的意思。

1124 埋堆
mai⁴ dœy¹ *(translit.)*
Put piles up. (lit.)
Form a small coterie/clique.
〔註〕搞小集團或拉幫結派。

1125 索油
sɔk³ jɐu⁴ *(translit.)*
Soak up oil. (lit.)
Intend to make a pass at a lady.
Tease a lady to amuse oneself.
〔註〕抱着不良動機有意接近女人，企圖佔便宜或調戲婦女。

1126 真金不怕洪爐火，石獅不怕雨滂沱
dzɐn¹ gɐm¹ bɐt⁷ pa³ huŋ⁴ lou⁴ fɔ², sɛk⁹ si¹ bɐt⁷ pa³ jy⁵ pɔŋ⁴ tɔ⁴ *(translit.)*
Genuine gold fears no fire and stone lions fear no heavy rain. (lit.)
A person of integrity can stand severe tests.
A person of ability can withstand all trials and tribulations.
〔註〕比喻正直或有才幹的人是經得起考驗。

1127 胭脂馬 —— 難騎
jin¹ dzi¹ ma⁵—nan⁴ kɛ⁴ (translit.)
A rouged horse—It is hard to be ridden. (lit.)
An uncontrollable person.
〔註〕比喻不受控制或難以駕馭的人。

1128 特登
dɐk⁹ dɐŋ¹ (translit.)
On purpose. (lit.)
Intentionally.
Deliberately.
On purpose.
For a special purpose.
〔註〕故意地或有目的地的意思。

1129 鬼五馬六
gwɐi² ŋ⁵ ma⁵ luk⁹ (translit.)
Ghost five and horse six. (lit.)
Act in a grotesque way.
Grotesque.
Shady-looking.
Be not serious.
〔註〕形容人或物樣子怪誕的或不正經的。

1130 鬼打鬼
gwɐi² da² gwɐi² (translit.)
Ghosts fight ghosts. (lit.)
Put up an internecine fight.
Be at odds with each other.
Have an internal dissension.
〔註〕內鬨。參閱"狗咬狗骨"條（0891）。

1131 鬼打都冇咁醒
gwɐi² da² dou¹ mou⁵ gɐm³ siŋ² (translit.)
A ghosts's strike is not so alarming.
Be on the alert.
〔註〕表示非常警覺。

1132 鬼拍後尾枕 —— 不打自招
gwɐi² pak⁸ hɐu⁶ mei⁵ dzɐm²—bɐt⁷ da² dzi⁶ dziu¹ (translit.)
A ghost taps one's occiput—confess oneself without being beaten. (lit.)
Confess without presure.
Make a confession without duresse.
Unintentionally reveal one's own secret to somebody.
〔註〕比喻自己承認罪狀或過失或不自覺地洩露自己的秘密，參閱"不打自招"（0234）條。

1133 鬼馬
gwɐi² ma⁵ (translit.)
Ghostly horse. (lit.)
Have a whole bag of tricks.
Be as crafty as a fox.
Be comical.
〔註〕形容人狡猾或滑稽。

1134 鬼鬼鼠鼠〈祟祟〉
gwɐi² gwɐi² sy² sy² (translit.)
Devilish and mischievous. (lit.)
Sneak around.
Be furtive in one's movement.

〔註〕鬼鬼祟祟或偷偷摸摸的意思。

1135　鬼揞/揜眼
gwɐi² ɐm² ŋan⁵　(translit.)
A ghost covers one's eyes with hands.　(lit.)
Be muddled to make a mistake.
A mistake slips in.
〔註〕比喻糊裏糊塗地出錯。

1136　鬼畫符
gwɐi² wak⁹ fu⁴　(translit.)
The incantations that ghosts draw.　(lit.)
Be like an illegible scrawl.
〔註〕諷刺筆迹潦草。

1137　鬼聲鬼氣
gwɐi² sɛŋ¹ gwɐi² hei³
(translit.)
Ghost's voice and breath.　(lit.)
Speak in strange voice.
〔註〕即怪聲怪氣。

1138　隻[眼]開,隻[眼]閉
dzɛk⁸ [ŋan⁵] hɔi¹ dzɛk⁸
[ŋan⁵] bɐi³　(translit.)
One [eye] opens and one [eye] shuts.　(lit.)
Wink at...
Close one's eyes to...
Turn one's blind eye to...
〔註〕相當於"睁一隻眼,閉一隻眼";假裝沒看見。

1139　悵/撐雞
tsaŋ⁴ gɐi¹　(translit.)
Be like a fighting cock.　(lit.)
Be passionate and violent.
Be shrewish.

〔註〕潑婦似的。

1140　悵/撐雞妹
tsaŋ⁴ gɐi¹ mui¹　(translit.)
A girl like a fighting cock.　(lit.)
A girl of passionate disposition and violent temper.
〔註〕指性情兇惡而又易怒的少女。

1141　借刀殺人
dzɛ³ dou¹ sat⁸ jɐn⁴　(translit.)
Borrow a knife to kill people.　(lit.)
Murder with a borrowed knife.
Make use of somebody/something to get rid of one's adversary.

1142　借咗聾陳隻耳
dzɛ³ dzɔ² luŋ⁴ tsɐn² dzɛk⁸ ji⁵
(translit.)
Borrow an ear from the deaf Mr. Chan.　(lit.)
Turn a deaf ear to somebody.
〔註〕比喻充耳不聞,參閱"亞聾送殯"條(0831)。

1143　借花敬佛
dzɛ³ fa¹ giŋ³ fɐt⁹　(translit.)
Borrow flowers to offer to Buddha.　(lit.)
Make use of the gift from another to show respect to sombody.
〔註〕即借花獻佛。

1144　借艇割禾
dzɛ³ tɛŋ⁵ tɔt⁸ wɔ⁴　(translit.)

Borrow a boat to cut paddies. (lit.)
Make use of somebody to profit oneself.
Enlist somebody's help to fulfill one's own purpose.
〔註〕指利用別人來謀取利益或借助別人的幫忙來實踐自己的企圖的一種手段。

1145 借題發揮
dzɛ³ tɐi⁴ fat⁸ fɐi¹ *(translit.)*
Take advantage of the subject to call into play. (lit.)
Make use of the subject under discussion to put over one's own ideas.
Seize on an incident/a subject to talk at/make an assault on somebody.

1146 倒吊冇滴墨水
dou³ diu³ mou⁵ dik⁹ mɐk⁹ sœy² *(translit.)*
Have not a drop of ink even being hung upside down. (lit.)
Be uncivilized.
Haven't been educated.
Be uneducated.
〔註〕形容人沒文化，沒受過教育。

1147 倒吊荷包
dou³ diu³ hɔ⁶ pau¹ *(translit.)*
Hang the purse upside down. (lit.)
Invite losses for oneself.
Stand in one's own light.
〔註〕比喻自招損失或甘願蝕本。參閱"倒米"條（1148）。

1148 倒米
dou² mɐi⁵ *(translit.)*
Dump rice. (lit.)
Cause oneself or one's own side to suffer a loss.
Stand in one's own light.
〔註〕表示使自己或自己一方蒙受損失或損害自己利益的意思。參閱"倒吊荷包"條（1147）。

1149 倒米壽星
dou² mɐi⁵ sɐu⁶ siŋ¹ *(translit.)*
The god of longevity dumps rice. (lit.)
The person who causes himself or his own side to suffer a loss.
A person who stands in his own light.
〔註〕比喻自招損失或損害自己一方利益的人。

1150 倒掛臘鴨——滿口/嘴油
dou³ gwa³ lap⁹ ap²/³—mun⁵ hɐu²/dzœy² jɐu⁴ *(translit.)*
A cured duck hung upside down—its bill is full of oil. (lit.)
Have a glib tongue.
Oil one's tongue.
〔註〕形容人油腔滑調。

1151 倒瀉籮蟹
dou² sɛ² lɔ⁴ hai⁵ *(translit.)*
Upset a bamboo-basket of

crabs.　(lit.)
Be all in a muddle.
Be very busy with either this or that.
〔註〕形容手忙腳亂的樣子。

1152　倒瓤冬瓜
dou² nɔŋ⁴ duŋ¹ gwa¹　(translit.)
A big hard-skinned wax gourd with rotten pulp.　(lit.)
A person who is strong in appearance but poor in health.
A person who is outwardly wealthy but inwardly poor.
〔註〕比喻外表壯碩但實際不健康的人或外表富有的窮措大。

1153　個蜆個肉
gɔ³ hin² gɔ³ juk⁹　(translit.)
A small clam has only one lump of flesh.　(lit.)
Just one for just one.
〔註〕相當於'一個蘿蔔一個坑'。

1154　俾人揸住痛腳
bei² jɐn⁴ dza¹ dzy⁶ tuŋ³ gœk⁸　(translit.)
Let somebody hold one's aching leg.　(lit.)
Give somebody a handle.
Become fair game.
〔註〕即給人抓住把柄或成爲被人有懈可擊的對象。

1155　俾心機
bei² sɐm¹ gei¹　(translit.)
Give heart to...
Pay attention to...
Concentrate on...

Devote one's time and effort to...
〔註〕表示留心或下功夫的意思。

1156　俾個心你食都當狗肺
bei² gɔ³ sɐm¹ nei⁵ sik⁹ dou¹ dɔŋ³ gɐu² fei³　(translit.)
The heart given you to eat is regarded as dog's lungs.　(lit.)
Not to know chalk from cheese.
Not to know what is good for one.
Be ignorant of good from bad.
〔註〕指對方不知好歹。

1157　俾個頭你
bei² gɔ³ tɐu⁴ nei⁵　(translit.)
Give you the head.　(lit.)
No, I won't give you.
I'll give you nothing.
〔註〕表面肯定實際是否定的賭氣語。真意是拒絕給對方東西。

1158　修游
sɐu¹ jɐu⁴　(translit.)
Unhurried.　(lit.)
Be calm and unhurried.
Lead an easy life.
〔註〕形容從容不迫或過着悠閑的生活。

1159　修游淡定
sɐu¹ jɐu⁴ dam⁶ diŋ⁶　(translit.)
Keep cool and calm.　(lit.)
Be calm and composed.
Keep one's head and make no hast.
〔註〕這句話只表示從容不迫的態

度。

1160 氣羅氣喘
hei³ lɔ⁴ hei³ tsyn² (translit.)
The air grasps. (lit.)
Be out of breath.
Grasp for air.
Be panting.
〔註〕即氣喘。

1161 笑到肚刺
siu³ dou³ tou⁵ tsɛk³ (translit.)
One's belly aches with laughter. (lit.)
Split one's sides with laughter.
Laugh one's head off.

1162 笋嘢
sœn² jɛ⁵ (translit.)
A very cheap thing. (lit.)
A real bargain.
A job with wide margin of profits.
〔註〕比喻好東西，真便宜的東西或利潤大的工作。

1163 狼過華秀隻狗
lɔŋ⁴ gwɔ³ wa⁴ sɐu³ tsɜk⁸ gɐu² (translit.)
More fierce than Wa Sɐu's dog. (lit.)
Be more rapacious than a hawk.
Stick out for something by hook or crook.
Be very ferocious.
Bare one's fangs.
〔註〕表示貪得無厭，不擇手段要……或露出兇相的意思。

1164 拿手好戲
na⁴ sɐu² hou² hei³ (translit.)
One's dexterous performance. (lit.)
One's strong suit.
Be expert in...

1165 針冇兩頭利
dzɐm¹ mou⁵ lœŋ⁵ tɐu⁴ lei⁶ (translit.)
Not a needle is sharp at both ends. (lit.)
There is no rose without a thorn.
Nothing is good for both respects.
Nothing can satisfy rival claims.
〔註〕比喻沒有十全十美的事，相當於"甘蔗沒有兩頭甜"。

1166 針唔拮到肉唔知痛
dzɐm¹ m⁴ gɐt⁷ dou³ juk⁹ m⁴ dzi¹ tuŋ³ (translit.)
One does not feel the ache until a needle stings one. (lit.)
No one but the wearer knows better where the shoe pinches.
Do not stand in the shoe that pinches.
〔註〕比喻不置身於痛苦的地位不知痛苦。

1167 針鼻削鐵
dzɐm¹ bei⁶ sœk⁸ tit⁸ (translit.)
Scrape iron off the nose of a needle. (lit.)
Gain the narrowest margin of

profit.
〔註〕利潤極少。

1168 師姑
si¹ gu² *(translit.)*
Master's aunt. *(lit.)*
A Buddhist nun.
〔註〕即尼姑。

1169 留得青山在，哪怕有柴燒
lɐu⁴ dɐk⁷ tsiŋ¹ san¹ dzɔ⁶, na⁶ pa³ mou⁵ tsai⁴ siu¹
(translit.)
As long as the green mountain exists, one need not worry about having no firewood to burn. *(lit.)*
Life is safe and gains will surely be safe.

1170 留番啖氣暖吓肚
lɐu⁴ fan¹ dam⁶ hei³ nyn⁵ ha² tou⁵ *(translit.)*
Reserve a puff of breath to warm the belly. *(lit.)*
Maintain a strict silence on...
Button up one's mouth.
Bite the tongue.
〔註〕表示保持緘默的意思。

1171 留番嚟攝灶罅
lɐu⁴ fan¹ lɐi⁴ sip⁸ dzou³ la³
(translit.)
Put by a daughter to fill in the gap of the furnace. *(lit.)*
Let one's own daughter stay unmarried.
〔註〕比喻任由自己女兒作老處女，終身不嫁。

1172 幫理不幫親
bɔŋ¹ lei⁵ bɐt⁷ bɔŋ¹ tsɐn¹
(translit.)
Defend the reason, but defend on relations. *(lit.)*
Be fair-minded.
See fair play.
〔註〕表示公平。

1173 烏卒卒
wu¹ dzœt⁷ dzœt⁷ *(translit.)*
All is black. *(lit.)*
Be at a complete loss.
Be entirely ignorant.
Be as black as one's hat.
Be as black as night.
〔註〕即無知，參閱"烏啄啄"（1177）及"烏蛇蛇"（1178）各條，但又表示漆黑的意思。

1174 烏狗得食，白狗當災
wu¹ gɐu² dɐk⁷ sik⁹, bak⁹ gɐu² dɔŋ¹ dzɔi¹ *(translit.)*
A black dog gains the food to eat but a white dog suffers from the disaster. *(lit.)*
Be a whipping boy.
Carry the can.
Be a scapegoat.
〔註〕比喻代人受過，做替罪羊。

1175 烏喱馬扠
wu¹ lei¹ ma⁵ tsa¹ *(translit.)*
Black out all and write at random. *(lit.)*
Be ellegible and sloppy.
〔註〕形容字跡潦草。

1176 烏喱單刀
wu¹ lei¹ dan¹ dou¹ *(translit.)*

Black out the single knife. (lit.)
Be all in a muddle.
Be in an awful state.
〔註〕一塌糊塗的意思。

1177 烏啄啄
wu¹ dœŋ¹ dœŋ¹ (translit.)
In the dark. (lit.)
Be at a complete loss.
Be entirely ignorant.
〔註〕懵然不知，參閱"烏卒卒"（1173）及"烏蛇蛇"（1178）條。

1178 烏蛇蛇（借音字）
wu¹ sœ²ᐟ⁶ sœ⁶ (translit.)
In the dark. (lit.)
Be at a complete loss.
Be entirely ignorant.
〔註〕參閱"烏卒卒"（1173）及"烏啄啄"（1177）條。

1179 烏煙瘴氣
wu¹ jin¹ dzœŋ³ hei³ (translit.)
Black smoke and malaria. (lit.)
Be all in a muddle.
Be in an awful state.

1180 烏龍
wu¹ luŋ² (translit.)
A black dragon. (lit.)
Make a muddle of...
Muddle something together.
A muddy thinker.
〔註〕指做事糊塗，錯誤百出。

1181 烏蠅摟馬尾 —— 一拍兩散
wu¹ jin¹ lɐu¹ ma⁵ mei⁵ — jɐt⁷ pak⁸ lœŋ⁵ san³ (translit.)
Flies gather to hold on the tail of a horse — one slap disperses two. (lit.)
Rather make a mess of something then let either side monopolize it.
Smash up a monopoly.
〔註〕寧可把事情搞糟兩方面都得不到好處或不讓人獨佔。

1182 迷頭迷腦
mei⁴ tɐu⁴ mei⁴ nou⁵ (translit.)
Bury one's head and brains. (lit.)
Indulge oneself in...
Concentrate one's attention on...
〔註〕表示沉迷於某事或全神貫注的意思，也有人說成"埋頭埋腦"。

1183 送羊入虎口
suŋ³ jœŋ⁴ jɐp⁹ fu² hɐu² (translit.)
Send a goat into the mouth of a tiger. (lit.)
Put oneself/somebody to death.
Put one's chick under the care of a wolf.
〔註〕提等於把……送死。

1184 送佛送到西
suŋ³ fɐt⁹ suŋ³ dou³ sɐi¹ (translit.)
See Buddha off, go with him to the west. (lit.)
Help somebody, help him from

end to end.
Help a lame dog, help it over the stile.
Carry something through to the end.
Be thorough in one's work.
〔註〕比喻幫人幫到底或做事要徹底。

1185 害人終害己
hɔi⁶ jɐn⁴ dzuŋ¹ hɔi⁶ gei² (translit.)
Hurting others will hurt oneself instead in the end. (lit.)
Harm watch, harm catch.
Harm set, harm get.

1186 害死亞堅
hɔi⁶ sɛi² a³ gin¹ (translit.)
Harm A Gin to death. (lit.)
Be encumbered by somebody.
Be encumbered with something.
Make somebody come to an end.
〔註〕比喻爲……所累或累死某人。

1187 家和萬事興
ga¹ wɔ⁴ man⁶ si⁶ hiŋ⁴ (translit.)
A family of peace can establish ten thousand things. (lit.)
Harmony makes a family prosperous.

1188 家家有本難唸的經
ga¹ ga¹ jɐu⁵ bun² nan⁴ nim⁴ dik⁷ giŋ¹ (translit.)
Every family has a Buddhist Scripture that one finds it difficult to chant. (lit.)
Each and every family has its own problems.

1189 家醜不可外傳
ga¹ tsɐu² bɐt⁷ hɔ² ŋɔi⁶ tsyn⁴ (translit.)
The shameful business of a family can not be exposed outside. (lit.)
It is an ill bird that fouls its own nest.
Not to wash dirty linen in public.

1190 酒後吐真言
dzɐu² hɐu⁶ tou³ dzɐn¹ jin⁴ (translit.)
Tell the truth after having wine. (lit.)
Truth is exposed in wine.

1191 酒醉三分醒
dzɐu² dzœy³ sam¹ fɐn¹ sɛŋ¹ (translit.)
Be drunk but still a little clear-minded. (lit.)
Be in wine but still a little conscous.
Be in muddle but still know what to do.

1192 冤有頭，債有主
jyn¹ jɐu⁵ tɐu⁴, dzai³ jɐu⁵ dzy² (translit.)
Enmity has cause and debt has its debitor. (lit.)
There must be an agent for what is done.
〔註〕比喻凡事都有原因或主使者。

1193 冤屈

jyn¹ wɐt⁷ (translit.)
A wrong. (lit.)
Grievance.
False charge.
〔註〕"冤枉"的同義詞。

1194 冤柱嚟瘟疫去
jyn¹ wɔŋ² nɐi⁴ wɐn¹ jik⁹ hœy³ (translit.)
Come from a wrong, go for plague. (lit.)
Ill gotten, ill spent.
〔註〕表示悖入悖出的意思。

1195 冤家
jyn¹ ga¹ (translit.)
An enemy. (lit.)
An opponent.
One's destined lover.
〔註〕指對立的人，有時又指自己命中注定的愛人或妻子。

1196 冤家宜解不宜結
jyn¹ ga¹ ji⁴ gai² bɐt⁷ ji⁴ git⁸ (translit.)
Enmity should be untied and should not be tied. (lit.)
It is better for enemies to have their hatred slaked than it is to contract enmity.
It is better to bury the hatchet.

1197 冤家路窄
jyn¹ ga¹ lou⁶ dzak⁸ (translit.)
Opponents in the narrow road. (lit.)
Enemies are bound to meet.

1198 冤豬頭都有盟鼻菩薩
jyn¹ dzy¹ tɐu⁴ dou¹ jɐu⁵ mɐŋ⁴ bei⁶ pou⁴ sat⁸ (translit.)
A foul pig's head would be appreciated by the god with bad nose. (lit.)
A lover has no judge of beauty.
Love is blind.
Beauty exists in a lover's eyes.
Beauty exists in a beholder.
〔註〕相當於"臭豬頭有爛鼻子來聞"，意為美麗是沒有準則的，參閱"情人眼裏出西施"條（1368）。

1199 冤孽
jyn¹ jip⁹ (translit.)
The curses for evil deeds. (lit.)
The retribution for ancestors' evil deeds.
Predestinated connection.
Evil connection.
〔註〕指上一代敗德所留下的報應或命中注定的關係。

1200 剃眼眉
tɐi³ ŋan⁵ mei⁴ (translit.)
Shave eyebrows. (lit.)
Not to spare somebody's sensibilities.
Not to save somebody's face.
Criticize somebody to his face.
Bring humiliation upon somebody.
〔註〕指令人丟臉，當面批評人或使人當場出醜的行為。

1201 高不成，低不就
gou¹ bɐt⁷ siŋ⁴, dɐi¹ bɐt⁷

dzɐu⁶ (translit.)
Neither achieve the height nor accomplish the low. (lit.)
Be neither willing to stoop to conquer nor able to match with...
Be neither unfit for a higher position nor willing to take a lower one.
〔註〕參閱"半天吊"（0505）條。

1202 高竇
goɐu¹ dɐu³ (translit.)
A high nest. (lit.)
Be as proud as a peacock.
Have not a word to throw at a dog.
〔註〕傲慢。

1203 消/宵夜
siu¹ jɛ² (translit.)
While away the night. (lit.)
Have a midnight snack.
Midnight supper.
Refreshments taken late at night.

1204 差唔多
tsa¹ m⁴ dɔ¹ (translit.)
Almost. (lit.)
Much of a muchness.
Be not very different from...
Be about the same.
Almost.
Nearly.
〔註〕表示很相像或相差不大，但亦表示幾乎的意思。

1205 痾尿遞草紙
ɔ¹ niu⁶ dɐi⁶ tsou² dzi² (translit.)
Offer toilet tissue to the one who is discharging one's urine. (lit.)
Offer an unnecessary help.
〔註〕比喻給予不必要的幫忙。

1206 痾屎唔出賴地硬，痾尿唔出賴風猛
ɔ¹ si² m⁴ tsœt⁷ lai⁶ dei⁶ ŋaŋ⁶, ɔ¹ niu⁶ m⁴ tsœt⁷ lai⁶ fuŋ¹ maŋ⁵ (translit.)
Put the blame on the hard ground for failure to defecate and on the strong wind for being unable to discharge one's urine. (lit.)
Bad workmen often blame their tools.
Lay the blame upon somebody/something.
〔註〕比喻歸咎某人/物或怪這怪那。相當於"拉不出屎賴茅房"。

1207 海上無魚蝦自大
hɔi² sœŋ⁶ mou⁴ jy⁴ ha¹ dzi⁶ dai⁶ (translit.)
Were there no fish in the sea, a shrimp would become the biggest. (lit.)
A dwarf in Liliput would be thought as a superbeing.

1208 烟（蔫）靭
jin¹ ŋɐn⁴/jɐn⁶ (translit.)
As tough as leather. (lit.)
Be heels over head in love with each other.
Enthuse each other over love.

〔註〕形容男女間的熱火纏綿。

1209 流口水
lɐu⁴/⁶ hɐu² sœy² (translit.)
Dribble mouth water. (lit.)
Lick one's chops.
Show greed for...
Be inferior.
Be of poor quality.
Be low-graded.
〔註〕表示饞涎欲滴。如形容物件為劣質時,"流"字作 lɐu⁶ 音。

1210 流馬尿
lɐu⁴/⁶ ma⁵ niu⁶ (translit.)
Flow horse's urine. (lit.)
Shed tears.
Cry out tears.
〔註〕譏諷人流淚。

1211 戙起幡竿有鬼到
duŋ⁶ hei² fan¹ gɔn¹ jɐu⁵ gwɐi² dou³ (translit.)
Set up the banner calling the soul home and ghosts will come. (lit.)
People will come as soon as they know the location.
〔註〕表示有人知所在地,自會前來的意思。

1212 財不可露眼
tsɔi⁴ bɐt⁷ hɔ² lou⁶ ŋan⁵ (translit.)
Money should not be exposed to eyes. (lit.)
Opportunity makes the thief.
〔註〕表示漫藏誨盜的意思。

1213 財可通神
tsɔi⁴ hɔ² tuŋ¹ sɐn⁴ (translit.)

Money can tempt gods. (lit.)
Money makes the mare go.
Money talks.
〔註〕參閱"有錢使得鬼推磨"條
(0567)。

1214 財到光棍手 —— 有去冇回頭
tsɔi⁴ dou³ gwɔŋ¹ gwɐn³ sɐu²—jɐu⁵ hœy³ mou⁵ wui⁴ tɐu⁴ (translit.)
The money reaches a swindler's hand—once go never come back. (lit.)
Give a bone to a dog.
No one can get it back when the bone is given to a dog.
〔註〕表示被騙的錢沒法收回,相當於"肉包子打狗 —— 一去不回頭"。

1215 唔三唔四
m⁴ sam¹ m⁴ sei³ (translit.)
Not three not four. (lit.)
Neither fish, flesh nor fowl.
Neither one thing nor the other.
Be nondescript.
〔註〕不倫不類的;形容不出的。

1216 唔化
m⁴ fa³ (translit.)
Not sublimate. (lit.)
Be too stubborn.
Be not enlightened/open-minded.
Be not liberal in one's views.
Not realize the ways of the world.
〔註〕固執,不開通或不覺醒的意

思。

1217 唔在行
m⁴ dzɔi⁶ hɔŋ⁴ (translit.)
Not in the trade. (lit.)
Be out of one's beat.
Be out of one's line.
〔註〕指自己不熟悉的事或並非自己本行業的範圍。

1218 唔打唔相識
m⁴ da² m⁴ sœŋ¹ sik⁷ (translit.)
No blows, no friendship grows. (lit.)
No discord, no concord.

1219 唔同床唔知被爛
m⁴ tuŋ⁴ tsɔŋ⁴ m⁴ dzi¹ pei⁵ lan⁶ (translit.)
One that does not sleep in the same bed does not know that the quilt is worn out. (lit.)
No one knows what the other side of the world looks like.
〔註〕比喻局外人難知局中事，參閱"一家唔知一家事"條（0039）。

1220 唔自在
m⁴ dzi⁶ dzɔi³ (translit.)
Be uneasy. (lit.)
Be unwell.
Feel awkward and ill at ease.
〔註〕表示不舒服或侷促不安。

1221 唔自量
m⁴ dzi⁶ lœŋ⁶ (translit.)
Not to measure oneself. (lit.)
Not to understand oneself.
Be ignorant of one's own ability/situation.

〔註〕表示不自量力的意思。

1222 唔見得光
m⁴ gin⁶ dɐk⁷ gwɔŋ¹ (translit.)
Can not see the light. (lit.)
Can not be exposed to the light of day.
〔註〕即不能公開的意思。

1223 唔見棺材唔流眼淚
m⁴ gin³ gun¹ tsɔi⁴ m⁴ lɐu⁴ ŋan⁵ lœy⁶ (translit.)
Not to shed a tear until seeing the coffin. (lit.)
Refuse to be convinced until facing the grim reality.
〔註〕不見到最後結果不死心或事到臨頭才知危害。

1224 唔見過鬼都唔怕黑
m⁴ gin³ gwɔ³ gwɐi² dou¹ m⁴ pa³ hɐk⁷ (translit.)
One that hasn't seen a ghost does not fear darkness. (lit.)
Any child that hasn't been burned dreads no fire.
A burned child dreads the fire.
〔註〕參閱"見過鬼就怕黑"條（0811）。

1225 唔志在
m⁴ dzi³ dzɔi³ (translit.)
Not mind about. (lit.)
Not to care a fig.
Not to mind.
〔註〕即不在乎的意思。

1226 唔知個"醜"字點寫
m⁴ dzi¹ gɔ³ tsɐu² dzi⁶ dim²

sɛ² *(translit.)*
Do not know how to write the Chinese character "醜". (lit.)
Be dead to shame.
Be thick-skinned.
〔註〕形容人厚顏無恥。

1227 唔怕官至怕管
m⁴ pa³ gun¹ dzi³ pa³ gun² *(translit.)*
Not to be afraid of the senior officials but afraid of the junior clerk who governs. (lit.)
Had better obey the person in direct charge.
A mouse fears nobody but the cat that would catch it.
〔註〕相當於"不怕官就怕管"。

1228 唔怪之得/唔怪得之
m⁴ gwai³ dzi¹ dɐk⁷/m⁴ gwai³ dɐk⁷ dzi¹ *(translit.)*
There is no wonder. (lit.)
Little wonder that...
...so that is why...
〔註〕難怪,引語,用於表忽然明白原因時而引出下句。

1229 唔抵得瘀
m⁴ dɐi² dɐk⁷ jy² *(translit.)*
Cannot stand the extravasated blood. (lit.)
Cannot bear the sight of...
Frown upon...
Cannot bear the waste.
〔註〕表示看不下去或捨不得浪費。

1230 唔抵得頸
m⁴ dɐi² dɐk⁷ gɛŋ² *(translit.)*
Cannot stand the neck. (lit.)
Cannot control one's temper.
Be unable to contain oneself for it.
〔註〕氣不過,忍不住性子或憋不住的意思。

1231 唔忿氣
m⁴ fɐn⁶ hei² *(translit.)*
Not to give the air up. (lit.)
Be unreconciled to...
Be reluctant to give in/up.
Be unwilling to confess the defeat.
〔註〕不服氣,不甘心於……或不願放棄/讓步/承認失敗的意思。

1232 唔使問亞貴
m⁴ sɐi² mɐn⁶ a³ gwei³ *(translit.)*
There is no need to ask A Gwai. (lit.)
Be as sure as eggs is eggs.
There is no need to ask if a duck will swim.
〔註〕比喻不言而喻或事情便是這樣,用不着問。

1233 唔使指擬
m⁴ sɐi² dzi² ji⁵ *(translit.)*
Not to depend upon. (lit.)
Hold no hope of it.
Have no fond dream about it.
〔註〕別指望或別夢想。

1234 唔使畫公仔畫出腸
m⁴ sɐi² wak⁹ guŋ¹ dzɐi² wak⁹ tsœt⁷ tsœn² *(trans-*

lit.)
It is not necessary to draw intestines while drawing a figure. (lit.)
It goes without saying in details.
It is not necessary to ask if a duck will swim.
〔註〕表示不言而喻的意思，參閱"唔使問亞貴"條（1232）。

1235 唔使擒擒青
m⁴ sɐi² kɐm⁴ kɐm² tsɛŋ¹ (translit.)
There is no need to be in such a hurry. (lit.)
First catch your hare, then cook him.
Easy does it.
There is no hurry about it.
〔註〕即不必着急。

1236 唔敢當
m⁴ gɐm² dɔŋ¹ (translit.)
Not so bold to deserve it. (a polite and humble expression spoken by the first person.) (lit.)
Thank you, but I feel ashamed to obtain my desert.
〔註〕不敢當。

1237 唔信命都信吓塊鏡
m⁴ sœn³ mɛŋ⁶ dou¹ sœn³ ha⁵ fai³ gɛŋ³ (translit.)
If one does not believe in one's own fate, one should believe in the mirror. (lit.)
It is wise to know oneself.

It is wise to have self-knowledge.
〔註〕表示要有自知之明的意思。

1238 唔係路
m⁴ hɐi⁶ lou⁶ (translit.)
Not the way. (lit.)
Be not on the right track.
It doesn't seem to be normal/rigth.
It doesn't seem to be encouraging.
It is far from good.
〔註〕即不對勁，不對頭或事情不妙的意思。

1239 唔係猛龍唔過江，唔係毒蛇唔打霧
m⁴ hɐi⁶ maŋ⁵ luŋ⁴ m⁴ gwɔ³ gɔŋ¹, m⁴ hɐi⁶ duk⁹ sɛ⁴ m⁴ da² mou⁶ (translit.)
If it were not a fierce dragon, it would not cross the river; if it were not a deadly snake, it would not breathe mist. (lit.)
He who dares to come is surely not a coward.
If one were not so despotic, one would not come.
Only the man of power dares to come.
〔註〕參閱"來者不善，善者不來"（0843）。

1240 唔咬弦
m⁴ ŋɐu⁵ jin² (translit.)
Do not bite the string of the musical instrument. (lit.)
Be out of tune with somebody.

Not to speak the same language.

Not to get along so well with somebody.

〔註〕比喻和某人談不來或合不來。

1241 唔要斧頭唔得柄甩

m⁴ jiu³ fu² tɐu² m⁴ dɐk⁷ bɛŋ³ lɐt⁷ (translit.)

Through the axe is not wanted any more, it is difficult to get its helve off. (lit.)

Hold a wolf by the ears.

Up a gum tree.

Cannot help carrying on.

〔註〕比喻欲罷不能。

1242 唔食羊肉一身臊

m⁴ sik⁹ jœŋ⁴ juk⁹ jɐt⁷ sɐn¹ sou¹ (translit.)

The whole body gets full of lamb odour without eating mutton. (lit.)

Invite unexpected trouble.

Be involved in an unexpected troublesome case.

〔註〕相當於"不吃羊肉空惹一身膻"。

1243 唔埋得個鼻

m⁴ mai⁴ dɐk⁷ gɔ³ bei⁶ (translit.)

Can not get near the nose. (lit.)

Make a long nose.

Turn up one's nose at...

Look down one's nose at...

〔註〕原意爲"臭不堪聞"，引伸爲對人表示鄙視，瞧不起。大致相當於"一錢不值"，"沒甚麼了不起"。

1244 唔理三七二十一

m⁴ lei⁵ sam¹ tsɐt⁷ ji⁶ sɐp⁹ jɐt⁷ (translit.)

Not to care if three times seven equal to twenty-one. (lit.)

Chance the duck.

Cast all caution to the wind.

Pay no regard to the consequences.

〔註〕表示不顧一切的意思。參閱"唔理得咁多"條（1245）。

1245 唔理得咁多

m⁴ lei⁵ dɐk⁷ gɐm³ dɔ¹ (translit.)

Not to care for such a good many. (lit.)

Cast all caution to the wind.

Pay no regard to the consequences.

Rain or shine.

For better or worse.

〔註〕相當於"唔理三七二十一"。

1246 唔做中唔做保，唔做媒人三代好

m⁴ dzou⁶ dzuŋ¹ m⁴ dzou⁶ bou², m⁴ dzou⁶ mui⁴ jɐn⁴ sam¹ dɔi⁶ hou² (translit.)

Neither being a middleman or a guarantor nor being a matchmarker will make three later generations better. (lit.)

He that does no business of a middleman and the like will have worthy descendence.

〔註〕這是勸人不要多管別人的事或做中間人的口頭語。

1247　唔湯唔水

m⁴ tɔŋ¹ m⁴ sœy² *(translit.)*

Neither soap nor water. (lit.)

Neither fish nor fowl.

Be done by halves.

Hang in half-way.

〔註〕表示不倫不類或工作做得一半而未徹底完成的意思。

1248　唔睇白鴿，都睇吓堆屎

m⁴ tɐi² bak⁹ gɐp⁸, dou¹ tɐi² ha² dœy¹ si² *(translit.)*

Not to look at the pegeon itself, but have to look at its manure. (lit.)

A straw shows which way the wind blows.

From his ostentation or extravagance, one can find a clue to how wealthy somebody is.

〔註〕比喻見微知著。（指從某人的排場便知某人的家世的意思。）

1249　唔睇僧面，都睇吓佛面

m⁴ tɐi² dzɐŋ¹ min⁶, dou¹ tɐi² ha² fɐt⁹ min⁶ *(translit.)*

Not to look at the face of a monk, look at the face of Buddha. (lit.)

Not for everybody's sake but for somebody's sake.

〔註〕這是用於懇求別人幫忙時的插語，意思即是說，"如你不賞臉給我，也請你賞臉給某人"。相當於"不看僧面看佛面"。

1250　唔嗲耕

m⁴ na¹ gaŋ¹ *(translit.)*

Have no relation. (lit.)

Have nothing to do with...

Bear no relation to...

Be not concerned in...

Be as different as chalk from cheese.

Beside the point.

Be wide of mark.

〔註〕表示毫不相干，和某人毫無關係，"不着邊際或不切題"的意思。

1251　唔經大腦

m⁴ giŋ¹ dai⁶ nou⁵ *(translit.)*

Not to pass through the cerebrums. (lit.)

Not to rack one's brains.

Leap without thinking.

〔註〕表示未經考慮便說出或做出某事的意思。

1252　唔該借一借

m⁴ gɔi¹ dzɛ³ jɐt⁷ dzɛ³ *(translit.)*

Please lend me a loan. (lit.)

Excuse me.

Give way to me, please.

Make room for me, please.

〔註〕參閱"唔該借歪啲"條（1253）。

1253　唔該借歪啲

m⁴ gɔi¹ dzɛ³ mɛ² di¹ *(translit.)*

Please, lend a little. (lit.)

Excuse me.

Give way to me, please.
Make room for me, please.
〔註〕意爲借光，請讓開一些！用於請對方"讓路"或"讓坐"。

1254 唔嗅米氣
m⁴ tsɐu³ mɐi⁵ hei³ (translit.)
Haven't yet smelt the odour of rice. (lit.)
One's mouth is full of pap.
Be too childish.
〔註〕比喻無知或幼稚。

1255 唔算數
m⁴ syn³ sou² (translit.)
Not to count the sum. (lit.)
Go back on one's words.
Play fast and loose.
〔註〕表示食言或反覆無常，參閱"唔認賬/數"條（1256）。

1256 唔認賬/數
m⁴ jiŋ⁶ dzœŋ³ (sou³) (translit.)
Deny the account (sum). (lit.)
Go back on one's words.
Play fast and loose.
〔註〕參閱"唔算數"條（1255）。

1257 唔嗲唔吊
m⁴ dɛ² m⁴ diu³ (translit.)
Neither care nor pay attention to... (lit.)
Be casual.
〔註〕相當於"大大咧咧的"，意指不緊不慢，愛理不理或對甚麼都無所謂的意思。

1258 唔黏家
m⁴ tsi¹ ga¹ (translit.)
Not to stick home. (lit.)
Not to be a home-bird.
Not to stick indoors.
〔註〕表示不喜歡或不經常留在家中的意思。

1259 唔覺眼
m⁴ gɔk⁸ ŋan⁵ (translit.)
Have no feeling in the eyes. (lit.)
Pay no attention to...
Not to keep one's eyes open.
〔註〕沒注意。

1260 唔覺意
m⁴ gɔk⁸ ji³ (translit.)
Have no feeling in the mind. (lit.)
Take no care.
One's mind is absent.
Have no intention of...
Not to mean to...
〔註〕不留神，不小心。

1261 蚊髀同牛髀
mɐn¹ bei² tuŋ⁴ ŋɐu⁴ bei² (translit.)
The leg of a mosquito and the leg of an ox. (lit.)
By long chalks.
Can not measure with each other.
There is no comparision between the two.
Not to be compared with each other.

〔註〕比喻無法作互相比較或有天淵之別。

1262 蚊都瞓
men¹ dou¹ fen³ *(translit.)*
Mosquitoes also sleep. (lit.)
It will be too late to...
〔註〕表示某人行動慢吞吞的，等到他做……時，爲時已晚了的意思。

1263 恩將仇報
jen¹ dzœŋ¹ tseu⁴ bou³ *(translit.)*
Revenge for kindness. (lit.)
Bite the hand that feeds.
Quit love for hate.

1264 茶瓜送飯 —— 好人有限
tsa⁴ gwa¹ sun³ fan³—hou² jen⁴ jeu⁵ han⁶ *(translit.)*
Have cooked-rice with cucumber stips in sugar-salted—Good men are limited. (lit.)
Not to behave oneself as well as one is expected.
Be not such a good person as expected.
〔註〕即斷非好人。病人（不是健康的好人）在禁口時，只好用茶瓜（一種糖水浸漬的瓜）送飯。反過來說，用茶瓜送飯的人決非好（健康好的）人。此"好人"和行爲良好的"好人"語帶雙關。

1265 骨子
gwet⁷ dzi² *(translit.)*
Smallboned. (lit.)
Be delicate and exquisite.

〔註〕形容嬌小玲瓏的意思。

1266 除笨有精
tsy⁴ ben⁶ jeu⁵ dzɛŋ¹ *(translit.)*
Besides foolishness, there is cleverness. (lit.)
Bait a hook with a small fish to catch a bigger one.
Make the best of a bad bargain.
〔註〕形容笨人偶爾也有聰明之處，或除了吃虧也會佔便宜。

1267 除褲疴屁 —— 多此一舉
tsy⁴ fu³ ɔ¹ pei³—dɔ¹ tsi² jet⁷ gœy² *(translit.)*
Take off trousers to break wind—take an unnecessary action. (lit.)
Carry coals to Newcastle.

1268 蒸生瓜
dziŋ¹ saŋ¹ gwa¹ *(translit.)*
An under-steamed cucumber. (lit.)
Be half-idiotic.
A simpleton.
〔註〕比喻半痴的，不靈活，笨頭笨腦。蒸煮不熟的瓜必碜（音sen⁵）。碜即不夠綿軟的意思，但廣東人把"碜"又作"痴"或"傻"解。

1269 紙紥下扒
dzi² dzat³ ha⁶ pa⁴ *(translit.)*
The paper chin. (lit.)
Talk at random.
Talk through one's neck.
Only cackle without laying an

egg.

〔註〕比喻大放厥詞，亂説一通或講空話。

十一畫

1270 豉油撈飯——整色水
si⁶ jɐu⁴ lou¹ fan⁶—dziŋ² sik⁷ sœy² *(translit.)*
Mix cooked-rice with soy sause—making colours. (lit.)
Stand upon one's dignity by intention.
Put on airs.
〔註〕比喻故作尊嚴或擺架子。

1271 現眼報
jin⁶ ŋan⁵ bou³ *(translit.)*
The visible recompense. (lit.)
Deserve an immediate retribution.
〔註〕指做了壞事，馬上得到報應。相當於"現世現報"。

1272 帶花
dai³ fa¹ *(translit.)*
Put on a flower. (lit.)
Stop a bullet.
〔註〕比喻受鎗傷或受傷。（多爲黑社會人語。）

1273 帶挈
dai³ hit⁸ *(translit.)*
Look after. (lit.)
Keep an eye on somebody.
Help somebody on.
Guide and support somebody.
〔註〕即關照或提攜。

1274 曹操都有知心友，關公亦有對頭人
tsou⁴ tsou¹ dou¹ jɐu⁵ dzi¹ sɐm¹ jɐu⁵, gwan¹ guŋ¹ jik⁹ jɐu⁵ dœy³ tɐu⁴ jɐn⁴ *(translit.)*
Tsou Tsou had his bosom friends and Gwan Guŋ had his enemies. (lit.)
Tsou Tsou—the person standing for craftiness.
Gwan Guŋ—the person standing for uprightness.
A devil has friends to sup with and a saint has foes worthy of his steel.
〔註〕比喻壞人有其支持者，而好人也有其反對者。

1275 爽手
sɔŋ² sɐu² *(translit.)*
Brisk hands. (lit.)
Be generous in giving money/consent/help...to others.
Be as nimble as a squirrel.
Be quick.
Quicken one's hands/steps.
〔註〕本義爲用手觸摸東西時，有軟滑舒服的感覺。但此語爲轉義詞形容人慷慨或爽快。這一語有人説成"手爽"。此外又形容人利索，敏捷。

1276 專登

dzyn¹ dɐŋ¹　*(translit.)*
In purpose.　(lit.)
Intentionally.
Deliberately.
On purpose.
For a special purpose.
〔註〕參閱"特登"條（1128）。

1277　執人口水溦
dzɐp¹ jɐn⁴ hɐu² sœy² mei¹/⁵
　(translit.)
Pick up somebody's mouth water.　(lit.)
Take a leaf out of somebody's book.
Say after somebody.
Follow the words of somebody.
Echo somebody.
Echo somebody's nonsense.
〔註〕人云亦云，拾人牙慧。

1278　執二攤
dzɐp¹ ji⁶ tan¹　*(translit.)*
Pick at a second-hand stall.　(lit.)
Have/Buy something second hand.
Marry a widow/a non-virgin/a loose woman.
〔註〕指購買二手貨；娶寡婦或非處女等爲妻。

1279　執手尾
dzɐp⁷ sɐu² mei⁵　*(translit.)*
Pick up the hand and tail.　(lit.)
Deal with the work left over.
Deal with the aftermath of...
〔註〕指收拾丟下未完的工作或清理善後。相當於"擇魚頭"。

1280　執死雞
dzɐp⁷ sei² gɐi¹　*(translit.)*
Pick up a dead hen.　(lit.)
Take what others give up.
Obtain a real bagain.
〔註〕比喻人棄我取或購得非常便宜的東西，買退票。

1281　執到襪帶累身家
dzɐp⁷ dou² mɐt⁹ dai³ lœy⁶ sɐn¹ ga¹　*(translit.)*
The garters picked up implicate the whole wealth.　(lit.)
Lose a pound for gaining a penny.
Penny wise and pound foolish.
〔註〕比喻因小失大。

1282　執笠
dzɐp⁷ lɐp⁷　*(translit.)*
Pick a bamboo basket.　(lit.)
Shup up the shop.
Go bankrupt.
Close down.
〔註〕即倒閉的意思。

1283　執輸
dzɐp⁷ sy¹　*(translit.)*
Pick up a loss.　(lit.)
Take no wind out of somebody's sails.
Miss the bus.
Lose an opportunity.
Not to take an immediate action in time.
〔註〕表示佔下風，吃虧，失去機會

或未採取立即行動的意思。

1284 執輸行頭，慘過敗家
dzɐp⁷ sy¹ hɐŋ⁴ tɐu⁴, tsam² gwɔ³ bai⁶ ga¹ *(translit.)*
It is more distressful not to pack up the baggage in time than it is to ruin a family. (lit.)
It would be disadvantageous not to take an immediate action in time.
〔註〕譏諷那些行動遲緩而讓人佔了上風的人。

1285 執頭執尾
dzɐp⁷ tɐu⁴ dzɐp⁷ mei⁵ *(translit.)*
Pick odds and ends. (lit.)
Do odd jobs.
〔註〕指無指定的工作做，做零碎工作。

1286 頂尖
diŋ² dzim¹ *(translit.)*
At the tip-top. (lit.)
To the queen's taste.
Choose the best.
Aim at perfection.
〔註〕表示務求盡善盡美的意思。

1287 頂包
diŋ² bau¹ *(translit.)*
Support the package. (lit.)
Take somebody's place by assuming his name.
Pass somebody/something off as...
〔註〕冒名頂替或以假充真。

1288 頂頭上司
diŋ² tɐu⁴ sœŋ⁶ si¹ *(translit.)*
The boss direct on one's head. (lit.)
One's direct superior.

1289 頂檔
diŋ² dɔŋ³ *(translit.)*
Support the stall. (lit.)
Serve as a stopgap.
〔註〕臨時代替，頂替。

1290 勒時間
lak⁹ si⁴ gan¹ *(translit.)*
Immediately. (lit.)
All at once.
All of a sudden.
Out of the blue.
〔註〕即忽然間，突然間。

1291 勒實褲頭帶
lak⁹ sɐt⁹ fu³ tɐu⁴ dai³ *(translit.)*
Tighten the belt of trousers. (lit.)
Tighten one's belt.
〔註〕暗喻忍受饑餓。

1292 斬腳趾避沙蟲
dzam² gœk⁸ dzi² bei⁶ sa¹ tsuŋ² *(translit.)*
Cut off the toes to avoid siphon-worm. (lit.)
Trim the toes to fit the shoes.
Abandon the greatest to save the smallest.
Make a sacrifice in order to avoid trouble.
〔註〕比喻爲了避免小麻煩，不惜作

較大犧牲。

1293 扎炮
dzat⁸ pau³　(translit.)
Tie up firecrackers.　(lit.)
Suffer from hunger.
Have nothing to eat.
〔註〕餓肚子。參閱"吊沙煲"條（0670）。

1294 扎扎跳
dzat⁸ dzat⁸ tiu³　(translit.)
Jump about.　(lit.)
Be all at sea.
Be like an ant on a hot griddle.
Be on the rack.
Jump the traces.
Kick over the traces.
Be in a rage.
Be hot with rage.
〔註〕表示感到極度不安，無定性且不受拘束及憤怒的意思。

1295 掘尾龍——攪風攪雨
gwɐt⁹ mei⁵ luŋ²—gau² fuŋ¹ gau² jy⁵　(translit.)
A blunt-tailed dragon — stirring wind and rain.　(lit.)
The person who stirs up strife.
The person who plays some ones off against one another.
〔註〕指煽風點火的人。

1296 挃拃
ŋa⁶ dza⁶　(translit.)
Infringe space.　(lit.)
Occupy too much space.
Be overbearing.
Occupy space with a high hand.

〔註〕形容東西佔地方，形容人霸道，以高壓手段霸佔地方。

1297 捩咁嚱
lɐi² gɐm³ hɛ³　(translit.)
Busy about.　(lit.)
Be all in a muddle.
Make a muddle of something.
Be all in a fluster.
〔註〕形容狼狽或手足無措的神態。

1298 捩橫折曲
lɐi² waŋ⁴ dzit⁸ kuk⁷　(translit.)
Turn round and bend.　(lit.)
Swear black is white.
Confound right with wrong.
〔註〕表示指鹿爲馬的意思。

1299 掛羊頭賣狗肉
gwa³ jœŋ⁴ tɐu⁴ mai⁶ gɐu² juk⁹　(translit.)
Hang a goat's head but sell dog's flesh.　(lit.)
Foist something on somebody.
Label vinegar as vintage.
Cry up wine and sell vinegar.

1300 掉忌
dzɐu⁶ gei⁶　(translit.)
It is too bad.　(lit.)
It is too bad.
It is under taboo.
〔註〕即不妙了的意思。

1301 推三推四
tœy¹ sam¹ tœy¹ sei³　(translit.)
Push three and push four.　(lit.)

Cook up a lame excuse.
Shift on to somebody else.
Decline with all sorts of excuses.
〔註〕藉詞推却的意思。

1302 推莊
tœy¹ dzɔŋ¹ (translit.)
Push the bank away. (lit.)
Decline.
Shirk one's duty towards...
Beat a retreat.
〔註〕表示拒絶，逃避對……的責任或放棄的意思，參閲"打退堂鼓"條（0433）。

1303 掟煲
dɛŋ³ bou¹ (translit.)
Throw down an earthen pot. (lit.)
Break up.
Break off.
〔註〕男女因感情破裂而分手的意思，相當於"吹了"。

1304 捱世界
ŋai⁴ sɐi³ gai³ (translit.)
Endure the world. (lit.)
Live from hand to mouth.
Keep the wolf from the door.
〔註〕熬苦日子。

1305 捱更抵夜
ŋai⁴ gaŋ¹ dɐi² jɛ⁶ (translit.)
Endure the beating of watchman's drum and bear the night. (lit.)
Sit up all night.
Sit up late.

Turn night into day.
〔註〕即"熬夜"。

1306 捱夜
ŋai⁴ jɛ² (translit.)
Endure the night. (lit.)
Sit up late.
〔註〕同"捱更抵夜"（1305）。

1307 捱騾仔
ŋai⁴ lœy⁴ dzɐi² (translit.)
Endure like an ass. (lit.)
Labour up to live on.
Work like a horse.
Be beaten like a mule.
〔註〕辛辛苦苦過日子。

1308 梗板
gɐŋ² ban² (translit.)
Rigid plank. (lit.)
Be inflexible.
Be as stiff as a poker.
〔註〕表示呆板，死板，或固定不變的意思。

1309 乾手淨脚
gɔn¹ sɐu² dzɛŋ⁶ gœk⁹ (translit.)
Dry hands and clean feet. (lit.)
Save trouble.
Make a snappy.
In a straightforward way.
With nothing to worry about in the days to come.
〔註〕表示省却麻煩，直截了當的意思。

1310 偷偷摸摸
tɐu¹ tɐu¹ mɔ² mɔ² (trans-

lit.)
Act stealthly. (lit.)
On the sly.
Do something under the rose.
Act surreptitiously.

1311 偷龍轉鳳
tɐu¹ luŋ⁴ dzyn² fuŋ⁶ (translit.)
Steal a dragon and change it for a phoenix. (lit.)
Make a secret substitution.
Substitute A for B.
〔註〕比喻以甲換乙。

1312 偷雞
tɐu¹ gɐi¹ (translit.)
Steal hens. (lit.)
Loaf on the job.
Be idle.
Avail oneself of a leisure moment.
Jery-build.
Scamp the work and stint materials.
〔註〕沒正當理由缺席，開小差，曠課，逃學，磨洋工或偷工減料。

1313 偷雞唔到蝕揸米
tɐu¹ gɐi¹ m⁴ dou² sit⁹ dza¹ mɐi⁵ (translit.)
Try to steal a hen but end up with a loss of a handful of rice. (lit.)
Go for wool and come home shorn.
〔註〕比喻得不到益處，反受損失。

1314 做日和尚唸日經
dzou⁶ jɐt⁹ wɔ⁴ sœŋ² nim⁶ jɐt⁹ giŋ¹ (translit.)
Be a day's monk, chant a day's Buddhist Sutra. (lit.)
Wear through the day.
Be a happy-go-lucky person.
Take a passive attitude towards one's work.
〔註〕相當於"做一天和尚撞一天鐘"。

1315 做世界
dzou⁶ sɐi³ gai³ (translit.)
Do the world. (lit.)
Do an evil deed.
Rob or steal.
〔註〕指爲非作歹，幹行兇，偷盜，搶劫等勾當。

1316 做好做醜
dzou⁶ hou² dzou⁶ tsɐu² (translit.)
Be both good and bad. (lit.)
Both coax and coerce.
With an iron hand in a velvet glove.
〔註〕軟硬兼施或又唱紅臉又唱白臉。

1317 做咗鬼會迷人
dzou⁶ dzɔ² gwɐi² wui⁵ mɐi⁴ jɐn⁴ (translit.)
Enchant people after becoming a ghost. (lit.)
Once a beggar is set on horse back, he will work for devils.
〔註〕喻小人得志便會害人。

1318 做鬼都唔靈

dzou⁶ gwɐi² dou¹ m⁴ lɛŋ⁴ (translit.)
Even though one becomes a ghost, one does not turn out to be marvellous. (lit.)
Be good-for-naught.
〔註〕形容人毫無長處。

1319 做磨心
dzou⁶ mɔ³ sɐm¹ (translit.)
Be an axis of a grinder. (lit.)
Be in a dilemma.
Have difficulty in taking the sides with both parties.
Find it difficult to be partial to either side.
Be an arbitrator.
〔註〕處於爲難境地，各方的關係不好處理，或作調停人的意思。

1320 做慣乞兒懶做官
dzou⁶ gwan³ hɐt⁷ ji⁴ lan⁵ dzou⁶ gun¹ (translit.)
Be too lazy to be an official because of being accustomed to being a beggar. (lit.)
Get used to living in idleness.
〔註〕表示安於目前悠閑自在或懶惰的生活。

1321 做薑唔辣，做醋唔酸
dzou⁶ gœŋ¹ m⁴ lat⁹, dzou⁶ tsou³ m⁴ syn² (translit.)
It is not hot if it is used as ginger; it is not sour if it is used as vinegar. (lit.)
It is far from sufficient for something/the purpose.

〔註〕距離所需要的數目太遠（尤指金錢方面）。

1322 做醜人
dzou⁶ tsɐu² jɐn² (translit.)
Be a bad person. (lit.)
Be scapegoat.
Carry the can.
Speak for somebody.
〔註〕當挨罵的人或替人説話或辯護。

1323 做咗人豬仔/俾人賣豬仔
dzou⁶ dzɔ² jɐn⁴ dzy¹ dzɐi²/ bei² jɐn⁴ mai⁶ dzy¹ dzɐi² (translit.)
Become somebody's piglet/Be sold as a piglet. (lit.)
Be sold/betrayed by somebody.
Be shanghaied into going to... (somewhere).
〔註〕指被人出賣或背叛或被人誘拐去……（地方）。

1324 得上床掀被冚
dɐk⁷ sœŋ⁵ tsɔŋ⁴ hin¹ pei⁵ kɐm² (translit.)
After being permitted to get into bed, one tries to pull a coverlet to cover oneself. (lit.)
Gain an inch and then take an ell.
Be greedy for gains.
〔註〕比喻得寸進尺，貪得無厭。

1325 得寸進尺
dɐk⁷ tsyn³ dzœn³ tsɛk⁸ (translit.)

Gain an inch and then go for a foot. *(lit.)*

Gain an inch and then take an ell.

Be greedy for gains.

1326　得米

dɐk⁷ mɐi⁵　*(translit.)*

Have got the rice. *(lit.)*

Meet with success.

Achieve one's goal.

〔註〕比喻得手或達到目的。

1327　得把聲

dɐk⁷ ba² sɛŋ¹　*(translit.)*

Have only the sound. *(lit.)*

Go on cackling without laying an egg.

In word but not in deed.

〔註〕諷刺人只會說而不見諸行動。

1328　得些好意須回手

dɐk⁷ sɛ¹ hou² ji³ sœy¹ wui⁴ sɐu²　*(translit.)*

Pull in one's hand after gaining a little profit. *(lit.)*

One should leave some leeway after having got some advantage.

Stop before going too far.

Not to overdo it.

〔註〕指得到好處便應留有餘地或勸人切勿過份。

1329　得咗

dɐk⁷ dzɔ²　*(translit.)*

Have got it. *(lit.)*

Come off with flying colours.

Meet with success.

〔註〕參閱"得米"（1326）條。

1330　得戚

dɐk⁷ tsik⁷　*(transit.)*

Get an imperial order. *(lit.)*

Have one's head swelled by being favoured.

Hold one's head high.

Crow over oneself.

〔註〕洋洋自得，得意忘形的意思。

1331　得啖笑

dɐk⁷ dam⁶ siu³　*(translit.)*

Have a puff of laughter. *(lit.)*

Laugh out of court.

Carry off with a laugh.

〔註〕即樂一樂。

1332　得棚牙

dɐk⁷ paŋ⁴ ŋa⁴　*(translit.)*

Have only the haw of teeth. *(lit.)*

Have a loose tongue.

Wag one's tongue.

〔註〕諷刺人絮絮叨叨地説話，但亦可和"得把聲"同義，參閱該條（1327）。

1333　得過且過

dɐk⁷ gwɔ³ tsɛ² gwɔ³　*(translit.)*

Pass and let oneself pass. *(lit.)*

Muddle along.

Fair to muddling.

Not to put undue stree on …

1334　剝光豬

mɔk¹ gwɔŋ¹ dzy¹　*(translit.)*

Make a pig bare. *(lit.)*

Strip oneself/somebody to the skin.

Gamble away.

Be robbed of all one's money.

Take somebody to the cleaners.

〔註〕比喻脫光衣服，輸光或被人搶劫光。

1335 剝花生

mɔk¹ fa¹ sɐŋ¹ (translit.)

Stripp off the husks of peanuts. (lit.)

Become a peanut when going with somebody to have a heavy date.

〔註〕比喻陪人去談情說愛，自己處於無聊的地位。

1336 笨手笨腳

bɐn⁶ sɐu² bɐn⁶ dœk⁸ (translit.)

Foolish hands and legs. (lit.)

One's fingers are all thumbs.

A stumblebum.

1337 笨頭笨腦

bɐn⁶ tɐu⁶ bɐn⁶ nou⁵ (translit.)

Foolish head and brains. (lit.)

Be block-headed.

1338 船到江心補漏遲

syn⁴ dou³ gɔŋ¹ sɐm¹ bou² lɐu⁶ tsi⁴ (translit.)

It is too late to plug a leak when the boat reaches the midstream. (lit.)

It is too late to mend.

It is too late to repent.

〔註〕比喻悔之已晚。

1339 船到橋頭自然直

syn⁴ dou³ kiu⁴ tɐu⁴ dzi⁶ jin⁴ dzik⁹ (translit.)

When the reaches the head of the bridge, it will be naturally straight. (lit.)

Let things slide.

Be submissive to God's will.

Leave it chance.

Don't cross the bridge until you come to it.

〔註〕比喻事到臨頭自然會有辦法，多用於安慰對方。相當"車到山前必有路"。

1340 船頭慌鬼，船尾慌賊

syn⁴ tɐu⁴ fɔŋ¹ gwɐi², syn⁴ mei⁵ fɔŋ¹ tsak⁹ (translit.)

Fear to see a ghost at the prow and a thief at the stern. (lit.)

One's heart misgives one about this and that.

Be between the devil and the deep sea.

Get into a hobble.

Be in a cleft stick.

〔註〕表示擔心這樣，又擔心那樣或進退兩難的意思。

1341 "貪"字變個"貧"

tam¹ dzi⁶ bin³ gɔ³ pɐn⁴ (transit.)

The Chinese character "貪" (read 'tam¹', means 'greed') changes to the character "貧" (read 'pɐn⁴', means 'poverty'). (lit.)

Grasp all, lose all.

〔註〕借兩個形狀近似的漢字來比喻貪心反而損失。

1342 貪得無厭

tam¹ dɐk⁷ mou⁴ jim³ (translit.)

Be too greedy to be insatiable. (lit.)

Be too greedy for gains.
Be as greedy as a hawk.

1343 貧不與富敵，富不與官爭

pɐn⁴ bɐt⁷ jy⁵ fu³ dik⁹, fu³ bɐt⁷ jy⁵ gun¹ dzaŋ¹ (translit.)

The poor can not match against the rich; the rich can not fight against the authorities. (lit.)

Money speaks louder and kings have long arms.

1344 移磡就船

ji⁴ hɐm³ dzɐu⁶ syn⁴ (translit.)

Move the bund to the ship. (lit.)

If the mountain will not come to Mohammed, Mohammed must go to the mountain.

〔註〕比喻女求男去男子的家中幽會或降貴屈尊去遷就某人。

1345 兜踎

dɐu¹ mɐu¹ (translit.)

Be in humble circumstances. (lit.)

Be poverty-striken.

Be shabby in dress.

〔註〕比喻貧困或衣衫襤褸。

1346 兜篤將軍

dɐu¹ duk⁷ dzœŋ¹ gwɐn¹ (translit.)

Turn around to discover check. (lit.)

Shoot a Parthian arrow.
Rip up the back of somebody.

〔註〕比喻向人背後放暗箭或背後中傷或攻擊。

1347 湊啱

tsɐu³ ŋam¹ (translit.)

By any chance. (lit.)

Happen to de something.
In the nick of time.
As luck would have it.

〔註〕剛好，湊巧或恰巧的意思，有時廣東人把"湊蹺"和"湊啱"互相換用。

1348 寅食卯糧

jɐn⁴ sik⁹ mau⁵ lœŋ⁴ (translit.)

At the third of the Twelve Earthly Branches (the period of the day from 3 a.m. to 5 a.m.), eat the cereals which are to be earned at the fourth of the twelve Earthly Banches (the period of the day from 5 a.m. to 7 a.m.). (lit.)

Anticipate one's wages/income.
Have one's corn in the blade.

〔註〕即提前使用工資的意思，參閱"先使未來錢"條（0634）。

1349 密底算盤
mɐt⁹ dɐi² syn³ pun⁴ (translit.)
An abacus with sealed bottom. (lit.)
Penny pincher.
A person who takes much count of every dollar.
〔註〕比喻精打細算的人。

1350 密斟
mɐt⁹ dzɐm¹ (translit.)
A secret talk. (lit.)
A private conversation.
Talk in secret.
〔註〕密談。

1351 密實姑娘假正經
mɐt⁹ sɐt⁹ gu¹ nœn⁴ ga² dziŋ³ giŋ¹ (translit.)
A girl of silent disposition has false seriousness. (lit.)
A girl of few words may not be so serious as she should be.
〔註〕"密實"即沉默寡言的意思。

1352 密鑼緊鼓
mɐt⁹ lɔ⁴ gɐn² gu² (translit.)
Beat the gong and drum very fast. (lit.)
The noose is hanging.
Be intense in preparation for an undertaking.

1353 望天打卦
mɔŋ⁶ tin¹ da² gwa³ (translit.)
Wish heaven to cast lots. (lit.)
Be left to the mercy of God.
Wish to be the mercy of God.
By the finger of God.
〔註〕靠天吃飯,希望上蒼垂憐的意思,參閱"摩囉差拜神"條(1791)。

1354 望長條頸
mɔŋ⁶ tsœŋ⁴ tiu⁴ gɛŋ² (translit.)
Hope makes a neck longer. (lit.)
Pin one's hopes on ...
Hanker after ...
Be looking forward to ...
〔註〕表示渴望的意思。

1355 混水摸魚
wɐn⁶ sœy² mɔ² jy⁴ (translit.)
Grope for fish in turbid waters. (lit.)
Fish in trouble waters.

1356 混吉
wɐn⁶ gɐt⁷ (translit.)
Give trouble. (lit.)
Do something in a haphazard way.
Ask [a shop-assistant] for this and that without making a purchase.
〔註〕表示瞎抓,瞎擺弄或看這樣看那樣而不購買的意思。

1357 混混/渾渾噩噩
wɐn⁶ wɐn⁶ ŋɔk⁹ ŋɔk⁹ (translit.)
Be unintelligent. (lit.)
Be as innocent as a baby.

Be chaotic-headed.
〔註〕表示頭腦渾沌無知的意思。

1358 淘古井
tou⁴ gu² dzɛŋ² *(translit.)*
Clean out an ancient well. (lit.)
Marry with a widow lady of great wealth.
〔註〕比喻娶富有的寡婦。

1359 粗人
tsou¹ jɐn⁴ *(translit.)*
Rough person. (lit.)
A vulgarian.

1360 粗口爛舌
tsou¹ hɐu² lan⁶ sit⁹ *(translit.)*
Rough mouth and rotten tongue. (lit.)
Speak contempible words.
Speak coarse language.
〔註〕即說下流粗鄙的話。

1361 粗心大意
tsou¹ sɐm¹ dai⁶ ji³ *(translit.)*
Careless mind and big idea. (lit.)
Be inadvertent.
〔註〕不細心，馬馬虎虎。

1362 粗手粗腳
tsou¹ sɐu² tsou¹ gœk⁸ *(translit.)*
Thick hands and thick feet. (lit.)
A clumsy person.
Have clumsy fingers.
〔註〕即笨手笨腳。

1363 粗枝大葉
tsou¹ dzi¹ dai⁶ jip⁹ *(translit.)*
Thick branches and big leaves. (lit.)
Be crude and careless.
Be slapdash.
A sloppy job.
〔註〕做事不認真，不細緻。

1364 粗重工夫
tsou¹ tsuŋ⁵ guŋ¹ fu¹ *(translit.)*
Heavy work. (lit.)
Heavy work.

1365 粗茶淡飯
tsou¹ tsa⁴ dam⁶ fan⁶ *(translit.)*
Bad tea and tasteless. cooked-rice. (lit.)
Simple fare.
A homely meal.
Fare plainly.
〔註〕即家常便飯。

1366 粗製濫造
tsou¹ dzɐi³ lam⁶ dzou⁶ *(translit.)*
Rough manufactured and indiscriminately done. (lit.)
Be slipshod in one's work.
Make something in a slipshod way.

1367 粗魯
tsou¹ lou⁵ *(translit.)*
Rough. (lit.)

Be rough and rude.

1368 情人眼裏出西施
tsiŋ⁴ jɐn⁴ ŋan⁵ lœy⁵ tsœt⁷ sɐi¹ si¹ (translit.)
Sɐi Si comes out of a lover's eyes. (lit.)
Sɐi Si — one of the four beauties in ancient China.
Love is blind.
Beauty exists in a lover's eyes.
〔註〕表示美麗是沒有標準的，參閱"兔豬頭都有盟鼻菩薩"條 (1198)。

1369 惦過碌蔗
dim⁶ gwɔ³ luk⁷ dzɛ³ (translit.)
Straighter than a sugar-cane. (lit.)
Come off well.
Have something in the bag.
Have not any trouble with...
Take a path strewn with roses.
〔註〕表示一切順利或生活安樂的意思。

1370 麻麻地
ma⁴ ma⁵ dei² (translit.)
Rather. (lit.)
Be neither good nor bad.
Exceptionally do one/somebody a favour to...
Make a virtue of necessity.
Be constrained to...
〔註〕表示尚好，例外地幫一幫忙或裝出非做不可的勉強。

1371 麻雀雖小，五臟俱全
ma⁴ dzœk⁸ sœy¹ siu², ŋ⁵ dzɔŋ⁶ kœy¹ tsyŋ⁴ (translit.)
A sparrow is small, but it has all five visera. (lit.)
There is a life in a mussel though it is small.

1372 眼大睇過籠/界
ŋan⁵ dai⁶ tɐi² gwɔ³ luŋ⁴/gai² (translit.)
The eyes are so big that they see beyond the line. (lit.)
Be too careless to see anything.
〔註〕心粗看不細。

1373 眼火爆
ŋan⁵ fɔ² bau³ (translit.)
The fire of eyes bursts. (lit.)
See red.
Fly into a rage.
〔註〕指看到令人氣憤的事而憤怒。

1374 眼中釘
naŋ⁵ dzuŋ¹ dɐŋ¹ (translit.)
The nail in the eye. (lit.)
A thorn in one's flesh.
A pain in the neck.

1375 眼坦坦
ŋan⁵ tan² tan² (translit.)
Show the whites of eyes. (lit.)
In a desperate state.
To an unbearable degree.
To the state of fatigue.
In a situation of complete defeat.
〔註〕照字面看，似和普通話的"翻白眼"同意。但廣東話的含義應爲在絕望中，到了難以忍受的地

步或處於完全失敗的境地。部分意義和"攤攤腰"同,參閱該條(1973)。

1376 眼甘甘
ŋan⁵ gɐm¹ gɐm¹ (translit.)
Look fixedly. (lit.)
Fix one's eyes upon...
Not to take one's eyes off...
〔註〕形容貪婪地,目不轉睛地盯看的樣子。

1377 眼紅
ŋan⁵ huŋ⁴ (translit.)
Eyes become red. (lit.)
Be jealous of...
Feel envy at...
〔註〕表示忌妒的意思。

1378 眼眉毛長過辮
ŋan⁵ mei⁴ mou⁴ tsœŋ⁴ gwɔ³ bin¹ (translit.)
The eyebrows are longer than a pigtail. (lit.)
Be very lazy.
Not to stir a finger.
〔註〕諷刺人懶得動也不動。

1379 眼眉毛雕通瓏
ŋan⁵ mei⁴ mou⁴ diu¹/tiu¹ tuŋ¹ luŋ² (translit.)
The eyebrows are carved to be tubular. (lit.)
Be up to snuff.
There are no flies on one.
Be sharp-witted.
Have a keen insight into matters.
〔註〕比喻精明,不易受騙或明察秋毫。

1380 眼唔見為伶俐
ŋan⁵ m⁴ gin³ wɐi⁴ liŋ⁴ lei⁶ (translit.)
Anything that is not seen by eyes is clear/clean. (lit.)
Out of sight, out of mind.
〔註〕相當於"眼不見,心不煩"。

1381 眼斬斬
ŋan⁵ dzam² dzam² (translit.)
The eyes wink. (lit.)
Be expressionless.
A dull look passes over one's face.
〔註〕指無表情或臉上顯出無可奈何的神色。

1382 眼淺
ŋan⁵ tsin² (translit.)
The eyes are shallow. (lit.)
Be narrow-minded.
Be intolerant of...
Be jealous of...
Be apt to be moved to tears.
〔註〕指人小氣,心胸狹窄,妒忌或易受感動而流淚。

1383 眼冤
ŋan⁵ jyn¹ (translit.)
The grievance of eyes. (lit.)
Be disgusted at...
Take an aversion to...
Feel a repugnance to...
〔註〕指看見不好的事物或情景就討厭,反感。

1384 眼䁖䁖

ŋan⁵ luk¹ luk¹　(translit.)
The eyes roll.　(lit.)
Look at somebody with angry eyes.
Glower at somebody.
〔註〕即怒目而視。

1385　眼闊肚窄
ŋan⁵ fut⁸ tou⁵ dzak⁸　(translit.)
Eyes are broad but the belly is narrow.　(lit.)
Bite off more than one can chew.
〔註〕表示貪心不足或心有餘而力不足的意思。

1386　眼噬噬
ŋan⁵ sɐi⁶ sɐi⁶　(translit.)
The eyes seem to swallow up.　(lit.)
Look sideways at somebody in order to prevent him from doing something.
〔註〕同"眼睭睭"條。

1387　眼掘掘
ŋan⁵ gwɐt⁹ gwɐt⁹　(translit.)
Keep the eyes fixed.　(lit.)
Glare hate at somebody.
Stare at somebody with hostility.
〔註〕表示以仇恨的眼光或敵意盯着人的意思。

1388　眼睭睭
ŋan⁵ lɐi⁶ lɐi⁶　(translit.)
Give a signal with eyes.　(lit.)
Look sideways at somebody in order to stop him from doing something.
〔註〕即斜視着某人意圖制止他某事。

1389　眼濕濕
ŋan⁵ sɐp⁷ sɐp⁷　(translit.)
The eyes are getting wet.　(lit.)
One's eyes are filled with tears.
〔註〕眼睛帶着淚花的樣子。

1390　啋
tsɔi¹　(translit.)
Go with you!　(lit.)
Bah!
〔註〕婦女多用以表示嫌棄或斥責的感嘆詞，相當於"去你的"。

1391　啞仔食雲吞——心中有數
a² dzɐi² sik⁹ wɐn⁴ tɐn¹ — sɐm¹ dzuŋ¹ jɐu⁵ sou³　(translit.)
A dumb eats stuffed dumplings — his mind knows the number.　(lit.)
Know what to do.
Know a thing or two.
Know what is what.

1392　啞仔食黃連——有苦自己知——有口難言
a² dzɐi² sik⁹ wɔŋ⁴ lin⁴ — jɐu⁵ fu² dzi⁶ gei² dzi¹ (—jɐu⁵ hau² nan⁴ jin⁴)　(translit.)
A dumb eats coptis roots — knowing the bitterness by

himself.
—having mouth but finding it hard to speak. (lit.)
Swallow the leek.
Have lost one's tongue.
Take the bitter without a word.

1393 啱心水「緒」
ŋam¹ sɐm¹ sœy² (translit.)
Suit one's heart. (lit.)
After one's own heart.
After one's fancy.
〔註〕表示合意的意思。參閱"合晒心水"條（0642）"合晒合尺"條（0643）。

1394 啱啱好
ŋam¹ ŋam¹ hou² (translit.)
Just right. (lit.)
To the turn of a hair.
Be as right as nails.
〔註〕表示剛好，絲毫不差或十分正確的意思。

1395 唱衰人
tsœŋ³ sœy¹ jɐn⁴ (translit.)
Sing somebody to be on the wane. (lit.)
Paint somebody in dark colour.
Put false colours upon somebody.
〔註〕説得人一錢不值的意思。

1396 崩口人忌崩口碗
bɐŋ¹ hɐu² jɐn⁴ gei⁶ bɐŋ¹ hɐu² wun² (translit.)
A man with hare-lip shuns the bowl with broken brim. (lit.)

Not to stroke somebody's hair the wrong way.
Avoid touching somebody on the raw.
Not to sting somebody to the quick.
〔註〕表示避諱或別觸及人的痛處，相當於"別當着矮人説短話"。

1397 患得患失
wan⁶ dɐk⁷ wan⁶ sɐt⁷ (translit.)
Worry about personal gains and losses. (lit.)
Be swayed by considerations of success and failure.

1398 患難見真情
wan⁶ nan⁶ gin³ dzɐŋ¹ tsiŋ⁴ (translit.)
Calamity exposes the true affection. (lit.)
A friend in need is a friend indeed.
Calamity is the true touch-stone.

1399 蛇有蛇路，鼠有鼠路
sɛ⁴ jɐu⁵ sɛ⁴ lou⁶, sy² jɐu⁵ sy² lou⁶ (translit.)
Snakes have their won way and mice also have their way. (lit.)
Gang one's own gait.
Play a lone hand.
Each follows his own bent.
〔註〕表示各有各的打算或各行各是的意思。

1400 蛇見硫磺

sɛ⁴ gin³ lɐu⁴ wɔŋ⁴ (translit.)
Snakes see sulphur. (lit.)
Everybody has his vanquisher.
Diamond cut diamond.
〔註〕表示各有相剋的意思，參閱
"一物治一物，糯米治木蝨"條
（0025）。

1401 蛇無頭不行
sɛ⁴ mou⁴ tɐu⁴ bɐt⁷ hɐŋ⁴
(translit.)
A snake can not crawl without a head. (lit.)
Without a man in the lead, all the others move no farther.
〔註〕表示沒有人帶頭，事情難成。

1402 蛇鼠一窩
sɛ⁴ sy² jɐt⁷ wɔ¹ (translit.)
Snakes and mice live together in the same den. (lit.)
Gang up with each other.
Be in collusion with each other.
Play booty.
〔註〕朋比爲奸的意思。

1403 蛇頭鼠眼
sɛ⁴ tɐu⁴ sy² ŋan⁵ (translit.)
Snake's head and rat's eyes. (lit.)
Be as crafty as a fox.
Be wily.
〔註〕相當於"鬼頭蛤蟆眼"。

1404 陪太子讀書
pui⁴ tai³ dzi² duk⁹ sy¹
(translit.)
Accompany the Crown Prince to study. (lit.)
Bear somebody company.
Do something with somebody for company.
〔註〕比喻陪人做某事。

1405 陰濕
jɐm¹ sɐp⁷ (translit.)
Both gloomy and wet. (lit.)
Be vicious.
Be insidious.
〔註〕形容人狡猾，陰險。

1406 陳皮
tsɐn⁴ pei⁴ (translit.)
Old skin. (lit.)
Dried orange peel.
Old-fashioned.
Be stale.
〔註〕"陳皮"本爲廣東三寶（陳皮、老薑及禾桿草）之一，是由柑皮曬乾而成，用作藥材。貯藏年份越久價值越高，正由此因，遂轉喻陳舊的或舊式樣。

1407 陳村種
tsɐn⁴ tsyn¹ dzuŋ² (translit.)
The clan of Tsɐn Tsyn. (lit.)
A fop with money to burn a hole in his pocket.
〔註〕比喻有錢便要花光的人。（陳村爲順德縣屬的一小村落）。

1408 陸雲庭睇相 —— 冇衰攞嚟衰——（冇衰整成衰）
luk⁹ wɐn⁴ tiŋ⁴ tɐi² sœŋ³ —
mou⁵ sœy¹ lɔ² lɐi⁴ sœy¹ —
mou⁵ sœy¹ dziŋ² sɐn⁴ sœy¹
(translit.)

A man named Luk Wɐn Tiŋ had his phylognomy read,
—not so poor but pretended to reduce to poverty.
—not in distress but invited the distress himself. (lit.)

Feign oneself to be poor.
Bring disgrace to oneself.
Offer an insult to oneself.
Pocket an insult.

〔註〕軍閥陸雲庭化裝成貧民去找一位享譽甚高的相士看相，目的想考驗那相士的相術，及知自己的前途，詎料該相士一看便看出他不是普通人，於是把他譏諷一番。"冇衰整成衰"意謂扮窮，"冇衰攞嚟衰"意謂被人譏諷或自取其辱。

1409 通水
tuŋ¹ sœy² (translit.)
Let out the water. (lit.)
Give information to somebody.
Disclose secret information.

〔註〕通風報信的意思。

1410 通氣
tuŋ¹ hei³ (translit.)
Ventilate. (lit.)
Have more sense than to hinder somebody.
Show sombody every consideration.

〔註〕形容人通情達理得不致於防礙別人或體貼人。

1411 蛋家婆打仔 —— 唔慌你走得上坦
dan⁶ ga¹ pɔ² da² dzɐi² —m⁴ fɔŋ¹ nei⁵ dzɐu² dɐk⁷ sœn⁵ tan² (translit.)
A Tanka (the boat people of Canton) woman beats her son—not fearing you can run to the sand. (lit.)
Put somebody at the dead end.
Drive somebody to bay.

〔註〕相當於"大缸擲骰子 —— 沒跑兒"，意謂"無路可走"。

1412 蛋家婆打醮 —— 冇壇「彈」
dan⁶ ga¹ pɔ² da² dziu³ —mou⁵ tan⁴ (translit.)
Tanka women celebrate the feast of 'All Souls'—No altar (no criticism). (lit.)
Be above criticism.
Be beyond reproach.

〔註〕蛋家以艇爲家，打醮酧神時，限於地方，不能擺設祭壇，"壇"和"彈"同音，借這諧音喻無可批評或指責。

1413 蛋家婆摸蜆 —— 第二篩「世」
dan⁶ ga¹ pɔ² mɔ² hin² —dɐi⁶ ji⁶ sɐi¹ᐟ³ (translit.)
Tanka women grope for clams—until next sieve (generation). (lit.)
Have hope in nine cases out of ten.
Have difficulties in realizing one's aspiration as long as one lives.

〔註〕比喻今生已成絕望,唯有希望來世(第二世)。"世"是"篩"的諧音,至於俚語的來源,有待查考。

1414 蛋家雞 —— 見水唔得飲
dan⁶ ga¹ gɐi¹ —— gin³ sœy² m⁴ dɐk⁷ jɐm² *(translit.)*
The chickens of Tanka — they are unable to drink the water in sight. (lit.)
The person who fails to obtain an advantage in spite of being in a favourable position.
Always have opportunities to near somebody one loves on the sly but never have an opportunity to win her/him.
〔註〕蛋家在艇上養雞,但雞並不因身處近水的地方而能喝到見到的水,因此這俚語在廣義上喻並不因自己身處有利的地位而得到好處,在狹義上則喻雖常有機會接近自己暗中熱戀的人,但從沒有機會得到她(他)。

1415 問師姑攞梳 —— 實冇
mɐn⁶ si¹ gu¹ lɔ² sɔ¹ —— sɐt⁹ mou⁵ *(translit.)*
Ask a nun for a comb — sure to have none. (lit.)
Ask the wrong person for something.
Come to the wrong shop.
〔註〕相當於"和尚廟裏借梳子 —— 走錯門了"。

1416 終須有日龍穿鳳
dzuŋ¹ sœy¹ jɐu⁵ jɐt⁹ luŋ⁴ tsyn¹ fuŋ⁶ *(translit.)*
A dragon will one day marry a phoenix. (lit.)
Every cloud has a silver lining.
Every dog has his day.
Everyone would have a chance to stand head and shoulder above others.
Will free oneself from misery one day.
〔註〕指人人皆有出頭日。

1417 細心
sɐi³ sɐm¹ *(translit.)*
Small-hearted. (lit.)
Be tender to attend upon somebody.
Be attentive to somebody/something.
Attend upon somebody with meticulous care.
〔註〕表示當心照料或體貼入微的意思。

1418 細水長流
sɐi³ sœy² tsœŋ⁴ lɐu⁴ *(translit.)*
A small stream flows long. (lit.)
Waste not, want not.
A bit at a time causes no letup.
〔註〕比喻節約,有計劃的用錢可保持不缺。有時也用來比喻經常不間斷地做某事。

1419 細時偷雞,大時偷牛
sɐi³ si⁴ tɐu¹ gɐi¹, dai⁶ si⁴ tɐu¹

ŋɐu⁴ *(translit.)*
Stealing hens in young days will lead to steal cows in the days of adulthood. (lit.)
Young pilferer, old robber.
A child who maltreats animals in his childhood will become a killer in his young days.
〔註〕比喻兒時犯錯，長大成人犯罪。

1420 細佬哥剃頭
sɐi³ lou² gɔ¹ tɐi³ tɐu⁴ *(translit.)*
A small child has his head shaved. (lit.)
Will be ready/finished in no time.
Will soon complete/finish...
〔註〕比喻事物很快便準備好/完成或很快便完成……（工作）。

1421 將……一軍
dzœŋ¹....jɐt⁷ gwɐn¹ *(translit.)*
Challenge somebody. (lit.)
Embarrass somebody.
Lay a complaint against somebody with...
〔註〕表示使某人窘迫或向……告某人一狀的意思。

1422 將/攞……嚟教飛
dzœŋ¹/lɔ²....lɐi⁴ gau³ fei¹ *(translit.)*
Look for somebody/something to be taught to fly. (lit.)
Put somebody/something to trial.
〔註〕指把某人/某物作試驗品。

1423 將心比己
dzœŋ¹ sɐm¹ bei² gei² *(translit.)*
Compare oneself with other's heart. (lit.)
Measure another's foot by one's own last.
Measure other's corn by one's own bushel.
〔註〕以己度人的意思。

1424 將佢拳頭抌佢嘴
dzœŋ¹ kœy⁵ kyn⁴ tɐu⁴ dɐm² kœy⁵ dzœy² *(translit.)*
Knock somebody's mouth with his own fist. (lit.)
Pay somebody back in his own coin.
Return like for like.
Turn somebody's battery against himself.
Give sombody a gift of the same value as that he has given out.
〔註〕比喻"以其人之道還治其人之身"，"以子之矛攻子之盾"或用同等價值的禮物回敬。

1425 將計就計
dzœŋ¹ gei³ dzɐu⁶ gei³ *(translit.)*
Let the plot be the plot. (lit.)
Turn somebody's tricks against him.

1426 將就
dzœŋ¹ dzɐu⁶ *(translit.)*

Compromise. (lit.)
Make do with...
Put up with...
Accommodate oneself to...
〔註〕勉強適應不滿意的事物或環境。

1427 將錯就錯
dzœŋ¹ tsɔ³ dzɐu⁶ tsɔ³
(translit.)
Let the mistake be the mistake. (lit.)
Make the best of a bad job.
Make the best of a mistake.
Over shoes over boots.
〔註〕既然錯了，索性利用錯誤去補償的意思。

十二畫

1428 惡人自有惡人磨
ɔk⁸ yɐn⁴ dzi⁶ jɐu⁵ ɔk⁸ jɐn⁴ mɔ⁴ (translit.)
An ill person will be ill-treated by other evil persons. (lit.)
Diamond cut diamond.
Devils devil devils.

1429 惡人先告狀
ɔk⁸ jɐn⁴ sin¹ gou³ dzɔŋ²ᐟ⁴
(translit.)
An evil man brings in an indictment first. (lit.)
Take a preemptive step.
〔註〕即先發制人，參閱"使銅銀夾

大聲"條（0902）。

1430 惡有惡報
ɔk⁸ jɐu⁵ ɔk⁸ bou³ (translit.)
Evil doings recompense evil returns. (lit.)
Sow the wind and reap the whirl-wind.
Curses come home to roost.
Recompense somebody for his misdeeds.

1431 惡到凸堆
ɔk⁸ dou³ dɐt⁹ dœy¹ (translit.)
Be ferocious to the top degree. (lit.)
Play the bully.
〔註〕形容恃強凌弱的姿態。

1432 惡恐人知便是大惡
ɔk⁸ huŋ² jɐn⁴ dzi¹ bin⁶ si⁶ dai⁶ ɔk⁸ (translit.)
The ferociousness that is hidden is a great piece of ferociousness. (lit.)
The sins dissembled are deadly sins indeed.

1433 朝上有人好做官
tsiu⁴ sœŋ⁶ jɐu⁵ jɐn⁴ hou² dzou⁶ gun¹ (translit.)
It is easy to be an official if one has a friend at court. (lit.)
Make convenience of a friend at court.
〔註〕自己的朋友有了地位或權力自己總得個方便或辦事容易。

1434 朝種樹，晚剝板

dziu¹ dzuŋ³ sy⁶, man⁵ gai³ ban² *(translit.)*

Plant trees in the morning and cut them into planks in the evening. (lit.)

Live from hand to mouth.
Live beyond one's means.

〔註〕比喻不足溫飽或朝食晚糧。

1435 替死鬼

tɐi³ sei² gwɐi² *(translit.)*

The ghost takes somebody's place to die. (lit.)

A whipping boy.
The person who carries the can.
A scapegoat.

〔註〕比喻代人受過的人,參閱"烏狗得食,白狗當災"(1174)或"做醜人"(1322)條。

1436 黃皮樹鷯哥 —— 唔熟唔食

wɔŋ⁴ pei⁴ sy⁶ liu¹ gɔ¹ —— m⁴ suk⁹ m⁴ sik⁹ *(translit.)*

The mynah on a whampee tree —It does not eat the unripe fruit. (lit.)

The person who swindles money out of his familiar friends.
The person who sells a pup to his close friends.

〔註〕歇後語中的"熟"字和"食"字,都是語帶雙關的。意為專欺騙熟人或向熟人推銷次品。

1437 黃泡髧熟

wɔŋ⁴ pɐu¹ dɐm³ suk⁹ *(translit.)*

Yellow and swollen. (lit.)

A swollen face with yellow complexion.

〔註〕形容人面目浮腫或臉色萎黃。

1438 黃馬褂

wɔŋ⁴ ma⁵ gwa³ *(translit.)*

A yellow riding jacket. (Yellow riding jackets were given to royalties by the emperors of the T'sing Dynasty as a mark of honour.) (lit.)

The clerk related to the boss.

〔註〕比喻和老闆有親屬關係的職員。由於"黃馬褂"為清代的一種官服,巡行扈從大臣,如御前大臣、內大臣、內廷王大臣、侍衞什長皆例准穿黃馬褂,有功大臣也特賜穿着,表璋他的功勳,因而得這口頭語。

1439 黃綠醫生

wɔŋ⁴ luk⁹ ji¹ sɐŋ¹ *(translit.)*

Yellow and green doctor. (lit.)

A charlatan.

〔註〕指庸醫,不學無術的大夫,醫術不高明,靠行醫騙錢。

1440 黃腫腳 —— 不消蹄「提」

wɔŋ⁴ dzuŋ² gœk⁸ —— bɐt⁷ siu¹ tɐi⁴ *(translit.)*

Dropsy leg —the swelling of the trotter is not dispersed. (lit.)

Make no mention of it.
(The character '蹄' which means 'trotter' is the homonyn to the

character '提' which means 'mention'.)

〔註〕借"蹄"字諧音作"提"用，意爲不必提了。

1441 硬晒骹
ŋaŋ²/⁶ sai³ tai⁵ (translit.)
The steer becomes stiff. (lit.)
Bring to a deadlock.
Be immovable.

〔註〕指事情鬧僵了，完全沒希望了。但又形容動彈不得。

1442 報效
bou³ hau⁶ (translit.)
Offer service. (lit.)
Be free of charge.

〔註〕即免費。

1443 越揼越出屎
jyt⁹ gɐm⁶ jyt⁹ tœt⁷ si²
(translit.)
The more presure, the more manure. (lit.)
The more one speaks, the more secret one lets out.
The harder somebody is pressed to say, the more secret he reveals.

〔註〕這俚語可用於主動或被動兩方面，主動意爲越講越洩漏多些內幕，被動則意爲被迫越甚，所洩漏的秘密也越多。

1444 越窮越見鬼，肚餓打瀉米
jyt⁹ kuŋ⁴ jyt⁹ gin³ gwɐi²
tou⁵ ŋɔ⁶ da² sɛ³ mɐi⁵
(translit.)
The poorer one is, the more ghosts one sees; one upsets all the rice when one feels hungry. (lit.)
Misfortunes never come singly.
Go from bad to worse.
So much the worse.

〔註〕表示更加糟糕或禍不單行的意思，參閱"屋漏更兼逢夜雨"條（1102）。

1445 趁手
tsɐn³ sɐu² (translit.)
Take advantage of the hand. (lit.)
In passing.
At one's convenience.
When it is convenient.
Take the opportunity.

〔註〕順手或乘機的意思。

1446 散更鑼
san³ gɐŋ³ lɔ⁴ (translit.)
The last alarm of a watchman's gong. (lit.)
A flourish of trumpets.
A horn-blower.
The person who bandies something about.
(The last alarm of watchman's gong is beaten at dawn, indicating that it is going to be daybreak.)

〔註〕比喻到處散播謠言或其他消息的人（尤指婦女）。往時廣東省各地有更夫報時，夜裏每隔一段時間便敲小鼓及小鑼，到黎明時，密敲小鑼，意味天明，這便

是"散更鑼"。

1447 散檔
san³ dɔŋ³ (translit.)
Disassemble the stall. (lit.)
Disband.
Break off the partnership with somebody.
Make trouble.
Undermine somebody.
〔註〕表示散伙或結束，但亦表示搗亂或拆臺的意思。

1448 搏一搏
bɔk⁸ jɐt⁷ bɔk⁸ (translit.)
Gamble for once. (lit.)
Take a risk.
Risk the jump.
〔註〕表示冒一冒險的意思。

1449 搏命
bɔk⁸ mɛŋ⁶ (translit.)
Fight for life. (lit.)
Make every effort.
For dear life.
〔註〕即拚命。

1450 搏亂
bɔk⁸ lun⁶ (translit.)
Make use of the confusion. (lit.)
Fish in trouble water.
Take advantage of the confused situation.
〔註〕即混水摸魚，參閱該條（1355）。

1451 搏懵
bɔk⁸ muŋ² (translit.)
Try to gain a muddle of something. (lit.)

Hope for an advantage by making use of somebody's negligence.
〔註〕即利用別人不留神，不警惕而得到好處。相當於"鑽空子"。

1452 搵……（人）過橋
wɐn²....gwɔ³ kiu² (translit.)
Look for somebody to walk across the bridge. (lit.)
Make use of somebody as a cat's paw.
Play upon somebody.
〔註〕用不正當手段利用別人達到自己目的。

1453 搵老襯
wɐn² lou⁵ tsɐn³ (translit.)
Look for a dupe. (lit.)
Attract somebody to rise to a bait.
Fool somebody into doing something.
Fool money out of somebody.
Make somebody fall into dupery.
〔註〕騙人；使人上當受騙；使人吃虧。

1454 搵丁
wɐn² diŋ¹ (translit.)
Look for the foolish ones. (lit.)
〔註〕同"搵老襯"（1453）。

1455 搵笨
wɐn² bɐn⁶ (translit.)
Look for the foolish ones. (lit.)

〔註〕騙人；騙；討便宜。同"搵丁"（1454）。

1456 搵得嚟使得去
wɐn² dɐk⁷ lɐi⁴, sɐi² dɐk⁷ hœy² *(translit.)*
Find it and spend it. (lit.)
Easy come, easy go.
Light come, light go.
〔註〕比喻金錢"來的容易去的快"。

1457 揦手唔成勢
la² sɐu² m⁴ siŋ⁴ sɐi³ *(translit.)*
Set a hand to something but fail to make a formation. (lit.)
Be tied up in knots due to lack of preview.
Find it difficult to work in a hopeless mess.
〔註〕棘手，難辦，或在一團糟的情形下，做起來樣樣事都棘手。

1458 揦西
la² sɐi¹ *(translit.)*
Rough out something. (lit.)
Scamp one's work.
〔註〕工作馬虎或隨便。

1459 揦起塊面
na²/la² hei² fai³ min⁶ *(translit.)*
Stretch the face tight. (lit.)
Pull a long face.
〔註〕相當於奓拉着臉。

1460 揦屎上身
la² si² sœŋ⁵ sɐn¹ *(translit.)*
Grasp manure and bring it on to the body. (lit.)
Invite trouble.
Wake a sleeping dog.
Make a rod for one's own back.
〔註〕比喻自找麻煩或自作自受，參閱"木匠擔枷"條（0244）。

1461 揦高肚皮
la² gou¹ tou⁵ pei⁴ *(translit.)*
Lift up the skin of belly. (lit.)
Give the show away.
Expose one's own weak sides.
〔註〕暴露自己弱點的意思。

1462 揦脷
la² lei⁶ *(translit.)*
Sting the tongue. (lit.)
Haggle over every penny.
Be high-priced.
Open one's mouth wide.
〔註〕比喻因要價過高或成本太高，受不了的意思。

1463 揭盅
kit⁷ dzuŋ¹ *(translit.)*
Lift up the cover of a teacup. (lit.)
Make known.
Bring to light.
〔註〕即揭鍋或披露。

1464 提心吊膽
tɐi⁴ sɐm¹ diu³ dam² *(translit.)*
Lift up the heart and hang the gall. (lit.)
Have one's heart in one's mouth.
Be in a blue funk.
Be on tenterhooks.

〔註〕形容非常擔心，害怕，慌恐不安。

1465 揞/拚住良心
ɐm³ dzy⁶ lœŋ⁴ sɐm¹ (translit.)
Cover the good heart with a hand. (lit.)
Be conscience-smitten.
Have the conscience to do something.
〔註〕表示自受良心責備或竟敢不顧良心而厚着臉皮去做……。

1466 揞/拚住嘴嚛笑
ɐm³ dzy⁶ dzœy² lɐi⁴ siu³ (translit.)
Cover the mouth with a hand and laugh. (lit.)
Laugh at somebody in one's sleeve.
〔註〕暗暗譏笑某人的意思。

1467 揸大葵扇
dza¹ dai⁶ kwɐi⁴ sin³ (translit.)
Hold a big fan made out of mallow leaves. (lit.)
Be a match-maker.
Act as a go-between.
〔註〕即作媒。在一般人心目中，至少在戲劇角色的造型上，大凡媒婆都手拿葵扇，象徵把男女雙方"撥成"（撮合）。

1468 揸住雞毛當令箭
dza¹ dzy⁶ gɐi¹ mou⁴ dɔŋ³ liŋ⁶ dzin³ (translit.)
Hold a fowl's feather as an arrow-token of authority. (lit.)
Steal the show of an authoritative person.
Put on airs.
Bully somebody on other's power.
〔註〕即"狐假虎威"，借別人的權勢唬人。

1469 揸頸就命
dza¹ gɛŋ² dzɐu⁶ mɛŋ⁶ (translit.)
Grasp the neck to procrastinate the life. (lit.)
Bear and forbear to save life.
Suffer from the patience of Job.
Submit to humiliation to cope with the situation.
〔註〕忍辱偷生或爲應付目前環境而忍氣吞聲的意思。

1470 揩牛黃
saŋ² ŋɐu⁴ wɔŋ⁴ (translit.)
Seize cow bezoa. (lit.)
Bully somebody and snatch something from him.
〔註〕強取或強佔他人的東西；勒索。

1471 揞金龜
dɐp⁸ gɐm¹ gwɐi¹ (translit.)
Knock a gold tortoise. (lit.)
Put the arm on one's wife.
Ask one's wife for money.
〔註〕指向妻子要錢花。

1472 揼堆
dɐm³ dœy¹ (translit.)

Lack of pace. *(lit.)*
Be both doddery and obtuse.
Be penniless and frustrated.
〔註〕形容老態龍鐘，參閱"論盡"（1784）條，但又表示貧困潦倒的意思。

1473 㧣爛塊面
wɛ²/wa² lan⁶ fai³ min⁶ *(translit.)*
Scratch the face and make it become rotten. *(lit.)*
Fly in the face of dignity.
Have the cheek to do something.
Have no sense of shame.
〔註〕抓破了臉皮或不顧羞恥的意思。

1474 棚尾拉箱
paŋ⁴ mei⁵ lai¹ sœŋ¹ *(translit.)*
Drag trunks at the end of a shed. *(lit.)*
Come to a disgraceful end.
Meet with an ignominious fate.
〔註〕指遭遇並不光榮的下場。粵劇演員叫演出的地方爲"戲棚"。如在演出時，開面，做手或唱工偶有出錯，便被對粵劇有認識的觀衆大喝倒彩，而這個演員就要下臺，靜靜悄悄地由後臺（棚尾）拉箱（搬走衣箱的意思）而去了。

1475 棋差一着
kei⁴ tsa¹ jɐt⁷ dzœk⁹ *(translit.)*

Make a careless move. *(lit.)*
Lose a move to somebody.

1476 棋高一着
kei⁴ gou¹ jɐt⁷ dzœk⁹ *(translit.)*
One move ahead. *(lit.)*
Be a stroke above somebody.

1477 棋逢敵手
kei⁴ fuŋ⁴ dik⁹ sɐu² *(translit.)*
Meet a rival in the chess tournament. *(lit.)*
Be well-matched.
Nip and tuck.
〔註〕旗鼓相當或技藝等不相上下的意思。

1478 腌尖
jim¹ dzim¹ *(translit.)*
Find faults. *(lit.)*
Strain at a gnat.
Split hairs over something.
Pick and choose.
Pick hole in something.
〔註〕愛挑剔的或好吹毛求疵的。

1479 腌悶
jim¹ mun⁶ *(translit.)*
Be vexed. *(lit.)*
Vex oneself.
Be upset.
〔註〕表示獨自煩惱或心煩的意思。如說對方爲"腌悶"時，則爲"腌尖腥悶"的簡畧語，見1480條。

1480 腌尖腥悶
jim¹ dzim¹ sɛŋ² mun⁶ *(translit.)*

Be hard to please. (lit.)
Be hard to please.
Be choosey.
Pick and choose.
〔註〕指難以取悦的或因愛挑剔，太講究而令人討厭的。

1481 無孔不入
mou⁴ huŋ² bɐt⁷ jɐp⁹ *(translit.)*
Not to enter where there is no hole. (lit.)
Seize every opportunity.
〔註〕表示把握每一個機會的意思，含貶義。

1482 無功不受祿
mou⁴ guŋ¹ bɐt⁷ sɐu⁶ luk⁹ *(translit.)*
Not to get a reward for not having merit. (lit.)
Refuse to be paid for doing nothing.

1483 無名小卒
mou⁴ miŋ⁴ siu² dzœt⁷ *(translit.)*
A nameless soldier. (lit.)
A mere nobody.
〔註〕指不見經傳的小人物。

1484 無私顯見私
mou⁴ si¹ hin² gin³ si¹ *(translit.)*
In spite of being not selfish, the selfish motives are clearly seen. (lit.)
Selfreveal one's own guilty conscience in spite of being irrelative with the trouble.
〔註〕表示事件雖和自己無關，但亦不經心地流露出自己的心虛的意思。

1485 無官一身輕
mou⁴ gun¹ jɐt⁷ sɐn¹ hiŋ¹ hɐŋ¹ *(translit.)*
It makes the body lighter to have no office. (lit.)
Without burden, without worriment.
Free from office, free from care.
〔註〕比喻一旦卸下責任，輕鬆得多。

1486 無事不登三寶殿
mou⁴ si⁶ bɐt⁷ dɐŋ¹ sam¹ pou² din⁶ *(translit.)*
If one had nothing, one would not go up to the temple-hall of Buddhist Trinity. (lit.)
Have an axe to grind.
〔註〕比喻沒有事不上門。

1487 無事生非
mou⁴ si⁶ saŋ¹ fei¹ *(translit.)*
Cause trouble out of nothing. (lit.)
Make trouble out of nothing.
〔註〕無緣無故挑起事端，製造麻煩。參閱"無風三尺浪"（1490）條。

1488 無事忙
mou⁴ si⁶ mɔŋ⁴ *(translit.)*
Busy for nothing. (lit.)
Make much ado about nothing.

Be busy with nothing.

1489 無事獻慇勤，非奸即盜

mou⁴ si⁶ hin³ jɐn¹ kɐn⁴, fei¹ gan¹ dzik⁷ dou⁶ (translit.)

When somebody pays attentions to you without any cause, he is either an artful villain or a thief. (lit.)

Too much solicitous hospitality without any cause would be considered as an ill deed.

1490 無風三尺浪

mou⁴ fuŋ¹ sam¹ tsɛk⁸ lɔŋ⁶ (translit.)

Three-foot-high waves rise without wind. (lit.)

Invent a baseless slander.

Make trouble out of nothing.

〔註〕參閱"無事生非"（1487）條。

1491 無風不起浪

mou⁴ fuŋ¹ bɐt⁷ hei² lɔŋ⁶ (translit.)

There are no waves without wind. (lit.)

There is no smoke without fire.

Nothing is stolen without hands.

Every why has its wherefore.

〔註〕比喻事出有因，參閱"石檳榔唔嗻得出汁"（0290）條。

1492 無情白事

mou⁴ tsiŋ⁴ bak⁹ si⁶ (translit.)

Have not anything. (lit.)

Without reason or cause.

All of a sudden.

〔註〕表示無緣無故或忽然間的意思，參閱"無端端"（1497），"無端白事"（1496）及"無啹啹"（1495）各條。

1493 無聊賴

mou⁴ liu⁴ lai⁶ (translit.)

Have not any resources. (lit.)

Feel bored.

Be dispirited.

Idle away one's time/days.

〔註〕無聊或無事可幹而虛度時光。

1494 無債一身輕

mou⁴ dzai³ jɐt⁷ sɐn¹ hiŋ¹ / hɛŋ¹ (translit.)

It makes the body lighter to have no debts. (lit.)

Out of debt, out of burden.

1495 無啹啹

mou⁴ ŋa¹ ŋa¹ (translit.)

Have not any hints. (lit.)

Without reason or cause.

All of a sudden.

〔註〕參閱"無端端"（1497），"無端白事"（1496）及"無情白事"（1492）各條。

1496 無端白事

mou⁴ dyn¹ bak⁹ si⁶ (translit.)

Have not any hints. (lit.)

Without reason or cause.

All of a sudden.

〔註〕參閱"無端端"（1497），"無情白事"（1492）及"無啹啹"（1495）各條。

1497 無端端

mou⁴ dyn¹ dyn¹　(translit.)
Have not any clues.　(lit.)
Without reason or cause.
All of a sudden.
〔註〕參閱"無端白事"（1496），
"無情白事"（1492）及"無啱啱"
（1495）各條。

1498　無端端發達
mou⁴ dyn¹ dyn¹ fat⁸ dat⁹
（translit.）
Suddenly become rich.　(lit.)
Stike oil.
Shake the pagoda tree.
〔註〕忽然發了大財的意思。

1499　無聲狗，咬死人
mou⁴ siŋ¹/sɐŋ¹ gɐu² ŋau⁵
sei² jɐn⁴　(translit.)
Noiseless dog bites a man to death.　(lit.)
A dumb's bite is worse than a barking dog's.
A man of no words gives it somebody hot.
〔註〕比喻不聲不響使用陰謀的人最可怕。

1500　無氈無扇，神仙難變
mou⁴ dzin¹ mou⁴ sin³, sɐn⁴
sin¹ nan⁴ bin³　(translit.)
Even a benignant spirit cannot change without a blanket and a fan.　(lit.)
No one can make bricks without straw.
No one can make a silk purse out of a sow's ear.

〔註〕比喻巧婦難為無米之炊。

1501　週身刀 —— 冇張利
dzɐu¹ sɐn¹ dou¹ — mou⁵
dzœŋ¹ lei⁶　(translit.)
There are knives on the whole body — no one is sharp.　(lit.)
Jack of all trades and master of none.
Jack-of-all-trades.
〔註〕比喻博而不專的人。

1502　週身唔聚財
dzɐu¹ sɐn¹ m⁴ dzœy⁶ tsɔi⁴
（translit.）
The whole body can not gather wealth.　(lit.)
Be uncomfortable/uneasy all over.
Be in a terrible fidget.
Fidget with one's tie.
〔註〕表示坐立不安的意思。

1503　爲口奔馳
wɐi⁶ hɐu² bɐn¹ tsi⁴　(translit.)
Run about for the mouth.　(lit.)
Labour for food in the field.
Be on the run to make a living.
〔註〕指為生活而奔波。

1504　爲食鬼
wɐi⁶ sik⁹ gwɐi²　(translit.)
A gluttonous ghost.　(lit.)
A glutton.
〔註〕即饞嘴者。

1505　衆事莫理，衆定莫企
dzuŋ³ si⁶ mɔk⁹ lei⁵, dzuŋ³

dɛŋ³ mɔk⁹ kei⁵　(translit.)
Neither handle public affairs nor stand at the public place. (lit.)
Put neither your hand between the bark and the tree nor yourself in a bustling place.
Neither poke your nose into everybody's business nor go with the crowd.
〔註〕這是老一輩的"獨善其身"的做人道理，表示不要理人家的事或大眾的事，也不要流連在熱鬧的地方。

1506　猴急
hɐu⁴ gɐp⁷　(translit.)
The monkey hurries. (lit.)
Be of a hasty disposition.
Be impetuous.
〔註〕指心急或性急，相當於"急性子"。

1507　猴擒
hɐu⁴ kɐm⁴　(translit.)
The monkey scatches. (lit.)
〔註〕同"猴急"（1056）。

1508　順口
sœn⁶ hɐu²　(translit.)
Smoothen the mouth. (lit.)
Read smoothly.
〔註〕表示（字句或文章等）唧唧上口而易讀的意思。

1509　順水人情
sœn⁶ sœy² jɐn⁴ tsiŋ⁴　(translit.)
The human nature with the downstream. (lit.)
The favour done at one's convenience.
〔註〕即順便的幫忙。

1510　順水推舟
sœn⁶ sœy² tœy¹ dzɐu¹　(translit.)
Push a boat with the downstream. (lit.)
Make use of an opportunity to win one's end.
Take advantage of the tide to...
Take advantage of the tide to refuse somebody's request.
〔註〕指趁着機會做……參閱"順風駛艍"條（1513），但亦表示乘機推却他人的請求的意思。

1511　順手
sœn⁶ sɐu²　(translit.)
At hand. (lit.)
Be handy.
With ease.
Without extra trouble.
Carry on with doing something.
Right after doing something.
〔註〕表示順便，方便，跟着做……或接着做……的意思。

1512　順手牽羊
sœn⁶ sɐu² hin¹ jœŋ⁴　(translit.)
Lead away the goat at hand. (lit.)
Go on the scamp.
Make away with something.
Make free with something.
Take something off on the sly.

〔註〕即乘人不備，順手拿走東西的行爲。

1513 順風駛悝

sœn⁶ fuŋ⁴ sɐi² lei⁵ *(translit.)*

Make sails in the favourable wind. *(lit.)*

Trim the sails.

Take advantage of the opportunity to do something.

Grasp at an opportunity.

〔註〕順着趨勢行事。參閱"順水推舟"條（1510）。

1514 順得哥情失嫂意

sœn⁶ dɐk⁷ gɔ¹ tsiŋ⁴ sɐt⁷ sou² dzi³ *(translit.)*

Obey elder brother's will but lose the idea of sister-in-law. *(lit.)*

Find it hard to be partial to either side of the two.

〔註〕左右爲難。

1515 順得「德」人

sœn⁶ dɐk⁷ jɐn² *(translit.)*

Yes man. *(lit.)*

A person who always says yes to everyone.

A person who never refuses.

A person who always complies with what he is asked to do.

〔註〕龍山和龍江本爲順德縣屬下的鄉鎮，但龍江鄉人和龍山鄉人從不承認他們的鄉鎮是隸屬於順德縣。所以有"兩龍不認順"的一句話。但順德縣人則常以"順德人"爲自豪。"德"和"得"爲一音之轉，意義便成"能夠順人意的人"的意思了。

1516 順眼

sœn⁶ ŋan⁵ *(translit.)*

Agree to the eyes. *(lit.)*

Be pleasing to the eyes.

Be pleasant to look at ...

〔註〕表示看起來悅目的意思。

1517 順喉

sœn⁶ hɐu *(translit.)*

Smoothen the throat. *(lit.)*

Be mild to the throat.

〔註〕形容味醇的（指煙酒等）。

1518 順攤

sœn⁶ tan¹ *(translit.)*

Be easy. *(lit.)*

Be smooth.

Can be dealt with without a hitch.

Be running smoothly/without a hitch.

〔註〕表示容易應付的（人）或順當（事）的意思。

1519 着起龍袍唔似太子

dzœk⁸ hei² luŋ⁴ pou⁴ m̄ tsi⁵ tai³ dzi² *(translit.)*

Not to look like the Crown Prince in spite of putting on an emperor's robe. *(lit.)*

A beggar in a dress-suit still looks like a beggar.

〔註〕比喻一個無才無貌或才貌不出衆的人，無論怎樣打扮或處於任何地位，也仍是庸才，難登大雅。

1520 着數

dzœk⁹ sou³　*(translit.)*
Profit oneself from something.　(lit.)
Gain extra advantage.
Take the lead in doing something.
Be favoured.
Be in a favourable situation.
Be reasonable in price.
Get one's money's worthwhile.
〔註〕表示獲得額外利益，在行動上佔優勢，處於有利地位或合算的意思。

1521　着緊
dzœk⁹ gɐn²　*(translit.)*
Care for.　(lit.)
Pay too much attention to ...
Give one's mind to ...
Care for ...
Be worried about ...
〔註〕表示對人特別關心或焦慮的意思。

1522　詐型
dza³ jiŋ⁴　*(translit.)*
Feign.　(lit.)
Put on an act.
Play the fool.
〔註〕即裝模作樣。

1523　詐假意
dza³ ga¹ ji¹　*(translit.)*
Pretend to be true.　(lit.)
Make believe.
Feign oneself to be/to do something.
Make a joke.
Be but a joke.
〔註〕假裝或鬧着玩的意思。

1524　詐［詐］諦［諦］
dza³　[dza³]　dɐi³　[dɐi³]　*(translit.)*
Pretend to know nothing.　(lit.)
Feign oneself to be ignorant of something.
Make a pretence of ignorance.
〔註〕假裝，裝作，相當於"裝蒜"。

1525　詐嬌
dza³ giu¹　*(translit.)*
Pretend to be pampered.　(lit.)
Pretend to get angry at displeasure.
Look somewhat displeased.
Behave like a spoiled child.
〔註〕即"撒嬌"。

1526　勞氣
lou⁴ hei³　*(translit.)*
Labour the breath.　(lit.)
Fly into a temper.
Show temper.
〔註〕即勞神，動氣的意思。

1527　勞嘈
lou⁴ tsou⁴　*(translit.)*
Be angry and noisy.　(lit.)
Make noisy clamour.
Get busy about ...
Be eager about ...
〔註〕大吵大鬧，生氣或急於……的意思。

1528　瓷器棺材 —— 不漏汁
tsi⁴ hei³ gun¹ tsɔi⁴—bɐt⁷ lɐu⁶ dzɐp⁷　*(translit.)*

A porcelain coffin — it does not leak juice. (lit.)

A person who haggles over every penny.

A person who profits nobody.

A person who preoccupies his own losses.

〔註〕比喻精打細算的人，斤斤計較的人或不會給人利益的人。

1529 補鑊唔見枳

bou² wɔk⁹ m⁴ gin³ dzɐt⁷ *(translit.)*

While mending a frying-pan, one loses a cotton-cork. (lit.)

Find oneself in a fix.

Be in a tight corner.

Be all in a fluster.

〔註〕比喻狼狽或手足無措。鑊即炒菜鍋。從前用以炒菜的鍋為生鐵製的。佛山為產地，用破了可以修補。廣州佛山兩地，常有鑄鑊的退休工人轉業上街替人補鑊，其法是把鐵沙燒熔後，先用布紮成的布塞（枳）放在要補的地方下面，再把鐵漿倒在上面，再用另一布塞（枳）把鐵漿壓平，俟其冷卻，便告修好。如果在這工序上失去布枳，情形怎樣，可以想見了。

1530 善財難捨，冤枉甘心

sin⁶ tsɔi⁴ nan⁴ sɛ², jyn¹ wɔŋ² gɐm¹ sɐm¹ *(translit.)*

It is difficult to give money for philanthropy, but pleased to spend it in a wrong way. (lit.)

Be reluctant to give money to some good purposes, but ready to play ducks and drakes with it.

〔註〕比喻寧揮霍也不願花錢花得有意義。

1531 春瘟雞

dzun¹ wɐn¹ gɐi¹ *(translit.)*

A plagued hen. (lit.)

A person who walks in a drunken manner.

A person who knocks round this way and that way.

〔註〕比喻行路像喝醉酒的人或亂碰亂撞的人。

1532 哼沉

ŋɐm⁴ tsɐm⁴ *(translit.)*

Be wordy. (lit.)

Be long-winded.

Keep on murmuring.

〔註〕形容人絮叨或多怨言。

1533 喎咗

wɔ⁵ dzɔ² *(translit.)*

All failed. (lit.)

Fell flat.

Fell down.

Fizzled out.

〔註〕表示完全失敗的意思。相當於"告吹了"。

1534 喱啦

li¹/lei¹ la¹ *(translit.)*

Shoot off the mouth. (lit.)

Run off at the mouth.

Have a loose tongue.

Be fond of gossip.

Be nosy.

〔註〕多嘴，順口開河，愛講閒話或多管閒事的意思。

1535 貼錯門神
tip³ tsɔ³ mun⁴ sɐn⁴ *(translit.)*
Stick the paper portrait of door gods in the wrong ways. (lit.)
There is no love between them.
Be at odds with each other.
Turn one's back upon somebody.
Be at loggerheads with each other.
〔註〕比喻彼此不和，互相仇視或互相敵對，相當於"反貼門神"。（按："門神"的正確貼法爲面對面左右分貼的。）

1536 貼錢買難受
tip³ tsin⁴ mai⁵ nan⁶ sɐu⁶ *(translit.)*
Pay out money to buy calamity to suffer. (lit.)
Pay for troubles.
〔註〕比喻付出代價，反惹麻煩。

1537 虛浮
hœy¹ fɐu⁴ *(translit.)*
Be both void and floating. (lit.)
Be impractical.
Be superficial.
〔註〕表示膚淺或不實際的意思。

1538 喺口唇邊
hɐi² hɐu² sœn⁴ bin¹ *(translit.)*
At the edge of lips. (lit.)
Have something at the tip of one's tongue.
〔註〕指一時想不起。

1539 喺乞兒兜揦飯食
hɐi² hɐt⁷ ji¹ dɐu¹ la² fan⁶ sik⁹ *(translit.)*
Snatch cooked-rice to eat out of a begging bowl. (lit.)
Rob the poor.
Juice the hay.
Squeeze wool for water.
〔註〕指打窮人的主意或壓搾窮人。

1540 喺孔夫子面前賣文章
hɐi² huŋ² fu¹ dzi² min⁶ tsin⁴ mai⁶ mɐn⁴ dzœŋ¹ *(translit.)*
Sell literary works before the face of Confucius. (lit.)
Teach one's grandmother how to suck eggs.
Display one's slight skill in the presence of an expert.
〔註〕即"班門弄斧"。

1541 喺門角落頭燒炮仗
hɐi² mun⁴ gɔk⁸ lɔk⁷ tɐu² siu¹ pau³ dzœŋ² *(translit.)*
Let off fireworks at the corner of the door. (lit.)
All dressed and nowhere to go.
〔註〕比喻炫耀自己的光彩不得其法。

1542 睇人口面
tɐi² jɐn⁴ hɐu² min⁶ *(translit.)*
Look at somebody's mouth and face. (lit.)

Consult somebody's wishes/pleasure.
Be dependent on other's pleasure.
Be slavishly dependent.
〔註〕看人臉色行事或仰仗他人。

1543 睇化
tɐi² fa³ (translit.)
See the solution of life. (lit.)
Understand one's life thoroughly.
Awaken to life.
Realize why life should be so.
〔註〕表示看透了世事的意思。相當於"看透了"。

1544 睇水
tɐi² sœy² (translit.)
Watch water. (lit.)
Keep watch.
Take a sharp lookout.
〔註〕把風，放風。

1545 睇白/睇死
tɐi² bak⁹/tɐi² sei² (translit.)
See the white./See the death. (lit.)
Can anticipate that ...
It is to be expected that ...
According to expectation,
Assert that ...
Stand to one's assertion that ...
〔註〕斷定，意料到……或正如所料的意思。（"睇白"多用於事後表示自己在事情發生前早就料到。"睇死"則帶有輕視態度於事前所作的斷定。）

1546 睇穿
tɐi² tsyn¹ (translit.)
See through. (lit.)
Gain an insight [into ...]
〔註〕表示對於……看得一清二楚的意思。

1547 睇唔過眼
tɐi² m⁴ gwɔ³ ŋan⁵ (translit.)
Not agree to the eyes. (lit.)
Cannot bear the sight of ...
Frown upon ...
〔註〕表示看不過去；有看見不公平的事氣不過的意思。

1548 睇差一皮
tɐi² tsa¹ jɐt⁷ pei⁴ (translit.)
Give a wrong look. (lit.)
Commit an error in judgement.
Form a wrong estimation of somebody/something.
〔註〕表示判斷錯誤的意思，參閱"有眼無珠"條（0588），"走眼"條（0713）及"跌眼鏡"（1556）各條，語出自"番攤"（賭博的一種）。

1549 睇開啲嚇！
tɐi² hɔi¹ di¹ la¹ (translit.)
See it open! (lit.)
Don't mind it!
Turn a blind eye to it!
〔註〕這是叫人"不要計較"或"裝看不見好了"的一句口頭語。

1550 睇起
tɐi² hei² (translit.)
See up. (lit.)
Regard somebody with special

favour.

Take a bright view of somebody.

〔註〕表示對某人瞧得起。

1551　睇嚟湊

tɐi² lai⁴ tsɐu³　(translit.)

See the condition.　(lit.)

It depends on the situation.

〔註〕看着辦，根據情況而定。

1552　睇餸食飯，睇蠋喃嘸〈謨〉

tɐi² suŋ³ sik⁹ fan⁶, tɐi² dzuk⁷ nam⁴ mɔ⁴　(translit.)

Watch the dainties to eat cooked-rice and watch the candle-sticks to say 'Namah' (Sanskrit, meaning 'to trust in Buddha').　(lit.)

Cut one's coat according to one's cloth.

Make both ends meet.

Live with one's means.

〔註〕表示量入爲出的意思，參閱"度住屎窟裁褲"（1068）條。

1553　買水咁嘅頭

mai⁵ sœy² gɐm² gɛ³ tɐu²　(translit.)

Be like the head of a mourning son who is buying water for his dead father.　(lit.)

Be crestfallen.

Be dejected.

Sing the blues.

〔註〕指垂頭喪氣的神態。（舊時俗例父母死後，長子必到附近河邊，投入銅錢，取些河水爲屍體抹臉，這便是"買水"，在去"買水"途中，身穿孝服，垂頭流涕，痛失至親，自不待言了。）

1554　跌咗個橙，執番個桔

dit⁸ dzɔ² gɔ³ tsaŋ², dzɐp⁷ fan¹ gɔ³ gɐt⁷　(translit.)

Drop an orange but pick up a tangerine in return.　(lit.)

Make up on the roundabouts what one loses on the swings.

Lose at sunrise and gain at sunset.

〔註〕比喻"失之東隅，收諸桑榆"。

1555　跌倒捫番揸沙

dit⁸ dou² la² fan¹ dza⁶ sa¹　(translit.)

Stumbled but pretended to pick up a handful of sand.　(lit.)

Invent a lame excuse to save face in spite of failure/making mistakes.

Put one's fault in the right side.

〔註〕比喻失敗或做錯也不承認，措詞來挽回面子或"文過飾非"。

1556　跌眼鏡

dit⁸ ŋan⁵ gɛŋ²ᐟ³　(translit.)

Drop the spectacles.　(lit.)

Have an error in judgement.

〔註〕相當於"走了眼"，參閱"走眼"（0713），"有眼無珠"（0558）及"睇差一皮"（1548）各條。

1557　跛腳鷯哥自有飛來蜢

bɐi¹ gœk⁸ liu¹ gɔ¹ dzi⁶ jɐu⁵ fei¹ lɔi⁴ maŋ²　(translit.)

A lame mynah naturally has grasshoppers flying to it.

(lit.)
God tempers the wind to the shorn lamb.
〔註〕指呆人有呆福。

1558 量地官
lœŋ⁴ dei⁶ gun¹ *(translit.)*
An official of measuring land. (lit.)
Be out of job.
A job hunter.
Be unemployed.
A person looking for an employment.
A person without a job.
〔註〕失業者的幽默解嘲語。

1559 單刀直入
dan¹ dou¹ dzik⁹ sɐp⁹ *(translit.)*
Enter straight with a single knife. (lit.)
Come straight to the point.
Speak out without beating about the bush.
〔註〕直截了當地說出目的，參閱"開門見山"（1580）條。

1560 單手獨拳
dan¹ sɐu² duk⁹ kyn⁴ *(translit.)*
Single hand and lone fist. (lit.)
Pull a lone oar.
〔註〕表示無人協助，單獨去做的意思。

1561 單身寡仔
dan¹ sɐn¹ gwa² dzɐi² *(translit.)*
Single body and widower boy. (lit.)
Be a single man/a bachelor.
Remain unmarried.
A celibate.
〔註〕即單身漢。

1562 單料銅煲
dan¹ liu² tuŋ⁴ bou¹ *(translit.)*
The water-boiler made of the thinnest plate copper. (lit.)
The person who instantly makes friends with a stranger.
The person who takes a stranger for an old friend at the first meeting.
〔註〕指跟陌生人一見如故的人，尤指女性。

1563 單單打打
dan¹ dan¹ da² da² *(translit.)*
Dash and dash and beat and beat. (lit.)
Satirize and make a mock of somebody.
Pour ridicule on somebody./Talk at somebody.
Make oblique accusations at somebody.
〔註〕指不明言地諷刺或嘲笑，指雞罵狗或指桑罵槐，參閱"指住禿奴罵和尚"條（1000）及"靠諦"條（1776）。

1564 單筷箸批（fɐk³ 音，攪拌也）豆腐——攪喎晒。

dan¹ fai³ dzi² fɐk³ dɐu⁶ fu⁶—gau² wɔ⁵ sai³ *(translit.)*
Stir bean curd with a single chopstick—it becomes muddy. (lit.)
Make a mess of things.
Muddle things up.
〔註〕比喻把事情弄糟。

1565 發毛
fat⁸ mou¹ *(translit.)*
Grow hair. (lit.)
Go mouldy.
〔註〕即發霉。

1566 發木獨
fat⁸ muk⁹ duk⁹ *(translit.)*
Be inflexible. (lit.)
Be in a trance.
Look like an idiot.
〔註〕發愕或發呆的意思,參閱"發吽哣"條(1569)。

1567 發矛
fat⁸ mau⁴ *(translit.)*
Raise a spear with anger. (lit.)
Fly into a rage.
Go off the hooks with anger.
〔註〕指人因過於衝動而不顧一切,紅了眼。參閱"發啷厲"條(1570)。

1568 發市
fat⁸ si⁵ *(translit.)*
Expand the market. (lit.)
Conclude an initial transaction of the day.
Get an initial winning after losing a lot.
〔註〕即"開市"或"開齋",參閱該條(B330)。

1569 發吽哣
fat⁸ ŋɐu⁶ dɐu⁶ *(translit.)*
With a silly look (lit.)
Be in a trance.
Look like an idiot.
〔註〕發愕,發呆。參閱"發木獨"條(1566)。

1570 發啷厲
fat⁸ lɔŋ¹ lɐi² *(translit.)*
Raise an anger. (lit.)
Suddenly fly into a rage.
Go off the hooks with anger.
Suddenly fly into temper with anger.
〔註〕突然發脾氣,大發雷霆。

1571 發盟憎
fat⁸ mɐŋ² dzɐŋ² *(translit.)*
Be displeased with oneself. (lit.)
Quarrel with one's own shadow.
〔註〕指莫明其妙地自己生自己的氣。

1572 發噏風
fat⁸ ŋɐp⁷ fuŋ¹ *(translit.)*
Issue the wind. (lit.)
Talk nonsense.
Throw the bull.
Talk through one's hat.
〔註〕胡説八道,胡言亂語。

1573 發窮惡
fat⁸ kuŋ⁴ ɔk⁸ *(translit.)*
Raise an anger of poverty. (lit.)

Be angered by poverty.

〔註〕因窮而心境不好，發脾氣來發洩。

1574 發錢寒

fat⁸ tsin² hɔn⁴ (translit.)

Shiver with the cold of money. (lit.)

Be infatuated with money.

〔註〕財迷心竅，想錢想瘋了。

1575 發爛渣

fat⁸ lan⁶ dza² (translit.)

Make dregs become ferment. (lit.)

Disregard one's dignity.

Be reckonless of consequences.

〔註〕這是比較新一點的口頭語，意謂不顧尊嚴或不顧後果。

1576 開大價

hɔi¹ dai⁶ ga³ (translit.)

Open a big price. (lit.)

Open one's mouth wide.

1577 開口及着脷

hɔi¹ hɐu² gɐp⁸ dzœk⁹ lei⁶ (translit.)

Bite the tongue as soon as the mouth is opened. (lit.)

Cause offence to somebody as soon as one begins to speak.

Talk at somebody as soon as one starts talking.

〔註〕指一開口便觸怒或諷刺某人。

1578 開心見誠

hɔi¹ sɐm¹ gin³ siŋ⁴ (translit.)

Open the heart to show sincerity. (lit.)

Show one's card on the table.

Be open-hearted.

Wear one's heart upon one's sleeve.

〔註〕表示開誠相見或毫不隱瞞的意思，參閱"開明車馬"條（1581）及"擺到明"條（1909）。

1579 開天索價，落地還錢

hɔi¹ tin¹ sak⁸ ga³, lɔk⁹ dei⁶ wan⁴ tsin⁴ (translit.)

One opens the sky to ask for a price and another comes down to the ground to cut the charge. (lit.)

Drive a hard bargain over something.

〔註〕指賣方要價很高，而買方則給予低價的一種討價還價行為。相當於"瞞天要價，就地還錢"。

1580 開門見山

hɔi¹ mun⁴ gin³ san¹ (translit.)

Opening the door, one sees the mountain. (lit.)

Come straight to the point.

Not to mince one's words.

Not to put too fine a point on it.

Put it bluntly.

〔註〕參閱"單刀直入"條（1559）。

1581 開明車馬

hɔi¹ miŋ⁴ gœy¹ ma⁵ (translit.)

Apparently move the chariot and horse. (lit.)

Be open-hearted.

Wear one's heart upon one's

sleeve.
Lay one's card on the table.
〔註〕說明意圖。參閱"開心見誠"條（1578）及"擺到明"條（1909）。

1582 開啱……嗰槓
hɔi¹ ŋam¹ ... gɔ²ᐟ³ luŋ⁵ *(translit.)*
Open the very trunk of somebody. (lit.)
Hit somebody's fancy.
Be after somebody's fancy.
To somebody's liking.
Hit one's very ability.
〔註〕正合某人心意或正是某人的所長的意思。

1583 開籠雀
hɔi¹ luŋ⁴ dzœk⁸ᐟ² *(translit.)*
The bird in the opened cage. (lit.)
Talk away.
Wag one's tongue.
〔註〕一開口便滔滔不絕。

1584 強中自有強中手
kœŋ⁴ dzuŋ¹ dzi⁶ jɐu⁵ kœŋ⁴ dzuŋ¹ sɐu² *(translit.)*
There is a stronger man among the strong. (lit.)
Catch a tartar.
〔註〕表示遇到勁敵的意思。

1585 幾大就幾大
gei² dai² dzɐu⁶ gei² dai² *(translit.)*
How big is how big./Not to care how big it is. (lit.)
For good or for evil.
In for a penny, in for a pound.

Rain or shine.
〔註〕無論如何或不顧一切。

1586 媽媽聲
ma¹ ma¹ sɛŋ¹ *(translit.)*
With the sound 'ma ma'. (lit.)
Swear like a pirate/trooper.
〔註〕粗口罵人或破口大罵。

十三畫

1587 斟盤
dzɐm¹ pun² *(translit.)*
Talk about the plan. (lit.)
Hold talks with somebody.
Negotiate with somebody about something.
Enter into negotiation with somebody.
Talk about business with somebody.
〔註〕表示和人協商，談判或談生意的意思。

1588 電燈膽——唔通氣
din⁶ dɐŋ¹ dam²－m⁴ tuŋ¹ hei³ *(translit.)*
a lamp bulb－not ventilate. (lit.)
Not to stand to sense.
〔註〕比喻人不通情達理或不知情識趣。

1589 塘邊鶴
tɔŋ⁴ bin¹ nɔk⁹ᐟ² *(translit.)*
The cane looking for food at

the edge of a pool.　(lit.)

The person who hastens to make away with his winnings/gains.

〔註〕比喻一有所獲便立即離去的人，尤指在賭博方面。

1590 鼓氣袋

gu² hei³ dɔi²ᐟ⁶　(translit.)

The bellows full of air.　(lit.)

A man of few words.

A man of reticence.

Be uncommunicative.

〔註〕比喻不愛交際而又沉默寡言的人。

1591 煮到嚟就食

dzy² dou² lɐi⁴ dzɐu⁶ sik⁹　(translit.)

Eat what is cooked for.　(lit.)

Submit oneself to the circumstances.

Adapt onself to what happens to one.

Submit oneself to one's own fate.

〔註〕使自己適應環境，對所發生的事處之泰然或順應天命的意思。

1592 煮鬼

dzy² gwɐi²　(translit.)

Boil a ghost.　(lit.)

Rip up the back of somebody.

Lay complaints against somebody.

Paint somebody in dark colour behind his back.

〔註〕表示在人背後指控的意思，參閱"煮重米"（1593）及"篤背脊"（1669）條。

1593 煮重米

dzy² tsuŋ² mɐi⁵　(translit.)

Cook much more rice.　(lit.)

Paint somebody in the darkest colour.

Lodge an exaggerated complaint against somebody.

〔註〕參閱"煮鬼"條（1592）。

1594 搗亂

dou² lyn⁶　(translit.)

Beat a mess.　(lit.)

Make trouble.

Cause a disturbance.

1595 搶手

tsœŋ² sɐu²　(translit.)

Seize hands.　(lit.)

Be most welcome to everybody.

Win popularity.

Be very popular with everybody.

Be sold like hot cakes.

〔註〕比喻暢銷，受人歡迎。

1596 搶眼

tsœŋ² ŋan⁵　(translit.)

Snatch eyes.　(lit.)

Dazzle the eyes.

Be dazzling and resplendent.

Offer attractions.

Attract attention.

〔註〕表示顯眼；奪目或吸引人。

1597 搬弄是非

bun¹ luŋ⁶ si⁶ fei¹　(translit.)

Carry right and wrong about.　(lit.)

Tell tales out school.

1598 揢手爛腳
syn² sɐu² lan⁶ gœk⁸ (translit.)
Injure the hands and spoil the feet. (lit.)
Suffer heavy losses.
〔註〕比喻招受重大損失。

1599 揿/撳地游水
gɐm⁶ dei⁶ jɐu⁴ sœy² (translit.)
Press on the ground to swim. (lit.)
Play safe.
Play for safety.
Go about steadily and surely.
〔註〕表示不做冒險的事。

1600 揿/撳鷓鴣
gɐm⁶ dzɛ³ gu¹ (translit.)
Press a partridge. (lit.)
Take somebody at advantage to practise extortion.
〔註〕指乘人一時疏忽來進行敲詐的行爲。

1601 搭沉船
dap⁸ tsɐm⁴ syn⁴ (translit.)
Make the ship sink. (lit.)
One's bad luck implicates others.
The person whose bad luck causes others to suffer a loss.
〔註〕比喻招致別人損失的不祥之人，參閱"陀衰家"條（0977）。

1602 搭單
dap⁸ dan¹ (translit.)
Join hands. (lit.)
Take advantage of somebody's convenience to ask him to do something.
Join as a partner.
Join in a bet.
〔註〕乘着別人之便請他也做……，搭伙或參加賭注的意思。

1603 搭錯賊船
dap⁸ tsɔ³ tsak⁹ syn⁴ (translit.)
Wrongly take a pirate ship. (lit.)
Be misled to suffer a loss.
Tread in somebody's wrong steps.
〔註〕因被誤導而招致損失或"跟錯風"的意思。

1604 搭錯綫
dap⁸ tsɔ³ sin³ (translit.)
Get in touch with the wrong line. (lit.)
Dial the wrong number.
Misunderstand what somebody means and give an irrelevant answer.
〔註〕本指撥錯電話號碼，但引伸比喻誤會別人意思而答非所問。

1605 搓得圓揿得扁
tsɔ¹ dɐk⁷ tyn⁴ gɐm⁶ dɐk⁷ bin² (translit.)
Can be rolled into a ball and pressed flat. (lit.)
Be as mild as a dove.
Be amiable.
〔註〕形容人性情溫和和靄可親。

1606 碰啱
puŋ³ ŋam¹ (translit.)

Bump right against. (lit.)
Coincide with ...
By a curious coincidence.
By chance.
As luck would have it.
〔註〕意爲"碰巧"，參閱"撞〔到〕正"（1759）及"撞啱"條（1761）。

1607 靳度
gɐn³ dou⁶ (translit.)
Be miserly. (lit.)
Be grudging.
Be very calculating.
Be scheming.
〔註〕表示靳而不予，善爲自己打算或工心計的意思。

1608 鼠入嚟
sy² jɐp⁹ lɐi⁴ (translit.)
Mouse in. (lit.)
Steal in/into ...
〔註〕表示溜進來的意思。

1609 鼠嘢
sy² jɛ⁵ (translit.)
Mouse things. (lit.)
Steal things.
〔註〕指偷東西。

1610 傾唔埋
kiŋ¹ m⁴ mai⁴ (translit.)
Cannot have a chat together. (lit.)
Be out of tune with somebody.
Do not speak the same language.
Do not get along well with somebody.
〔註〕即話不投機。

1611 傾唔埋欄
kiŋ¹ m⁴ mai⁴ lan¹ (translit.)
Disagree with ... (lit.)
Not to reach an agreement with somebody.
Fail to carry one's point.
Not to speak the same language.
Be out of tune with somebody.
〔註〕表示未能達成協議，無法說服對方同意，或話不投機的意思，後義參閱"傾唔埋"（1610）條。

1612 僅僅夠（一）
gɐn² gɐn² gɐu³ (translit.)
Just enough. (Indicates small quantity) (lit.)
Be just sufficient.
〔註〕指數量方面的足夠。

1613 僅僅夠……（二）
gɐn² gɐn² gɐn³ ... (translit.)
Just enough ... (Indicates low degree). (lit.)
Be just ... enough.
〔註〕指程度方面的足夠。

1614 煲冇米粥
bou¹ mou⁵ mɐi⁵ dzuk⁷ (translit.)
Boil riceless congee. (lit.)
Be all talk.
Make an idle talk.
The business ends in talk.
〔註〕指閒談（無目的），或商談沒有成果的生意。

1615 會錯意
wui⁶ tsɔ³ ji³ (translit.)
Get the wrong idea. (lit.)
Misunderstand somebody's in-

tention.
Wrongly take a hint.
〔註〕誤會別人的意圖。

1616　飲咗門官茶
jɐm² dzɔ² mun⁴ gun¹ tsa⁴ (translit.)
Have drunk the tea offered to the god of door.　(lit.)
Split one's sides with laughter.
Always wear a smiling face.
〔註〕即笑口常開。

1617　飲頭啖湯
jɐm² tɐu⁴ dam⁶ tɔŋ¹ (translit.)
Drink the first sip of soup.　(lit.)
Gain the initial advantage.
Take a first sip of somebody's soup.
〔註〕比喻獲得他人尚未得到的好處，相當於"試頭水兒"。

1618　鈴鈴鋹鋹都丟埋
liŋ¹ liŋ¹ tsa⁴ tsa² dou¹ diu¹ mai⁴ (translit.)
Throw away the bell and cymbals.　(lit.)
Meet with a crushing defeat.
Be at the end of one's tether.
Be at one's wit's end.
〔註〕廣東人稱銅鈸爲"鋹鋹"。鈴和鈸爲道士作法的法寶，當道士作法時，如遇鬼魅法力較道士爲強，則道士便要丟掉法寶而逃。所以這句話是喻遭到極大的失敗或"智窮才盡"。

1619　筲箕打水——一場空
sau¹ gei¹ da² sœy²—jɐt⁷ tsœŋ⁴ huŋ¹ (translit.)
Draw water with a sieve.— vanish into the void.　(lit.)
Draw water with a sieve.
〔註〕喻希望成空。

1620　筲箕冚鬼一窩神
sau¹ gei¹ hɐm⁶ gwɐi² jɐt⁷ wɔ¹ sɐn⁴ (translit.)
Cover ghosts with a sieve to form a den of gods.　(lit.)
Be hand and glove with each other.
Be in cahoots with each other.
Devils gang up with devils
〔註〕表示同流合污的意思。

1621　亂晒坑
lyn⁶ sai³ haŋ¹ (translit.)
The pit gets confused.　(lit.)
Be at sixes and sevens.
Be thrown into confusion.
Muddle things up.
〔註〕相當於亂了套。

1622　亂籠
lyn⁶ luŋ⁴ (translit.)
Disorderly cages.　(lit.)
〔註〕同"亂晒坑"（1621）。

1623　腦囟/顖未生埋
nou⁵ sœn² mei⁶ saŋ¹ mai⁴ (translit.)
The forehead has not closed yet.　(lit.)
One's mouth is full of pap.
〔註〕形容人年幼無知或乳臭未乾。

1624　滾水淥腳
gwɐn² sœy² luk⁹ gœk⁸

(translit.)
Dip the feet in boiling water. (lit.)
Hurry one's pace.
Hurry off.
〔註〕表示去得匆匆的意思。

1625 滾水淥豬腸——兩頭縮
gwɐn² sœy² luk⁹ dzy¹ tsœŋ²—lœŋ⁵ tɐu⁴ suk⁷ (translit.)
Dip the pig's intestines in boiling water—both ends shrink. (lit.)
Lose out one both sides.
〔註〕表示兩頭損失的意思。

1626 話唔埋
wa⁶ m⁴ mai⁴ ... (translit.)
Can hardly say ... (lit.)
Perhaps.
Maybe.
It is beyond expectation that ...
〔註〕說不定；難以預料。參閱"話唔定"條（B349）。

1627 話晒事
wa⁶ sai³ si⁶ (translit.)
Say all the things. (lit.)
Wield the sceptre.
〔註〕作主，說了算，掌握大權。

1628 該釘就釘，該鐵就鐵
gɔi¹ dɛŋ¹ dzɐu⁶ dɛŋ¹, gɔi¹ tit⁸ dzɐu⁶ tit⁸ (translit.)
Nails should be nails and iron should be iron. (lit.)
Call a spade a spade.
〔註〕表示事情不能模棱兩可的意思。

1629 該煨咯！
gɔi¹ wui¹ lɔk⁸ (translit.)
It should be roasted in ashes! (lit.)
Just my luck!
What a bad luck!
Too bad!
〔註〕意爲糟糕了（帶有可憐，心痛的感情）。

1630 滋油
dzi¹ jɐu⁶ (translit.)
Slow at movement. (lit.)
Act or speak leisurely and unhurriedly.
〔註〕指談吐及行動慢條斯理的。不慌不忙，悠然自得。

1631 滋油淡定
dzi¹ jɐu⁴ dam⁶ diŋ⁶ (translit.)
Slow and calm at movements. (lit.)
A slow coach.
Of phlegmatic temperament.
〔註〕指從容不迫的態度，亦即"慢條斯理"的意思。

1632 滋陰/滋微
dzi¹ jɐm¹/dzi¹ mei¹ (translit.)
Nourish the negative element in the body./Nourish the slightest. (lit.)
Pinch pennies.
Haggle over every penny.
〔註〕表示精打細算或斤斤計較的意思。

1633 㷫起/着個火頭

lat⁸ hei²/dzœk⁶ gɔ³ fɔ² tɐu⁴ *(translit.)*
Light up the fire-head. (lit.)
Stir up the dust./Stir up somebody to mischief.
Throw the situation into confusion.
Set the situation on fire.
Agitate for something to inflame popular feeling.
〔註〕喻煽動，煽動某人胡鬧，造成局面混亂或爲……而進行鼓動來激動羣衆情緒等。

1634 新屎坑三日香
sɐn¹ si² haŋ¹ sam¹ jɐt⁹ hœŋ¹ *(translit.)*
A new lavatory smells of fragrance for three days. (lit.)
A new broom sweeps clean.
Prevail for a time.
Be all the rage for a while.
〔註〕比喻成爲一時時尚或風靡一時。

1635 辣撻人有辣撻福
lat⁹ tat⁸ jɐn⁴ jɐu⁵ lat⁹ tat⁸ fuk⁷ *(translit.)*
Dirty persons have dirty bliss. (lit.)
God tempers the wind to the shorn lamb.
Happiness often comes to mediocre persons.
〔註〕表示庸人多厚福的意思，參閱"跛腳鷯哥自有飛來蜢"條（1557）。

1636 道高一尺，魔高一丈
dou⁶ gou¹ jɐt⁷ tsɛk⁸, mɔ¹ gou¹ jɐt⁷ dzœŋ⁶ *(translit.)*
The magical arts of Taoist grow one foot high but the glamour of the devil grows to ten feet. (lit.)
Offenders are a stroke above law-makers.
Where there are laws, there are fierce offensives against them.
〔註〕表示一法立，一弊生的意思。

1637 稟神都冇句真
bɐn² sɐn⁴ dou¹ mou⁵ gœy³ dzɐn¹ *(translit.)*
Not a sentence is true even as praying down. (lit.)
Often tell the tale.
Lie in one's teeth.
Live a lie.
Lie like a gas meter.
〔註〕強調（某人）講話沒一句真的，慣於説謊。

1638 慌失失
fɔŋ¹ sɐt⁷ sɐt⁷ *(translit.)*
Get frightened. (lit.)
Be all in a fluster.
Be in a flurried manner.
〔註〕慌手慌腳；慌慌張張，參閱"失失慌"條（0491）。

1639 塞古盟憎
sɐk⁷ gu² mɐŋ⁴ dzɐŋ¹ *(translit.)*
Suddenly. (lit.)
All of a sudden.
Before you could say Jack Robinson.

〔註〕表示忽然間，轉眼之間。

1640　塞竇窿
sɐk⁷ dɐu⁶ luŋ¹　(translit.)
Something to fill up the hole of the drain.　(lit.)
A little child.
A kid.
〔註〕喻小孩的諧趣語。

1641　過口癮
gwɔ³ hɐu² jɐn⁵　(translit.)
Satisfy the addict of the mouth.　(lit.)
Have snack to ease the mouth.
Talk at random.
Talk nonsense.
Cook up a tale.
〔註〕本意指吃零食，但引伸指瞎聊，胡謅。

1642　過水濕腳
gwɔ³ sœy² sɐp⁷ gœk⁸　(translit.)
Wet one's feet as soon as one wades across the water.　(lit.)
Taste another's broth with one's finger.
Draw water to one's mill.
Nose a job in everything.
Whatever one does, one plays for one's own hand.
〔註〕表示無論做甚麼也要佔點兒便宜的意思。

1643　過夾吊頸
gwɔ³ gap⁸ diu³ gɛŋ²　(translit.)
Hang oneself with a rope round one's armpits.　(lit.)
Handle everything with great care.
Make two bites at a cherry.
〔註〕比喻做事過分小心，參閱"落住屎窟吊頸"條（1652）。

1644　過咗海就神仙
gwɔ³ dzɔ² hɔi² dzɐu⁶ sɐn⁴ sin¹　(translit.)
Crossing the sea, one becomes a celestial being.　(lit.)
Sail under false colours.
Succeed in practising deception on somebody.
〔註〕表示瞞天過海的意思。

1645　過骨
gwɔ³ gwɐt⁷　(translit.)
Pass through the bones.　(lit.)
Get throuth/over ...
Pass a test.
Slide through ...
Scrape through/past ...
〔註〕過關或通過的意思。

1646　過氣老倌
gwɔ³ hei³ lou⁵ gun¹　(translit.)
A behindhand actor.　(lit.)
An actor who was once famous.
A used-to-be.
〔註〕本義為過去紅極一時的老藝人，但引伸作失去權勢地位或資財的人。

1647　過得去
gwɔ³ dɐk⁷ hœy³　(translit.)
Just can pass.　(lit.)
Be not too bad.

Be just passable.
So-so.
〔註〕還可以的意思。

1648　過橋抽板
gwɔ³ kiu⁴ tsɐu¹ ban² (translit.)
Pull up the board after crossing the bridge. (lit.)
Kick down the ladder.
Once on shore, pray no more.
〔註〕比喻成功後便忘了幫忙的人，相當於"過河拆橋"。參閱"打完齋唔要和尚"條（0425）。

1649　落……棚牙
lɔk⁷ ... paŋ⁴ ŋa⁴ (translit.)
Pull down the jaws of teeth of somebody. (lit.)
Draw somebody's teeth.
Make somebody lose face.
Bring somebody down a peg or two.
Sheer off somebody's plume.
〔註〕打掉（某人的）傲氣；殺（某人的）威風。

1650　落力
lɔk⁹ lik⁹ (translit.)
Put physical strength to. (lit.)
Spare no effort.
Make an effort.
With one's strength.
Tooth and nail.
〔註〕表示努力，認真，盡所能或賣力的意思。

1651　落手打三更
lɔk⁹ sɐu² da² sam¹ gaŋ¹
(translit.)
Begin to beat the third interval on the drum. (lit.)
Begin with a wrong move.
Put one's foot in one's own mouth at the start.
〔註〕比喻一開始便出錯。

1652　落住屎窟吊頸
lɔk⁹ dzy⁶ si² fɐt⁷ diu³ gɛŋ²
(translit.)
Hang oneself with one's hips supported by a net. (lit.)
Handle everything with great care.
Make two bites at a cherry.
〔註〕參閱"過夾吊頸"條（1643）。

1653　落定
lɔk⁹ dɛŋ⁶ (translit.)
Put a downpayment. (lit.)
Pay down.
Pay the deposit.
〔註〕給定錢。

1654　落雨賣風爐——越擔越重
lɔk⁹ jy⁵ mai⁶ fuŋ¹ lou²—jyt⁶ dam¹ jyt⁶ tsuŋ⁵ (translit.)
Sell earthen stoves in the rain—the longer they are carried on a shoulder, the heavier they become. (lit.)
One's burden becomes heavier and heavier.
Be heavy-laden day by day.
〔註〕意思是表示一個人所承擔的責任，一天重過一天。

1655　落雨擔遮——顧前唔顧

後

lɔk⁹ jy⁵ dam¹ dzɛ¹—gu³ tsin⁴ m⁴ gu³ hɐu⁶ *(translit.)*

Raise an umbrella in the rain—care for the front not for the back *(lit.)*

Pay no regard to the future.

Be regardless of the consequence.

〔註〕比喻不理將來或不顧後果。

1656 落狗屎

lɔk⁹ gɐu² si² *(translit.)*

Drop dog's manure. *(lit.)*

It rains dogs and cats.

〔註〕形容滂沱大雨。

1657 落膈

lɔk⁹ gak⁸ *(translit.)*

Down the diaphragm. *(lit.)*

Stick to somebody's/one's fingers.

Line one's own pockets.

Misappropriate.

〔註〕原指吃東西後休息片刻，讓食物在胃裏穩定下來的意思，此處引伸爲侵吞欸項的意思。

1658 萬事俱備，只欠東風

man⁶ si⁶ kœy¹ bei⁶, dzi² him³ duŋ¹ fuŋ¹ *(translit.)*

Ten thousand things are all ready to wait for the eastern wind. *(lit.)*

Ready to the last gaiter button.

All is ready except what is crucial.

〔註〕表示一切均已做好準備，只差最後一個重要條件。

1659 萬事起頭難

man⁶ si⁶ hei² tɐu⁴ nan⁴ *(translit.)*

It is difficult to begin the head of ten thousand things. *(lit.)*

It is difficult to begin a new business.

1660 萬無一失

man⁶ mou⁴ jɐt⁷ sɐt⁷ *(translit.)*

There is not a miss in ten thousand times. *(lit.)*

There is no risk to worry about.

Be as sure as a surefooted horse.

〔註〕絕對不會出差錯。

1661 萬變不離宗

man⁶ bin³ bɐt⁷ lei⁴ dzuŋ¹ *(translit.)*

Ten thousand changes cannot get rid of the origin. *(lit.)*

Myriads of changes base themselves on the origin.

〔註〕無論形式怎樣千變萬化，但最基本的東西沒有變或無論事情怎樣變化其宗旨（目的）不變。

1662 賊公計，狀元才

tsak⁹ guŋ¹ gɐi³, dzɔŋ⁶ jyn⁴ tsɔi⁴ *(translit.)*

The trick of thieves and the talent of 'dzɔŋ jyn' *(lit.)*

Know a trick worth two of that.

Each exercises his own wit.

〔註〕比喻有更妙的方法或各顯才能。

'Dzɔŋ jyn'—a title conferred on the one who came first in the highest imperial examination in Ming and Tsing Dynasties.

1663 賊亞爸
tsak⁹ a³ ba¹ (translit.)
Father of thieves. (lit.)
A thief of thieves.
A person who extorts money from rascals.
〔註〕指賊中之賊或專向發不義之財的人敲榨的人。

1664 賊佬試砂煲
tsak⁹ lou² si³ sa¹ bou¹ (translit.)
A thief tries an earthen tea-pot. (lit.)
Put forth a feeler.
Pry about the reaction of others.
Make a trial beforehand.
〔註〕表示試探別人的反應或先來一試的意思。

1665 賊眉賊眼
tsak⁹ mei⁴ tsak⁹ ŋan⁵ (translit.)
Thievish eyebrows and eyes. (lit.)
Thievish looking.
Look like a thief.

1666 賊過興兵
tsak⁹ gwɔ³ hiŋ¹ biŋ¹ (translit.)
Raise an army after the thief has gone. (lit.)

Lock the stable door after the horse is stolen.
〔註〕表示事後才謀補救或防範的意思。

1667 照單執藥
dziu³ dan¹ dzɐp⁷ jœk⁹ (translit.)
Pick medicinal herbs according to the prescription. (lit.)
Follow the beaten track.
Act as listed above/below.
〔註〕表示要人按照開列事項去做的意思。

1668 照板煮碗
dziu³ ban² dzy² wun² (translit.)
Cook for a bowl in accordance with the sample. (lit.)
Follow the beaten track.
Make one like the given sample.
Give an eye for an eye; a tooth for a tooth.
〔註〕表示依樣畫葫蘆，要人按照所交出的樣板去做。又可引伸作以牙還牙。

1669 督背脊
duk¹ bui³ dzɐk⁸ (translit.)
Pierce the back. (lit.)
Rip up the back of somebody.
Speak ill of somebody behind his back.
〔註〕即背後説人壞話，參閱"煮鬼"條（1592）。

1670 督眼督鼻
duk¹ ŋan⁵ duk¹ bei⁶ (trans-

lit.)
Pierce eyes and nose. *(lit.)*
Irritate to the eyes.
Have a thorn in one's flesh.
Detest to see somebody/something.
〔註〕視作眼中釘的意思。

1671　暈得一陣
wɐn⁴ dɐk⁷ jɐt⁷ dzɐn⁶ *(translit.)*
Faint away for a while. *(lit.)*
Be intoxicated by one's beauty.
Be enchanted with honey words.
〔註〕被某人的美色或甜言蜜語所陶醉的意思。

1672　暗啞抵
ɐm³ a¹ dɐi² *(translit.)*
Bear without a word. *(lit.)*
Suffer in silence.
Swallow the leek.
〔註〕表示被迫忍辱而說不出聲來的意思。

1673　盟塞
mɐŋ⁴ sɐk⁷ *(translit.)*
Be unclever. *(lit.)*
Be as stupid as an owl.
Be poor at understanding.
〔註〕指愚蠢或理解力弱。

1674　㗳頭近
gɔ² tɐu⁴ kɐn⁵/gɐn⁶ *(translit.)*
That end is near. *(lit.)*
Have one's foot in the grave.
Be at death's door.
〔註〕喻接近死亡。

1675　㗳單嘢
gɔ² dan¹ jɛ⁵ *(translit.)*
That matter. *(lit.)*
The business between you, me and the gatepost.
The matter of that.
〔註〕那檔事兒，指彼此心知的事情。

1676　嗌通街
ai³ tuŋ¹ gai¹ *(translit.)*
Scold the whole street. *(lit.)*
Bandy words with everyone.
〔註〕指到處都和人吵架。

1677　當時得令
dɔŋ¹ si⁴ dɐk⁷ liŋ⁶ *(translit.)*
Be seasonable. *(lit.)*
Be in season.
Be the main trend of today.
Win popularity.
〔註〕表示合時令的，當時風行的或當紅的意思。

1678　跪地餵/餵豬乸 —— 睇錢份上
gwɐi⁶ dei⁶ hei³/wɐi³ dzy¹ ŋa²—tɐi² tsin²/⁴ fɐn⁶ sœŋ⁶ *(translit.)*
Kneel down to feed a sow — for money's sake. *(lit.)*
Money makes the mare go.
For the sake of money.
Money talks.
〔註〕表示為了金錢，甚麼也做或為了金錢甘於低三下四的意思。

1679　隔山買牛
gak⁸ san¹ mai⁵ ŋɐu⁴ *(translit.)*
Buy an ox at a separate moun-

1680 隔夜油炸鬼

gak⁸ jɛ⁶ jɐu⁴ dza³ gwɐi² (translit.)

The deep-fried dough-strip of last evening. (lit.)

A milk sop.

A person who never turns a hair.

A person who never gets angry.

A person of both unhurried and unperturbed dispositions.

〔註〕比喻懦弱的人，從不發怒的人或慢條斯理的人。

1681 隔夜素馨釐戥秤

gak⁸ jɛ⁶ sou³ hiŋ¹ lei⁴ dɐŋ² tsiŋ³ (translit.)

The jasimine left over night is weighted on beam and scales. (lit.)

The outmoded are sometimes outvalued.

〔註〕表示過時的東西反而更貴，更有價值的意思。

1682 隔岸觀火

gak⁸ ŋɔn⁶ gun¹ fɔ² (translit.)

Watch a fire at other side of the bank. (lit.)

Show indifference towards somebody's trouble.

〔註〕指對別人的不幸等，毫不關心採取從旁看熱鬧的態度。

1683 隔靴捎痕/癢

gak⁸ hœ¹ ŋau¹ hɐn⁴/jœŋ³ (translit.)

Scratch an itch outside the boot. (lit.)

Work out no effective solution to the problem.

Hit beside the mark.

Not to keep to the point.

〔註〕比喻說話做事沒有觸到要害，不解決問題。

1684 隔牆有耳

gak⁸ tsœŋ⁴ jɐu⁵ ji⁵ (translit.)

The separate wall has ears. (lit.)

Walls have ears.

Pitchers have ears.

1685 叠埋心水（緒）

dip⁹ mai⁴ sɐm¹ sœy² (translit.)

Fold up the mind. (lit.)

Not to think oneself into a dilemma any more.

〔註〕表示專心致志，集中精神，不胡思亂想的意思。

1686 裝假狗

dzɔŋ¹ ga² gɐu² (translit.)

Install a false dog. (lit.)

Be under the guise.

Make believe.

Camouflage something with ...

〔註〕偽裝或弄虛作假。

1687 裝彈弓

dzɔŋ¹ dan⁶ guŋ¹ (translit.)

Install a spring. (lit.)

Make an ambush.

十三畫

Set a trap.
Drop a pinch of salt on the tail of a horse.
〔註〕即設圈套。

1688 嫌棄
jim⁴ hei³　(translit.)
Dislike.　(lit.)
Be displeased at somebody/something.
Turn a cold shoulder to somebody.

十四畫

1689 壽仔
sɐu⁶ dzɐi²　(translit.)
A long-living guy.　(lit.)
A fool.
A spoon.
〔註〕指傻瓜，白癡。

1690 壽星公吊頸 —— 嫌命長
sɐu⁶ siŋ¹ kuŋ¹ diu³ gɛŋ² — jim⁴ mɛŋ⁶ tsœŋ⁴　(translit.)
The god of longevity hangs himself — dislike long life.　(lit.)
Tempt one's fate.
Do something at the risk of one's life.
Run risk of life.
〔註〕歇後語。比喻人不顧危險幹某事，"玩兒命"。

1691 壽頭
sɐu⁶ tɐu⁴　(translit.)
A long-living head.　(lit.)
A blockhead.
A spoon.
〔註〕傻瓜，呆子。

1692 壽頭壽腦
sɐu⁶ tɐu⁴ sɐu⁶ nou⁵　(translit.)
A long-living head with long-living brains.　(lit.)
Be foolish-looking.
Be muddled-headed.
〔註〕形容人呆頭呆腦。

1693 趕到……絕
gɔn² dou³ ... dzyt⁹　(translit.)
Drive to the cliff.　(lit.)
Drive somebody to the wall.
〔註〕令某人陷於絕境。

1694 魂不守舍
wɐn⁴ bɐt⁷ sɐu² sɛ³　(translit.)
The soul does not stay in.　(lit.)
Lose one's head.
Be distracted.
Be perplexed.
Be out of one's wits.
〔註〕指人不知所措，迷迷惘惘或心不在焉的姿態。

1695 魂不附體
wɐn⁴ bɐt⁷ fu⁶ tɐi²　(translit.)
The soul does not attach to the body.　(lit.)
Lose one's head.

Be distracted.
Be at a loss.
To be scared (almost) to death.
Be out of one's wits.
〔註〕形容人受到極大的震驚，恐懼萬分。

1696 誓神劈願
sɐi⁶ sɐn⁴ pɛk⁸ jyn⁶ *(translit.)*
Swear by God and trust forth a will (lit.)
Take an oath and call God to witness.
〔註〕起誓，發誓。

1697 誓願當食生菜
sɐi⁶ jyn⁶ dɔŋ³ sik⁹ saŋ¹ tsɔi³ *(translit.)*
Swear like eating lettuce. (lit.)
Get used to making false oath.
Take an easy oath.
〔註〕比喻隨便起誓，但是從來不履行。

1698 駁嘴
bɔk⁸ dzœy² *(translit.)*
Reverse the mouth. (lit.)
Answer back.
Talk back.
〔註〕頂嘴。

1699 輕枷重罪
hɛŋ¹/hiŋ¹ ga¹ tsuŋ⁵ dzœy⁶ *(translit.)*
The wooden collar is light but the crime is serious. (lit.)
Be burdened with the work of a moment.
〔註〕表示工作不多，但責任重大的意思。

1700 輕佻
hiŋ¹ tiu¹ *(translit.)*
Not serious. (lit.)
Be frivolous.
Be skittish.

1701 輕浮
hiŋ¹ fɐu⁴ *(translit.)*
Light and floating. (lit.)
Be frivolous.
Have the indiscretion.

1702 摸門釘
mɔ² mun⁴ dɛŋ¹ *(translit.)*
Touch the door-nail. (lit.)
Kiss the doorpost.
〔註〕指到親友家找不到人。

1703 摟蓆
lɐu¹ dzɛk⁹ *(translit.)*
Put on a mat. (lit.)
Become a beggar.
〔註〕比喻做了乞丐。

1704 摟錯人皮
lɐu¹ tsɔ³ jɐn⁴ pei⁴ *(translit.)*
Wrongly put on a human skin. (lit.)
Behave oneself like a beast.
Be man and beast.
〔註〕指人行爲不端或毫無人性。相當於"白披了張人皮"。

1705 監人食死貓
gam¹ jɐn⁴ sik⁹ sei² mau¹ *(translit.)*
Force somebody to eat a dead cat. (lit.)
Lay the blame upon somebody

for the fault.
Compel somebody to confess to having done something.
〔註〕表示把過失歸咎某人或強迫某人承認曾經做過……的意思。

1706　監人賴厚
gam¹ jɐn⁴ lai²/⁵ hɐu⁶ *(translit.)*
Force somebody to be intimate. (lit.)
Shamelessly take oneself for somebody's intimate.
〔註〕諷刺人不知羞恥地把自己當作某人的知己。

1707　疑心生暗鬼
ji⁴ sɐm¹ saŋ¹ ɐm³ gwɐi² *(translit.)*
Suspicion produces invisible ghost. (lit.)
Misgivings / Suspicions often bring about imaginary fears.

1708　鳳凰無寶不落
fuŋ⁶ wɔŋ⁴ mou⁴ bou² bɐt⁷ lɔk⁹ *(translit.)*
A male or a female phoenix does not come to the place where there is no treasure. (lit.)
Draw water to one's mill.
Where there is profit, there is one's trace.
〔註〕喻有利益的地方,便有某人的足跡。

1709　算死草
syn³ sei² tsou² *(translit.)*
Calculate the grass to death. (lit.)
Pinch and scrape.
Pinch pennies.
Be misery.
A penny-pincher.
〔註〕喻精打細算或吝嗇,有時亦喻精打細算的人。

1710　領嘢
lɛŋ⁶ jɛ⁵ *(translit.)*
Accept something. (lit.)
Rise to a bait.
Swallow the bait.
Be swindled.
Be caught with chaff.
〔註〕相當於"上當"(即被騙)。

1711　銅銀買病豬 —— 大家偷歡喜
tuŋ⁴ ŋɐn⁴ mai⁵ bɛŋ⁶ dzy¹ dai⁶ ga¹ tɐu¹ fun¹ hei² *(translit.)*
Buy a sickly pig with copper-silver coins (false money) — both sides feel happy on the sly. (lit.)
Each of the two hugs himself on having cheated the other.
Each of the two laughs in his sleeve in spite of being deceived by the other.
〔註〕買方用僞幣,而賣方以次貨充好貨,及至雙方交易成功,彼此認爲自己詭計得逞而暗自歡喜。因此這俚語便喻以爲自己騙了別人,不知自己也是受騙者。

1712　飽死
bau² sei² *(translit.)*

Die of eating to fill. (lit.)
Be exasperated against somebody.
Be irritated by somebody's ...
Be ruffled./Be annoyed for ...
〔註〕這是輕蔑或挖苦別人的口頭語，意爲"氣死"或"氣壞"，有時又可說成"飽死荷蘭豆"，參閱該條（B381）。

1713 認低威
jiŋ⁶ dɐi¹ wɐi¹ (*translit.*)
Confess to be low-dignified. (*lit.*)
Say uncle.
Confess to be unworthy.
Admit to be inferior to somebody.
〔註〕意指服輸，甘拜下風。

1714 滿肚密圈
mun⁵ tou⁵ mɐt⁹ hyn¹ (*translit.*)
The belly is full of close circles. (*lit.*)
Be full of wrinkles.
Have full confidence to overcome the difficulties.
Be sure of the success.
〔註〕表示足智多謀，自信可克服困難或對成功有把握。

1715 漏氣
lɐu⁶ hei³ (*translit.*)
Leak air. (*lit.*)
Be unhurried and unperturbed.
Be sluggish.
〔註〕形容人做事拖沓或慢吞吞的。

1716 漏罅
lɐu⁶ la³ (*translit.*)
Leaking gap. (*lit.*)
A loophole.
A leak.
Slip over.
Miss out.
〔註〕作名詞用時，指漏洞；差錯，但作動詞時，表示疏忽或遺漏的意思。

1717 滲氣
tsɐm³ hei³ (*translit.*)
Talky-aired. (*lit.*)
Be long-winded.
Be wordy.
〔註〕表示絮絮叨叨的意思，參閱"啍沉"條（1532）。

1718 寡母婆死仔——冇晒希望
gwa² mou⁵ pɔ² sei² dzɐi²——mou⁵ sai³ hei¹ mɔŋ⁶ (*translit.*)
The sole son of a widow died — have not any hope. (*lit.*)
Be driven to despair.
Be in a desperate state.
Pin one's hope on nobody.
〔註〕表示沒了希望的意思。

1719 寡母婆咁多心
gwa² mou⁵ pɔ² gɐm³ dɔ¹ sɐm¹ (*translit.*)
Have as many minds as a widow. (*lit.*)
Hang in doubt.
Be in two minds.
Shilly-shally.
〔註〕參閱"三心兩意"（0139），

"心多多"(0345)及"十五個銅錢分兩份"(0077)各條。

1720 寧犯天條，莫犯衆憎
niŋ⁴ fan⁶ tin¹ tiu⁴, mɔk⁹ fan⁶ dzuŋ³ dzɐŋ¹ (translit.)
Rather commit an offence against heaven disciplines than cause the hatred of the public monks. (lit.)
It is wise not to offend the public.
〔註〕勸人不要犯衆怒的警誡語。

1721 寧食開眉粥，莫食愁眉飯
niŋ⁴ sik⁹ hɔi¹ mei⁴ dzuk⁷, mɔk⁹ sik⁹ sɐu⁴ mei⁴ fan⁸ (translit.)
Prefer to eat congee of happiness rather than cooked-rice of sadness. (lit.)
Had rather be poor but happy than become rich but anxious.
Prefer to be under-paid for good treatment rather than well-paid for being ill-treated.
〔註〕表達個人寧貧而樂，勝於富而憂或寧受低薪而受良好待遇於高薪而受不良待遇的心情。

1722 寧欺白鬚公，莫欺鼻涕蟲
niŋ⁴ hei¹ bak⁹ sou¹ guŋ¹, mɔk⁹ hei¹ bei⁶ tɐi³ tsuŋ⁴ (translit.)
Rather insult a white-bearded man than a snivel-worm (small boy). (lit.)
A colt may make a good horse.
Kids are full of promise.

〔註〕表示後生可畏，不容輕視。

1723 實牙實齒
sɐt⁹ ŋa⁴ sɐt⁹ tsi² (translit.)
Say with solid teeth. (lit.)
Exhort again and again.
Clinch one's instruction.
〔註〕表示千叮嚀萬囑咐的意思。

1724 實食冇黐牙
sɐt⁹ sik⁹ mou⁵ tsi¹ ŋa⁴ (translit.)
Sure to eat without sticking to the teeth. (lit.)
Be in the bag.
Be well in hand.
Be sure of the success.
Have the ball at one's feet.
〔註〕表示完全有把握，十拿九穩。

1725 實鼓實鑿
sɐt⁹ gu² sɐt⁹ dzɔk⁹ (translit.)
Real drums and real chisels. (lit.)
Be neither garish nor gaudy.
Be solid worth.
〔註〕即並非花裏胡哨的，並無虛飾的或有實際價值的。

1726 瘟瘟沌沌
wɐn¹ wɐn¹ dɐn⁶ dɐn⁶ (translit.)
Be dazzled. (lit.)
Lose one's consciousness.
Lapse into delirium.
Have a perplexed look.
Be at a loss.
〔註〕指迷迷糊糊，頭腦不大清醒或惘然若失的樣子。

1727 對牛彈琴

doey³ ŋɐu⁴ tan⁴ kɐm⁴ *(translit.)*

Play the harp to a cow. *(lit.)*

Speak to the wrong audience.

Sing to a mule.

〔註〕比喻對愚蠢的人講深刻的道理或用來譏笑說話的人不看對象。

1728 端端度度

dyn¹ dyn¹ dɔk⁹ dɔk⁹ *(translit.)*

Scrutinize and measure. *(lit.)*

Have evil intention.

Have ulterior motives.

Be calculating.

Have one's own calculation.

Be in quest of ...

〔註〕表示心懷鬼胎，老在打算着或心存謀取……的意思。

1729 精人出口，笨人出手

dzɛŋ¹ jɐn⁴ tsœt⁷ hɐu², bɐn⁶ jɐn⁴ tsœt⁷ sɐu² *(translit.)*

A wise man give words but a foolish man takes action. *(lit.)*

Words are cleverer than action.

1730 精打細算

dziŋ¹ da² sɐi³ syn³ *(translit.)*

Reckon cleverly and calculate carefully. *(lit.)*

Pinch and scrape.

Pinch pennies.

1731 精到出骨

dzɛŋ¹ dou³ tsœt⁷ gwɐt⁷ *(translit.)*

Cleverness comes out of bones. *(lit.)*

Act cleverly from selfish motives.

〔註〕形容人十分善於爲自己打算，非常自私。

1732 精埋一便

dzɛŋ¹ mai⁴ jɐt⁷ bin⁶ *(translit.)*

Be clever at one side. *(lit.)*

Be clever only at ill doings.

〔註〕指專把聰明用於做壞事，或爲自己打算。

1733 精歸左

dzɛŋ¹ gwɐi¹ dzɔ² *(translit.)*

Be clever at the left side. *(lit.)*

〔註〕同"精埋一便"（1732）。

1734 塵埃落定

tsɐn⁴ ɔi¹ lɔk⁹ diŋ⁶ *(translit.)*

The dust has come down. *(lit.)*

All is fixed.

Everything is decided.

The outcome has come to a conclusion.

〔註〕表示一切已定或大局已定的意思。

1735 慢工出細貨

man⁶ guŋ¹ tsœt⁷ sɐi³ fɔ³ *(translit.)*

Slow work produces fine goods. *(lit.)*

Soft fire makes sweet malt.

〔註〕指精雕細刻才做成的精緻的作品。

1736 肇慶荷包 ── 陀衰人
siu⁶ hiŋ³ hɔ⁴ bau¹ ─ tɔ⁴ sœy¹ jɐn⁴ (translit.)
The purse made in Siu Hiŋ — bring distress to people (lit.)
A person who involves somebody in a disastrous state.
A person who causes somebody to suffer a loss.
〔註〕參閱"陀衰家"（0977）及"搭沉船"（1601）條。肇慶除以"端硯"馳名外，草蓆亦為名產，從前使用硬幣，出外購物，因硬幣重，甚感不便，遂有"荷包"出現，製造"荷包"材料，有布或皮革等，但肇慶荷包為用水草織成，因該地盛產水草，就地取材，不過由於不夠耐用，配帶者常因荷包破而招損失，遂有這俚語。

1737 嘥
sai¹ (translit.)
Speak ironically. (lit.)
Play down somebody.
Depreciate somebody.
Give a dig at somebody.
Go to waste.
〔註〕表示貶低，挖苦，誹謗人或浪費糟蹋東西。

1738 嘥心機
sai¹ sɐm¹ gei¹ (translit.)
Waste the mental labour. (lit.)
Flog a dead horse.
Plough the sand.
Shoe the goose.
All the mental care expends to no purpose.
Bark up the wrong tree.
〔註〕白費勁。

1739 嘥鬼氣嘑
sai¹ gwɐi² hei³ la¹ (translit.)
Waste air. (lit.)
It wastes energy/breath.
Waste one's words.
It is of no use.
〔註〕表示白費唇舌的意思。（1738條指腦力而這條則指唇舌方面。）

1740 嘥燈賣油
sai¹ dɐŋ¹ mai⁶ jɐu⁴ (translit.)
Waste the lamp and sell the oil. (lit.)
A game not worth a candle.
Let the gas go to waste.
〔註〕表示不值得花工夫去做的意思。

1741 嘥聲壞氣
sai¹ sɛŋ¹ wai⁶ hei³ (translit.)
Waste the sound and spoil the air. (lit.)
〔註〕同嘥鬼氣嘑（1739）。

1742 嘥撻
sai¹ tat⁸ (translit.)
Waste. (lit.)
Go to waste.
Squander.
〔註〕浪費，糟蹋。

1743 踎墩

mɐu¹ dɐn¹　(translit.)
Squat on a mound.　(lit.)
Out of work.
Be unemployed.
〔註〕喻失業，相當於"家蹲兒"。

1744　聞見棺材香
mɐn⁴ gin³ gun¹ tsɔi⁴ hœŋ¹
(translit.)
Smell the fragrance of the coffin.　(lit.)
Have one's foot in the grave.
Be at the death's door.
Live to a great age.
〔註〕喻離死不遠（用於對老年人的刻薄話）。

十五畫

1745　賣大包
mai⁶ dai⁶ bau¹　(translit.)
Sell big steamed stuffed-buns. (lit.)
Bargain away.
Price-war.
Play up to somebody.
Curry favour with somebody.
〔註〕表示廉價出售的意思。從前廣州有所謂"二釐館"者（下級茶館，茶價只收二釐錢），光顧的人，多爲貧苦大衆，這些二釐館爲了爭取顧客，特在每日早晨推出一種大包，內有燒肉，雞，叉燒，鹹蛋等物。而體積有若大飯碗，且售價僅爲一分二釐（等於今日一角的六份之一），普通人吃一個足够一餐。因這樣大包收到生意興隆之效，不少茶館，甚至較高級的也爭相效尤，遂又含有廉價出售，"減價戰"的意思。進而引伸成爲賣人情，"迎合別人"，或"希望得人歡心"的口頭語了。

1746　賣口乖
mai⁶ hɐu² gwai¹　(translit.)
Sell the cleverness of the mouth. (lit.)
Oil one's tongue.
Say holiday words.
Talk glibly.
Boast somebody to the skies.
〔註〕表示用甜言蜜語或稱讚的話來取悅人的意思。

1747　賣仔莫摸頭
mai⁶ dzɐi² mɔk⁹ mɔ¹ tɐu⁴
(translit.)
While selling a son, do not touch his head.　(lit.)
Be very sorry to bargain away something that one loves most.
Be heart-struck to sell one's favourite at a bargain price.
Sell one's hen on a rainy day.
Express regret at being forced to sell one's favourite.
〔註〕表示忍痛把自己的心愛東西賤價出售的意思。

1748　賣花姑娘插竹葉
mai⁶ fa¹ gu¹ nœŋ⁴ tsap⁸ dzuk⁷ jip⁹　(translit.)

The girl who sells flowers puts on bamboo leaves. (lit.)

A tailor makes the man but he clothes himself in rags.

〔註〕表示自己捨不得用自己所賣的東西或薄於自奉的意思。

1749 賣花讚花香
mai⁶ fa¹ dzan³ fa¹ hœŋ¹ (translit.)

Those who sell flowers praise their flowers for fragrance. (lit.)

There is nothing like leather.
Sing one's own praises.
Make a boast of oneself.

〔註〕自己稱讚自己的意思，相當於"老王賣瓜自賣自誇"。

1750 賣面光
mai⁶ min⁶ gwɔŋ¹· (translit.)

Sell the light of the face. (lit.)

Curry favour with somebody.
Ingratiate oneself into somebody's favour.

〔註〕意指買好，拍馬屁或討好。

1751 賣剩蔗
mai⁶ dziŋ⁶/siŋ⁶ dzɛ³ (translit.)

The sugar-cane left over unsold. (lit.)

A girl/daughter who remains unmarried off.
A person without a dancing partner in the ball.
The article(s) left over and unsold.

〔註〕比喻剩下未嫁的女兒，舞會中沒有舞伴的人或剩下而賣不去的貨物。

1752 賣鹹酸菜 —— 畀面
mai⁶ ham⁴ syn¹ tsɔi³ —— bei² min² (translit.)

Sell pickles — give face. (lit.)

Give face to somebody.
Show respect for somebody.

〔註〕表示給某人面子的意思。鹹酸菜是一層一層疊在埕或缸內，賣時絕不能翻亂，必須從上層按次序賣出，所以有"畀面（上層）"的說法，這是語帶雙關的俚語。

1753 熱氣飯
jit⁹ hei³ fan⁶ (translit.)

The cooked-rice causing fever. (lit.)

The devil to pay.
A difficult job.

〔註〕比喻可怕的後果，未來的麻煩或不容易做的工作。

1754 熱煮不能熱食
jit⁹ dzy² bɐt⁷ nɐŋ⁴ jit⁹ sik⁹ (translit.)

Cannot eat anything that is boiling hot. (lit.)

Fool's haste is no speed.
Be patient to wait.

〔註〕喻欲速則不達。

1755 墟冚
hœy¹ hɐm⁶ (translit.)

Bustle. (lit.)

Be as bustling as a market.
Be bustling with noise and excitement.
Be in a bustle.

Spread around.
Give publicity to something.
〔註〕形容人聲嘈雜，亂哄哄的像集市一樣。但如作動詞時，則表示張揚的意思。

1756 撞火
dzɔŋ⁶ fɔ² *(translit.)*
Knock against fire. (lit.)
Make one get angry.
Become furious.
〔註〕表示生氣，發火兒。

1757 撞手神
dzɔŋ⁶ sɐu² sɐn⁴ *(translit.)*
Meet the luck with a hand. (lit.)
Try one's luck.
Take a chance.
〔註〕碰運氣的意思（一般用於與手的動作有關的活動，如賭博，抓鬮等）。參閱"撞彩"條(1760)。

1758 撞死馬
dzɔŋ⁶ sei² ma⁵ *(translit.)*
Bump into a horse to death. (lit.)
A person who jostles his way in hot haste.
〔註〕比喻橫衝直撞的人。

1759 撞〔到〕正
dzɔŋ⁶ [dou]³ dzɛn³ *(translit.)*
Bump right against. (lit.)
Coincide with ...
By a curious coincidence.
By chance.
As luck would have it.
〔註〕意爲碰巧，參閱"撞啱"（1761）及"碰啱"條（1606）。

1760 撞彩
dzɔŋ⁶ tsɔi² *(translit.)*
Take a luck. (lit.)
Try one's luck.
Take a chance.
〔註〕指碰運氣的意思，而廣東人有時説成"碰吓彩數"（puŋ³ ha² tsɔi² sou³）。參閱"撞手神"條（1757），不過"撞彩"又被引伸作"撞啱"用，參閱該條（1761）。

1761 撞啱
dzɔŋ⁶ ŋam¹ *(translit.)*
Bump right against. (lit.)
Coincide with ...
By a curious coincidence.
By chance.
As luck would have it.
〔註〕意爲碰巧，參閱"撞〔到〕正"（1759）及"碰啱"條（1606）。

1762 撞鬼
dzɔŋ²/⁶ gwɐi² *(translit.)*
Meet with a ghost. (lit.)
Have come up against fantasticality.
Be down on one's luck.
〔註〕即活見鬼或倒霉。

1763 撚化
nɐn² fa³ *(translit.)*
Twist. (lit.)
Play a trick on somebody.
Twist somebody around one's finger.
Trick somebody into doing something.

〔註〕表示捉弄或愚弄的意思，參閱"整蠱"條（1811）。

1764　撩是鬥非
liu⁴ si⁶ dɐu³ fei¹　(translit.)
Tease right and provoke wrong. (lit.)
Stir up a quarrel.
Pick a quarrel.
Wake a sleeping dog.
〔註〕表示尋衅的意思。

1765　撇脫／撇撇脫脫
pit⁸ tyt⁸／pit⁸ pit⁸ tyt⁸ tyt⁸　(translit.)
Cast way. (lit.)
Be prompt in action.
Fish or cut the bait.
Make a prompt decision.
Not to muddle away.
Bring to a quick decision.
〔註〕形容做事爽快，絕不拖泥帶水。

1766　撐／蹭枱腳
tsaŋ³／jaŋ³ tɔi² gœk⁸　(translit.)
Prop against the legs of a table. (lit.)
Have a meal with one's wife/lover.
〔註〕形容和妻子或愛人共同進餐的情形。

1767　撈賸水
lou¹ dziŋ⁶ sœy²　(translit.)
Get the remnents (of the spails). (lit.)
Obtain an unnoticed advantage.
Gain the profit to which nobody pays attention.
Have all to oneself.
〔註〕比喻從別人不大注意的地方，或看不起的事物中，得到很大好處或利益。

1768　撈過界
lou¹ gwɔ² gai³　(translit.)
Do business beyond the demarcarcation line. (lit.)
Have a foot in another's domain.
〔註〕表示串地盤，侵入別人的勢力範圍的意思。

1769　擒青／擒擒青
kɐm⁴ tsɛŋ¹／kɐm⁴ kɐm² tsɛŋ¹　(translit.)
In a hurry. (lit.)
Be in a tearing hurry.
Be short-tempered.
Be too impatient to wait.
Leap without thinking.
Be rash.
〔註〕表示忽忽忙忙的樣子，魯莽，莽撞。

1770　撬牆腳
giu⁶ tsœŋ⁴ gœk⁸　(translit.)
Prize off the foot of a wall. (lit.)
Carry off somebody's lover.
Snatch the business from one's competitor.
〔註〕指把別人的情人佔為己有或奪去別人的生意的一種行為。

1771　標青
biu¹ tsɛŋ¹　(translit.)
Shoot out the green. (lit.)

Be tip-top.
Be outstanding.
Have good looks.
〔註〕出衆，拔尖兒，亦表示美貌出衆。

1772 標參
biu¹ sɐm¹ *(translit.)*
Snatch the ginseng. (lit.)
Kidnap a person for a king's ransom.
Hold somebody to ransom.
〔註〕即綁票。

1773 標松柴
biu¹ tsuŋ⁴ tsai⁴ *(translit.)*
Shoot off pine wood. (lit.)
Embezzle somebody's money.
Line one's pockets with somebody's money.
Divert somebody's money to one's own pockets.
〔註〕表示侵吞，中飽或把別人的錢據爲己有的意思。

1774 靠呃
kau³ ŋɐk⁷ *(translit.)*
Rely on deceiving. (lit.)
Live by getting something on the cross.
Double-cross somebody to earn one's living.
Sell somebody down the river.
〔註〕表示以欺騙爲生或欺騙。

1775 靠害
kau³ hɔi⁶ *(translit.)*
Do harm. (lit.)
Lead somebody into a trap.
Entrap somebody into a difficult situation.
〔註〕誘使人陷入困境的意思，相當於"坑人"。

1776 靠諦
kau³ dɐi³ *(translit.)*
Make use of scathing satire. (lit.)
Talk at somebody.
Pout ridicule on somebody.
〔註〕表示冷嘲熱諷的意思，參閱"單單打打"條（1563）。

1777 劉備借荆州 —— 有借冇回頭
Lɐu⁴ Bei²ᐟ⁶ dzɛ³ Giŋ¹ Dzɐu¹—jɐu⁵ dzɛ³ mou⁵ wui⁴ tɐu⁴ *(translit.)*
Lau Bei borrowed Kingchow — borrowing it but never returning it (lit.)
Not to discharge/return the borrowing.
The loan once given never comes back.
Lau Bei — the emperor of the Minor Han (Hɔn³) Dynasty in the period of The Three Kingdoms 221 A.D.
〔註〕指借出的東西永沒有歸還或從不歸還借來的東西。

1778 蝨乸都要檐枷
sɐt⁷ ŋa² dou¹ jiu³ dam¹ ga¹ *(translit.)*
Even all the fleas have to put on wooden collars. (lit.)
Deserve a very severe punishment.

Even one's family are implicated in a severe punishment.

〔註〕表示除個人應受極嚴厲的懲罰外，甚至連家人也得受嚴厲的懲罰。

1779 蝕底

sit⁹ dɐi² *(translit.)*

Diminish the bottom by encroachment. (lit.)

Suffer losses.

Be in unfavourable situation.

Come to grief.

Get the worst of it.

〔註〕遭受損失，處於不利地位或吃虧。

1780 膝頭哥撟眼淚

sɐt⁷ tɐu⁴ gɔ¹ giu² ŋan⁵ lœy⁶ *(translit.)*

Wipe tears with a knee. (lit.)

Commit a gross error and shed sad tears.

〔註〕表示"鑄成大錯而傷心流淚"的意思。

1781 潮州音樂 ── 自己顧自己

tsiu⁴ dzɐu¹ jɐm¹ ŋɔk⁹—dzi⁶ gei¹ᐟ² gu³ dzi⁶ gei¹ᐟ² *(translit.)*

Chiuchow music—one looks after oneself. (lit.)

Take care of oneself.

Near is my shirt, but nearest us my skin.

Pay one's bill for oneself.

Pay for something at one's own expense.

〔註〕自己照顧自己或各自付賬的意思，相當於"老西兒拉胡琴──自顧自"。

1782 潑冷水

put⁸ laŋ⁵ sœy² *(translit.)*

Sprinkle cold water. (lit.)

Throw cold water on somebody.

Discourage somebody from doing something.

Throw a wet blanket over somebody.

〔註〕表示掃興，使人洩氣或打擊人（做某事）的熱情。

1783 潑辣

put⁸ lat⁹ *(translit.)*

Be shrewish-tempered. (lit.)

Be both shrewish and violent.

〔註〕形容人兇悍而不講理。

1784 論盡

lœn⁶ dzœn⁶ *(translit.)*

Slow-moving. (lit.)

Be both doddery and obtuse.

Be not smart enough.

It is too bad.

Burdensome / cumbersome.

〔註〕形容老年人遲鈍，老態龍鍾；年青人舉止不靈活；物件累贅，笨重而不方便的意思。除此之外，還作感歎詞作糟糕意思用。

1785 諗縮數

nɐm² suk⁷ sou³ *(translit.)*

Think of shrinking account. (lit.)

Be petty and scheming.

Pursue selfish interests.

〔註〕爲自己打如意算盤或謀私利的

意思。

1786 諗爛心肝
nɐm² lan⁶ sɐm¹ gɔn¹ *(translit.)*
Deep thinking makes the heart and livers be rotten. *(lit.)*
Chew the cud.
Ponder deeply over ...
Take counsel of one's pillow.
〔註〕表示反覆思量或思考得不能入睡的意思。

1787 窮到燶
kuŋ⁴ dou³ luŋ¹ *(translit.)*
Being poor up to the degree of being scorched. *(lit.)*
Be as poor as a church mouse.
Have not a feather to fly with.
Have not a bean.
Be down on one's uppers.
〔註〕比喻一貧如洗。

1788 窮寇莫追
kuŋ⁴ kɐu³ mɔk⁹ dzœy¹
(translit.)
Do not run after a foe too far. *(lit.)*
Not to try to run after the hard-pressed enemy.
〔註〕原指圍殲敵人時要講究策畧，對於陷入絕境的敵人不可逼得太緊，否則它會困獸搏鬥，造成己方不必要的損失。後引伸爲不追無路可走的敵人。

1789 熠熟狗頭
sap⁹ suk⁹ gɐu² tɐu⁴ *(translit.)*
A well-boiled dog's head.

(lit.)
Be on the broad grin.
Have a face beaming with smiles.
〔註〕形容人笑得齜牙咧嘴的樣子。

1790 熟人買破鑊
suk⁹ jɐn⁴ mai⁵ pɔ³ wɔk⁹ *(translit.)*
A familiar friend buys a broken frying-pan. *(lit.)*
Be sold a pup by one's friend.
Be imposed by one's friend.
〔註〕指被熟人以次貨欺騙，上熟人的當。

1791 摩囉差拜神 —— 睇天
mɔ¹ lɔ¹ tsa¹ bai³ sɐn⁴—tɐi² tin¹ *(translit.)*
Indians worship their god — look at the sky. *(lit.)*
Be under the mercy of God.
Take notice of the change of weather.
It depends on the weather.
〔註〕表示一切望上蒼庇佑，（參閱1353"望天打卦"條）或視天氣情況而定的意思。

1792 瘦田有人耕，耕親有人爭
sɐu³ tin⁴ mou⁵ jɐn⁴ gɐŋ¹, gɐŋ¹ tsɐn¹ jɐu⁵ jɐn⁴ dzaŋ¹ *(translit.)*
No man ploughs a barren field, but if it is ploughed, others will fight for it. *(lit.)*
Once a wasteland is inhabited, a rush for an occupation is insisted.

〔註〕暗喻一向沒人歡迎的東西，一旦有人垂注，便立即成爲爭取的對象。

1793 數還數，路還路
sou³ wan⁴ sou³, lou⁶ wan⁴ lou⁶　*(translit.)*
A sum is a sum and a road is a road.　(lit.)
Balance accounts with somebody in spite of intimates.
〔註〕即人情是人情，數目要算清。

1794 踩着/倒芋荵都當蛇
tsai² dzœk⁹/dou² wu⁶ hap³ dou¹ dɔŋ³ sɛ⁴　*(translit.)*
Stepping on a leaf-stalk of taro is thought as stepping on a snake.　(lit.)
Take every bush for a bugbear.
〔註〕表示杯弓蛇影的意思。

1795 踩親……條尾
tsai² tsɐn¹ ... tiu⁴ mei⁵　*(translit.)*
Tread somebody's tail.　(lit.)
Cause offence to somebody.
Touch somebody to his pain.
〔註〕表示觸怒某人或觸犯了某人的忌諱。

1796 踩死蟻
tsai² sei² ŋai⁵　*(translit.)*
Tread ants to death.　(lit.)
Walk at a snail's pace.
Be snail-slow.
〔註〕比喻慢吞吞的走路。

1797 劏死牛
tɔŋ¹ sei² ŋɐu⁴　*(translit.)*
Slaughter a dead cow.　(lit.)

Highjack.
〔註〕即攔路搶劫。參閱"打腳骨"（0440）條。

1798 劏光豬
tɔŋ¹ gwɔg¹ dzy¹　*(translit.)*
Butcher naked pig.　(lit.)
All the pieces (chessmen) have been taken by the opponent.
〔註〕比喻下棋時，棋子全被對方吃光。

1799 暴富難睇
bou⁶ fu³ nan⁴ tɐi²　*(translit.)*
A parvenu is unpleasing to look at.　(lit.)
Set a beggar on horse-back and he'll ride to the devil.
〔註〕指暴發户猖狂。

1800 幡竿燈籠——照遠唔照近
fan¹ gɔn¹ dɐŋ¹ luŋ⁴—dziu³ jyn⁵ m⁴ dziu³ kɐn⁵　*(translit.)*
The lantern on the banner pole calling the soul home—It illuminates far, not near.　(lit.)
Benefit any other persons than close ones.
Rather help outsiders than insiders.
〔註〕表示寧關照外人而不關照自己人的意思。

1801 踏兩頭船
dap⁹ lœŋ⁵ tɐu⁴ syn⁴　*(translit.)*

Stand on two boats. (lit.)
Play both ends against the middle.
Attempt to profit oneself in two ways.
Fall between two stools.
Seek favour with opposing parties.

〔註〕參閱"一腳踏兩船"條（0055）。

1802 劈炮
pɛk⁸ pau³　*(translit.)*
Chop a cannon. (lit.)
Quit from one's job.

〔註〕這是較新的口頭語，意爲辭職不幹。

1803 劈〔殟〕揞鑿
pɛk⁸ nɐn² dzɔk²　*(translit.)*
In spite of being cloven, one makes the chisel dirty. (lit.)
A person who swears black is white.
A person who denies having done something.

〔註〕比喻顛倒是非或否認幹過某事的人。迷信者相信雷神會劈那些不忠不孝或不義的人，對於那些顛倒是非或幹過壞事也否認的人，即使受雷神劈了也會弄污他的鑿。"揞"廣東人除作"玩弄"意思外，還借音作"弄污"解。

十六畫

1804 融洽

juŋ⁴ hɐp⁷　*(translit.)*
On friendly terms. (lit.)
Get along well with each other.
Be harmonious with each other.

1805 豬頭骨
dzy¹ tɐu⁴ gwɐt⁷　*(translit.)*
A pig's skull. (lit.)
A job/workpiece without profit-margin.
A bad job.

〔註〕"豬頭骨"無肉可食，即使吃之也費時，因此以此比喻無利可圖的工作或白費勁的工作。

1806 豬欄報數——又一隻
dzy¹ lan¹ bou³ sou³—jɐu⁶ jɐt⁷ dzɛk⁸　*(translit.)*
A wholesaler of pigs reports the number—one more. (lit.)
One more has died.

〔註〕比喻又多死了一人。

1807 豬籠入水
dzy¹ luŋ⁴ jɐp⁹ sœy²　*(translit.)*
The water comes into a pig's bamboo cage. (lit.)
One's money comes from everywhere.
One's financial resources come from all directions.

〔註〕比喻某人財源廣進。

1808 整古做怪
dziŋ² gu² dzou⁶ gwai³　*(translit.)*
Make strangeness and do peculiarities. (lit.)
Make a face.

Make mystery of something.
Wrap something in mystery.
〔註〕表示做鬼臉故意出洋相或故弄玄虛的意思。

1809 整色整水
dziŋ² sik¹ dziŋ² sœy² *(translit.)*
Make colours and water. (lit.)
Put on an act.
〔註〕裝模作樣。

1810 整定
dziŋ² diŋ⁶ *(translit.)*
Be determined. (lit.)
Be destined.
Destinies grasp one's fate.
〔註〕即某種客觀規律決定，注定。

1811 整蠱
dziŋ² gu² *(translit.)*
Make noxious worms. (lit.)
Play a trick on somebody.
Play pranks upon somebody.
Trick somebody into doing something.
Frame up somebody.
Catch somebody in a trap.
〔註〕表示捉弄或惡作劇，參閱"撚化"條（1763）或陷害的意思。

1812 頭痛醫頭，腳痛醫腳
tɐu⁴ tuŋ³ ji¹ tɐu⁴, gœk⁸ tuŋ³ ji¹ gœk⁸ *(translit.)*
Cure the head when it aches; cure the leg when it aches. (lit.)
Take only a stopgap measure, not a radical one.

〔註〕比喻治標不治本的方法。

1813 頭頭碰着黑
tɐu⁴ tɐu⁴ puŋ³ dzœk⁸ hɐk⁷ *(translit.)*
Meet with black in every direction. (lit.)
Strike a snag everywhere.
Run into snags in all directions.
Meet with difficulties whatever one does.
〔註〕到處碰壁的意思。

1814 頭髮尾浸浸涼
tɐu⁴ fat³ mei⁵ dzɐm³ dzɐm³ lœŋ⁴ *(translit.)*
All the ends of hair become cool. (lit.)
Gloat over somebody's/one's enemy's misfortune.
〔註〕參閱"心都涼晒"條（0355）及"幸災樂禍"條（0850）。

1815 靜靜雞/靜雞雞
dziŋ⁶ dziŋ² gɐi¹/dziŋ⁶ gɐi¹ gɐi¹ *(translit.)*
Keep silence. (lit.)
Keep one's hair on.
Keep one's countenance without a word.
Bite one's lips.
Act in silence.
〔註〕指保持鎮靜，不露聲色或靜悄悄地行事。

1816 霎眼嬌
sap⁸ ŋan⁵ giu¹ *(translit.)*
Instant beauty. (lit.)
Appear to be beautiful at a

glance.

〔註〕乍看起來，似乎漂亮的意思。

1817　雯戀！

sap⁸ ŋɔŋ⁶! *(translit.)*

Scoundrel! (lit.)

(You) preposterous Bastard!

〔註〕即"傻瓜"，"荒謬"或"混賬"。

1818　輸蝕

sy¹ sit⁹ *(translit.)*

Suffer losses. (lit.)

Be inferior to ...
Be lower-graded than ...
Be on a lower level.
Let another boat eat the wind out of one's own.
Let somebody gain the wind.

〔註〕差；差勁；吃虧或讓人佔上風的意思。

1819　軟皮蛇

jyn⁵ pei⁴ sɛ⁴ *(translit.)*

A soft-skinned snake. (lit.)

A person who neither cuts up stiff nor reacts to blames.
A person who acts in a slick way.

〔註〕比喻對譴責無反應及不易發怒的人或疲疲杳杳，對甚麼都無所謂的人。

1820　擔屎都唔偷食

dam¹ si² dou¹ m⁴ tɐu¹ sik⁹ *(translit.)*

While carrying manure with a pole on a shoulder, one does not steal any of it to eat.

(lit.)

Be very honest in deed.

〔註〕形容人誠實可靠。

1821　擔戴

dam¹ dai³ *(translit.)*

Carry and bring something on the shoulder. (lit.)

Undertake responsibility.

〔註〕表示擔待；承擔責任的意思。

1822　搣/捵衫尾

mɐŋ¹ sam¹ mei⁵ *(translit.)*

Drag the tail of a coat. (lit.)

Ask gambling winners for money/tips outside the casino.

〔註〕指在賭館門外向贏錢賭客乞取賞錢的行為（也有人說成拉衫尾）。

1823　擇使

dzak⁹ sɐi² *(translit.)*

Trouble with. (lit.)

Be troublesome.
Have some trouble in doing something.
It is a headache.
It embarrasses one.
Put one to inconvenience.
Have difficulty in dealing with ...

〔註〕表示麻煩，傷腦筋，難辦或不好使用，不方便。

1824　樹大有枯枝，族大有乞兒

sy⁶ dai⁶ jɐu⁵ fu¹ dzi¹, dzuk⁹ dai⁶ jɐu⁵ hɐt⁷ ji⁴ *(translit.)*

Big trees have decayed

branches; big clans may have beggars. (lit.)

There is a black sheep in every fold.

〔註〕意即十個指頭有長短；哪裏都有害羣之馬。

1825　樹大招風
sy⁶ dai⁶ dziu¹ fuŋ¹　(translit.)

Big trees catch much wind. (lit.)

A person of reputation is liable to become the envy of others.

〔註〕比喻名聲大或地位高的人在社會上特別顯眼，往往容易給自己招來麻煩或招人嫉妒。

1826　樹倒猢猻散
sy⁶ dou² wu⁴ syn¹ san³　(translit.)

When a tree falls, all the monkeys scatter about. (lit.)

Rats leave a sinking ship.

As soon as an influential person falls from his position, all his hangers-on disperse.

〔註〕比喻人一失勢，追隨者亦隨而分散。

1827　樹高千丈，落葉歸根
sy⁶ gou¹ tsin¹ dzœŋ⁶, lɔk⁹ jip⁹ gwɐi¹ gɐn¹　(translit.)

Though a tree is ten thousand feet tall, the fallen leaves come back to its roots. (lit.)

No matter whether it is east or west, home is the best.

〔註〕上了年紀的國人，鄉土觀念甚強，無論在何處謀生，到了一個時期，總是忘不了故里而作鳥倦知還之想。這就是"樹高千丈，落葉歸根"的道理。

1828　橫九唔十
waŋ⁴ gɐu² dim⁴ sɐp⁹　(translit.)

The breadth is nine and the length is ten. (lit.)

Such being the case.

In any case.

In for a penny, in for a pound.

〔註〕這口頭語的意義是相當籠統的，既可表事實既然如此，又可表無論如何或橫豎，參閱"橫唔"條（1831），更可作"一不做，二不休"的意思。

1829　橫手
waŋ⁴ sɐu²　(translit.)

Cross hand. (lit.)

The person who acts underhand for somebody.

〔註〕指秘密代理某人的人。

1830　橫行霸道
waŋ⁴ hɐŋ⁴/haŋ⁴ ba³ dou⁶　(translit.)

Walk on the cross and act in tyrannous manner. (lit.)

Play the bully.

〔註〕仗勢欺人，做壞事；不講理。

1831　橫唔
waŋ⁴ dim⁶　(translit.)

Breadth and length. (lit.)

In any case.

Anyhow.

Anyway.
〔註〕表示無論如何，反正或橫豎的意思。

1832 橫哄都喺一樣
waŋ⁴ dim⁶ dou¹ hɐi⁶ jɐt⁷ jœŋ⁶ (translit.)
Breadth and length are the same. (lit.)
It is all the same to somebody.
It is the very same thing whether ...
〔註〕表示"對……而言，都是一樣"或作強調來表示"是否……也是完全一樣"的意思。

1833 橫衝直撞
waŋ⁴ tsuŋ¹ dzik⁹ dzɔŋ⁶ (translit.)
Rush horizontally and knock straightly. (lit.)
Collide in every direction.
Jostle and elbow one's way through a crowd.
〔註〕亂衝亂闖的意思。

1834 橫蠻無理
waŋ⁴ man⁴ mou⁴ lei⁵ (translit.)
Be beastly and reasonless. (lit.)
Be savage like a beast.

1835 醒水
siŋ² sœy² (translit.)
Wake the water. (lit.)
Come to realize ...
Be awake to ...
〔註〕即醒覺的意思。

1836 貓衣/兒毛 —— 順捏
mau¹ ji¹ mou⁴—sœn⁴ nip⁹ (translit.)
Kitten's hair—give it a smooth according to its natural tendency. (lit.)
Stroke the fur the right way.
Cater to smebody's tendency.
Beguile somebody with honeyed words.
〔註〕指對吃軟不吃硬的人的哄騙手段。

1837 貓哭老鼠 —— 假慈悲
mau¹ huk⁷ lou⁵ sy²—ga² tsi⁴ bei¹ (translit.)
A cat weeps for the rat—false mercy. (lit.)
Shed crocodile tears.

1838 錯有錯着
tsɔ³ jɐu⁵ tsɔ³ dzœk⁹ (translit.)
Take advantage of the mistake. (lit.)
Have a fault on the right side.
〔註〕因禍得福的意思。

1839 錯蕩
tsɔ³ dɔŋ⁶ (translit.)
Have a wrong stroll. (lit.)
Be honoured by the undeserved visit/presence.
Be glad to have the undeserved visit/presence.
〔註〕這是見到自己親朋忽然來訪時，一見面説的客套語，意爲承蒙枉顧，實感榮幸，愧不敢當。

1840 獨家村
duk⁹ ga¹ tsyn¹ (translit.)

One man's village. (lit.)
A person of uncommunicative and eccentric disposition.
An unsociable and eccentric person.
A lone wolf.
〔註〕比喻不好交際離羣獨居或難與爲友的人。

1841 餓死老婆燻臭屋
ŋɔ⁶ sei² lou⁵ pɔ⁴ fɐn¹ /wɐn¹ tsɐu³ uk⁷ (translit.)
Make a wife die of hunger and let her corpse vaporize the house to be foul. (lit.)
Cannot earn enough bread to get married.
One's income is too poor to have a wife.
Make one's wife suffer hunger due to insufficiency of income.
〔註〕表示收入不足以養妻室。

1842 餓狗搶屎
ŋɔ⁶ gɐu² tsœŋ² si² (translit.)
Hungry dogs fight to seize manure. (lit.)
Compete against each other for something.
〔註〕形容人搶奪東西時的醜態。

1843 餓鬼投胎
ŋɔ⁶ gwɐi² tɐu⁴ tɔi¹ (translit.)
A hungry ghost reincarated. (lit.)
Devour like a hungry tiger pouncing its prey.
Wolf down.
〔註〕形容人的吃相醜，意爲狼吞虎嚥的樣子。

1844 燒冷竈
siu¹ laŋ⁵ dzou³ (translit.)
Burn a cold stove. (lit.)
Back the wrong horse.
〔註〕比喻支持失勢的人，希望他重獲財勢時，獲得好處。

1845 燒到……嗰疊
siu¹ dou³ ... gɔ² dap⁹ (translit.)
The fire spreads to ... (lit.)
The spearhead is directed to somebody.
Drag somebody in ...
Transfer the subject of conversation to somebody.
〔註〕表示矛頭指向……身上，把某人拉進……之内或把話題轉移到某人身上的意思。

1846 燒枱炮
siu¹ tɔi⁴ pau³ (translit.)
Fire the big gun on the table. (lit.)
Thump the table/desk and heap abuse on somebody.
〔註〕拍桌子大罵。

1847 燒壞瓦
siu¹ wɐi⁶ ŋa⁵ (translit.)
An ill-burned tile. (lit.)
Can not adjust oneself to others.
Can not mate with others.
Not suit well with others.

〔註〕比喻和人合不來的人。

1848　燈芯搣成鐵
dɐŋ¹ sɐm¹ liŋ¹ siŋ⁴/sɛŋ⁴ tit⁸
(translit.)
Take a lamp wick for a long time and it will become iron. (lit.)
A straw shows its weight when it is carried a long way.
〔註〕比喻最輕的東西，拿上一段時間，也會變重。

1849　諸事
dzy¹ si⁶ (translit.)
Like to interfere in all matters. (lit.)
Like to poke one's nose into ...
Have an oar in every man's boat.
Poke and pry.
〔註〕指好管閒事。（"諸事"和"滋事"音義有別，"諸"爲dzy¹音，"滋"爲dzi¹音，但南海順德及小欖等地人士，則"諸""滋"兩音一樣作dzy¹音，"滋事"爲無事生非的意思。參閱1487條）。

1850　諸事理
dzy¹ si⁶ lei¹ (translit.)
A meddler. (lit.)
A Nosy Parker.
A meddler.
〔註〕指好管閒事的人。

1851　親力親爲
tsɐn¹ lik⁹ tsɐn¹ wɐi⁴ (translit.)
Do by oneself. (lit.)
Do the job all by oneself.

〔註〕親自動手的意思。

1852　親生仔不如近身錢
tsɐn¹ saŋ¹ dzɐi² bɐt⁷ jy⁴ gɐn⁶ sɐn¹ tsin⁴ (translit.)
A begotten son is not so good as the money in pocket. (lit.)
Money is the nearest relation.
〔註〕表示靠自己的積蓄勝過依靠兒子的意思。

1853　糖黏豆
tɔŋ⁴ tsi¹ dɐu² (translit.)
Beans stuck with sugar. (lit.)
Form a close connextion with each other.
Hand and glove.
〔註〕喻彼此友好關係密切。

1854　龍床唔似狗竇
luŋ⁴ tsɔŋ⁴ m⁴ tsi⁵ gɐu² dɐu³
(translit.)
A dragon (an imperial bed) is not like a dog's kennel. (lit.)
There is no place sweeter than home.
A man gets used to his own bed /kennel.
〔註〕相當於"金窩銀窩，不及自己的草窩"。

1855　龍游淺水遭蝦戲
luŋ⁴ jɐu⁴ tsin² sœy² dzou¹ ha¹ hei³ (translit.)
A dragon swimming in shallow water is fooled by shrimps. (lit.)
No man is a hero to his valet.
Out of one's sphere of influ-

ence, out of one's power.
〔註〕參閱"虎落平陽被犬欺"條
（0975）。

1856 褪舦
tɐn³ tai⁵ (translit.)
Turn back the steer. (lit.)
Beat a retreat.
Shrink back.
〔註〕即放棄，退縮或"打退堂鼓"參
閱該條（0433）。

1857 暫吓眼
dzam² ha² ŋan⁵ (translit.)
Wink the eyes. (lit.)
In a twinkle.
In a flash.
In an instant.
〔註〕一眨眼功夫，轉瞬之間。

1858 躁蹄躁爪
dɐm⁶ tɐi⁴ dɐm⁶ dzau²
(translit.)
Stamp both hoofs and paws. (lit.)
Stamp the floor in deep sorrow/in anger.
〔註〕形容傷心或憤怒時搥胸頓足的神態。

1859 頻倫
pɐn⁴ lɐn⁴ (translit.)
Hurry. (lit.)
Be in a tearing hurry.
Be hurry-scurry.
Hurry through something.
〔註〕匆匆忙忙；手忙腳亂。

1860 頻倫唔得入城
pɐn⁴ lɐn⁴ m⁴ dɐk⁷ jɐp⁹ sɛŋ⁴
(translit.)
Too hasty to enter the city. (lit.)
More haste, less speed.
A watched pot never boils.
〔註〕欲速則不達的意思。

1861 頻撲
pɐn⁴ pɔk⁸ (translit.)
Be busy running about. (lit.)
Have a run for one's money.
Shuttle back and forth for one's living.
〔註〕奔波或為生活東奔西走。

1862 險過剃頭
him² gwɔ³ tɐi³ tɐu⁴ (translit.)
More dangerous than shaving a head. (lit.)
Hang by a hair.
Be in great danger.
Be in the hour of peril.
〔註〕表示千鈞一髮的意思。

1863 遲到好過冇到
tsi⁴ dou³ hou² gɔ³ mou⁵ dou³
(translit.)
Coming lately is better than not coming. (lit.)
Rather late than never.
〔註〕表示晚到比不到要好。

1864 遲嚟先上岸
tsi⁴ lɐi⁴ sin¹ sœŋ⁵ ŋɔn⁶
(translit.)
Come late but go ashore first. (lit.)
The last comer becomes the first goer.
The person who comes first is

not like the one who comes all by a happy coincidence.

〔註〕相當於"來得早不如來得巧"。

1865 閻羅王揸攤 —— 鬼買

jim⁴ lɔ⁴ woŋ⁴ dza¹ tan¹ — gwɐi² mai⁵ *(translit.)*

The king of Jim Lɔ holds 'Fantan' (The king of hell is the bank of 'Fantan' — a form of gambling.) — ghosts bet. (lit.)

Nobody buys.

〔註〕真意為無人購買。

1866 閻羅王嫁女 —— 鬼要

jim⁴ lɔ⁴ woŋ⁴ ga³ nœy⁵ — gwɐi² jiu³ *(translit.)*

The king of Jim Lɔ (The king of hell) marries off his daughters — ghosts want. (lit.)

Nobody wants (it).

〔註〕表示沒有人要的意思。

十七畫

1867 聰明一世，蠢鈍一時

tsuŋ¹ miŋ⁴ jɐt⁷ sɐi³, tsœn² dœn⁶ jɐt⁷ si⁴ *(translit.)*

Be clever all the life but foolish for once. (lit.)

A smartie is not always as smart as a steel trap.

Be clever all the time but become a fool this once.

〔註〕表示一時糊塗的意思。

1868 聲大夾冇準

sɛŋ¹ dai⁶ gap⁸ mou⁵ dzœn² *(translit.)*

The voice is loud but not correct. (lit.)

Much cry and little wool.

〔註〕形容一個人說話很多，但沒一句是對的。

1869 聲大夾惡

sɛŋ¹ dai⁶ gap⁸ ɔk⁸ *(translit.)*

Be big-voiced and ferocious. (lit.)

Come the bully over somebody.

1870 擦錯鞋

tsat³ tsɔ³ hai⁴ *(translit.)*

Brush the wrong shoe. (lit.)

Stroke the fur the wrong way.

〔註〕比喻本來想討好某人，但結果適得其反。

1871 擰到骨罅都刺埋

sɛŋ³/sɐn³ dou³ gwɐt⁷ la³ dou¹ tsɛk⁸ mai⁴ *(translit.)*

Utter moans until the articulations of the bones ache. (lit.)

Make a constant complaint for having paid so much for something.

〔註〕指因付出代價太多而發出怨言，參閱"擰到樹葉都落埋"條（1872）。

1872 擰到樹葉都落埋

sɛŋ³/sɐn³ dou³ sy¹ jip⁹ dou¹ lɔk⁹ mai⁴ *(translit.)*

Utter moans until all the leaves

have fallen. (lit.)
Express one's repentance for having paid for something worthless.
Make a constant complaint for having paid so much for something.
Feel sorry for having missed a chance.

〔註〕大致和"擝到骨罅都刺埋"同義，但這句更表示因花了錢購得無用的東西而懊悔或因失去機會而難過的意思。

1873 擝笨
sɐŋ³/sɛn³ bɐn⁶ (translit.)
Utter moans for stupidity. (lit.)
Show repentance for having been stupid/fooled.
Feel sorry for having missed the opportunity.

〔註〕表示因自己過去愚昧，被騙或失去機會而後悔的意思。

1874 膽大心細
dam² dai⁶ sɐm¹ sɐi³ (translit.)
The gall is big and the heart is small. (lit.)
Be bold but cautious.
Be courageous but attentive.

1875 膽正命平
dam² dzɛŋ³ mɛŋ⁶ pɛŋ⁴/dam² dziŋ³ miŋ⁶ pɛŋ⁴ (translit.)
The gall is upright and the life is cheap. (lit.)
Have too much spunk to care for one's own life.

〔註〕勇氣十足，不顧生命危險。

1876 臊臊都係羊肉，爛爛/舊舊都係絲綢
sou¹ sou¹ dou¹ hɐi⁶ jœŋ⁴ juk⁹, lan⁶ lan⁶/gɐu⁶ gɐu⁶ dou¹ hɐi⁶ si¹ tsɐu⁴ (translit.)
It is still mutton though it is rank-smelling; it is still silk though it is worn out/though it is very old. (lit.)
Gold is gold no matter whether it glitters or not.

〔註〕比喻不論外表怎樣，價值始終是價值。

1877 艻竇
lɛk⁹ dɐu³ (translit.)
A thorny den. (lit.)
Be hard to make contact with ...
Be hard to get along with.
Be hard to please.
Dirty work.
A hard job./A profitless job.
Gain no profit from the job.
Work for a dead horse.

〔註〕比喻難以打交道的（人）或無利可圖的（工作），這方面和"豬頭骨"大致相同。參閱（1805）條。

1878 簍休
lɐu¹ jɐu¹ (translit.)
Untidy (lit.)
Be in one's shirt sleeves.
Not to tidy oneself up.
Be slovenly.

〔註〕表示不修邊幅的意思。

1879 濕水棉胎 —— 冇得彈
sɐp⁷ sœy² min⁴ tɔi¹ — mou⁵ dɐk⁷ tan⁴ *(translit.)*
The cotton-padding soaked in water—it cannot be fluffed (criticized). (lit.)
Be above criticism.
Be beyond reproach.
〔註〕指無可指責或批評。本來"彈"字意爲"把棉花抖鬆"的意思。但廣東人把"指責或批評"也叫做"彈"，參閱"蛋家婆打醮"條（1412）。

1880 濕水欖核 —— 兩頭標
sɐp⁷ sœy² lam² wɐt⁹ — lœŋ² tɐu⁴ biu¹ *(translit.)*
A wet kernel of olive—it slides this way and that way. (lit.)
Be fleet of foot.
Kick over the traces.
A person who leaves no trace.
〔註〕比喻轉眼便不見人，不受約束或難以尋其行踪的人。

1881 濕星
sɐp⁷ siŋ¹ *(translit.)*
Petty things. (lit.)
Odds and ends.
Skin disease or the like.
〔註〕零零碎碎的東西或皮膚病之類。

1882 濕滯
sɐp⁷ dzɐi⁶ *(translit.)*
Damp and impeded. (lit.)
Be impeded.
Meet with hinderance.
Meet with a hitch.
Be unfavourable.
Find it hard to deal with ...
Troublesome
Knotty / Thorny
〔註〕"濕滯"本爲中醫術語，意爲腸胃不適，不好消化。廣東人借以喻有梗阻，不順利，不好辦；難對付。

1883 濟軍
dzɐi³ gwɐn¹ *(translit.)*
Lung Tsaikwong's soldiers. (lit.)
A regular mischief.
A person who runs wild.
〔註〕"濟軍"爲"龍濟光的軍隊"的簡稱，龍濟光爲民國早年的軍閥，他所率領的軍隊，軍紀全無，無惡不作，後來人便用"濟軍"這稱號來喻"惡作劇"或"無法無天的人"。

1884 講心啫
gɔŋ² sɐm¹ dʒɛ¹ *(translit.)*
Talk about heart. (lit.)
Take each other to bosom.
Have a heart-to-heart talk.
〔註〕推心置腹的意思。

1885 講多錯多
gɔŋ² dɔ¹ tsɔ³ dɔ¹ *(translit.)*
The more one speaks, the more mistakes one makes. (lit.)
The least said, the soonest mended.

1886 講咗/過就算〔數〕
gɔŋ² dzɔ²/gwɔ³ dzɐu⁶ syn³

十七畫

[sou³]　(translit.)
What is said is in real earnest.
(positive)
What is said is null and voil.
(negative)　(lit.)
One means what one says.
No sooner said than done.
Go back on one's words.
Only say without deeds.
〔註〕這口頭語有正反兩義，正義爲說得出，做得到。反義爲只是説説便算。

1887　講明就陳顯南
gɔŋ² miŋ⁴ dzɐu⁶ tsɐn⁴ hin² nam²　(translit.)
It is repetitious to say clearly.
(lit.)
It is a tiresome repetition to make oneself clear.
There is no need to ask if a duck will swim.
It is understood without an explanation.
〔註〕指不言而喻或不必再加解釋也明白了。參閱"唔使問亞貴"條（1232）及"唔使畫公仔畫出腸"條（1234）。

1888　講來/嚟講去都係三幅被
gɔŋ² lɔi⁴/lɐi⁴ gɔŋ² hœy³ dou¹ hɐi⁶ sam¹ fuk⁷ pei⁵
(translit.)
What one talks again and again is only but a three-sheet quilt.
(lit.)
Sing the song of burden.
Repeat oneself.

〔註〕表示不斷重覆説。

1889　講起嚟一定布咁長
gɔŋ² hei² lɐi⁴ jɐt⁷ pɐt⁷ bou³ gɐm³ tsœŋ⁴　(translit.)
Telling in details is like as long as a bolt of cloth.　(lit.)
It is like telling a long story.
〔註〕即説來話長。

1890　講得出就講
gɔŋ² dɐk⁷ tsœt⁷ dzɐu⁶ gɔŋ²
(translit.)
Say what one wants to say.
(lit.)
Have a loose tongue.

1891　講開又講
gɔŋ² hɔi¹ jɐu⁶ gɔŋ²　(translit.)
Mention while speaking.
(lit.)
By the way.
〔註〕意即順便説説。

1892　講就易，做就難
gɔŋ² dzɐu⁶ ji⁶, dzou⁶ dzɐu⁶ nan⁴　(translit.)
Saying is easy but doing is difficult.　(lit.)
Easier said than done.

1893　糟質
dzou¹ dzɐt⁷　(translit.)
Spoil.　(lit.)
Slander somebody.
Abuse/Ill treat somebody.
Play the fool of somebody.
Make fool of somebody.
Waste/Spoil something.
〔註〕表示虐待，作弄，誹謗人或糟

踢東西的意思。

1894　窿窿罅罅
luŋ¹ luŋ¹ la³ la³　(translit.)
Holes and gaps.　(lit.)
Nook and corner.
Crannies.
〔註〕即"嘰里旮旯兒兒"或"旮旯旮旯兒兒"。

1895　臨天光瀨尿
lɐm⁴ tin¹ gwɔŋ¹ lai⁶ niu⁶
(translit.)
Have an unvoluntary passage of urine at daybreak.　(lit.)
There is many a slip 'twixt the cup and the lip.'
Suffer failure when success is within one's grasp.
〔註〕表示功虧一簣的意思。

1896　臨老學吹打
lɐm⁴ lou⁵ hɔk⁹ tsœy¹ da²
(translit.)
Begin to learn blowing and beating when getting old.　(lit.)
An old dog begins to learn new tricks.
〔註〕比喻到年紀大時才學習。

1897　嬲到彈起
nɐu¹ dou³ dan⁶ hei²　(translit.)
Spring up for anger.　(lit.)
Hit the roof.
〔註〕表示勃然大怒，發火。

1898　嬲爆爆
nɐu¹ bau³ bau³　(translit.)
Get angry.　(lit.)

Be filled with anger.
Be hot with rage.
〔註〕氣鼓鼓的。

1899　點算好
dim² syn³ hou²　(translit.)
How to reckon?　(lit.)
What is to be done?
What shall we/I do?
How shall it be done?
〔註〕即怎麼辦？

1900　孻仔拉心肝，孻女拉內臟
lai¹ dzɐi² lai¹ sɐm¹ gɔn¹, lai¹ nœy⁵ lai¹ nɔi⁶ dzɔŋ⁶
(translit.)
The youngest son pulls heart and liver; the youngest daughter pulls internal viscera.　(lit.)
The youngest child often gains majority of parents' love.
〔註〕指父母多數溺愛最小的子女。

1901　擘網巾
mak⁸ mɔŋ⁵ gɐn¹　(translit.)
Tear up the silk kerchief.　(lit.)
Break off friendly relation with somebody.
Sever connections with somebody.
〔註〕表示和人絕交的意思。

1902　縮沙
suk⁷ sa¹　(translit.)
Retreat.　(lit.)
Beat a retreat.
Shrink back.
〔註〕表示臨時反口，臨陣退縮。參

閱"打退堂鼓"條（0433）。

1903　縮數
suk⁷ sou³　*(translit.)*
A shrinking sum.　(lit.)
Be calculating.
Selfish calculations.
〔註〕打小算盤或好爲自己打算的意思。

十八畫

1904　騎牛搵馬
kɛ⁴ ŋɐu⁴ wɐn² ma⁵　*(translit.)*
Ride a bull to look for a horse.　(lit.)
Seek for the better while holding on to one.
Use one's present position as a stepping stone.
〔註〕比喻保有目前手上的東西，另找一個較好的或以目前的職位作基礎而另找較高的職位。

1905　騎硫磺馬
kɛ⁴ lɐu⁴ wɔŋ⁴ ma⁵　*(translit.)*
Ride a sulphuric horse.　(lit.)
Divert somebody's money/public funds to one's own purpose.
〔註〕把別人的錢財或公款據爲己有的意思。

1906　轉呔
dzyn³ tai⁵　*(translit.)*
Turn the steer.　(lit.)
Change one's mind.
Make a change of heart.
Make a change in ...
〔註〕改變主意。

1907　轉膞
dzyn³ bɔk⁸　*(translit.)*
Change to another shoulder.　(lit.)
Make an appropriate adaption.
Accommodate oneself to ...
Be flexible.
〔註〕隨機應變的意思。

1908　擺明車馬
bai² miŋ⁴ gœy¹ ma⁵　*(translit.)*
Openly set out the chariots and horses.　(lit.)
Before somebody's very eyes.
Play fair and square.
〔註〕參閱"明刀明槍"條（0957）及"開明車馬"條（1581）。

1909　擺到明
bai² dou³ miŋ⁴　*(translit.)*
Clearly display.　(lit.)
Expose one's intention.
Make a display of someone's purpose.
Show one's card on the table.
Wear one's heart on one's sleeve.
〔註〕指把意圖或目的開誠佈公地擺出來或流露出來，參閱"開心見誠"條（1578）。

1910　擺烏龍
bai² wu¹ luŋ²　*(translit.)*

Display a black dragon. (lit.)
Make a mistake.
Confuse A with B.
Confuse black and white.
〔註〕弄錯或搞誤會的意思。

1911 擺欵
bai² fun² (translit.)
Put up the style. (lit.)
Put on airs.
Give oneself airs.
〔註〕擺架子。

1912 雞手鴨腳
gɐi¹ sɐu² ap⁸ gœk⁸ (translit.)
Hen's hands and duck's legs. (lit.)
One's fingers are all thumbs.
Have two left feet.
〔註〕笨手笨腳，或毛手毛腳的意思，參閱"十指孖埋"（0079）條。

1913 雞仔媒人
gɐi¹ dzɐi² mui⁴ jɐn⁴ (translit.)
A match-maker for chickens. (lit.)
A nosy intermediator.
〔註〕指愛多管閒事的人。

1914 雞噉腳
gɐi¹ gɐm³ gœk⁸ (translit.)
Be like hens' legs. (lit.)
Be fleet of foot.
Show leg.
Take to one's legs.
Walk at a good pace.
〔註〕諷刺人聞風先逃或急急忙忙走路。

1915 雞春咁密都襟出仔
gɐi¹ tsœn¹ gɐm³ mɐt⁹ dou¹ bou⁶ tsœt⁷ dzɐi² (translit.)
Though eggs are so dense, they can be hatched chickens. (lit.)
No secret can be kept.
The cat will at last be let out of the bag.
〔註〕比喻秘密終會洩漏。

1916 雞春摸過都輕四両
gɐi¹ tsœn¹ mɔ¹ gwɔ³ dou¹ hɛŋ¹ sei³ lœŋ² (translit.)
The egg that is touched by somebody becomes four taels lighter. (lit.)
Do damage to whatever somebody handles.
Take some small gains out of whatever somebody deals with.
〔註〕指責人用過的東西必受損害或無論經手做甚麼也要佔點便宜。

1917 雞疴尿 —— 少有/少見
gɐi¹ ɔ¹ niu⁶—siu² jɐu⁴/siu² gin³ (translit.)
Chickens pass urine — this doesn't exist/it is seldom seen. (lit.)
Seldom or never.
Rarely.
Be seldom seen./Once in a blue moon.
〔註〕表示少有或罕見的意思。

1918 雞食放光蟲 —— 心知肚明

gɐi¹ sik⁹ fɔŋ³ gwɔŋ¹ tsuŋ² — sɐm¹ dzi¹ tou⁵ miŋ⁴ *(translit.)*

A hen eats the worm that glistens — its heart knows and belly understands. (lit.)

Have a clear mind.
Know what is what.

〔註〕比喻心中知道得一清二楚。

1919 雞啄唔斷

gɐi¹ dœŋ¹ m⁴ tyn⁵ *(translit.)*

Cannot be cut off by the beak of a hen. (lit.)

Talk somebody's ear off.
Rattle on without stopping.

〔註〕不停地說話的意思。

1920 雞髀打人牙骹軟

gɐi¹ bei² da² jɐn⁴ ŋa⁴ gau³ jyn⁵ *(translit.)*

A hen's leg beats a man's jaws soft. (lit.)

Beat a dog with a bone and it will not howl.
Serve him with nice food and the contention will cease.
Grease the palm of his and you will be able to make a convenience of him.

〔註〕表示以利益相誘對方，行事無往而不利的意思。

1921 歸根到底

gwɐi¹ gɐn¹ dou³ dɐi² *(translit.)*

Come back to the roots. (lit.)
In the last analysis.
In the end.
Reverting to the origin.

1922 翻渣茶葉 —— 有鹽味道

fan¹ dza¹ tsa⁴ jip⁹ — mou⁵ lei⁴ mei⁶ dou⁶ *(translit.)*

Infused tea leaves — they have not a bit of taste. (lit.)

Be as insipid as water.

〔註〕比喻飲料淡而無味。

1923 獵狗終須山上喪

lip⁹ gɐu² dzuŋ¹ sœy¹ san¹ sœn⁶ sɔŋ³ *(translit.)*

A hunting dog will at last die in the mountain. (lit.)

He who plays with fire will get burned at last.
A great swimmer is likely to meet his fate in the water.

〔註〕表示善騎者死於馬的意思。

1924 雜崩唥

dzap⁹ bɐŋ¹ nɐŋ¹ *(translit.)*

Assorted things. (lit.)

Odds and ends of miscelanious things.

〔註〕相當於"雜八湊兒"。

1925 蹟直

gwɐn³ dzik⁹ *(translit.)*

Stumble flat. (lit.)

Be completely defeated.
Meet a lost cause.

〔註〕喻已告失敗。

1926 藉/借啲意/藉/借頭藉/借路

dzɛ³ di¹ ji²/dzɛ³ tɐu⁴ dzɛ³

lou⁶ (translit.)
Borrow some ideas/Borrow both the head and the way. (lit.)
Jump at the chance.
Seize the opportunity.
Take advantage of the favourable situation.
Cook up a lame excuse.
〔註〕表示乘機，趁勢或製造假藉口。

1927 蟻多搜死象
ŋɐi⁵ dɔ¹ lɐu¹ sei² dzœŋ⁶ (translit.)
Too many ants can swarm an elephant to death. (lit.)
Union gives strength.
The united efforts of the masses can fight for the accomplishment of the purpose.
〔註〕比喻團結就是力量。

1928 斷市
tyn⁵ si⁵ (translit.)
Break the market. (lit.)
Be out of stock.
Be sold out.
〔註〕脫銷。

1929 斷估
dyn³ gu² (translit.)
Depend on an estimation. (lit.)
By guess and by gosh.
Make a wild guess.
〔註〕表示瞎猜，瞎矇。

1930 斷尾
tyn⁵ mei⁵ (translit.)

Cut the tail. (lit.)
Effect a thoroughgoing cure.
Be thoroughly cured.
〔註〕表示徹底醫好（疾病），不再復發。相當於"除根兒"。

1931 繡花枕頭
sɐu³ fa¹ dzɐm² tɐu⁴ (translit.)
An embroidered pillow. (lit.)
All that glitters is not gold.
Ginger bread.
〔註〕比喻華而不實的人或物。

1932 繞起
kiu² hei² (translit.)
Wind up. (lit.)
Beat somebody.
〔註〕參閱"臘起"條（1938），意爲"難倒"。

十九畫

1933 難兄難弟
nan⁴ hiŋ¹ nan⁴ dɐi⁶ (translit.)
Difficult elder brother and difficult younger brother. (lit.)
Be in the same boat.
Be in the same box.
Fellow sufferers.
Two of a kind.
〔註〕比喻處境相同或同患難，但亦比喻同流合污的人。

1934 顛倒是非

din¹ dou² si⁶ fei¹ *(translit.)*
Confound right with wrong. *(lit.)*
Swear black is white.

1935　穩打穩紮
wɐn² da² wɐn² dzat⁸ *(translit.)*
Be staid to fight and to take root. *(lit.)*
Go ahead steadily and strike sure blows.
Play safe.
Take no risk.
〔註〕指求穩或不冒險，參閱"搣地游水"條（1599）。

1936　穩如鐵塔
wɐn² jy⁴ tit⁸ tap⁸ *(translit.)*
As firm as an iron pagoda. *(lit.)*
Be as firm as it is founded on the rock.
Be secure against assult.
Be sure of success.
〔註〕喻"固若金湯"，但亦喻"肯定成功"。

1937　穩陣
wɐn² dzɐn⁶ *(translit.)*
Be firm enough. *(lit.)*
Steady.
Stable.
Safe/reliable.
Staid/Sedate.
〔註〕穩當，安全可靠的（物）或穩重的（人）。

1938　臘起
lap⁹ hei² *(translit.)*
Cure up. *(lit.)*
Beat somebody.
Baffle somebody.
〔註〕參閱"繞起"條（1932）。

1939　懶人多屎尿
lan⁵ jɐn⁴ dɔ¹ si² ŋiu⁴ *(translit.)*
A lazy person has more manure and urine. *(lit.)*
A lazybones cooks up more lame excuses.
〔註〕相當於"懶驢上磨屎尿多"，意指懶人諸多藉口拒絕做事或拖拉。

1940　懶佬工夫
lan⁵ lou⁵ guŋ¹ fu¹ *(translit.)*
A lazy man's work. *(lit.)*
The work that saves labour.
〔註〕容易做的工作；不費功夫的工作。

1941　懵盛盛
muŋ² siŋ⁶ siŋ⁶ *(translit.)*
Be muddled. *(lit.)*
Have a thick skull.
Be ignorant.
Sheer ignorance of something.
Have no inkling as to the real cause.
〔註〕懵懵懂懂；糊里糊塗；對事實真相一無所知。

1942　懵懵閉/懵閉閉
muŋ² muŋ² bɐi³/muŋ² bɐi³ bɐi³ *(translit.)*
Be muddled. *(lit.)*
〔註〕"同懵盛盛"（1942）。

1943 瀟湘
siu¹ sœŋ¹　(translit.)
As delicate as a bamboo. (lit.)
Be slim.
Have a slim figure.
〔註〕喻女性秀氣，身材苗條。

1944 藤扔瓜，瓜扔藤
tɐŋ⁴ lɐŋ³ gwa¹, gwa¹ lɐŋ³ tɐŋ⁴　(translit.)
A melon hangs on the vine and the vine winds round and round the melon. (lit.)
Get entangled with each other.
An entangled affair.
〔註〕指互相糾纏不清或糾纏不清的事。

1945 羅通掃北
lɔ⁴ tuŋ¹ sou³ bɐt⁷　(translit.)
Lɔ Tuŋ (an ancient warrior's name) swept the north. (lit.)
Make a clean sweep of everything.
Finish all the dish on the table.
Sweep the board.
〔註〕以歷史人物的事件來喻一掃而光或譜喻把桌上食物吃個精光。

1946 關人
gwan¹ jɐn⁴　(translit.)
It doesn't concern me. (lit.)
None of my business.
There is nothing to do with me.
I won't concern myself with it.
I take no interest in it.
〔註〕這爲第一人稱説的口頭語，意爲與我無關或我不願過問此事。

廿　畫

1947 露出馬腳
lou⁶ tsœt⁷ ma⁵ gœk⁸　(translit.)
Expose a horse's leg. (lit.)
Give the show away.
Show the cloven foot.
〔註〕不留意暴露出弱點，秘密或罪行等等的意思。

1948 糯米屎窟
nɔ⁶ mɐi⁵ si² fɐt⁷　(translit.)
Glutinous rice hips. (lit.)
A visitor who sticks like a bur.
A visitor who overstays his welcome.
〔註〕謔喻賴着捨不得告辭的客人。

1949 竈君上天 —— 有嘅句講嘅句
dzou³ gwɐn¹ sœŋ⁵ tin¹—jɐu⁵ gɔ² gœy³ gɔŋ² gɔ² gœy³　(translit.)
Kitchen god goes up to heaven —he says the sentences he has in his mind. (lit.)
Say what one has to say.
〔註〕有什麼説什麼的意思。

1950 蘇州屎
sou¹ dzɐu¹ si²　(translit.)
Sou Dzɐu manure. (lit.)
The trouble left behind.
〔註〕比喻遺下的麻煩。

1951 蘇州過後冇艇搭

sou¹ dzɐu¹ gwɔ³ hɐu⁶ mou⁵ tɛŋ⁵ dap⁸ *(translit.)*

There is not a sampan to take beyond Sou Dzɐu. *(lit.)*

The opportunity once missed will never come back.

〔註〕表示失去的機會，永不再來。

1952 鹹魚

ham⁴ jy² *(translit.)*

Salted fish. *(lit.)*

Corpse.

〔註〕喻死屍。

1953 鹹魚番生

ham⁴ jy⁴ fan¹ saŋ¹ *(translit.)*

A salt-fish restored to life. *(lit.)*

The person falling into disgrace comes to fame again.

Rehabilitate oneself.

〔註〕比喻失去財勢的人重獲地位。

1954 鹹濕

ham⁴ sɐp⁷ *(translit.)*

Salty and wet. *(lit.)*

Be salacious/bawdy.

〔註〕（指書，畫，言談等）誨淫的，猥褻的，下流的，黃色的；（指人）好色的。

1955 獻世

hin³ sɐi³ *(translit.)*

Offer oneself to bear hardship. *(lit.)*

Be penanced for one's ill deeds.

〔註〕表示因曾做壞事而被上蒼懲罰以捱苦行贖罪的意思。

1956 獻醜不如藏拙

hin³ tsɐu² bɐt⁷ jy⁴ tsɔŋ⁴ dzœt⁸ *(translit.)*

Showing one's weak points is not so good as hiding one's ignorance. *(lit.)*

It is wiser to conceal one's stupidity than it is to show oneself up.

廿一畫

1957 趯更

dɛk⁸ gaŋ¹ *(translit.)*

Run away. *(lit.)*

Desert.

Show a clean pair of heels.

Take to one's legs.

Make away./Make away with …

Run away.

〔註〕開小差；逃跑；逃命。參閱"走路"（0714）條。

1958 鐵沙梨——咬唔入

tit⁸ sa¹ lei²—ŋau⁵ m⁴ jɐp⁹ *(translit.)*

A russet pear made of iron—It cannot be bitten. *(lit.)*

A person from whom nobody can obtain any profit.

A great miser.

Be very stingy.

〔註〕從歇後語"咬唔入"來解釋，意為"任何人無法從他身上得到好處的人"，但亦同時喻非常吝嗇

的人。相當於"鐵公雞 —— 一毛
不拔"。

1959 鐵杵磨成針
tit⁸ tsy⁵ mɔ⁴ siŋ⁴ dzɐm¹
(translit.)
An iron pillar can be ground
into a needle. (lit.)
Little strokes fell great oaks.
Intestinal fortitude will prevail.
〔註〕表示堅穩終能成功的意思。

1960 鐵嘴雞
tit⁸ dzœy² gɐi¹ (translit.)
An iron-beaked hen. (lit.)
**A lady with a silver and bitter
tongue.**
〔註〕比喻口才流利，嘴很厲害的女
人。

1961 鐸叔
dɔk⁹ suk⁷ (translit.)
Uncle Dɔk. (lit.)
A niggard.
A miser.
〔註〕對"吝嗇鬼"的稱呼。

1962 顧得頭嚟/來腳反筋
gu³ dɐk⁷ tɐu⁴ lɐi⁴/lɔi⁴ gœk⁸
fan² gɐn¹ (translit.)
While caring for the head, the
leg becomes spastic. (lit.)
**Attend to one thing and neglect
another.**
**Aim at another bird in the bush
and the one in hand is choked.**
**Cannot take care of so many
things at the same time.**
〔註〕顧此失彼的意思。

1963 爛口

lan⁶ hou² (translit.)
Rotten mouth. (lit.)
Obscene language.
Be foul-mouthed.
〔註〕下流話；愛講下流話。

1964 爛市
lan⁶ si⁵ (translit.)
Rotten market. (lit.)
Be unsalable.
Be dull of sale.
〔註〕表示賣不掉，滯銷。

1965 爛尾
lan⁶ mei⁵ (translit.)
Rotten tail. (lit.)
**Be irresponsible for what one
should do.**
Give up half-way.
Leave one's work unfinished.
**Not to go on with one's work to
the end.**
〔註〕相當於"拆爛污"或半途而廢。

1966 爛泥扶唔上壁
lan⁶ nɐi⁴ fu⁴ m⁴ sœŋ⁵ bik⁸
(translit.)
Thin mud cannot be put on to
the wall. (lit.)
Be good-for-nothing.
**A silk purse cannot be made out
of sow's ears.**
Be not worthy to be favoured.
**No pillars are made out of
decayed timbers.**
〔註〕形容人低能，不堪造就的意
思。

1967 爛笪笪
lan⁶ dat⁸ dat⁸ (translit.)

Rotten to the core. *(lit.)*
Be unbridled.
Make no scruple.
Throw all restraints to the wind.
〔註〕形容人放肆，無所顧忌，或稀巴爛的意思。

1968 爛鬥爛
lan⁶ dɐu³ lan⁶ *(translit.)*
Being rotten for being rotten. (lit.)
Give tit for tat.
Give stick for stick and carrot for carrot.
〔註〕表示以打對打，以拉對拉，針鋒相對，一報還一報。

1969 爛船拆埋都有三斤釘
lan⁶ syn⁴ tsak⁸ mai⁴ dou¹ jɐu⁵ sam¹ gɐn¹ dɛŋ¹ *(translit.)*
There are three catties of nails left when a ship is disassembled. (lit.)
Even the wrecks of a boat are still of some surplus value.
〔註〕比喻有錢人雖破產，但比窮人還是有錢（或有辦法）。相當於"船破有底"。

1970 爛頭蟀
lan⁶ tɐu⁴ dzœt⁷ *(translit.)*
A broken-headed cricket. (lit.)
A person who cares for nothing.
A person who works for somebody without regard to his own life.
〔註〕比喻破罐破摔，無所顧忌的人或爲人賣命的人。

廿二畫

1971 攤直
tan¹ dzik⁹ *(translit.)*
Lie straight. (lit.)
Have met with one's death.
Have fallen flat.
〔註〕已經死去的詼諧説法，參閲"瓜直"條（0479）。

1972 攤凍至嚟食
tan¹ duŋ³ dzi³ lɐi⁴ sik⁹ *(translit.)*
Wait till it is cold and then eat it. (lit.)
It is unnecessary to make haste to enjoy the prey.
Have taken a firm hold of something.
〔註〕表示已掌握中，不必急於……的意思。

1973 攤攤腰
tan¹ tan¹ jiu¹ *(translit.)*
With a straightened backbone. (lit.)
To an unbearable degree.
To the state of fatigue.
To an extent of disability to stand up again.
In a situation of complete defeat.
〔註〕這是用表達程度的口頭禪，例如説，"做嘢做到我～"，"佢俾

人打到～"，"熱到我～"或"餓到我～"等等。用處甚廣，意義不同，大致言之，不外到了難忍的程度，到了疲倦已極的地步，到了沒法站得住腳的地步或到了慘敗的地步等。

1974 攞皮宜

lɔ² pei⁴ ji²/⁴ (translit.)

Make a joke. (lit.)

Jolly with somebody to amuse oneself.

Take somebody at advantage to make a pass at her.

Seek undue advantage.

〔註〕表示跟人開玩笑以自娛；對婦女非禮，討便宜。

1975 攞豆

lɔ² dɐu² (translit.)

Get beans. (lit.)

Meet one's fate.

Go west.

Come to an untimely end.

〔註〕喻死亡。

1976 攞命

lɔ² mɛŋ⁶ (translit.)

Take away the life. (lit.)

Ride one to death.

〔註〕即要命。

1977 攞朝唔得晚

lɔ² dziu¹ m⁴ dɐk⁷ man⁶ (translit.)

What is earned in the morning is not sufficient for the evening. (lit.)

Live from hand to mouth.

Be unable to make both ends meet.

〔註〕現掙現吃或收支不相抵的生活狀況。

1978 攞景

lɔ² giŋ² (translit.)

Angle a camera. (lit.)

Say/Do something to enrage somebody during his disappointment.

〔註〕這本爲攝影時找鏡頭的一種動作，後來轉義爲趁人家失意，説或做一些事來氣他。

1979 攞景定贈興/慶？

lɔ² giŋ² diŋ⁶ dzɐŋ⁶ hiŋ³ (translit.)

Do you give trouble or help in the fun? (lit.)

Do you make a mock or add trouble?

〔註〕當甲在失意或處於不幸時，而乙做些事或説些話觸怒了他，甲便會説，"你究竟攞景定贈慶？"意思即是説"你嘲笑抑或增加麻煩？"。

1980 攞嚟衰

lɔ² lɐi⁴ sœy¹ (translit.)

Make oneself decline. (lit.)

Bring disgrace on oneself.

Lay the blame on oneself.

〔註〕即自找麻煩；自討苦吃。

1981 攞嚟賤

lɔ² lɐi⁴ dzin⁶ (translit.)

Make oneself cheap. (lit.)

Make a rod for one's back.

Work for one's destruction.

〔註〕表示自找麻煩或自暴自棄的意

1982 攞膽

lɔ² dam² *(translit.)*

Take away the gall. *(lit.)*

Take away one's life.

Ride somebody to death.

〔註〕即"要命"的意思參閱"攞命"條（1976）。

Awfully.

Extremely.

〔註〕作程度副詞用，例如"熱到～"，或"咳到～"，意爲極，很，非常。

What a bad luck!

What a nuisance!

〔註〕用作感歎詞，但通常説成"真攞膽"，意爲"真不幸！"或"多麼的討厭！"。

1983 聽價唔聽斗

tɛŋ¹ ga³ m⁴ tɛŋ¹ dɐu² *(translit.)*

Listen to the price but not to the unit of dry measure for grain. (lit.)

Care for whether the price is cheap or high but neglect the quality or quantity.

〔註〕意指只顧價錢貴賤，不理所購的東西的質量。

1984 鑑硬

gam³ ŋaŋ² *(translit.)*

Act by force. (lit.)

Make forcible demand for ...

Force-feed somebody to ...

Act blindly/recklessly.

〔註〕"鑑粗"和"鑑硬"同樣表示硬來，蠻幹。

1985 鑑粗

gam³ tsou¹ *(translit.)*

Act insistently. (lit.)

By force.

Make forcible demand for ...

Do something with violence/by force.

Do something at one's insistence.

〔註〕參閱"鑑硬"條（1984）。

1986 囉唆

lɔ¹ sɔ¹ *(translit.)*

Speak too much. (lit.)

Be long-winded.

Be wordy.

Talk the hind leg off a donkey.

〔註〕即嘮叨。

1987 囉囉攣

lɔ¹ lɔ¹ lyn¹ *(translit.)*

Be anxious about this and that. (lit.)

Be restless with anxiety.

Be anxiety-ridden.

〔註〕表示焦躁不安或憂心忡忡的意思。

廿三畫

1988 攪手

gau² sɐu² *(translit.)*

A hand of stir. (lit.)

A sponsor.

〔註〕即發起人或主辦者。

1989 攪出個大頭鬼/佛

gau² tsœt⁷ gɔ³ dai⁶ tɐu⁴ gwɐi²/fɐt⁹ (translit.)
Make out a big-headed ghost/Buddha. (lit.)
Put all the fat in the fire.
Scale something up.
〔註〕比喻把事情搞糟或把事情擴大了。

1990 攪屎棍
gau² si² gwɐn³ (translit.)
A club for stirring up manure. (lit.)
The person who stirs up trouble/strife/hatred.
The person who fans the flame.
Play somebody off against one another.
Stir up the dirt.
Make a mountain out of a molehill.
〔註〕比喻愛挑撥離間，搬弄是非的人，愛出壞主意搗亂的人或愛小題大做的行為。

1991 籠裏雞作反
luŋ⁴ lœy⁵ gɐi¹ dzɔk⁸ fan² (translit.)
The chickens in the same bamboo-cage rebel against each other. (lit.)
Have an internal dissension.
〔註〕即內鬨。

1992 變卦
bin³ gwa³ (translit.)
Change divinstion diagram. (lit.)
Change one's mind.
Retract one's promise.
Go back on one's words.
Break an agreement.
〔註〕改變主意，毀約或不遵守諾言；已定的事忽然改變。

1993 齜牙棒爪
ji¹ na⁴ baŋ⁴ dzɐu² (translit.)
Show teeth and spread out arms. (lit.)
Be elated at something.
Laugh a hearty laugh.
〔註〕指高興到裂嘴大笑，這話有人說成"齜牙嘩齒"（ji¹ na⁴ baŋ⁴ tsi²）或"齜牙鬆肛"（ji¹ na⁴ suŋ¹ gɔŋ⁴）。

1994 曬命
sai³ mɛŋ⁶ (translit.)
Dry one's own life in the sun. (lit.)
Cry up one's own fortune.
Crow over one's own life.
Sing one's own glorious song.
〔註〕誇耀自己良好際遇的意思。

廿四畫

1995 攬住一齊死
lam² dzy⁶ jɐt⁷ tsɐi⁴ sei² (translit.)
Embrace together to die. (lit.)
End in common ruin.
〔註〕比喻同歸於盡。

1996 攬頭攬頸
lam² tɐu⁴ lam⁵ gɛŋ² *(translit.)*
Embrace necks and heads. (lit.)
Be on intimate terms with each other.
Be as close as lips to teeth.
〔註〕比喻彼此相好。

1997 鹽倉土地 —— 鹹夾濕
jim⁴ tsɔŋ¹ tou² dei² — ham⁴ gap⁸ sɐp⁷ *(translit.)*
The local god of soil in a salt storehouse — He is salty and wet. (lit.)
Be salacious.
A luster.
A man of a bawdy disposition.
〔註〕喻好色之徒。

1998 躝屍趷路
lan¹ si¹ gɐt⁹ lou⁶ *(translit.)*
You corpse, crawl away!
Scram!
Get out!
Beat it!
Get out of my sight!
〔註〕斥責或罵人的話，即滾蛋。參閱 B260"趷路"及 B468"躝屍"各條。

廿五畫

1999 籮底橙
lɔ⁴ dai² tsaŋ² *(translit.)*
The orange at the bottom of a bamboo basket. (lit.)
The girl/article of nobody's choice.
A left-over.
A person of low level.
The article of poor quality.
〔註〕比喻無人願娶的女子，無人要的東西，剩下的人或物，水平低的人或質量不好的東西等。

廿八畫

2000 掹掹緊
maŋ¹ maŋ¹ gɐn² *(translit.)*
Be tightly mounted. (lit.)
Be in straitened circumstances.
Scarecely make both ends meet.
Be out at elbows.
〔註〕生活貧困，收支僅能相抵或甚至捉襟見肘的情形。

2001 掹唔番
may¹ m⁴ fan¹ *(translit.)*
Fail to drag back. (lit.)
Be incorrigible.
Be incurable.
Be beyond remedy.
〔註〕無法糾正，無可救藥，或無可補救的意思。

2002 鑿大
dzɔk⁹ dai⁶ *(translit.)*
Chisel big. (lit.)
Make an exaggerated report.
Make an overstatement.
Overstate something.
〔註〕誇大，言過其實的意思。

補遺

一畫

B001 一五一十
jɐt⁷ ŋ⁵ jɐt⁷ sɐp⁹ (translit.)
One five and one ten. (lit.)
Go into details.
Spill one's guts.
In full detail.
〔註〕詳盡地或把自己所知的原原本本地説出來。

B002 一本萬利
jɐt⁷ bun² man⁶ lei⁶ (translit.)
One capital earns ten thousand profits. (lit.)
Gain big profits with a small capital.
〔註〕以小本獲取大利。

B003 一向
jɐt⁷ hœŋ³ (translit.)
Always. (lit.)
Consistently.
All along.
〔註〕一貫，始終或向來。

B004 一次過
jɐt⁷ tsi³ gwɔ³ (translit.)
One time past. (lit.)
At one go.
In one breath.
Without a break.
Once for all.
Once and away.
No more than once.
〔註〕表示"一氣"參閱該條（B011）或限於這一次的意思。

B005 一把火
jɐt⁷ ba² fɔ² (translit.)
A column of fire. (lit.)
Be filled with rage.
Be hot with rage.
〔註〕滿肚子怒氣或冒火的意思。

B006 一面之詞
jɐt⁷ min⁶ dzi¹ tsi⁴ (translit.)
One-faced remarks. (lit.)
One-sided statement.

B007 一言驚醒夢中人
jɐt⁷ jin⁴ giŋ¹ siŋ² muŋ⁶ juŋ¹ jɐn⁴ (translit.)
One word wakes up a dreaming person. (lit.)
Put one wise.
Give a wise word to a fool.

B008 一息間
jɐt⁷ sik⁷ gan¹ (translit.)
One minute. (lit.)
A little while.
In a moment.
One moment.
〔註〕和"一陣間"同，參閱該條（正篇0032）。

B009 一時時
jɐt⁷ si² si⁴ (translit.)
Sometimes. (lit.)
Sometimes for a single moment.
〔註〕不經常，只有時一次，參閱"一陣陣"條（B013）。

B010 一時唔偷雞做父老/保長
jɐt⁷ si⁴ m⁴ tɐu¹ gɐi¹ dzou⁶ fu⁶ lou⁵/bou² dzœŋ² (translit.)

When a hen-stealer doesn't steal for only once, he becomes an elder of a country/the head of a hundred households. (lit.)

A rogue goes so far as to moralize to another rogue.

〔註〕比喻一時不做壞事便假裝正人君子。

B011 一氣

jɐt⁷ hei³ (translit.)

One breath. (lit.)

At one go.

Without a break.

In one breath.

〔註〕一口氣，一直或沒稍停的意思。

B012 一就一，二就二

jɐt⁷ dzɐu⁶ jɐt⁷, ji⁶ dzɐu⁶ ji⁶ (translit.)

One is one and two is two. (lit.)

It should be unequivocal.

It should be perfectly clear. / as clear as noonday.

〔註〕不容模棱兩可或應要清清楚楚的意思。

B013 一陣陣

jɐt⁷ dzun² dzun⁶ (translit.)

Sometimes. (lit.)

Sometimes for a single moment.

〔註〕指次數而言，和"一時時"同，參閱該條（B009）。

B014 一坺迾

jɐt⁷ pɛk⁹ lɛk⁶ (translit.)

Be muddled up. (lit.)

Be as thick as paste.

Make a mess of something.

Be all muddled up.

〔註〕本意爲稠得像糊狀，但又表示把事情弄糟得不可收拾的意思。

B015 一箸夾中

jɐt⁷ dzy⁶ gap⁸ dzuŋ³ (translit.)

Pick up the right food with chopsticks. (lit.)

Hit the right nail on the head.

Make a right guess.

〔註〕表示一語道破或一猜便中。

B016 一龍去，二龍追

jɐt⁷ luŋ⁴ hœy³, ji⁶ luŋ⁴ dzœy¹ (translit.)

One dragon goes and two dragons pursue. (lit.)

While one (A) goes to fetch/look for somebody (B) along one route, he (B) comes back along the other.

〔註〕指當甲從這處去接或找乙時，乙從別路回來。

B017 一雞死，一雞鳴

jɐt⁷ gɐi¹ sei², jɐt⁷ gɐi¹ miŋ⁴ (translit.)

When one cock dies, another cook crows. (lit.)

Qualified successors come forth one after another.

Persons of a kind come forth in succession.

Waves urge waves.

There is always a successor regime.

〔註〕後繼有人，同類者一個接替一個，後浪推前浪或常有人接着上台的政權。

二　畫

B018　十五十六
sɐp⁹ ŋ⁵ sɐp⁹ luk⁹　*(translit.)*
Fifteen and sixteen.　(lit.)
Be of two minds.
Feel some hesitation in doing something.
〔註〕參閱正篇"十五個銅錢分兩份"（0077）及"三心兩意"（0139）各條。

B019　二打六
ji⁶ da² luk⁹　*(translit.)*
Two beats six.　(lit.)
Be inferior.
Be low-graded.
Be of poor quality.
A junior member of the staff.
Be low-levelled.
〔註〕形容東西質量低劣或低檔，形容人爲低級職員或水平低。

B020　二四六八單 —— 冇得變
ji⁶ sei⁴ luk⁹ bat⁸ dan¹ —— mou⁵ dɐk⁷ bin³　*(translit.)*
Two, four, six, eight and single —— they have no change.　(lit.)
It is unchangeable.
Be decided/fixed/settled.
Reach a final decision.
It is a foregone conclusion.
〔註〕比喻已成定局或事情已定難以改變。這是以天九牌作"鬥牛"賭博的術語，賭法爲每人手上有五隻牌，三隻作"牛蔃"，其餘兩隻作"牛幾"，最大爲"牛㪟"，最小爲"牛釘"，十一點是"牛釘"，十二點或二十點爲"牛㪟"。如手上的牌爲地二（二點），板櫈四（四點），長衫六（六點），人八（八點）及七點則無法變爲"牛蔃"了。

B021　人多熠狗唔焓
jɐn⁴ dɔ¹ sap⁹ gɐu² m⁴ nɐm⁴　*(translit.)*
Too many persons can not cook dog's meat soft.　(lit.)
Too many cooks spoil the broth.
〔註〕參閱正篇"人多手腳亂"條（0104），兩者意義相同。

B022　八仙過海 —— 各顯神通
bat⁸ sin¹ gwɔ³ hɔi² —— gɔk⁸ hin² sɐn⁴ tuŋ¹　*(translit.)*
Eight Immorals cross the sea —— each shows his magical powers.　(lit.)
Each has his merits.
Each dispays his special powers.
Each shows his strong points/abilities.
〔註〕各出奇謀，各有千秋或各顯所長的意思。

B023　入埋……（某人）嘅數
jɐp⁹ mai⁴…gɛ³ sou³　*(trans-*

lit.)
Enter into somebody's account. (lit.)
Charge it to somebody's account.
Lay the blame on somebody.
Attribute the guilt/fault/success etc. to someboby.
Impute the guilt/responsibility...to somebody.
〔註〕表示記入某人的賬（這是本意），或把事情歸咎某人所爲。

三　畫

B024　大人大姐
dai⁶ jɐn⁴ dai⁶ dzɛ² (*translit.*)
A big man and a big girl. (lit.)
An adult.
Grown-up.
〔註〕成年人的意思。

B025　大丈夫能屈能伸
dai⁶ dzœŋ⁶ fu¹ nɐŋ⁴ wɐt⁷ nɐŋ⁴ sɐn¹ (*translit.*)
A real man can both bow and stand up. (lit.)
Stretch one's leg according to one's own blanket.
Be ready to accept either a higher or a lower post.
Be ready to give one's head for the washing or hold one's head high.
〔註〕形容人能隨機應變，能任高職或低職或既可俯首受辱復可趾高氣揚的意思。

B026　大把
dai⁶ ba² (*translit.*)
A big grasp. (lit.)
A great deal of.
A good/great many.
〔註〕有的是；很多。

B027　大命
dai⁶ mɛŋ⁶ (*translit.*)
Big life. (lit.)
Escape with bare life.
Turn all ill luck into a good one.
〔註〕亦即"命大"，表示死裏逃生，僅以身免或逢凶化吉的意思。

B028　大食有指擬
dai⁶ sik⁹ jɐu⁵ dzi² ji⁵ (*translit.*)
Have dependence to gluttonize. (lit.)
Have a firm backing to do such a deed/for one's extravagance.
〔註〕比喻一個人敢於去幹一種行爲或敢去花錢，當有其背後支持或背景。

B029　大拿拿
dai⁶ na⁴ na⁴ (*translit.*)
A big sum. (lit.)
A considerable sum of money.
〔註〕表示大大的一份或可觀的金額的意思。

B030　大種乞兒

dai⁶ dzuŋ² hɐt⁷ ji¹ᐟ⁴ *(translit.)*
A big-raced beggar. *(lit.)*
A person who refuses to accept a handout in contempt.
A person who disregards small gains.
〔註〕比喻不願接受嗟來之食的人或不屑小利的人。

B031 大難友
dai⁶ nan⁴ jɐu² *(translit.)*
A big lazy guy. *(lit.)*
An idler.
A lotus-eater.
A gluttonous lazybones.
〔註〕指遊手好閒的人，貪圖安逸者或好吃懶做的人。

B032 大癲大廢
dai⁶ din¹ dai⁶ fɐi³ *(translit.)*
Big insaneness and big rubbish. *(lit.)*
Be playsome.
Be casual.
Be too optimistic to care anything.
〔註〕形容人大大咧咧，漫不經心，好玩或樂觀。

B033 下氣
ha⁶ hei³ *(translit.)*
Lower the air. *(lit.)*
Humble oneself.
Humble one's own pride.
Be out of rage.
〔註〕表示低聲下氣，把自己的氣焰壓下去或怒氣全消的意思。（和中醫的術語"下氣"或抽薪止沸的

"下氣"完全無關）。

B034 山水有相逢
san¹ sœy² jɐu⁵ sœŋ¹ fuŋ⁴ *(translit.)*
Mountains and waters have chance to meet each other. *(lit.)*
It is likely for somebody to meet each other again in travels one day.
〔註〕比喻總有一天會再相逢或彼此總會有機會再相見。

B035 上咗岸
sœŋ⁵ dzɔ² ŋɔn⁶ *(translit.)*
Have gone ashore. *(lit.)*
Have earned more than enough.
Have struck oil.
Have made one's fortune.
〔註〕賺夠了或發了大財。

B036 女人纏腳布 —— 又長又臭
nœy⁵ jɐn² dzin⁶ gœk⁸ bou³ —— jɐu⁶ tsœŋ⁴ jɐu⁶ tsɐu³ *(translit.)*
A woman's foot-binding cloth-tapes — they are both long and stinking. *(lit.)*
Be long and tiresome. (of lecture/speech or composition)
〔註〕諷喻人的演講或文章長而使人厭煩。

四 畫

B037 不至於

bɐt⁷ dzi³ jy¹   (translit.)

Not as to ...   *(lit.)*

Be unlikely ...

It is unlikely that ...

It is not likely that ...

〔註〕表示不可能會的意思。

B038 不留

bɐt⁷ lɐu¹/⁵   (translit.)

Regularly.   *(lit.)*

Often.

Constantly.

Frequently.

〔註〕經常，一直的意思。

B039 比上不足比下有餘

bei² sœŋ⁶ bɐt⁷ dzuk⁷ bei² ha⁶ jɐu⁵ jy⁴   (translit.)

It is insufficient when one is compared to the uppermost but it is more than enough when one is compared to the lowest.   *(lit.)*

Be worse as compared with the best but better as compared with the worst.

B040 冇一定

mou⁵ jɐt⁷ diŋ⁶   (translit.)

Have no fixture.   *(lit.)*

It is unfixable.

It is irregular.

〔註〕表示不固定的意思。

B041 冇出息

mou⁵ tsœt⁷ sik⁷   (translit.)

Have no interest to let out.   *(lit.)*

Be futureless.

Be go for nothing.

〔註〕表示沒有前途或飯桶似的。

B042 冇行

mou⁵ hɐŋ⁴   (translit.)

Have no hope.   *(lit.)*

There is no hope.

It is hopeless.

〔註〕表示沒有希望。

B043 冇彎轉

mou⁵ wan¹ dzyn³   (translit.)

There is no bend to turn.   *(lit.)*

There is no leeway to save the situation.

There is no way to break a deadlock.

Reach an impasse.

Have no room for manoeuvre.

〔註〕沒有轉彎的餘地，沒有補救的辦法或陷入僵局的意思。

B044 牛一

ŋɐu⁴ jɐt⁷   (translit.)

Cow and one.   *(lit.)*

Birthday.

〔註〕這是拆字式的俚語。"牛"字下加"一"字便成"生"字，因此便借以喻生日。

B045 欠債還錢

him³ dzai³ wan⁴ tsin⁴   (translit.)

Repay the debt.   *(lit.)*

Promise a debt.

B046 勿歇

mɐt⁹ hit⁸   (translit.)

Without a pause.   *(lit.)*

Unceasingly.

Continuously.
Without a pause.
〔註〕表示不停地或不斷地。

B047 手作仔
sɐu² dzɔk⁸ dzɐi² *(translit.)*
Hand-working guy. (lit.)
Craftsman.
〔註〕手藝人，工匠。

B048 手尾長
sɐu² mei⁵ tsœŋ⁴ *(translit.)*
The hand and tail is long. (lit.)
The trouble lasts long.
The trouble is endless for the future.
〔註〕後患無窮的意思。

B049 手指罅疏
sɐu² dzi² la³ sɔ¹ *(translit.)*
The gaps between fingers are estranged. (lit.)
Money burns a hole in one's pocket.
Spend money like water.
Can hardly save any money.
〔註〕表示有錢便花光或揮金如土沒有什麼積蓄的意思。

B050 反口咬一啖
fan² hɐu² ŋau⁵ jɐt⁷ dam⁶
(translit.)
Turn around the mouth and give a bite. (lit.)
Trump up a countercharge against somebody.
Turn around and hit back.
〔註〕表示反咬一口或反戈一擊的意思。

B051 片面之詞
pin³ min⁶ dzi¹ tsi⁴ *(translit.)*
One-faced remarks. (lit.)
One-sided statement.

B052 文雀
mɐn⁴ dzœk⁸ *(translit.)*
Gentle bird. (lit.)
Pickpocket.
〔註〕指扒手。

B053 心抱
sɐm¹ pou⁵ *(translit.)*
Hearted embrace. (lit.)
Daughter-in-law.
〔註〕即兒媳婦。廣東人叫"兒媳婦"為"心抱"，為"新婦"的變音。

B054 心都實
sɐm¹ dou¹ sɐt⁹ *(translit.)*
The heart becomes solid. (lit.)
Be downhearted.
Be depressed.
Be melancholic.
Mope oneself.
〔註〕表示鬱鬱不樂或悶悶不樂的意思。

B055 日久見人心
jɐt⁹ gɐu² gin³ jɐn⁴ sɐm¹
(translit.)
A person's heart can be seen in long course of time. (lit.)
Time makes one understand a person.
It takes a long time to understand a person's heart.

五　畫

B056　未有來
　　mei⁶ jɐu⁵ lɔi¹ᐟ²　(translit.)
　　Not yet.　(lit.)
　　It is still a long time before ...
　　It is quite a while before ...
　　〔註〕表示要很久才會……或離……還早的意思。參閱"有排"條（097）。

B057　可大可小
　　hɔ² dai⁶ hɔ² siu²　(translit.)
　　It may be either big or small.　(lit.)
　　It may be either serious or unimportant.
　　〔註〕表示事情可能嚴重，也可能不重要的意思。

B058　正話
　　dziŋ³ wa⁶　(translit.)
　　Just.　(lit.)
　　Just now.
　　A moment ago.
　　Just.
　　Happen to ...
　　As it happens.
　　〔註〕表示正要，剛才或剛剛的意思。

B059　打店
　　da² dim³　(translit.)
　　Beat a shop.　(lit.)
　　Put up for the night in an inn or an/a hotel.
　　〔註〕表示在旅館或酒店投宿的意思。

B060　打掂
　　da² dim⁶　(translit.)
　　Beat uprightness.　(lit.)
　　Set/Put something upright.
　　Set/Put something with one end upward and the other downward.
　　With the head/one end northward and the feet/the other end southward.
　　〔註〕表示把東西垂直或直立放或一端向北另一端向南平放的意思。

B061　打底
　　da² dɐi²　(translit.)
　　Beat the bottom.　(lit.)
　　Give somebody a hint beforehand.
　　〔註〕表示先給人一個暗示或露些口風的意思。
　　Put something under something.
　　〔註〕墊底，先在某些東西下放些另外的東西的意思。
　　Eat something before having wine.
　　〔註〕有些不慣喝酒的人很易醉酒，據説先吃些東西然後喝酒，便不易飲醉，這又説是"墊底"。

B062　失魂
　　sɐt⁷ wɐn⁴　(translit.)
　　Lose soul.　(lit.)
　　Be in a trance.
　　Be absent-minded.
　　Be all in a fluster.
　　Be scared out of one's wits.
　　〔註〕表示精神恍惚，魂飛魄散或慌

B063 生水芋頭

saŋ¹ sœy² wu⁶ tɐu²ᐟ⁴ (translit.)

Water-bearing taro. (such a taro is not soft and floury even it is well-cooked.) (lit.)

Be foolish-looking.
Be block-headed.
A simpleton.
A blockhead.

〔註〕芋頭在煮熟後，應該是綿軟而粉的，但"生水芋頭"則否，雖然煮得很熟，仍是"腎"（讀高上聲 sɐn²）的，所謂"腎" sɐn² 意即不够綿軟而粉的，後以一音之轉，把"腎"讀作 sɐn⁵ 音（低上聲），同時 sɐn⁵ 又喻作傻氣的或傻氣的人。此語比喻傻裏傻氣，不機靈或神經不大正常的人。

B064 生息

saŋ¹ sik⁷ (translit.)

Bear interest. (lit.)

Bear interest.
Build up one's own.

〔註〕表示或金錢存放銀行或貸給別人收取利息或樹立自己勢力的意思。

B065 生色

saŋ¹ sik⁷ (translit.)

Bear colours. (lit.)

Add lustre to ...
Add colour to ...

〔註〕增添光彩的意思。

B066 生步

saŋ¹ bou² (translit.)

Unfamiliar space. (lit.)

New to somebody.
Strange.
Unfamiliar.

〔註〕陌生的意思。

B067 生晒

saŋ¹ sai³ (translit.)

Come to life. (lit.)

Recover one's health/energy.
Rehabilitate oneself.
Resume one's spirits.

〔註〕恢復健康或體力，恢復自己的地位或名譽或重新振作起來的意思。

B068 ……生晒

saŋ¹ sai³ (translit.)

Continuously. (lit.)

Keep on...
Without a pause.
Continuously.

〔註〕放在動詞後；表示老是……或不斷……的意思，例如"嘈生晒"（老是吵鬧）或"催生晒"（不斷地催促）等。

B069 生猛

saŋ³ maŋ⁵ (translit.)

Living and fierce. (lit.)

Vigorous.
Lively.
Energetic.
Living.

〔註〕表示精力充沛，生龍活虎或活生生的意思。

B070 生鬼

saŋ¹ gwɐi² *(translit.)*
Of living ghost. *(lit.)*
Jocular.
Comical.
〔註〕詼諧或滑稽。

B071 生番哂
saŋ¹ fan¹ sai³ *(translit.)*
Come to life again. *(lit.)*
Recover one's health/energy.
Rehabilitate oneself.
Resume one's spirits.
〔註〕意和"生哂"（B067）同，不過意義較強一些。

B072 生曬
saŋ¹ sai³ *(translit.)*
Be dried while living. *(lit.)*
Be dried in the sun while something is living/alive/raw.
〔註〕這"生曬"和"生哂"音同異義，"生曬"的意思是當一種動物或其肉未經煮熟或仍是活生生的便在太陽下曬乾，多作表語或形容詞用，例如"這片豬肉是生曬的"或"生曬的豬肉"等。

B073 冚到密/實
kɐm² dou³ mɐt⁹/sɐt⁹ *(translit.)*
Cover tight. *(lit.)*
Block the passage of information.
Keep one's mouth shut.
Not to breathe a word about...
〔註〕表示封鎖消息，秘而不宣或對……一言不發/隻字不提的意思。

B074 冚檔
kɐm² dɔŋ³ *(translit.)*
Cover the stall. *(lit.)*
Close down.
Mop up the den (of illegal business).
〔註〕表示倒閉或掃蕩非法經營的地方的意思。

B075 冚唪呤（借音字）
hɐm⁶ baŋ⁶ laŋ⁶ *(translit.)*
All. *(lit.)*
All...
The whole of...
In all.
One and all.
All told.
Altogether.
〔註〕表示全部，一共或總額共……的意思。

B076 卡罅
ka³ la² *(translit.)*
A gap. *(lit.)*
The crevice between two things.
Either this or that.
Be equivocal.
〔註〕表示兩物之間的縫隙（這是本意）或兩可之間。

B077 四正
si³/sei³ dzɛŋ³/dziŋ³ *(translit.)*
Square-shaped. *(lit.)*
Regular-featured (of appearance).
〔註〕表示端正不差（指外型）。

B078 加料
ga¹ liu² *(translit.)*
Add more material. *(lit.)*

Feed more raw material(s) to something.
Add one/some more.
Reinforce something with...
Be reinforced with something.
Make a greater effort.
Put one's back into something.
Add some more (to the meal).
〔註〕意即增加原料，加倍努力，加勁或在吃飯時加菜。

B079 加埋……
ga¹ mai⁴... (translit.)
Add into... (lit.)
Include.
Add up to...
〔註〕包括或總共計起來的意思。

B080 出山
tsœt⁷ san¹ (translit.)
Go out of the mountain. (lit.)
Hold a funeral procession.
〔註〕即出殯。

B081 出口成文/章
tsœt⁷ hɐu² siŋ⁴ mɐn⁴/dzœŋ¹ (translit.)
What is out of the mouth becomes a composition. (lit.)
Keep a civil tongue in one's head.
Words out of the mouth are like those written by the pen of a writer.
〔註〕誇獎別人說話措詞謹慎或文謅謅的。

B082 出手
tsœt⁷ sɐu² (translit.)
Show out the hand. (lit.)
Raise a hand to blow.
Hit out.
〔註〕即動手打架。

B083 出年
tsœt⁷ nin²ʹ⁴ (translit.)
Go beyond the year. (lit.)
Next year.
〔註〕即明年。

B084 出色
tsœt⁷ sik⁷ (translit.)
Let the colour out. (lit.)
Acquit oneself well.
Make oneself remarkable.
Outstanding.
〔註〕表示使自己表現良好，顯出光芒或突出的意思。"出息"為音同異義的另一句俚語，參閱正篇（0522條）。

B085 出身
tsœt⁷ sɐn¹ (translit.)
Comt out of the body. (lit.)
One's family background.
Begin the world.
Start earning one's living.
〔註〕指家庭背景，或表示開始謀生。

B086 出便
tsœt⁷ bin⁶ (translit.)
Out of somewhere. (lit.)
Outside.
〔註〕即外面。

B087 出門
tsœt⁷ mun⁴ (translit.)
Go out of the door. (lit.)
Be away from home.

Be married out.
Marry to a man.
Marry off.
〔註〕表示離家遠去；姑娘出門子或出嫁。

B088 出馬
tsœt^7 ma^5 *(translit.)*
Take out the horse. (lit.)
Take the field.
Deal with.
〔註〕開戰，開始打鬥，應付或處理的意思。

B089 出嚟搵食
tsœt^7 lɐi^4 wɐn^2 sik^9 *(translit.)*
Come out to find something to eat. (lit.)
Come into the world to earn a living. (of both male and female)
Prostitute oneself (of female only).
Make easy money.
〔註〕表示在社會上掙錢（正當職業）；當娼妓或掙不正當的錢。

B090 出嚟撈
tsœt^7 lɐi^4 lou^1 *(translit.)*
Come out to scoop up. (lit.)
1. of male
  Drift about in the world to engage in dishonest work.
〔註〕指男人時，意為從事不正當的勾當，混飯吃。
2. of female
  Prostitute oneself.
  Earn one's living by becoming a social butterfly.
〔註〕指女人時，意為當娼妓或當交際花謀生。

B091 出爾反爾
tsœt^7 ji^5 fan^2 ji^5 *(translit.)*
Come out of you and go back to you. (lit.)
Go back on one's words.
Go back on one's promise.
〔註〕指說了又翻悔，或說了不照着做，表示言行前後自相矛盾。

六 畫

B092 在意
dzɔi^6 ji^3 *(translit.)*
Lay an idea on. (lit.)
Pay attention to...
Take notice of...
Use caution.
〔註〕表示留心，注意或謹慎的意思。（同義的有"為意"一語，參閱B307條。）

B093 有人做咗手腳
jɐu^5 jɐn^4 dou^6 dzɔ^2 sɐu^2 gœk^8 *(translit.)*
There is a man having done hands and feet. (lit.)
Somebody has secretly got up to little tricks.
Somebody has secretly done damage to somthing.
〔註〕表示別人暗中做了些小動作或背地破壞的意思。

B094 有毛有翼
jɐu⁵ mou⁴ jɐu⁵ jik⁹ *(translit.)*
Have feathers and wings. *(lit.)*
Be tameless.
Be uncontrollable.
〔註〕比喻孩子長大不順從父母或難以駕御的意思。相當於"翅膀硬了"。

B095 有行
jɐu⁵ hɔŋ⁴ *(translit.)*
Have hope. *(lit.)*
There is hope.
It is hopeful.
Be in the money.
〔註〕表示有希望，有辦法或有錢的意思。

B096 冇尾學人跳，冇尾又學人跳
jɐu⁵ mei⁵ hɔk⁹ jɐn⁴ tiu³, mou⁵ mei⁵ jɐu⁶ hɔk⁹ jɐn⁴ tiu³ *(translit.)*
Learn to jump with a tail and also do the same even without a tail. *(lit.)*
Blindly imitate somebody.
Act like a copycat.
Imitate somebody without measuring one's own capability.
〔註〕指人盲目仿效或不自量力去仿效別人。

B097 有排
jɐu²/⁵ pai²/⁴ *(translit.)*
For a long time. *(lit.)*
It is long before ...

〔註〕表示還有很長時間才……的意思，參閱"未有來"條（056）。

B098 有幾何呀？
jɐu⁵ gei² hɔ² a¹ *(translit.)*
How many times？ *(lit.)*
Seldom or never.
Seldom, if never.
Not so often.
〔註〕和"冇幾何"意同。見正篇該條（0278），"有幾何"用於反詰式的疑問句而"冇幾何"則用於否定式的陳述句，其實都是表達"不經常"的意思。

B099 有聲氣
jɐu⁵ sɛŋ¹ hei³ *(translit.)*
Have sound and air. *(lit.)*
There is hope.
It is hopeful.
Be in the money.
〔註〕和"有行"意同，參閱該條（B095）。

B100 有蹺蹊
jɐu⁵ kiu¹ kei¹ *(translit.)*
There is a trick. *(lit.)*
There are some tricks.
There is something secret about ...
There are some clever devices.
Have other fish to fry.
There is something fishing about ...
〔註〕內有乾坤，內有巧妙，另有他圖或裏面有鬼的意思。

B101 至多唔係……
dzi³ dɔ¹ m⁴ hai⁶ *(translit.)*
At most ... *(lit.)*

If the worst comes to worst...
When things are at their worst ...
〔註〕表示"大不了"或"頂多是"。

B102 至到……
dzi³ dou³ (translit.)
As to ... (lit.)
As to ...
〔註〕表示到；及至；至於的意思，不過如果説"不至於"時，則意爲"不會"，參閲該條（B037）。

B103 至話
dzi³ wa⁶ (translit.)
Just. (lit.)
Just now.
A moment ago.
Just.
Happen to.
As it happens.
〔註〕和"正話"同，參閲該條（B058）。

B104 至無……
dzi³ mou⁴ (translit.)
Even if ... (lit.)
Even if ...
Even so, ...
〔註〕和"甚至無"同，參閲該條（B179）。

B105 老人院都唔收
lou⁵ jɐn⁴ jyn² dou¹ m⁴ sɐu¹ (translit.)
Shelters for the old do not accept. (lit.)
One's remarks are too superfluous.
Be long-winded.

Be garrulous.
Repeat to a tiresome extent.
〔註〕喋喋不休或長氣，參閲正篇"滲氣"條（1717）。

B106 老積
lou⁵ dzik⁷ (translit.)
Old-aged accumulation. (lit.)
Be young but steady.
Have an old head on young shoulders.
〔註〕年少老成的意思，參閲正篇"年少老成"（0638）條。

B107 行運一條龍，失運一條蟲
haŋ⁴ wɐn⁶ jɐt⁷ tiu⁴ luŋ⁴, sɐt⁷ wɐn⁶ jɐt⁷ tiu⁴ tsuŋ⁴ (translit.)
A person having good luck is a dragon but a man having ill luck is only but a worm. (lit.)
A man in luck walks heavy but a man out of luck cowers with humility.
〔註〕比喻走運的人，趾高氣揚，但倒霉的人則不敢見人。

B108 行路打倒退
haŋ⁴ lou⁶ da² dou³ tɐn³ (translit.)
Go backward while walking. (lit.)
Fall on evil days.
Misfortunes never come singly.
〔註〕全句本爲"衰起上嚟有頭有路，行路都會打倒退嘅"，意思是説"當一個人倒霉時，甚至走路也會後退的"，但因爲句子太長了，廣東人多只説"行路打倒

退",簡單譯出來,便是"倒霉"或"禍不單行",參閱正篇"打倒退"(0429)條。

B109 先排
sin¹ pai² *(translit.)*
Previous days. (lit.)
Not long ago.
In the earlier days.
〔註〕和"前嗰排"意同,參閱該條(B193)。

B110 先斬後奏
sin¹ dzam² hɐu⁶ dzɐu³ *(translit.)*
Behead a man first and then report to the emperor. (lit.)
Act before reporting.
Do something first and then tell somebody about it.
〔註〕比喻先做完某事,造成既成事實,再向上級或有關方面報告。

B111 企喺城樓睇馬打
kei⁵ hɐi² siŋ⁴/sɛŋ⁴ lɐu⁴ tɐi² ma⁵ da² *(translit.)*
Stand on the gate tower to watch horses fighting. (lit.)
Make oneself stay out of the matter.
Keep oneself out of the affair.
〔註〕表示使自己置身度外。

B112 自梳
dzi⁶ sɔ¹ *(translit.)*
Self comb. (lit.)
Make up one's mind to marry to no man.
Decide to be an old maid all one's life.
Remain a maid all one's life.
Live in maidenhood all one's life.
〔註〕從前廣東順德、番禺、南海等縣的女子有終身不嫁的風氣,到了成年時,將辮子梳成髮髻,表示從此不嫁人,叫"自梳"或"梳起"。並且集合志同道合者,組織所謂"姑婆屋",以備年老時互相照顧。

B113 同一個鼻哥窿出氣
tuŋ⁴ jɐt⁷ gɔ³ bei⁶ gɔ¹ luŋ¹ tsœt⁷ hei³ *(translit.)*
Breathe from the same nose. (lit.)
Sing the same tune.
Echo somebody's nonsense.
〔註〕表示同某人有同一意見或跟人瞎說的意思。

B114 同……有路
tuŋ⁴ ... jɐu⁵ lou⁶ *(translit.)*
Have road with ... (lit.)
Commit adultery with somebody.
Have illicit intercourse with somebody.
〔註〕即和某人通奸。

B115 同……行得好埋
tuŋ⁴ ... haŋ⁴ dɐk⁷ hou² mai⁴ *(translit.)*
Walk very closely with somebody. (lit.)
Be on very familiar terms with somebody.
Get along very well with somebody.

〔註〕和某人極為友好或和某人相處得很好。

B116　同……行埋咗
tuŋ⁴ ... haŋ⁴ mai⁴ dzɔ² *(translit.)*
Have walked closely with somebody. (lit.)
Have had a sexual intercourse with somebody.
Have made love with/to somebody.
〔註〕諱言和人發生了性關係的委婉語，但如果只說"同……行"時，則表示和……戀愛的意思而已（見下）。
Have somebody's steady date.
Fall in love with somebody.

B117　收山
sɐu¹ san¹ *(translit.)*
Put away the mountain. (lit.)
Retire from one's work.
Retire from the world.
Live in retirement.
Wash one's hands of somebody.
〔註〕表示退休，退隱，過退隱生活或洗手不幹的意思。

B118　好心地
hou² sɐm¹ dei² *(translit.)*
Good heart ground. (lit.)
Be kind-hearted.
〔註〕即心地善良。

B119　好見飯
hou² gin³ fan⁶ *(translit.)*
See the cooked-rice well. (lit.)
The rice rises well when it is cooked.
〔註〕即"出飯"意指以同等份量的一種米煮飯，比同等份量的另一種米出的飯多。

B120　好話唔好聽
hou² wa⁶ m⁴ hou² tɛŋ¹ *(translit.)*
Words are good but they are not good to listen to. (lit.)
Frankly speaking.
Be quite honest about it.
In a manner of speaking.
〔註〕此為插入語，表示說實在的，老實說或不妨說的意思。

七　畫

B121　走趯
dzɐu² dɛk⁸ *(translit.)*
Walk and run about. (lit.)
Run about.
Walk this way and that way.
Rush about on errands.
Be on the busy come-and-go.
Do legwork.
Play a role of bit.
Be a legman/a utility man.
〔註〕表示四處走動，但引伸表示替人活動，奔波，做人跑腿或跑龍套的意思。

B122　找晦氣
dzau² fui³ hei³ *(translit.)*
Look for gloomy air. (lit.)
Go/Come to blame somebody to vent one's spite.

Seek a quarrel.
Denounce somebody for his...
〔註〕表示譴責某人以洩憤，尋衅或痛斥某人。

B123 夾手夾腳
gɐp³ sɐu² gɐp³ gœk⁸ (translit.)
Link hands and feet together. (lit.)
Co-operate closely with each other.
〔註〕緊密合作的意思。

B124 夾計
gap⁸/gɐp⁸ gei² (translit.)
Put the plots together. (lit.)
Lay our/your/their heads together.
Gang up with somebody.
Plot together.
Collude with somebody.
〔註〕即和某人聯合起來，串謀或串通。

B125 把火
ba² fɔ² (translit.)
A column of fire. (lit.)
Be filled with rage.
Be hot with rage/anger.
〔註〕意和"一把火"同，參閱該條（B005）。

B126 把幾火
ba² gei² fɔ² (translit.)
More than a column of fire. (lit.)
Flare out.
Be hot with rage.
Burn with anger.

Be filled with rage.
〔註〕大致上意和"一把火"（B005）及"把火"（B125）同，但意思和語氣較強。

B127 抙心抙肺
jiu¹ sɐm¹ jiu¹ fɐi³ (translit.)
Pierce both the heart and the lungs. (lit.)
Break somebody's heart.
Go to somebody's heart.
〔註〕令人很傷心的意思。

B128 求先
kɐu⁴ sin¹ (translit.)
Just now. (lit.)
A moment ago.
Just now.
〔註〕表示片刻之前或剛才的意思，和"頭先"同義，參閱該條（B421）。"頭先"和"求先"之分，是由於鄉音問題而已。

B129 扯頭纜
tsɛ² tɐu⁴ lam⁶ (translit.)
Draw the first cable. (lit.)
Take the lead.
〔註〕帶頭的意思，但有人說成"拉頭纜"的，參閱該條（B158）。

B130 扯綫'
tsɛ² sin²/³ (translit.)
Draw the line. (lit.)
Establish a relationship for both parties.
〔註〕給雙方拉關係。

B131 扯綫公仔
tsɛ² sin²/³ guŋ¹ dzɐi² (translit.)
A wooden figure dragged by

threads. (lit.)
A marionette.
A puppet.
A person who is led by the nose.
〔註〕即"牽綫木偶"或"傀儡",喻受人擺佈或支配的人。

B132 批中
pɐi¹ dzuŋ³ *(translit.)*
Give a right criticism. (lit.)
As expected.
Anticipate the result.
〔註〕在意料中或估計到的意思。

B133 告枕頭狀
gou³ dzɐm² tɐu⁴ dzɔŋ² *(translit.)*
Bring in a pillow indictment. (lit.)
Lay a complaint against somebody in the presence of one's husband.

B134 你/佢有寶呀?
nei⁵/kœy⁵...jɐu⁵ bou² a⁶ *(translit.)*
Do you/Does he...have treasured objects? (lit.)
What is unusual about you/him...?
Who cherishes you/him...?
Who cares about you/him...?
〔註〕這是對人表示輕蔑的用語,意爲你/他有甚麼了不起,或誰稀罕你/他。

B135 你/佢真開胃
nei⁵/kœy⁶ dzɐn¹ hɔi¹ wɐi⁶ *(translit.)*
You really have/He really has a good appetite. (lit.)
You are/He is too avaricious/greedy.
〔註〕即你/他真貪得無厭或貪婪。

B136 你/佢想點就點
nei⁵/kœy⁵ sœŋ² dim² dzɐu⁶ dim² *(translit.)*
Mark as you like/he likes to mark. (lit.)
Do/Does what you want/he wants to.
You/He can do what you/he can at random.
Do/Does as you like/he likes to.
Do/Does as you see/he sees fit.
Do/Does as your/his convenience.
〔註〕大意和"隨便你/佢"條同,參閱該條(B431)或"隨得……"(B432)。

B137 成日
sɛŋ⁴ jɐt⁹ *(translit.)*
A whole day. (lit.)
All day long.
All the day.
Nearly a whole day.
Always.
〔註〕表示"整天"或"老是"的意思。

B138 成數
siŋ⁴ sou³ *(translit.)*
Percent. (lit.)
Percent/Percentage.
It is likely that/whether...
There is possibility that...
By any possibility...

〔註〕表示百分率或有……可能的意思。

B139 佛口蛇心
fɐt⁹ hɐu² sɛ⁴ sɐm¹　*(translit.)*
Buddha's mouth but snake's heart.　*(lit.)*
Be kind-mouthed but vicious-hearted.
Be hypocritical and malignant.
〔註〕表示口慈心毒或口蜜腹劍。

B140 私己
si¹ gei²　*(translit.)*
Personal effects.　*(lit.)*
Private savings.
Personal effects.
〔註〕即私房錢或私有財產（尤指家中婦女所積蓄的財物）。

B141 足水
dzuk⁷ søy²　*(translit.)*
Enough water.　*(lit.)*
Be contented with one's luck.
Be pleased with oneself.
〔註〕表示心滿意足或自鳴得意。

八　畫

B142 抁頭
fiŋ⁶ tɐu²/⁴　*(translit.)*
Shake the head.　*(lit.)*
Shake one's head over something.
Say no.
Shake one's head to show disgust/to express sorry feeling.
〔註〕即搖頭，表示不答應，否認，厭惡或難過的意思（有時說成抁頭抁髻）。

B143 事頭
si⁶ tɐu²　*(translit.)*
The head of matters.　*(lit.)*
The boss.
A proprietor.
〔註〕對東家或老闆的稱呼。

B144 事頭婆
si⁶ tɐu⁴ pɔ⁴　*(translit.)*
The woman of the head of matters.　*(lit.)*
A proprietress.
〔註〕對老闆娘的稱呼。

B145 兩頭蛇
lœŋ⁵ tɐu⁴ sɛ⁴　*(translit.)*
A two-headed snake.　*(lit.)*
A tale teller.
A discord sower.
A fence sitter/rider.
A Jack on both sides.
〔註〕比喻挑撥是非的人或騎牆派。

B146 長腳蜢
tsœŋ⁴ gœk⁸ maŋ²　*(translit.)*
Long-legged grasshoppers.　*(lit.)*
A person with long legs
Be long-legged.
Be much of a walker.
〔註〕比喻長腿的人，走得快或善於走路的人。

B147 奉旨「子」成婚
tuŋ⁶ ji² siŋ⁴ fɐn¹　*(translit.)*
Be forced to get married under

an imperial decree「by a child」. (lit.)

Take a shotgun marriage.

〔註〕取"旨"和"子"的諧音來嘲人因有孕而不得不結婚。

B148 東莞佬賣蓆 —— 你生定死㗎？

duŋ¹ gun² lou² mai⁶ dzɛk⁹—nei⁵ saŋ¹ diŋ⁶ sei² ga³ *(translit.)*

Natives of Dun Gun sell mats — you are live or dead? *(lit.)*

Stretch one's legs according to one's own blanket.

〔註〕傳言東莞人短小精幹所製臘腸，亦短而粗大，同時所織草蓆亦較他地出產品較短，苟有人問他們為甚麼這樣短的，他們便反問說"你生定死㗎！"彼等意思是"死人則直卧，便不夠長，活人則可屈膝而卧，即便夠長的。"後來被人轉義為"人是能屈能伸的"更而喻"人是要隨機應變的"。參閱"大丈夫能屈能伸"條（B025）。

B149 亞蘭賣豬 —— 一千唔賣，賣八百

a³ lan²/⁴ mai⁶ dzy¹—jɐt⁷ tsin¹ m⁴ mai⁶, mai⁶ bat⁸ bak⁸ *(translit.)*

A Lan sells pigs — she doesn't sell them for one thousand dollars but for only eight hundred. *(lit.)*

Be forced to devalue something/oneself after having missed an opportunity.

Bargain away something.

Sell something at sale price.

〔註〕指錯過機會後，被迫把自己降低聲價或把物件賤價出售，但亦可簡單意為賤價把物件出賣。

B150 亞保亞勝

a³ bou² a³ siŋ³ *(translit.)*

A Bou and A Sing. *(lit.)*

Every Tom, Dick and Harry.

〔註〕泛指任何一個人，即"張三李四"的意思。

B151 到埗

dou³ bou⁶ *(translit.)*

Reach the wharf. *(lit.)*

Arrive (at/in ...).

〔註〕即到達。

B152 枕住

dzɐm² dzy⁶ *(translit.)*

Rest on. *(lit.)*

〔註〕同"枕長"（B153）。

B153 枕長

dzɐm² tsœn⁴ *(translit.)*

Rest for long. *(lit.)*

Often.

Throughout.

All along.

Year in and year out.

〔註〕經常地，長期，一貫地或長年累月地的意思。

B154 林沈

lɐm³/⁶ sɐm² *(translit.)*

Odds and ends. *(lit.)*

Something nondescript.

Odds and ends.

Something like skin disease.

〔註〕即不三不四的東西，零零碎碎的東西或皮膚病之類。

B155 拉埋……落水
lai¹ mai⁴ ... lɔk⁹ sœy² *(translit.)*
Drag ... into the water. *(lit.)*
Lay part of the blame upon somebody(for something).
Include one/somebody in the subject of conversation.
Drag somebody in ...
Involve one/somebody in the trouble.
Make somebody join in ...
〔註〕即拉人下水，表示把部分責任歸咎某人，把某人包括在話題內或把某人拉進（行動/事情）內的意思。

B156 拉頭纜
lai¹ tɐu⁴ lam⁶ *(translit.)*
Pull the first cable. *(lit.)*
Take the lead.
〔註〕意和"扯頭纜"同，參閱該條（B129）。

B157 制唔過
dzɐi³ m⁴ gwɔ³ *(translit.)*
Not worth doing. *(lit.)*
It doesn't pay...
It is not to one's profit.
〔註〕和"唔制得過"意同，參閱該條（B253）。

B158 依時依候
ji¹ si⁴ ji¹ hɐu⁶ *(translit.)*
According to time. *(lit.)*
On time.
In time.
Be punctual.
According to schedule.
〔註〕表示按時，準時或按照預定時間。

B159 和尚食狗肉 —— 一件穢，兩件又穢
wɔ⁴ sœn² sik⁹ gɐu² juk⁹ jɐt⁷ gin⁶ wɐi³, lœg⁵ gin⁶ jɐu⁶ wɐi³ *(translit.)*
A monk eats dog's flesh — it is sinful to eat one piece or two pieces. *(lit.)*
It is equally disgraceful to do such an ill deed for once or even once more again.
〔註〕比喻做一次壞事和再做多一次是一樣不光彩的。

B160 爭
dzaŋ¹ *(translit.)*
Contend for. *(lit.)*
Strive for ...
Scramble for ...
Differ from ...
Fall short of ...
Be out of balance.
Owe somebody something.
〔註〕表示爭取某人/物或差，欠，缺，短的意思。

B161 爭交
dzaŋ¹ gau¹ *(translit.)*
Strive for negotiation. *(lit.)*
Stop people from fighting with each other.
Dissude people from fighting each other.
〔註〕表示勸架或勸阻打架的意思。

B162 争住……
dzaŋ¹ dzy⁶ ... *(translit.)*
Strive for ... *(lit.)*
Show partiality to somebody.
Be behind with something.
Owe somebody something.
Be in arrears with one's payment.
Vie with each other in doing something.
〔註〕表示偏袒某人，拖欠或爭先做……的意思。

B163 争住先
dzaŋ¹ dzy⁶ sin¹ *(translit.)*
Strive first. *(lit.)*
Be behind with something temporarily.
Owe somebody something temporarily.
Be in arrears with one's payment temporarily.
〔註〕暫時拖欠的意思。

B164 夜長夢多
jɛ⁶ tsœŋ⁴ muŋ⁶ dɔ¹ *(translit.)*
A long night brings many dreams. *(lit.)*
Too long a delay causes hitches.
〔註〕指事情拖得太長便會引起障礙。

B165 夜遊神
jɛ⁶ jɐu⁴ sɐn⁴ *(translit.)*
A night-strolling god. *(lit.)*
A night owl.
〔註〕喻深宵不睡的人或過慣夜生活的人。"夜貓子"。

B166 油瓶
jɐu⁴ pɛŋ² *(translit.)*
An oil jar. *(lit.)*
Stepchild on mother's side.
〔註〕指隨母改嫁的孩子，含貶意。

B167 放水
fɔŋ³ sœy² *(translit.)*
Let out the water. *(lit.)*
Make an exception to favour somebody.
Accommodate somebody with good intention.
Convenience somebody for private reason.
〔註〕表示作出例外以利某人，故意通融或私下給人方便的意思。

B168 炕沙
hɔŋ³ sa¹ *(translit.)*
Be stranded on the sand. *(lit.)*
Go aground.
Come to a deadlock.
Be in low water.
Be immovable.
〔註〕本義爲船隻擱淺，比喻作陷入僵局，拮据或動彈不得（指物）。

B169 花紅
fa¹ huŋ⁴ *(translit.)*
Flowery red. *(lit.)*
Bonus.
Dividend.
〔註〕即紅利或獎金。

B170 阿箇
ɔ¹ gɔ⁶ *(translit.)*
Overdo. *(lit.)*

Be extremely unnatural and affected.
Overdo in affected manners.
Be inflexible.
Be restrained.
Be overscrulous.
〔註〕表示過分矯揉造作，拘束，或過分拘泥細節的意思。

B171 屈尾十
wɐt⁷ mei⁵ sɐp⁹ (translit.)
Bend the tail to ten. (lit.)
Turn around and come back.
〔註〕表示掉頭回來的意思。

B172 姑勿論……
gu¹ mɐt⁹ lœn⁶ (translit.)
Temporarily speak nothing. (lit.)
Not to speak of...
〔註〕暫且不說……的意思。

九畫

B173 挼埋
lɐt⁸ mai⁴ (translit.)
Hide somewhere. (lit.)
Hide oneself.
Hide out. / Cover up one's tracks.
Be on the dodge.
〔註〕和"匿埋"同義（B264），不過"挼埋"較爲粗鄙。

B174 挼吓鼓邊
lat⁸ ha⁵ gu² bin¹ (translit.)
Beat the rim of a drum. (lit.)
Have a small talk with somebody to sound out his reaction/the actual situation.
Sound somebody out on a question.
〔註〕表示用說話試探某人的反應或事情的眞相或試探某人對一個問題的意見。參閱"敲鼓邊"條（B385）。

B175 相睇
sœŋ¹ tɐi² (translit.)
See one another. (lit.)
Make a blind date.
〔註〕以前民風保守，婚嫁多由媒人安排男女雙方在一個地方相會，這便是"相睇"。二三十年代，廣州西關的"陶陶居"茶樓二樓，幾乎成爲此類"相睇"的固定地點。

B176 胡帝胡天／胡天胡帝
wu⁴ dɐi³ wu⁴ tin¹/wu⁴ tin¹ wu⁴ dɐi³ (translit.)
Mess up both the sky and the emperor. (lit.)
Behave foolishly.
Be mischievous.
Run wild.
〔註〕表示胡鬧，亂搞亂鬧。

B177 胡胡混混
wu⁴ wu⁴ wɐn⁶ wɐn⁶ (translit.)
Muddle away the life. (lit.)
Live a mediocre life.
Lead an aimless life.
〔註〕庸庸碌碌或無目的的生活的意思。

B178 指冬瓜話葫蘆

dzi² duŋ¹ gwa¹ wa⁶ wu⁴ lou⁴ (translit.)
Point at a hard-skinned cucumber and say it is a cucurbit. (lit.)
Talk nonsense.
Call black white.
Confound right with wrong.
Distort the facts.
〔註〕意即胡說八道，顛倒黑白（或是非）或歪曲事實。

B179 甚至無……
sɐm⁶ dzi³ mou⁴... (translit.)
Even if ... (lit.)
Even though ...
Even if ...
Even so,
〔註〕即使，甚至或就算是……的意思。

B180 風生水起
fuŋ¹ saŋ¹ sœy² hei² (translit.)
The wind blows and the water rises. (lit.)
Be prosperous.
Be getting on in life.
Have a rise in the world.
Be prospering with each passing day.
Have one's day.
〔註〕表示正在發迹，飛黃騰達或正在得意之時。

B181 食君之禄，擔君之憂
sik⁹ gwɐn¹ dzi¹ luk⁹, dam¹ gwɐn¹ dzi¹ jɐu¹ (translit.)
Eat emperor's emolument, undertake emperor's worriments. (lit.)
Do one's duty/Take somebody's duty since one is paid.
〔註〕指既受人用，應盡己責。

B182 食咗人隻豬
sik⁹ dzɔ² jɐn⁴ dzɛk⁸ dzy¹ (translit.)
Have eaten somebody's pig. (lit.)
Have raped/seduced a maid/virgin.
〔註〕喻奸污了一個處女的委婉語。

B183 食得鹹，就要抵得渴
sik⁹ dɐk⁷ ham⁴, dzɐu⁶ jiu³ dɐi² dɐk⁷ hɔt⁸ (translit.)
Since one can eat very salty food, one must be able to stand thirst. (lit.)
Since one has the courage of one's convictions, one must be prepared to accept the consequences.
〔註〕即"敢做敢當"的意思。喻一個人既然敢做出自己認爲正確的事，便要準備承擔後果。

B184 食齋不如講正話
sik⁹ dzai¹ bɐt⁷ jy⁴ gɔŋ² dziŋ³ wa⁶ (translit.)
It is better to speak correct words than it is to go vegetarian. (lit.)
It is better to be truthful.
It is better to speak the truth.

B185 香爐墩
hœŋ¹ lou⁴ dɐn² (translit.)

The mound of an incense burner (an earthen pot for holding incense sticks). *(lit.)*
One's sole inheritor/heir.
One's sole son to carry on ancestral traditions.
〔註〕即唯一的繼承的兒子或接續香烟的獨子。

B186 信邪
sœn³ tsɛ² *(translit.)*
Believe in evil spirits. *(lit.)*
Have belief in meeting with misfortune.
〔註〕表示相信會遭遇不幸。

B187 重係……
dzuŋ⁶ hɐi⁶... *(translit.)*
Be still ... *(lit.)*
All the same.
Nevertheless.
Had better ...
〔註〕仍是，仍然或還是的意思。但如果說"重係（接動詞）好"時，則表示還是……的好或最好莫如……的意思。

B188 皇帝女 —— 唔憂嫁
wɔŋ⁴ dɐi³ nœy²—m⁴ jɐu¹ ga³ *(translit.)*
An emperor's daughter—she doesn't worry about her marriage. *(lit.)*
A hoard/A person/A commodity/An object/Something everybody strives for/makes every endeavour to obtain.
〔註〕比喻爲人極力爭取的珍品/人/商品/對象或東西，亦即所謂奇貨可居。

B189 洒手擰頭
sa² sɐu² niŋ⁶ tɐu² *(translit.)*
Wave the hand and shake the head. *(lit.)*
Shake one's head (over something).
Say no.
Give a flat refusal.
〔註〕大致上和"抹頭"（B142）及"擰頭"同義（B436），但此語還含有"斷然拒絕"的意思。

B190 度水
dɔk⁶ sœy² *(translit.)*
Measure water. *(lit.)*
Ask for money.
〔註〕即要錢（詼諧的說法）。

B191 姜太公封神 —— 漏咗自己
gœŋ¹ tai³ guŋ¹ fuŋ⁴ sɐn⁴—lɐu⁶/lai⁶ dzɔ² dzi⁶ gei² *(translit.)*
Grand Duke Gœŋ offered gods high posts—omitting himself. *(lit.)*
Leave out/Omit oneself.
〔註〕歇後語便是註腳。凡分配，點名等等忘了自己那一份，廣東人便說"姜太公封神"，源自封神榜中的一段故事。

B192 前言不對後語
tsin⁴ jin⁴ bɐt⁷ dœy³ hɐu⁶ jy⁵ *(translit.)*
Previous words do not accord with the later ones. *(lit.)*
One's words do not hang

together.
One's remarks are incoherent.
One's accounts are self-contradictory.
〔註〕指所說的話，前後不符或自相矛盾。

B193 前嗰排
tsin⁴ gɔ² pai²/⁴ (translit.)
The other days. (lit.)
Not long ago.
In the earlier days.
〔註〕前些日子的意思。

B194 恃熟賣熟
tsi⁵ suk⁹ mai⁶ suk⁹ (translit.)
Rely on familiarity and sell familiarity. (lit.)
Be too familiar with each other to stand on ceremony.
〔註〕由於彼此很熟而不拘禮節的意思。

B195 穿煲/穿崩
tsyn¹ bou¹/tsyn¹ bɐŋ¹ (translit.)
Punch a hole in an earthen pot./Punch and break apart. (lit.)
Let the cat out of the bag./Spill one's guts.
Spill the beans./Split on an accomplice.
Expose the flaw/fault/sham.
〔註〕不慎洩露了秘密，說漏了嘴，告發同犯，露出破綻的意思。（嚴格說來，"穿煲"和"穿崩"是有些分別的。前者多指事情或秘密方面，而後者較着重指表演技藝方面。）

B196 穿櫃桶底
tsyn¹ gwɐi⁶ tuŋ² dɐi² (translit.)
Puncture the bottom of the drawer. (lit.)
Embezzle/Misappropriate the funds of the shop/store/company...
〔註〕表示挪用或侵吞公司/店舖款項的意思。（"穿櫃桶底"和"櫃桶底穿"兩者的分別是前者爲主動，後者爲被動。）

B197 計正
gɐi³ dzɛŋ³/dziŋ³ (translit.)
Count right. (lit.)
In the course of nature.
In the ordinary course of things.
Under normal conditions.
Accurately speaking.
〔註〕即按理說；本來；在正常情形下或準確地說。

B198 苦瓜乾咁嘅面口
fu² gwa¹ gɔn¹ gɐm² gɛ³ min⁶ hɐu² (translit.)
The face as well as the mouth looks like a dried bitter gourd. (lit.)
Pull a long face.
〔註〕即"哭喪着臉"，"耷拉着臉"的樣子。

B199 是必要……
si⁶ bit⁷ jiu³ (translit.)
Must ... (lit.)
Must ...

Ought to ...
Have to ...
Be bound to ...
〔註〕表示一定要,應該要或必須的意思。

B200 思思縮縮
si¹ si¹ suk⁷ suk⁷ *(translit.)*
Cower and cower. *(lit.)*
Have not an easy manner.
Do not carry oneself with ease and confidence.
Walk gingerly.
Cower with cold.
Be indecisive/hesitant.
〔註〕拘束;躡手躡腳;冷得打哆嗦或舉棋不定的意思。

B201 飛
fei¹ *(translit.)*
Flying. *(lit.)*
Be sharp/formidable. (of person with meaning of condemnation)
Be smart/clever. (of person with meaning of praise.)
〔註〕在貶義方面意爲厲害的或難以駕御的,在褒義方面,意爲精明能幹的或聰明的,試觀下列兩例:(1)"你而家飛咯",意爲"你現在不受駕御了"。這是貶義,但(2)"你嗰個女好飛嘅"意爲"你的女兒很精明能幹的"這是褒義。褒貶之分,視乎語氣而定。

B202 閂後門
san¹ hɐu⁶ mun² *(translit.)*
Bolt the back door. *(lit.)*
Express one's own poor situation beforehand in order to stop somebody from asking for a loan.
Feign oneself to live in poverty before somebody begins to borrow money.
〔註〕指預先哭窮,以免對方開口借錢。

B203 架步
ga³ bou⁶ *(translit.)*
The step of a shelf. *(lit.)*
Den.
Vice spots.
Unlicensed brothel.
Unlicensed gambling den.
〔註〕這"架步"和那"架步"(見該條B416)音同義異,這"架步"意爲進行非法活動的地方或巢穴,或非法妓寨及賭館之類。

B204 架勢
ga³ sɐi³ *(translit.)*
Posture of superiority. *(lit.)*
Magnificent.
Gorgeous.
Luxurious.
Swell with pride.
Terrific.
〔註〕南北皆有"架勢"這口語。但兩者意義不同。廣東人的所謂"架勢"意爲堂皇;威風;豪華;華麗或了不起的意思。

B205 架樑
ga³ lœŋ² *(translit.)*
Erect a beam. *(lit.)*
Pour oil on the flames.
Try to help one of the fighting

B206 紅光滿面
huŋ⁴ gwɔŋ¹ mun⁵ min⁶ (translit.)
The face is full of red light. (lit.)
One's face glows with health.

B207 紅鬚軍師
huŋ⁴ sou¹ gwɐn¹ si¹ (translit.)
Red-breaded military counsellor. (lit.)
A thoughtless adviser.
A misadviser.
〔註〕指給人錯誤指導的人。

十　畫

B208 捉蟲入屎窟
dzuk⁸ tsuŋ⁴ jɐp⁹ si² fɐt⁷ (translit.)
Catch a worm and put it into anus. (lit.)
Invite or ask for trouble.
Bring vexation on oneself.
〔註〕表示自尋煩惱，自討苦吃或自找麻煩的意思。但亦可説成"挑蟲入屎窟"。參閱正篇該條（0997）。

B209 捉錯用神
dzuk⁸ tsɔ³ juŋ⁶ sɐn⁴ (translit.)

sides.
〔註〕表示推波助瀾或幫助打架的一方的意思。

Wrongly catch the idea. (lit.)
Misunderstand somebody's intention.
〔註〕表示誤解別人用意，或"表錯情"。

B210 埋櫃
mai⁴ gwɐi² (translit)
Close the counter (lit)
Close the turnover of day.
Phunder a shop of its turnover of the day
〔註〕表示結算當天的營業額，也被引伸作搶劫商店的意思。

B211 班馬
ban¹ ma² (translit.)
Collect horses. (lit.)
Call for more persons ...
Gang up with more persons ...
〔註〕表示糾集多些人參加行動的意思。

B212 馬仔
ma⁵ dzɐi² (translit.)
Baby horse. (lit.)
Hatchet man.
Bodyguard.
Page.
Retinue.
Attendant.
〔註〕凡"打手"，"保鏢"或"侍從"之類，廣東人皆通稱之爲"馬仔"。

B213 起快（起筷）
hei² fai² (translit.)
Raise fast. (Raise chopsticks.) (lit.)
Help yourself to the food.

Cut and come again.

〔註〕"起快"亦即"起筷"。"起筷"其實是"起箸",廣東省多水上人(艇户),"箸"和"住"同音,"住"有停滯的意思,彼等迷信如"停滯不前",則屬不吉,何況"箸"又稱"筷箸",因此索性改稱爲"起快"取順風順水,進行快速之意。"快"和"筷"同音,而"筷"爲正字,漸逐成爲"起筷",意爲不要客氣隨便夾菜或較粗俗的説隨便盡量吃罷。

B214 起飛腳
hei² fei¹ gœk⁸ (translit.)
Raise a flying leg. (lit.)
Intend to fly high over somebody.
Rise in rebellion/revolt against somebody.
Try to flaunt one's superiority and outshine somebody.
〔註〕指懷有雄心,企圖超越某人。

B215 倔情
gwɐt⁹ tsiŋ⁴ (translit.)
Blunt feeling. (lit.)
Be unamiable.
Be unamenable to reason.
〔註〕指對人冷淡的;不易親近的或不近人情的。

B216 俾蕉皮/西瓜皮人踩
bei² dziu¹ pei⁴/sɐi¹ gwa¹ pei⁴ jɐn⁴ tsai² (translit.)
Give somebody banana skin/the skin of water-melon to tread on. (lit.)
Make somebody meet with failure/loss ...
Make somebody stand on slippery ground.
Make somebody slip up.
〔註〕指使人遭受失敗,損失或站在不可靠的地步或令人犯錯誤。

B217 臭檔
tsɐu³ dɔŋ³ (translit.)
Stinking stall. (lit.)
Be notorious.
A notorious scoundrel.
A stinkard.
〔註〕形容人臭名昭著,卑鄙,或聲名狼藉。

B218 鬼食泥噉聲
gwɐi² sik⁹ nɐi⁴ gɐm² sɛŋ¹ (translit.)
Make the sound like a ghost eating mud. (lit.)
Give utterance to one's complaint/rage.
Murmur against...
〔註〕形容人口中唸唸有詞,發出怨言或絮絮不休的自言自語的神態。

B219 鬼打你
gwɐi² da² nei⁵ (translit.)
The ghost beats you. (lit.)
You are possessed/obsessed.
〔註〕罵人話,即"活見鬼","鬼迷心竅"。

B220 鬼猾
gwɐi² wɐt⁹/wat⁹/wak⁹ (translit.)
Ghostly cunning. (lit.)
Crafty.

Be as crafty as a fox.
Cunning.
〔註〕狡猾或詭計多端的意思。

B221　拿拿聲
na⁴ na²ᐟ⁴ sɛŋ¹　(translit.)
Make a sound of 'na⁴ na⁵'.　(lit.)
Make haste to do something.
In haste.
Quicken one's steps to do something.
〔註〕形容趕快或加快步伐。

B222　兇神惡煞
huŋ¹ sɐn⁴ ɔk⁸ sat⁸　(translit.)
Brutal god and fierce devil.　(lit.)
Be fiendish and devilish.
〔註〕形容人"兇暴的"的樣子。

B223　狼
lɔŋ⁴　(translit.)
Wolf-natured.　(lit.)
Be ferocious.
〔註〕形容人兇狠,兇猛。

B224　狼忙
lɔŋ⁴ mɔŋ⁴　(translit.)
As busy as a wolf.　(lit.)
Be in a hurry.
Be in a hurry-skurry.
〔註〕表示急忙,忽忙或慌張,手忙腳亂。

B225　狼胎
lɔŋ⁴ toi¹　(translit.)
Wolf-foetused.　(lit.)
Be both fierce and malicious.
Be both ferocious and relentless.
Be too covetous.
〔註〕形容兇狠或過分貪婪。

B226　海水沖倒龍王廟 —— 自己人不識自己人
hɔi² sœy² tsuŋ¹ dou² luŋ⁴ wɔŋ⁴ miu² — dzi⁶ gei² jɐn⁴ bɐt⁷ sik⁷ dzi⁶ gei² jɐn⁴　(translit.)
Seawater washes down the Temple of the Dragon King of the sea (Chinese Neptune) — One's own man does not know one's own man.　(lit.)
Not to recognize another member/other members on one's own side.
Not to know the person(s) belonging to the same group.

B227　家有一老,如有一寶
ga¹ jɐu⁵ jɐt⁷ lou⁵, jy⁴ jɐu⁵ jɐt⁷ bou²　(translit.)
Having an old person at home is like having a gem.　(lit.)
An old-timer in the family is an adviser of rich experience.
〔註〕指家中的老人是一個經驗豐富的顧問。

B228　淨係
dziŋ⁶ hɐi⁶　(translit.)
Only.　(lit.)
Alone.
Only.
Merely.

Simply.

〔註〕意和"單係"同，參閱該條（B319）。

B229 流嘢

lɐu⁶ jɛ⁵ (translit.)

Poor thing. (lit.)

An article of poor quality.
Be low-graded.
Be low-levelled.

〔註〕形容成績或質量低劣，差。

B230 粉板/牌字──唔啱就抹咗佢

fɐn² ban²/pai² dzi⁶—m⁴ ŋam¹ dzɐu⁶ mut⁸/mat⁸ dzɔ² kœy⁵ (translit.)

Words/Characters on the blackboard—wipe them away if they are incorrect. (lit.)

Forget it if what is said is incorrect/disapproved.

〔註〕當你表達意見，不知對方是否同意或所說的是否正確，因此借黑板（廣東人叫做粉板或粉牌）上的字來表示所說的可以隨時不算或作廢。

B231 逆次次

ŋak⁹ tsi³ tsi³ (translit.)

Go against. (lit.)

Feel embarrassed not to comply with somebody's request.
Be not amenable to reason.
Rebel against somebody's will.

〔註〕表示由於不順應他人意思而感爲難或逆人意向的意思。

B232 差一皮

tsa¹ jɐt⁷ pei⁴ (translit.)

Fall short of a skin-depth. (lit.)

Be inferior (to ...)
Be lower-graded (than ...)
Be on a lower level.

〔註〕即差一等或低一級。

B233 差遲

tsa¹ tsi⁴ (translit.)

Error. (lit.)

Fault.
Mistake.
Slip.

〔註〕過失，差錯，失誤，漏洞或意外事故的意思。

B234 神主牌都會郁

sɐn⁴ dzy² pai² dou¹ wui⁵ juk⁷ (translit.)

Ancestral tablets can also move. (lit.)

Play big luck.
Meet with one's fortune.

〔註〕比喻人走了大運。

B235 神主牌都會擰轉面

sɐn⁴ dzy² pai² dou¹ wui⁵ niŋ³ dzyn³ min⁶ (translit.)

Ancestral tablets also turn round their faces. (lit.)

Once one becomes a leper, one brings disgace on one's forefathers.

〔註〕麻瘋病患者，爲人避之唯恐不及，甚至連祖宗也蒙羞，這句話便是含有這個意思。

B236 神前桔──陰乾

sɐn⁴ tsin⁴ gɐt⁷—jɐm¹ gɔn¹

(translit.)
The tangerines placed at the presence of gods,—they are dried in the shade. *(lit.)*
The longer the sum of money is saved, the smaller and smaller it becomes.
The longer something is kept, the smaller and smaller/the less and less it becomes.
The older one grows, the thinner and thinner one gets.
〔註〕比喻越放越少（金錢或物）或越長越瘦（人）。

B237 唔……罷就
m⁴ ... ba⁶ dzɐu⁶ *(translit.)*
Drop the matter if not... *(lit.)*
Forget it/Drop it/Let it pass if/since somebody does/will not...
〔註〕即不……便算了。

B238 唔一定
m⁴ jɐt⁷ diŋ⁶ *(translit.)*
Can not fix yet. *(lit.)*
Be not sure.
It is indefinite.
Can give no affirmative answer.
No definite answer can be given.
〔註〕表示不肯定的意思。

B239 唔止……重兼……
m⁴ dzi² ... dzuŋ⁶ gim¹ ... *(translit.)*
Not only...but also... *(lit.)*
Not only...but also...
〔註〕此爲連接詞，有人說成"不特……重兼/而且……"。

B240 唔中用
m⁴ dzuŋ¹ juŋ⁶ *(translit.)*
Be not useful. *(lit.)*
Be good for nothing.
Be ne'eve-do-well.
Won't do.
〔註〕表示不管用，無能，不成器或不行的意思。

B241 唔爭在……
m⁴ dzaŋ¹ dzɔi⁶ *(translit.)*
Not to fight for it. *(lit.)*
Can do without.
Can dispense with...
〔註〕不差，不計較或沒有也行的意思。

B242 唔爭氣
m⁴ dzaŋ¹ hei³ *(translit.)*
Not to fight for air. *(lit.)*
Fail to live up to one's expectation.
Disappoint somebody.
Let one down.
〔註〕表示不符期望，令人失望或辜負期望的意思。

B243 唔好手腳
m⁴ hou² sɐu² gœk⁸ *(translit.)*
Hands and feet are not good. *(lit.)*
Have a tendency of theft.
Get used to stealing.
〔註〕即"手腳不乾淨"，有偷竊傾向或慣於偷竊。

B244 唔淨只……
m⁴ dziŋ⁶ dzi² ... *(translit.)*

Not only... *(lit.)*
Not only...
〔註〕相當於"不單只"。

B245 唔使慌
m⁴ sɐi² fɔŋ¹ *(translit.)*
Don't be scared. *(lit.)*
Don't be afraid.
Don't worry about...
Take it easy.
Pin none of one's hope.
Pin no hope on th fact that...
〔註〕表示不必害怕（本義），不用擔心或不必發愁的意思。當説此語而帶勉強的語氣時，則是表示别指望了的幽默反義語。

B246 唔使恨
m⁴ sɐi² hɐn⁶ *(translit.)*
Have no wish for. *(lit.)*
Cherrish no hope for somebody/something.
Pin none of one's hope on somebody/something.
〔註〕表示不用指望，對某人/物不抱有希望的意思。

B247 唔似樣
m⁴ tsi⁵ jœn² *(translit.)*
Not alike. *(lit.)*
It is most imporper.
It is unreasonable for somebody to ...
It is outrageous that ...
Bear no resemblance to somebody/something.
〔註〕指在禮貌上要别人做……不成體統或太不像話，或指在别人的行爲或態度上，有令人難以容忍的含義。此外又表示在外表方面和……不類似的意思。

B248 唔食得豬
m⁴ sik⁹ dɐk⁷ dzy¹ *(translit.)*
Eat no pigs. *(lit.)*
Be non-virginal.
A maid without moral integrity of virginity.
〔註〕南番順各地，向重女性貞操，故迎娶時，慣例必有燒豬回門，以示新娘仍屬處女，若回門時，不備燒豬，藉作暗示新娘已非原璧。因此這俚語便用以婉說一個女子並非處女，倘女子被人説"你唔食得豬"時，便認爲莫大的侮辱。

B249 唔通……
m⁴ tuŋ¹ ... *(translit.)*
Could ... ? *(lit.)*
Isn't it that ... ?
Could ... possibly ... ?
〔註〕即難道。多用於疑問句中以加強語氣。

B250 唔通氣
m⁴ tuŋ¹ hei² *(translit.)*
Not to let air out. *(lit.)*
Be not sensible.
Not to know to behave in a delicate situation.
〔註〕表示不知趣（妨礙别人）的意思。參閲正篇"電燈膽"（1588）條。

B251 唔計帶
m⁴ gɐi³ dai³ *(translit.)*
Neither count nor bring. *(lit.)*
Do not mind.

Do not care about...
Do not haggle about.
〔註〕表示不介意或不計較的意思。

B252 唔話得
m⁴ wa⁶ dɐk⁷ *(translit.)*
Have nothing to say. *(lit.)*
Have nothing to complain of...
Be really good.
〔註〕表示沒有甚麼可說的，沒有可埋怨的話或確實是好人的意思。（對人或事表示滿意，提不出甚麼意見。）

B253 唔制得過
m⁴ dzɐi³ dɐk⁷ gwɔ³ *(translit.)*
Not worth doing. *(lit.)*
It doesn't pay...
It is not to one's profit.
〔註〕即不劃算或劃不來的意思，參閱"制唔過"條（B157）。

B254 唔恨
m⁴ hɐn⁶ *(translit.)*
Without wish. *(lit.)*
Not to care about.
Do not mind.
〔註〕表示不稀罕，不想或不在乎的意思。

B255 唔啱蕎
m⁴ ŋam¹ kiu² *(translit.)*
With wrong ideas. *(lit.)*
Do not get along well with each other.
Do not sing the same tune.
Be at odds with each other.
〔註〕即合不來或意見不合的意思。

B256 唔係是必要……
m⁴ hɐi⁶ si⁶ bit⁷ jiu³ ...
(translit.)
Need not ... *(lit.)*
Do not need to ...
There is no need for somebody to ...
It is not necessary for somebody to ...
〔註〕即不必要。

B257 唔係講玩
m⁴ hɐi⁶ gɔŋ² wan² *(translit.)*
Not speaking to play. *(lit.)*
It is no joke.
〔註〕不是玩兒的或這不是開玩笑的事的意思。

B258 剒
tsɔk³ *(translit.)*
Jerk. *(lit.)*
Jerk.
Tease somebody to tell the truth / to say that ...
Coax somebody into telling the truth / saying that ...
〔註〕表示用力一拉（本意）或逗引人說出真相或講出……

B259 剒住度氣
tsɔk³ dzy⁶ dou⁶ hei³ *(translit.)*
Jerk the breath. *(lit.)*
Be forced to swallow the leek.
Be compelled to hold back one's rage.
Be forced to submit to humiliation.
〔註〕被迫忍氣吞聲。

B260 跛路
gɐt⁶ lou⁶ *(translit.)*
Walk in the road with a limp! (lit.)
Scram!
Get out!
Beat it!
Get out of my sight!
〔註〕參閱"躝屍"條（B468）及"躝屍跛路"條（正篇1988）。

B261 骨痹
gwɐt⁷ bei³ *(translit.)*
The bones become numbled. (lit.)
Be filled with nausea.
Cause somebody to be disgusting.
〔註〕即令人肉麻的意思。

B262 戙起牀板
duŋ⁶ hei² tsɔŋ⁴ ban² *(translit.)*
Stand the bed-plates. (lit.)
Burn the midnight oil.
〔註〕表示工作至深夜的意思，參閱"開夜車"條（B327）。

B263 紗紙
sa¹ dzi² *(translit.)*
Gauze paper. (lit.)
A certificate.
A diploma.
〔註〕沙紙（sand paper）和紗紙（gauze paper）音同異義，前者爲用以打磨木器的一種用品，而後者爲中國特產，因其像紗布，故名"紗紙"，這種紙富有韌性，不易折斷，而且歷久不霉，古時書寫契約或字據之類文件，必用這種紙張，後人遂引伸喻作文憑或證書。

十一畫

B264 匿埋
lei¹ mai⁴ *(translit.)*
Hide somewhere. (lit.)
Hide oneself.
Hide out./Cover up one's tracks.
Be on the dodge.
〔註〕即藏起來或無固定住處以逃避拘捕。參閱"拗埋"條（B173）。

B265 梳起
sɔ¹ hei² *(translit.)*
Comb up. (lit.)
Make up one's mind to marry to no man.
Decide to be an old maid all one's life.
Remain a maid all one's life.
Live in maidenhood all one's life.
〔註〕同"自梳"，參閱該條（B112）。

B266 牽腸掛肚
hin¹ tsœŋ⁴ gwa³ tou⁵ *(translit.)*
Drag intestines and hang abdomen. (lit.)
Feel deep anxiety about somebody.

〔註〕即掛念（某人）。

B267 頂肚
diŋ² tou⁵　(translit.)
Fill up the abdomen.　(lit.)
Have something to appease one's hunger.
Allay one's hunger with something.
〔註〕即充飢，解餓。

B268 頂唔住
diŋ² m⁴ dzy⁶　(translit.)
Can not support.　(lit.)
Can not stand it.
Fail to put up with...
Be unable to...any more.
〔註〕表示受不了，吃不消或再不能……了的意思，參閱"頂唔順"條（B269）。

B269 頂唔順
diŋ² m⁴ sœn⁶　(translit.)
Can not support any more.　(lit.)
Can not stand it.
Fail to put up with...
Be unable to...any more.
〔註〕同"頂唔住"，參閱該條（B268）。

B270 頂硬上
diŋ² ŋaŋ⁶ sœn⁵　(translit.)
Tolerate the torment.　(lit.)
Compel oneself to do something against one's own will.
Brace oneself up and bear with it.
〔註〕表示硬着頭皮頂着或忍耐着，忍受着的意思。

B271 頂頭陣
diŋ² tɐu⁴ dzɐn⁶　(translit.)
Support the heading formation.　(lit.)
Set out in anticipation to make arrangements.
Act as a pioneer.
Take the lead.
Be in the van of movement/fight.
〔註〕指打前站或打頭陣，參閱前篇"打頭陣"條（0444）。

B272 頂頸
diŋ² gɛŋ²　(translit.)
Support the neck.　(lit.)
Squabble with somebody.
Quarrel with somebody.
Refute.
Talk back.
Retort sarcasm for sarcasm.
〔註〕表示雙方的拌嘴、抬槓或單方的反唇相譏的意思，參閱正篇1698"駁嘴"條。

B273 頂撞
diŋ² dzɔŋ⁶　(translit.)
Support and knock against.　(lit.)
Offend somebody.
Offer an affront to somebody.
〔註〕指冒犯或當衆侮辱。

B274 頂籠
diŋ² luŋ²　(translit.)
Support the cage.　(lit.)
Fulfil the quota.
Full-loaded.
Full up.

Full house.
Reach the limit.
〔註〕表示滿額，滿員，滿座，全滿，引伸作齊全。

B275 乾時緊月
gɔn¹ si⁴ gɐn² jyt⁹ (translit.)
Dry time and tight months. (lit.)
Be hard up for money.
〔註〕指手頭拮据。

B276 乾塘
gɔn¹ tɔŋ⁴ (translit.)
The pool becomes dry. (lit.)
Be in low water.
Fall short of money.
Be penniless.
〔註〕水塘乾涸則無水，以水喻錢，因此"乾塘"意即"不名一文"。

B277 執番條命
dzɐp⁷ fan¹ tiu⁴ mɛŋ⁶ (translit.)
Pick back the life. (lit.)
Escape with bare life.
〔註〕即死裏逃生。

B278 推心置腹
tœy¹ sɐm¹ dzi³ fuk⁷ (translit.)
Push the heart and place it into another's belly. (lit.)
Place confidence in somebody.
Take somebody into one's confidence.
〔註〕表示絕對信任某人或把某人當作知心人。

B279 推波助瀾
tœy¹ bɔ¹ dzɔ⁶ lan⁴ (trans-lit.)
Push small waves and help big waves. (lit.)
Pour oil on the flames.
Make waves.

B280 掛臘鴨
gwa³ lap⁹ ap⁸ (translit.)
Hang a cured duck. (lit.)
Hang oneself.
〔註〕謔喻上吊自殺。（掛臘鴨時，是用繩子繫着鴨頸的。）

B281 斬纜
dzam² lam⁶ (translit.)
Cut the rope. (lit.)
Break off with somebody.
Make a clean break with somebody.
Break off relations with somebody / between A and B.
〔註〕比喻和人一刀兩斷，分手或絕交，參閱正篇"掟煲"條(1303)。

B282 偏心
pin¹ sɐm¹ (translit.)
Slenting-hearted. (lit.)
Be biassed (towards...)
Show partiality to somebody.
〔註〕即對某人偏袒。

B283 得個吉
dɐk⁷ gɔ³ gɐt⁷ (translit.)
Gain an emptiness. (lit.)
Come to nothing.
End up with nothing.
Draw water with a sieve.
〔註〕表示落空或毫無收獲，參閱正篇"筲箕打水"條(1619)。

B284 兜住

dɐu¹ dzy⁶　(translit.)
Wrap up.　(lit.)
Save somebody from embarrassment.
Help somebody out of an awkward position.
Bring about a change of somebody's wrong remarks in order to save his face.
〔註〕表示幫助別人從尷尬局面中解脫或扭轉別人的誤說而挽回他的面子。

B285　夠皮
gɐu³ pei²　(translit.)
Have enough skin.　(lit.)
Just sufficient to cover the cost.
Just sufficient to pay one's expenses.
Have had enough.
It is too much for one.
More than one can ...
〔註〕賺夠消費之用，夠本或多得吃不消了的意思。

B286　逢場作興
fuŋ⁴ tsœŋ⁴ dzɔk⁸ hiŋ³　(translit.)
Enjoy oneself for once.　(lit.)
Join in the enjoyment on occasion.
〔註〕碰到一定的場合，湊湊熱鬧，樂呵樂呵。

B287　羞家
sɐu¹ ga¹　(translit.)
Shame the family.　(lit.)
For shame!
Shame on you/him ... !

Make somebody die of shame.
〔註〕羞，羞人，丟臉的意思。

B288　添食
tim¹ sik⁹　(translit.)
Add more to eat.　(lit.)
Ask for one/some more.
Do once more again.
Get an encore.
Give an encore.
〔註〕要多一些，再來一次或重演/奏的意思。

B289　清官難審家庭事
tsiŋ¹ gun¹ nan⁴ sɐm² ga¹ tiŋ⁴ si⁶　(translit.)
It is hard for an upright official to bring family affairs to trial.　(lit.)
Outsiders find it hard to understand the cause of a family quarrel.
〔註〕指外人無法明白別人的家庭糾紛。

B290　晦氣
fui³ hei³　(translit.)
Gloomy air.　(lit.)
Show somebody a querulous and discontent attitude.
Be too querulous and discontented to be friendly.
〔註〕表示對人不滿及滿腹牢騷的態度。（廣東人說的"晦氣"和普通話說的"晦氣"意義不同。）

B291　啲咁多
di¹ gɐm³ dɔ¹　(translit.)
A little.　(lit.)
A little bit.

A wee bit.
〔註〕表示極少，一點點兒，一丁點兒。

B292 啱啱
ŋam¹ ŋam¹ *(translit.)*
Just. (lit.)
Just as ...
Just now.
Only ...
〔註〕即剛剛的意思。

B293 荳丁
dɐu⁶ diŋ¹ *(translit.)*
Small like a bean. (lit.)
Tiny.
Bean-like.
A little chap.
〔註〕表示小得可憐或小傢伙意思，含有輕蔑的意思。

B294 通天
tuŋ¹ tin¹ *(translit.)*
Open the sky. (lit.)
Expose something without any reserve.
Make no secret of something.
The secret has been let out.
〔註〕表示毫無保留地把事件暴露出來，對事情毫不掩飾或秘密已經洩露了的意思。

十二畫

B295 靱皮
ŋɐn⁶ pei⁴ *(translit.)*
Tough-skinned. (lit.)
Naughty.
Mischievous.
Disobedient.
〔註〕皮，頑皮或調皮。参閱"跳皮"條（B363）但又含有不服從的意義。

B296 惡死能登
ɔk⁸ si²/sei² nɐŋ⁴ dɐŋ¹ *(translit.)*
Give a fierce look. (lit.)
Be ferocious/vicious.
〔註〕即惡狠狠的。

B297 惡揎揎
ɔk⁸ tɐn⁴ tɐn⁴ *(translit.)*
Fierce. (lit.)
Look ferocious (usually of women).
〔註〕（樣子）很兇的（常指女人）。

B298 挳
saŋ² *(translit.)*
Brush. (lit.)
Brush up something with sand/sand-paper/cleanser...
Rebuke somebody.
Dress down somebody.
〔註〕表示用沙之類刷洗（本義），但引伸表示訓斥某人的意思。

B299 挳到（人）鑞鑞睖
saŋ² dou³ ... lap⁸ lap⁸ liŋ³ *(translit.)*
Brush ... to shine brightly. (lit.)
Scathingly denounce somebody.
Sharply dress somebody down.
〔註〕痛斥某人一頓或狠狠地揍某人

一頓的意思。

B300 揸鐵筆

dza¹ tit⁸ bɐt⁷ (translit.)

Hold an iron pen. (lit.)

Carry off somebody's lover.

Cut the ground from under somebody's feet.

Snatch the business from one's competitor.

〔註〕比喻奪人的愛人或生意。相當於"挖牆腳"，參閱正篇"撬牆腳"條（1770）。

B301 揸鑊鏟

dza¹ wɔk⁹ tsan² (translit.)

Hold a frying-spade. (lit.)

Be a cook.

Wake up a heavy sleeper.

〔註〕指任廚子職位的自嘲説法，但又喻，喚醒不易起床的懶人的諧趣語。

B302 喪家狗

sɔŋ³ ga¹ gɐu² (translit.)

Homeless dog. (lit.)

Be in a state of anxiety.

Be seized with fear.

〔註〕比喻失魂落魄或惶惶不可終日的人。（"喪"字廣東人多誤讀爲 sɔŋ¹ 音。）

B303 搏唔過

bɔk³ m⁴ gwo³ (translit.)

Not worth to bet. (lit.)

It is not worth while running such a risk.

〔註〕表示不值得冒險的意思。

B304 黃面婆

wɔŋ⁴ min⁶ pɔ²/⁴ (translit.)

A yellow-faced woman. (lit.)

One's old woman.

One's wife.

〔註〕指男人自稱自己妻子的謔稱。

B305 散水

san³ sœy² (translit.)

Disprese the water. (lit.)

Escape in every direction.

Everybody takes his way.

〔註〕表示各自逃走的意思，參閱正篇"田鷄過河"條（0514）。

B306 爲食貓

wɐi⁶ sik⁹ mau¹ (translit.)

A gluttonous cat. (lit.)

A glutton.

〔註〕比喻饞嘴的人，參閱正篇"爲食鬼"條（1504）。

B307 爲意

wɐi⁴ ji³ (translit.)

Pay attention to. (lit.)

〔註〕同"在意"。（B092）

B308 傍友

bɔŋ⁶ jɐu² (translit.)

A dependant. (lit.)

A hanger-on.

A person sponging upon his friend/boss.

〔註〕指食客或依賴朋友或上司生活的人。

B309 炃善

nɐm⁴ sin⁶ (translit.)

Soft and kind. (lit.)

Be good and kind.

Be of an even temper.

〔註〕表示善良或性情平和。

B310 善靜

sin⁶ dziŋ⁶ *(translit.)*
Good and silent. (lit.)
Be kind and silent.
〔註〕善良且沉靜的意思。

B311 渣嘢
dza² jɛ⁵ *(translit.)*
Poor thing. (lit.)
An article of poor quality.
Be low-graded.
Be low-levelled.
〔註〕參閱"流嘢"條（B229）及"二打六"條（B019）。

B312 就嚟
dzɐu⁶ lɐi⁴ *(translit.)*
Come soon. (lit.)
Coming.
Just a second.
〔註〕用於答覆對方的催促時説的一句口頭語，表示正在要來了的意思。

B313 就嚟……
dzɐu⁶ lɐi⁴… *(translit.)*
Will … soon. (lit.)
Will/Shall … quite/very soon.
〔註〕當後面接上動詞時，意爲快要……了，例如"佢就嚟搬屋咯"（他快要搬家了）或"就嚟落雨喇"（天快要下雨了）等。

B314 睇小
tɐi² siu² *(translit.)*
Look small. (lit.)
Look down on somebody.
Despise somebody/something.
Belittle somebody/something.
〔註〕即小看或輕視。

B315 睇衰
tɐi² sœy¹ *(translit.)*
Look at the wane. (lit.)
Look down on somebody.
Despise somebody.
Belittle somebody.
〔註〕蔑視，看不起，小看。大意和"睇小"相同。但分別處爲"睇小"可用於人或物，而"睇衰"則只限用於人。

B316 異相
ji⁶ sœŋ³ *(translit.)*
Odd-looking. (lit.)
Unsightly.
Odd-looking.
〔註〕形容人或物難看或樣子古怪。

B317 黑口黑面
hɐk⁷ hɐu² hɐk⁷ min⁶ *(translit.)*
Black-mouthed and black-faced. (lit.)
Look displeased.
Nurse a grievance.
〔註〕形容人滿臉不高興的樣子或心懷不滿的神色。

B318 買生不如買熟
mai⁵ saŋ¹ bɐt⁷ jy⁴ mai⁵ suk⁹ *(translit.)*
Buying from a stranger is not like buying from a familiar. (lit.)
Feel secure to make a purchase in a familiar shop.
〔註〕指在熟識的店買東西較可靠。

B319 單係
dan¹ hɐi⁶ *(translit.)*
Only. (lit.)

Alone.
Only.
Merely.
Simply.
〔註〕表示光是，只是等意思，參閱 "淨係" 條（B228）。

B320 單眼仔睇榜 —— 一目了然
dan¹ ŋan⁵ dzɐi² tɐi² bɔŋ² — jɐt⁷ muk⁹ liu⁵ jin⁴ *(translit.)*
A single-eyed guy looks at the list of successful candidates — one eye makes clear. *(lit.)*
See with half an eye.
See at a glance.
Be clear at a glance.
〔註〕"亞單睇榜" 的另一說法，參閱正篇（0821）該條。

B321 發吟發話
fat⁸ ŋɐm⁴ fat⁸ wa²ᐟ⁶ *(translit.)*
Issue words. *(lit.)*
Talk rubbish.
Talk nonsense.
〔註〕即說廢話或胡說八道。參閱正篇 "發噏風" 條（1572）。

B322 發夢冇咁早
fat⁸ muŋ⁶ mou⁵ gɐm³ dzou² *(translit.)*
It is too early to be in a dream. *(lit.)*
It is not the time for somebody to talk nonsense / to rave.
Not to have a fond dream in the day time.
〔註〕即別說夢話。

B323 開刀
hɔi¹ dou¹ *(translit.)*
Open knife. *(lit.)*
Perform an operation on a patient.
Fleece somebody of his money.
Cut down.
Reduce.
Fire somebody. (of workers or staff)
Dismiss somebody. (-do-)
〔註〕表示在病人身上動手術（本義），向人敲竹槓，勒索金錢，或裁減或開除的意思。

B324 開口埋口都話……
hɔi¹ hɐu² mai⁴ hɐu² dou¹ wa⁶ *(translit.)*
Whenever opening and shutting the mouth, say that ... *(lit.)*
Whenever one speaks, one says that ...
Always sing the same old tune that ...
〔註〕老是說……的意思。

B325 開古
hɔi¹ gu² *(translit.)*
Reveal the story. *(lit.)*
Make known.
Reveal the answer to the riddle.
Let the cat out of the bag.
〔註〕表示揭曉，揭謎底或揭露秘密。參閱正篇 "揭盅" 條（1463）。

B326 開埋井俾人食水
hɔi¹ mai⁴ dzɛŋ² bei² jɐn⁴ sik⁹ sœy² *(translit.)*

Excavate a well for somebody to drink water. *(lit.)*
Do pioneering work with great labour but let somebody sit with folded arms and enjoy the results.
〔註〕比喻努力創業，但任人坐享其成。

B327 開夜車
hɔi¹ jɛ⁶ tsɛ¹ *(translit.)*
Drive a night train. (lit.)
Work late into the night.
Burn midnight oil.
〔註〕參閱"戙起牀板"條（B262）。

B328 開通
hɔi¹ tuŋ¹ *(translit.)*
Be opened and ventilated. (lit.)
Be liberal.
Be enlightened.
〔註〕即開明或不守舊。

B329 開荒牛
hɔi¹ fɔŋ¹ ŋɐu⁴ *(translit.)*
A bull opening up wasteland. (lit.)
A person who does pioneering work.
〔註〕比喻開基創業的先驅者。

B330 開齋
hɔi¹ dzai¹ *(translit.)*
Break fast. (lit.)
Conclude an initial transaction of the day.
Get an initial winning after losing a lot.
〔註〕表示達成一天的第一宗交易或輸了不少錢後才第一次贏錢的意思，參閱"發市"條（正篇1568）。

B331 閒閒地
han⁴ han⁴ dei² *(translit.)*
Easily. (lit.)
Easily.
Casually.
Without any difficulties.
Without making an effort.
It is a cinch that ...
〔註〕表示輕而易舉地，隨隨便便地或沒問題地的意思。

B332 幾乎
gei¹ fu⁴ *(translit.)*
Almost. (lit.)
Almost.
Nearly.
By a hair's breadth.

B333 幾係幾係，五郎救弟
gei² hɐi⁶ gei² hɐi⁶, ŋ⁵ lœŋ⁴ gɐu³ dɐi⁶ *(translit.)*
It was hard to bear when Brother V saved his younger brother. (lit.)
It is considerably/fairly cold to-day.
〔註〕這句口語真是令人難解的，原來意爲今天多麼冷啊。"五郎"爲坊間小說"楊門女將"或劇目"楊家將"中的"楊五郎"，故事家喻戶曉，至於爲甚麼竟轉義成爲"今天很冷"則無從考證了。

B334 幾係㗎
gei² hɐi⁶ ga³ *(translit.)*
Considerably. (lit.)

It is a little too much to bear.
It is too much to cope with.
It is hard to bear.
It is quite an ordeal.
〔註〕表示"有些那個","夠甚麼的","夠受的"或"夠勁兒"的意思。用於表達已經達到相當程度,但甚麼程度又不明言,例如說"呢間酒家收費都幾係㗎"(夠高了),又或"今日行咗好遠路,幾係㗎"(夠受了)等等。

B335 幾難先至……
gei² nan⁴ sin¹ dzi³ ... (translit.)
Have difficulties before... (lit.)
Have a hard time before...
Meet with great difficulty before...
〔註〕即好容易才……。

B336 幾難至得……
gei² nan⁴ dzi³ dɐk⁷ ... (translit.)
Have difficulties before gaining... (lit.)
〔註〕和"幾難先至……"同義,參閱該條(B335)。

十三畫

B337 塘水滾塘魚
tɔŋ⁴ sœy² gwɐn² tɔŋ⁴ jy⁴ (translit.)
Pool water boils the fish in the same pool. (lit.)
Members of the same group gain profits from each other.
〔註〕喻自相謀取利益。

B338 塘底特
tɔŋ⁴ dɐi² dɐk⁹ (translit.)
The stick at the bottom of a pool. (lit.)
The person who shows himself while he is in low water or otherwise who covers his tracks.
〔註〕水塘底的木杵,水乾時才見,以水喻錢,因此借喻沒有錢時便露面,否則便不易被人找到的人。

B339 想話……
sœŋ² wa⁶ ... (translit.)
Want to ... (lit.)
Be just going to ...
Intend to ...
〔註〕即打算……或正要……(後接動詞)。

B340 零舍……
liŋ⁴ sɛ³ ... (translit.)
Especially ... (lit.)
Extraordinarily.
Particularly.
Especially.
〔註〕即特別或分外。(通常後接形容詞或副詞。)

B341 勢利
sɐi³ lei⁶ (translit.)
Have blind faith in power and profits. (lit.)
Be snobbish.

〔註〕表示諂上欺下的意思。

B342 遊車河
jɐu⁴ tsɛ¹ hɔ² *(translit.)*
Stroll the car river. *(lit.)*
Go for a drive in a car.
〔註〕坐車遊覽或兜風。

B343 煲老藕
bou¹ lou⁵ ŋɐu⁵ *(translit.)*
Stew old lotus-roots. *(lit.)*
Marry with an aged woman.
〔註〕比喻娶老婦爲妻的意思。

B344 滾友
gwɐn² jɐu² *(translit.)*
A boiling friend. *(lit.)*
A fast counter.
An imposter.
A swindler.
A person who talks nonsense.
An irresponsible person.
〔註〕即騙子，胡說八道的人或不負責的人。

B345 滾紅滾綠
gwɐn² huŋ⁴ gwɐn² luk⁹
(translit.)
Boil red and green. *(lit.)*
Talk nonsense.
Make fast-talk.
Make irresponsible remarks.
〔註〕表示胡說八道，信口胡吹。

B346 滑頭
wat⁹ tɐu² *(translit.)*
A slippery head. *(lit.)*
Be shifty.
A sly fellow.
A slippery customer.
〔註〕即狡猾或狡猾的傢伙。

B347 該死
gɔi¹ sei² *(translit.)*
Should die. *(lit.)*
Deserve it.
〔註〕相當於"該當"，但和普通話的"該死"有別。

B348 話名係……
wa⁶ mɛŋ² hɐi⁶ … *(translit.)*
Say the name to be … *(lit.)*
In name only.
Nominally.
〔註〕即名義上，相當於"應名兒"。

B349 話唔定……
wa⁶ m⁴ diŋ⁶ … *(translit.)*
Not to fix the saying … *(lit.)*
Perhaps.
Maybe.
It is beyond expectation that …
〔註〕說不定，或難以預料的意思。

B350 話落
wa⁶ lɔk⁹ *(translit.)*
Say down. *(lit.)*
Leave message.
Leave words.
Bid somebody to … at departure.
Say at/before one's departure.
〔註〕交代，留言或吩咐的意思。

B351 ……（某人）話事偈
… wa⁶ si⁶ gɐi² *(translit.)*
As what is said by somebody. *(lit.)*
As what somebody says.
〔註〕即正如（某人）所說。

B352 話極都……
wa⁶ gik⁹ dou¹ *(translit.)*

Say by every possible means but ... (lit.)

Keep on advising somebody but ...

〔註〕指不斷地勸告某人，但他……。例如說，"我話極佢都唔肯做呢項工作"（我不斷地勸他，但他不肯做這項工作）。

B353 話實

wa⁶ sɐt⁹ (*translit.*)

Say firmly. (*lit.*)

Make sure that ...

Be definite in saying that ...

Surely.

〔註〕即說定或肯定地說。

B354 ……（某人）話齋

... wa⁶ dzai¹ (*translit.*)

As what is said by somebody. (*lit.*)

〔註〕同"話事偈"（B351）。

B355 過水

gwɔ³ sœy² (*translit.*)

Pass over the water. (*lit.*)

Give somebody the money.

Pay somebody.

Grease somebody's hand.

〔註〕指付錢或向人行賄的行為。

B356 過火

gwɔ³ fɔ³ (*translit.*)

Over fire. (*lit.*)

Overstep the bounds.

Go too far.

To excess.

〔註〕大致上和"過份"同，參閱該條（B357）。

B357 過份

gwɔ³ fɐn⁶ (*translit.*)

Over quantity. (*lit.*)

Overstep the bounds.

Go too far.

To excess.

〔註〕即出圈兒或超越……的意思。

B358 過身

gwɔ³ sɐn¹ (*translit.*)

Pass off the body. (*lit.*)

Pass out.

Pass away.

Pay one's debt to nature.

Meet one's death.

〔註〕死亡的委婉語。

B359 嗲吊

dɛ² diu³ (*translit.*)

Be laggard. (*lit.*)

Be sluggish and dilatory.

〔註〕形容人做事拖沓。

B360 嘞氣

sɔk⁸ hei³ (*translit.*)

Suck air. (*lit.*)

Lose one's breath./Be out of breath.

Be tired out.

Be in straitened circumstances.

〔註〕表示喘不過氣來，呼吸困難或引伸作十分疲勞或處於貧困境地。

B361 跣人

sin³ jɐn⁴ (*translit.*)

Slip somebody. (*lit.*)

〔註〕同俾蕉皮/西瓜皮人踩。又"跣人"和"線人"音同異義。後者為供給警方線索的人。

('Professional informer or Pro-

fessional clue informer').

B362 路數
lou⁶ sou³ (translit.)
The number of a road. (lit.)
Social connections.
The pull to find a job.
〔註〕即門路，參閱"頭路"條（B422）。

B363 跳皮（調皮）
tiu³ pei²ʼ⁴ (translit.)
Jumping-skinned. (lit.)
Mischievous.
Naughty.
〔註〕即淘氣，頑皮或調皮。

B364 落……（某人）嘅面
lɔk⁹ ... gɛ³ min² (translit.)
Put ... (somebody's) ... face down. (lit.)
Bring disgrace on somebody.
Make somebody lose face.
〔註〕表示使某人丟臉。

B365 落手
lɔk⁹ sɐu² (translit.)
Place the hand. (lit.)
Put one's hand to the plough.
Set one's hand to ...
Begin/Start.
Lay hands on somebody.
〔註〕下手，着手開始或對……動武的意思。

B366 落手落腳
lɔk⁹ sɐu² lɔk⁹ gœk⁸ (translit.)
Put hands and feet. (lit.)
Do something oneself.
Do something with/by hands.
〔註〕表示親自去做或用手去做（指有別於機器）的意思。

B367 落形
lɔk⁹ jiŋ⁴ (translit.)
Put down the body. (lit.)
Become thin.
Bet emaciated.
〔註〕表示嚴重消瘦以致變了樣兒。

B368 落井下石
lɔk⁹ dzɛŋ² ha⁶ sɛk⁹ (translit.)
Drop a stone on somebody that has fallen into a well. (lit.)
Persecute somebody while he is down.
〔註〕比喻趁別人遭遇麻煩或不幸時再加以迫害。

B369 落面
lɔk⁹ min² (translit.)
Put the face down. (lit.)
Lose face.
Be disgraced.
〔註〕即丟臉。

B370 落嘴頭
lɔk⁹ dzœy² tɐu⁴ (translit.)
Lay down mouth-head. (lit.)
Go about selling an idea.
Persuade somebody into doing something.
Fawn upon somebody.
〔註〕表示遊說或奉承的意思。

B371 當堂
dɔŋ¹ tɔŋ⁴ (translit.)
All at once. (lit.)
On the spot.
Red-handed.

At once.
Right away.
Immediately.
〔註〕表示當場，就地或馬上，立即的意思。

B372　當黑
dɔŋ¹ hɐk⁷　(translit.)
Meet the black.　(lit.)
Be down on one's luck.
Be out of luck.
〔註〕比喻倒霉或倒運。

B373　隔籬飯香
gak⁸ lei⁴ fan⁶ hœŋ¹　(translit.)
Neighbour's cooked-rice is fragrant.　(lit.)
The grass at the other side of one's own fence looks greener.
〔註〕和"本地薑唔辣"（正篇0391）同義，但此語應用範圍較窄，多只用於表示孩子們多數喜歡吃鄰居的飯。

B374　嫁雞隨雞，嫁狗隨狗
ga³ gɐi¹ tsœy⁴ gɐi¹, ga³ gɐu² tsœy⁴ gɐu²　(translit.)
Follow a cock after marrying to a cock; follow a dog after marrying to a dog.　(lit.)
Become a subordinate to one's husband once married.
〔註〕封建時代，婦女要三從四德，所謂三從，即未嫁從父，既嫁從夫，夫死從子，這句俗語是根據既嫁從夫演譯出來。

十四畫

B375　趕狗入窮巷
gɔn² gɐu² jɐp⁹ kuŋ⁴ hɔŋ⁶　(translit.)
Drive a dog into a blind alley.　(lit.)
Compel somebody to strike back in self-defence.
Make somebody do whatever he can to defend himself.
〔註〕表示迫使人因自衞而反擊或使人做出可能做的事來自衞的意思。

B376　趕工
gɔn² guŋ¹　(translit.)
Rush into work.　(lit.)
Work overtime.
〔註〕即加班。

B377　趕唔切
gɔn² m⁴ tsit⁸　(translit.)
Fail to rush into action.　(lit.)
Have not enough time to do something.
It is too late for somebody to do something.
〔註〕來不及的意思。

B378　趕住投胎
gɔn² dzy⁶ tɐu⁴ tɔi¹　(translit.)
Rush into reincarnation.　(lit.)
Rush oneself off one's own feet.
Be in a hurry.
In a hot haste.

十四畫

Make a hot haste.
〔註〕表示倉促行動，急急忙忙的意思。（多用於斥責別人行動太急。）

B379 鼻屎好食，鼻囊挖穿
bei⁶ si² hou² sik⁹, bei⁶ nɔŋ⁴ wat⁸ tsyn¹ *(translit.)*
Since nasal muck is good to eat, the nasal cavity is excavated through. (lit.)
Everybody strives for profitable business.
Where there are profits, there is a keen trade competition between/among competitors.
A wide margin of profit has a strong appeal to tradesmen.
〔註〕比喻利之所在，人爭趨之或利潤大的生意，競爭必大。

B380 飽唔死餓唔親
bau² m⁴ sei² ŋɔ⁶ m⁴ tsɐn¹ *(translit.)*
Neither die of being full nor suffer from hunger. (lit.)
Earn no more than what one needs.
Have sufficient for one's needs.
Lead a passable life.
〔註〕表示過着僅够溫飽或過得去的生活。

B381 飽死荷蘭豆
bau² sei² hɔ⁶ lan¹ dɐu² *(translit.)*
Dutch pods die of being overfilled. (lit.)
Be irritated at somebody's ...
Be ruffled.
Be annoyd for ...
〔註〕和"飽死"同義，參閱該條（正篇1712）。

B382 認數
jiŋ⁶ sou³ *(translit.)*
Recognize the number. (lit.)
Acknowledge the debt/account.
Admit what one has said or done.
〔註〕表示承認債項或承認自己所說或做過的事。

B383 認賬
jiŋ⁶ dzœŋ³ *(translit.)*
Recognize the account. (lit.)
〔註〕同"認數"（B382）。

B384 漏口風
lɐu⁶ hɐu² fuŋ¹ *(translit.)*
Let the wind of mouth leak. (lit.)
Be inadvertent to blurt out.
Blurt out a secret.
〔註〕表示無意中脫口而出或無意中洩漏秘密的意思。

B385 敲鼓邊
hau¹ gu² bin¹ *(translit.)*
Beat the rim of a drum. (lit.)
〔註〕和"捌鼓邊"意思一樣。參閱該條（B174）。

B386 煽風點火
sin³ fuŋ¹ dim² fɔ² *(translit.)*
Fan the wind and light up the fire. (lit.)
Stir up troubles.
Whip up waves.
Incite trouble and create confu-

B387 塵氣
tsɐn⁴ hei³ (translit.)
Dusty air. (lit.)
Put on airs.
Be arrogant.
〔註〕形容神氣十足，擺架子或驕傲自大的神態。

B388 跟跟腳
ŋɐn³ ŋɐn²/³ gœk⁸ (translit.)
Shake the legs up and down. (lit.)
Lead a rose-coloured life.
Lie in a bed of flowers.
Live well.
〔註〕"跟"廣東話的意思是彈動。跟腳即彈腿，比喻過着安逸的生活。

十五畫

B389 嘩鬼
wa¹ gwɐi² (translit.)
Clamourous ghosts. (lit.)
Noise maker(s).
Clamour maker(s).
Bustling guy(s).
〔註〕指狂叫的人或喧嘩者。

B390 嘰嘰趷趷
gi⁶ gi¹ gɐt⁹ gɐt⁹ (translit.)
Stammer and obstruct. (lit.)
Stutter out.
Be troubled with stammer.
Be in the way.
Obstruct somebody from doing something.
Hinder somebody this way and that way.
Be a hind rance.
〔註〕表示結結巴巴地説，阻撓人做……或（行動方面）礙手礙腳的意思（有時只說"嘰趷"）。

B391 撈
lou¹ (translit.)
Scoop up. (lit.)
Fish for dishonest money.
Engage in dishonest work.
〔註〕指從事不正當職業或謀取不正當的錢財。

B392 撈女
lou¹ nœy² (translit.)
Lady-scooper. (lit.)
Street-walker.
Unlicensed prostitute.
A hoodette.
Social butterfly.
A girl earning dishonest money.
〔註〕指妓女，暗娼，女流氓，交際花或賺取不正當錢財的女人的通稱。

B393 撈家
lou¹ ga¹ (translit.)
Scooper. (lit.)
A man engaging in dishonest work.
A man earning dishonest profits.
〔註〕指沒有正當職業，靠偷拐詐騙

賺收不正當財物的人。

B394 撈家仔
lou¹ ga¹ dzɐi² *(translit.)*
Scooper Jr. *(lit.)*
〔註〕同"撈家"（B393）條。

B395 撈家婆
lou¹ ga¹ pɔ²/⁴/⁶ *(translit.)*
A woman scooper. *(lit.)*
A woman engaging in dishonest work.
A woman earning dishonest profits.
〔註〕指從事不正當職業或賺取不正當錢財的女人。

B396 撈起
lou¹ hei² *(translit.)*
Scoop up. *(lit.)*
Stick oil.
Earn good money.
Make a fortune.
Coin money.
Have a rise in life.
〔註〕表示發迹，高升或飛黃騰達的意思。

B397 撲水
pɔk⁸ sœy² *(translit.)*
Catch water. *(lit.)*
Go for a loan of money.
Go for rush money.
〔註〕比喻到處去找錢或借錢。

B398 撒賴
sat⁸ lai⁶ *(translit.)*
Scatter blames. *(lit.)*
Raise hell.
Make a scene with an intention to shift the blame to other shoulders.
Raise hell to lay the blame on the wrong shoulder.
〔註〕表示大吵大嚷企圖把責任推到別人身上的意思。

B399 撒/殺手鐧
sat⁸ sɐu² gan² *(translit.)*
A killer's mace. *(lit.)*
One's trump card.
〔註〕即必勝的手段或最後的一着。

B400 磅水
bɔŋ⁶ sœy² *(translit.)*
Weigh the water. *(lit.)*
Give somebody the money.
Pay soembody.
Grease somebody's hand.
〔註〕意和"過水"同，參閱該條（B355）。

B401 虢礫嘩嘞
gwik⁷ lik⁷ gwak⁷ lak⁷
(translit.)
Kwick lick kwark lark. *(lit.)*
Odds and ends.
A gross medley of miscellaneous things.
Crackle /Rattle /Crackling / Rattling.
〔註〕即雜七雜八的東西，但亦作象聲詞，表示物件相撞的聲音。（作象聲詞時，語音爲 gik⁶ lik⁶ gwak⁶ gwak⁶）。

B402 潤
jœn⁶ *(translit.)*
Lubricate/Moisten. *(lit.)*
Give somebody ironical remarks.

It is meant to be a dig at somebody.
Hold somebody to ridicule.
Profit somebody.
〔註〕表示挖苦或諷刺別人或給人利益的意思。（前義和B434"㞓"大致同義，不過"㞓"有激發而沒有給人利益的意思。）

B403 誰不知……
sœy⁴ bɐt⁷ dzi¹ (translit.)
Who does not know ... (lit.)
Who would have thought that ...
It turned out to be that ...
〔註〕這句口頭語用於發現了實情後說的，意爲誰會料到……或原來是……。

B404 熟能生巧
suk⁹ nɐŋ⁴ sɐŋ¹/saŋ¹ hau² (translit.)
Proficiency can generate skills. (lit.)
Practice makes perfect.

B405 熟讀唐詩三百首，唔會吟詩也會偸
suk⁹ duk⁹ tɔŋ⁴ si¹ sam¹ bak⁸ sɐu², m⁴ wui⁵ jɐm⁴ si¹ ja⁵ wui⁵ tɐu¹ (translit.)
Having thoroughly read three hundred poems in the Tong Poetry, one can imitate the way how they were composed even though one can not compose one. (lit.)
Practice makes perfect.
Skill comes from constant practice.

All genuine knowledge originates in direct experience.
〔註〕從經驗學得，從長久練習學成或熟能生巧的意思。

B406 熟客仔
suk⁹ hak⁸ dzɐi² (translit.)
A familiar vistor. (lit.)
A frequent caller/customer.
〔註〕熟客，常客，熟主顧。

B407 熟檔
suk⁹ dɔŋ³ (translit.)
Familiar stall. (lit.)
Be adept in...
Know a lot about...
〔註〕即内行；熟悉。

B408 熟行
suk⁹ hɔŋ⁴ (translit.)
Familiar trading. (lit.)
Be adept in...
Be skilled.
〔註〕内行；在行；熟練。

B409 熟性
suk⁹ siŋ³ (translit.)
Familiar-natured. (lit.)
Be reasonable.
Offer bribes to somebody.
Grease the palm of somebody.
〔註〕表示通情達理或向人行賄。

B410 熟落
suk⁹ lɔk⁹ (translit.)
Ripe enough to come down. (lit.)
Be skilled in...
Know a lot about...
Be on familiar terms with somebody.

〔註〕表示熟練，對……很熟悉或和某人很稔熟的意思。

B411 墨七
mɐk⁹ tsɐt⁷　(translit.)
Ink stick VII.　(lit.)
A burglar.
〔註〕即夜盜。

B412 弊家伙
bɐi⁶ ga¹ fɔ²　(translit.)
How bad!　(lit.)
What a bad luck!
How terrible!
〔註〕表示"糟糕了！"的意思。

B413 賤格
dzin⁶ gak⁸　(translit.)
Cheap style.　(lit.)
Be bese-minded.
Make oneself cheap.
Be too mean to be favoured.
〔註〕提即下賤，做有損自己名譽的事或不識抬舉的意思。

B414 踢竇
tɛk⁸ dɐu³　(translit.)
Kick the den.　(lit.)
Gather together a bunch of women to create a disturbance in the house of one's husband's mistress/adulteress.
〔註〕婦女發覺丈夫在外養了小老婆或情婦，糾集一羣婦女去其住處搗亂洩憤，這種舉動，廣東人稱之爲"踢竇"。

B415 墮角
dɔ⁶ gɔk⁸　(translit.)
Degenerate corner.　(lit.)
Be out-of-the-way.
Be remote.
〔註〕即偏僻。

B416 駕步
ga³ bou⁶　(translit.)
The pace of cart.　(lit.)
Haughty manner/airs.
Noble-postured.
Be arrogant.
〔註〕駕勢或架子的意思，和"架步"音同異義，參閱"架步"條（B203）。

十六畫

B417 醒
siŋ²　(translit.)
Awaking.　(lit.)
Clever.
Smart.
Quick-witted.
Terrific.
Swell with pride.
〔註〕大致和"醒目"同義，又有"了不起"、"神氣"的意思。參閱該條（B418），有時又說"醒神"（siŋ² sɐn⁴）。

B418 醒目
siŋ² muk⁹　(translit.)
Awaking-eyed.　(lit.)
Clever.
Smart.
Be as smart as a steel trap.
Attractive.

Attract attention.
〔註〕表示聰明伶俐，機警或形象明顯引人注目。

B419 醒定啲
siŋ² diŋ⁶ di¹　(translit.)
Be awaken.　(lit.)
Take care.
Be careful.
Take yourself/himself...into account.
〔註〕表示當心（用於勸告）或提防……的性命（用於警告或威嚇）的意思，參閱"因住"（B117）。

B420 賴貓
lai³ mau¹　(translit.)
A counterfeit cat.　(lit.)
Make a denial/disavowal.
Disavow.
Play tricks.
〔註〕抵賴，不承認或耍手段欺騙的意思。

B421 頭先
tɐu⁴ sin¹　(translit.)
Just now.　(lit.)
A moment ago.
Just now.
〔註〕即剛才，和"求先"同。參閱該條（B128），原因是有些廣州人帶些鄉音，把"頭"音發成"求"音。

B422 頭路
tɐu⁴ lou⁶　(translit.)
The heading road.　(lit.)
A pull.
A way.
The ropes shown to somebody.

〔註〕即門路，竅門或途徑的意思。參閱"路數"條（B362）。

B423 豬朋狗友
dzy¹ pɐŋ⁴ gɐu² jɐu⁵　(translit.)
Piggy and doggy friends.　(lit.)
Friends of bad characters.
Bad companions.
〔註〕即不三不四的朋友。

B424 豬嘜
dzy¹ mak¹/mɛk¹　(translit.)
Pig mark.　(lit.)
Be stupid.
Be as foolish as an ass.
An ass.
An idiot.
〔註〕形容人像豬一樣蠢或逕意為極端愚蠢。

B425 錫住
sɛk³ dzy⁶　(translit.)
Give love to...　(lit.)
Cherish a deep love for somebody.
Use something sparingly/cautiously.
Make the best use of something.
Stint the/one's money.
〔註〕表示愛惜（人），善用（物）或吝惜（金錢）的意思。

B426 親自出馬
tsɐn¹ dzi⁶ tsœt⁷ ma⁵　(translit.)
Take out the horse personally.　(lit.)

Act in one's capacity.
Take up the matter by oneself.

B427 辦蟹
ban⁶ hai⁵ *(translit.)*
Tie a crab. *(lit.)*
Tie somebody up.
Bind somebody's hands behind him.
Be tied up./ Be bound up.
Be trussed up.
〔註〕表示把某人綁住，被人綁住或拘押的意思。

B428 蕩失路
dɔŋ⁶ sɐt⁷ lou⁶ *(translit.)*
Lose the way while strolling. *(lit.)*
Lose one's way.
Be lost (somewhere).
〔註〕即迷途。

B429 賭氣
dou² hei² *(translit.)*
Make a bet with air. *(lit.)*
Do something in a fit of pique.
Do something rashly for being put in the wrong.
〔註〕表示因不滿而做出……或因受了委屈而草率地做出……的意思。

B430 隨便
tsœy⁴ bin² *(translit.)*
Follow convenience. *(lit.)*
Be casual.
Casually.
Be informal.
Informally.
Make yourself at home.
〔註〕表示不拘形式或禮節或隨意地的意思。此外在客套語中，又有請對方不要客氣的含義。

B431 隨便你/佢
tsœy⁴ bin² nei⁵/kœy⁵ *(translit.)*
Follow your/his convenience. *(lit.)*
Do/Does what you want/he wants to.
You/He can do what you/he can at random.
〔註〕表示任從你/他怎樣做便怎樣做的意思，參閱"隨得……"條（B432）及"你/佢想點就點"條（B136）。

B432 隨得……
tsœy²/⁴ dɐk⁷ … *(translit.)*
Give rein to … *(lit.)*
As one/somebody likes.
As one/somebody sees fit.
At one's/somebody's convenience.
〔註〕表示隨便，或任便，參閱"隨便你/佢"條（B431）。

十七畫

B433 臨時臨急
lɐm⁴ si⁴ lɐm⁴ gɐp⁷ *(translit.)*
When emergency comes. *(lit.)*
At the last moment.

Not...until an emergency.
〔註〕表示到了最後時刻或非到緊急時刻不……的意思。

B434 齮

ɐi³ *(translit.)*

Satirize. (lit.)

Hold somebody to ridicule.

Give somebody ironical remarks.

It is meant to be a dig at somebody.

Pour ridicule on somebody.

Prodding/Annoy/Enrage somebody with derision.

〔註〕挖苦，以嘲笑來激發或激怒的意思。

B435 戴綠帽

dai³ luk⁹ mou² *(translit.)*

Wear a green hat. (lit.)

A cuckold.

A man whose wife commits adultery with another man.

Be cuckolded.

〔註〕即戴上綠頭巾。

B436 韓信點兵 —— 多多益善

hɔn⁴ sɵn³ dim² biŋ¹—dɔ¹ dɔ¹ jik⁷ sin⁶ *(translit.)*

Han Sun called for soldiers — the greater the number the better. (lit.)

The more the better.

Han Sun was one of the three persons of great endowments in the Early Hon Dynasty.

〔註〕表示"越多越好"的意思。

B437 講到話……

gɔŋ² dou³ wa⁶... *(translit.)*

Say to the words ... (lit.)

As to/for ...

〔註〕表示至於……或就……方面來說。

B438 講倒話

gɔŋ² dou³ wa²/⁴ *(translit.)*

Say reversed words. (lit.)

Say to the contrary.

Speak an irony.

〔註〕說反話（用以譏諷人的反話）。

B439 薄皮

bɔk⁹ pei² *(translit.)*

Thin-skinned. (lit.)

Be apt to cry. (of person)

Be prone to blush. (of person)

〔註〕即臉皮薄，容易哭或容易臉紅。

B440 薄削

bɔk⁹ sœk⁸ *(translit.)*

Thin and soft. (lit.)

Thin and soft (of cloth/paper ...).

〔註〕指布料或紙張等很薄，稀疏。

B441 蟊

mau⁴ *(translit.)*

Pest-like. (lit.)

Malicious/Maliciously.

Unruly (unrulily).

〔註〕"蟊"的本義爲害蟲之類的動物，但粵人借以喻人狠惡的或做事兇狠，同時又喻在賭博或遊戲中不守規則。

B442 縮骨

suk⁷ gwɐt⁷ *(translit.)*

Shrinkable bone. *(lit.)*
Be self-centred.
Act from selfish motives.
Be treacherous.
〔註〕含有貶義，形容人自私自利或詭計多端。

B443 縮頭龜
suk⁷ tɐu⁴ gwɐi¹ *(translit.)*
Shrinking-headed tortoise. (lit.)
A coward.
〔註〕同作罵人語。比喻膽怯或懦弱的人。

B444 擦鞋
tsat⁸ hai⁴ *(translit.)*
Shine shoes. (lit.)
Flatter somebody.
Fawn upon somebody.
Toady somebody.
〔註〕表示奉承別人的意思。

十八畫

B445 轉吓眼
dzyn²ᐟ³ ha⁵ ŋan⁵ *(translit.)*
Turn eyes for once. (lit.)
Like winking.
In a wink.
〔註〕即一轉眼，轉瞬之間的意思，和"斬吓眼"同，參閱正篇該條（1857）。

B446 轉死性
dzyn³ sei² siŋ³ *(translit.)*
Change the nature to death. (lit.)
Turn oneself into a person of different nature.
Suddenly change one's disposition.
Suddenly change one's tune.
〔註〕指性情改變或態度轉變（尤指在愛好上忽然有較明顯的改變）。

B447 櫃桶底穿
gwɐi⁶ tuŋ² dɐi² tsyn¹ *(translit.)*
The bottom of the drawer is punctured. (lit.)
The funds of the shop/store/ company...are embezzled/ misappropriated.
〔註〕店舖/公司的欵項被人侵吞或挪用，參閱"穿櫃桶底"條（B196）。

B448 鬆毛鬆翼
suŋ¹ mou⁴ suŋ¹ jik⁹ *(translit.)*
Slack both feathers and wings. (lit.)
Burst with joy.
Sing and dance for joy.
Be elated.
〔註〕表示心花怒放，高興得載歌載舞或得意洋洋的意思。

B449 翻抄
fan¹ tsau¹ *(translit.)*
Re-copy. (lit.)
Reproduce.
〔註〕再製，再生或複製的意思。

B450 翻炒

fan¹ tsau²　(translit.)
Fry again.　(lit.)
Repeat.
Reproduce.
Reprint.
〔註〕即重覆，重影，重演或重印。

B451　翻閹
fan¹ jim¹　(translit.)
Be castrated again.　(lit.)
Sing the same old tune.
Do the old job once again.
Stage a comeback.
〔註〕比喻"重操舊業"，"東山再起"。

B452　舊底
gɐu⁶ dɐi²　(translit.)
Old bottom.　(lit.)
Formerly.
In the past.
Once upon a time.
〔註〕即從前，以前或過去的意思。

B453　舊時
gɐu¹ si²/⁴　(translit.)
Old time.　(lit.)
〔註〕同"舊底"（B452）。

B454　斷窮根
tyn⁵ kuŋ⁴ gɐn¹　(translit.)
Break up the roots of poverty.
　(lit.)
Strike oil.
Not to live in poverty any more.
〔註〕表示一朝發達或生活不再窮困的意思。

十九畫

B455　識人眉頭眼額
sik⁷ jɐn⁴ mei⁴ tɐu⁴ ŋan⁵ ŋak⁹
　(translit.)
Know somebody's brows, eyes and forehead.　(lit.)
Be good at knowing somebody's intentions.
Be quick at understanding what somebody intends to do.
〔註〕表示善解人意。

廿畫

B456　鹹龍
ham⁴ luŋ²　(translit.)
Salty dragon.　(lit.)
Hongkong dollar/money.
Hongkong currency.
〔註〕指港幣。（民國初期未把白銀收歸國有前，市面的通貨，仍沿用前清鑄造的雙毫，面值爲二毫，幣之一面，刻有龍紋，俗稱爲龍毫。"龍"因此喻作貨幣，香港爲鹹水地區，"鹹龍"因而得名。）

廿一畫

B457　顧/因住
gu³/jɐn¹ dzy⁶　(translit.)
Be careful.　(lit.)
Take care of oneself.

Restrain oneself.
Control one's emotion.
Not to exceed the limit.
Beware of one's life.
Take one's life into account.
〔註〕即留心，小心，抑制感情，作有限度的使用，或警告人當心……性命。

B458 霸拏
ba³ ŋa⁶ *(translit.)*
Lord over. *(lit.)*
Be despotic.
Play the bully.
Seek hegemony.
〔註〕即霸道。

廿二畫

B459 聽話
tɛŋ¹ wa⁶ *(translit.)*
Listen to saying. *(lit.)*
Be obedient.
Be subordinate to ...
〔註〕表示服從的意思。

B460 聽講話……
tɛŋ¹ gɔŋ² wa⁶ *(translit.)*
Hear speaking. *(lit.)*
Be told that ...
Hear that ...
〔註〕即聽說……

B461 聽落有骨
tɛŋ¹ lɔk⁹ jɐu⁵ gwɐt⁷ *(translit.)*
There is a bone in the hearing. *(lit.)*
More is meant than meets the ear.
〔註〕指某人的話，實在另有言外之意。

B462 讀壞詩書包壞腳
duk⁹ wai⁶ si¹ sy¹ bau¹ wai⁶ gœk⁸ *(translit.)*
Badly read poems and books and badly wrapped the feet. *(lit.)*
Be not understanding and considerate.
Be pedantic.
Be learned but immoral/shameless.
〔註〕諷刺人迂腐或不通情理。如果說時帶有輕蔑語氣時，則指人文而無行了。

廿三畫

B463 攪風攪雨
gau² fuŋ¹ gau² jy⁵ *(translit.)*
Give a stir to both wind and rain. *(lit.)*
Stir up troubles.
Make trouble.
〔註〕製造紛亂或搗蛋的意思，前義參閱正篇"掘尾龍"條（1295）及"煽風點火"條（B386）。

B464 驚住會……
gɛŋ¹ dzy⁶ wui⁵ ... *(translit.)*

Fear that ... (lit.)
Feel anxious that ...
Be afraid that ...
〔註〕即擔心會……的意思。

B465 驚青
gɛŋ¹ tsɛŋ¹ (translit.)
Give oneself a scare. (lit.)
Be in a flurry manner.
Run scared.
Be flustered.
Be all in a fluster.
〔註〕慌張，驚慌失措的意思。

廿四畫

B466 靈神不用多致燭，好鼓不用多槌
liŋ⁴ sɐn⁴ bɐt⁷ juŋ⁶ dɔ¹ dzi³ dzuk⁷, hou² gu² bɐt⁷ juŋ⁶ dɔ¹ tsœy⁴ (translit.)
Neither put too many candlesticks to offer an efficacious god nor strike too many strokes on a good drum. (lit.)
Put a word to the wise./A word is enough to the wise.
〔註〕表示智者一言已足的意思。

B467 蠶蟲師爺
tsam⁴ tsuŋ² si¹ jɛ⁴ (translit.)
A silkworm private adviser. (lit.)
A person who is caught in his own trap.
A person who gets enmeshed in his own web.
〔註〕即作繭自縛的人。

B468 躝屍
lan¹ si¹ (translit.)
Let your corpse creep away! (lit.)
Scram!
Get out!
Beat it!
Get out of my sight!
〔註〕相當於滾蛋。用於驅逐對方時的一種喝令句，但通常又說成"躝屍趷路！"或"趷路"。參閱該相關條目（正篇1998）及（B260）。

廿五畫

B469 鬥
dɐu³ (translit.)
Fight. (lit.)
Touch.
Vie with somebody/Compete against somebody for.../in doing something.
Enter into rivalry with somebody for ...
Resort to manoeuvres with somebody.
Have a battle of wits with somebody.
Be at odds with somebody.
〔註〕表示觸摸，和人競爭……／

做……，和人角逐……，和人耍花招，和人鬥智，或和人鬧別扭等意思。

B470 鬭氣

dɐu³ hei³   (translit.)

Fight for airs.   (lit.)

Be at odds with somebody.

Have the sulks.

Do something in a fit of pique.

Take a pique against somebody.

〔註〕賭氣，慪氣，鬧別扭或和人有爭執的意思。

B471 鬭嘥

dɐu³ sai¹   (translit.)

Have a battle if waste.   (lit.)

Slander/Defame/Calumniate each other.

Vie with somebody in squandering something.

〔註〕表示互相詆毀，互相誹謗或和人爭相浪費……的意思。

B472 鬭踩

dɐu³ tsai²/jai²   (translit.)

Vie to tread on each other.   (lit.)

Slander/Defame/Calumniate each other.

〔註〕意和"鬭嘥"同，參閱該條（B471），但和競相浪費絕無關係。

條目筆畫索引

一　畫

〔一起〕

一人計短二人計長	0001
一人做事一人當	0002
一人得道雞犬升天	0003
一了百了	0004
一刀兩斷	0005
一山不能藏二虎	0006
一口咬定/實	0007
一子錯滿盤皆落索	0008
一弓射兩箭	0009
一不做，二不休	0010
一手一腳	0011
一天光晒	0012
一生兒女債半世老婆奴	0013
一件還一件	0014
一死了之	0015
一次生兩次熟	0016
一字咁淺	0017
一竹篙打死一船人	0018
一言為定	0019
一言難盡	0020
一言驚醒夢中人	B007
一五一十	B001
一本萬利	B002
一向	B003
一次過	B004
一把火	B005
一身蟻	0021
一沉百踩	0022
一波三折	0023
一波未平一波又起	0024
一物治一物糯米治木蝨	0025
一息間	B008
一枝公	0026
一面屁	0027
一面之詞	B006
一哥	0028
一隻乙噉	0029
一隻手掌拍唔響	0030
一隻屐噉	0031
一陣間	0032
一陣陣	B013
一理通百理明	0033
一氣	B011
一就一二就二	B012
一埲迾	B014
一箸夾中	B015
一動不如一靜	0034
一喊都冇	0035
一清二楚	0036
一時一樣	0037
一時時	B009
一時唔偷雞做父老/保長	B010
一家皮宜兩家着數	0038
一家唔知一家事	0039
一個做好一個做醜	0040
一個夠本兩個有利	0041
一個餅印噉	0042
一喙沙糖一喙屎	0043
一部通書睇到老	0044
一條鎖匙唔聞聲兩條鎖匙冷冷響	0045
一眼關七	0046
一場歡喜一場空	0047
一朝天子一朝臣	0048
一筆勾銷	0049
一筆還一筆	0050
一傳十十傳百	0051
一網打盡	0052
一腳牛屎	0053
一腳踢	0054
一腳踏兩船	0055
一模一樣	0056
一碌木噉	0057
一樣米養百樣人	0058
一輪嘴	0059
一磚豆腐想升仙	0060
一擔擔	0061
一龍去二龍追	B016
一雞死一雞鳴	B017
一頭霧水	0062
一講曹操曹操就到	0063
一蟹不如一蟹	0064
一嚿飯噉	0065
一鑊泡	0066
一鑊撟起	0067
一鑊熟	0068

二　畫

〔一起〕

二一添作五	0069	人有失手馬有失蹄	0102	又試	0133
二口六面	0070	人同此心心同此理	0103		
二仔底	0071	人多手腳亂	0104		
二世祖	0072	人多燶狗唔烚	B021	三　畫	
二打六	B019	人多好做作	0105		
二四六八單	B020	人老心不老	0106	〔一起〕	
二叔公割禾	0073	人老精鬼老靈	0107		
十人生九品	0074	人爭一口氣佛爭一爐香	0108	三十六度板斧都出齊/埋	0134
十三點	0075	人怕出名豬怕壯	0109	三十六着走爲上着	0135
十月芥菜	0076	人要衣裝佛要金裝	0110	三九兩丁七	0136
十五個銅錢分兩份	0077	人急智生	0111	三[九]唔識七	0137
十五十六	B018	人面獸心	0112	三口兩脷	0138
十年唔逢一閏	0078	人情世故	0113	三心兩意	0139
十年唔耕九年唔種	0079	人情物理	0114	三不管	0140
十指孖埋	0080	人細鬼大	0115	三水佬睇走馬燈	0141
十拿九穩	0081	人望高處水往低流	0116	三分顔色當大紅	0142
十隻手指有長短	0082	人渣	0117	三句不離本行	0143
十個甕缸九個蓋	0083	人無千日好	0118	三扒兩撥	0144
十劃都未有一撇	0084	人算不如天算	0119	三更窮，四更富	0145
丁文食件	0085	人窮志不窮	0120	三長兩短	0146
七七八八	0086	人窮志短	0121	三枝桅	0147
七老八十	0087	人講你又講	0122	三姑六婆	0148
七國咁亂	0088	入境問禁	0123	三隻手	0149
七零八落	0089	入埋……嘅數	B023	三羣五隊	0150
七嘴八舌	0090	入鄉隨俗出水隨灣	0124	三腳櫈	0151
七竅生煙	0091	八十歲番頭嫁	0125	三歲定八十	0152
		八仙過海	B022	三頭六臂	0153
〔丿起〕		八卦	0126	工多藝熟	0154
		八婆	0127	下扒輕輕	0155
人一世物一世	0092			下馬威	0156
人山人海	0093			下欄	0157
人比人比死人	0094	〔丨起〕		下氣	B033
人心不足蛇吞象	0095			大一歲長一智	0158
人心肉做	0096	刁/丢眼角	0128	大人物	0159
人心隔肚皮	0097	刁/丢喬扭擰	0129	大人大姐	B024
人生路不熟	0098	刁/丢蠻	0130	大小通吃	0160
人在人情在	0099	也都[係]假	0131	大大話話	0161
人有三衰六旺	0100	又姣又怕痛，見人仔又眼紅	0132	大方	0162
人有三急	0101				

條目筆畫索引　319

大王眼	0163	大碌藕	0194	口疏疏	0224
大石責死蟹	0164	大槽	0195	口輕輕	0225
大好沉香當爛柴	0165	大驚小怪	0196	上天無路，入地無門	0226
大好鮮花插在牛屎裏	0166	大纜絞唔埋	0197	上氣唔接下氣	0227
大行其道	0167	士「事」急馬行田	0198	上得山多終遇虎	0228
大光燈	0168	土鯪魚	0199	上當	0229
大耳窿	0169			上樑唔正下樑歪	0230
大泡和	0170	〔丿起〕		上咗岸	B035
大枝野	0171				
大事化小，小事化無	0172	千年道行一朝喪	0200	〔𠃍起〕	
大花面撟眼淚	0173	千里送鵝毛，物輕情義重	0201		
大花筒	0174			也文也武	0231
大食唔窮倒算窮	0175	千金小姐當作丫鬟賣	0202		
大食細	0176	千真萬確	0203	〔乚起〕	
大食有指擬	B028	千揀萬揀揀着個爛燈盞	0204		
大丈夫能屈能伸	B025			女人纏腳布	B036
大把	B026	〔丨起〕			
大命	B027				
大拿拿	B029	小心駛/使得萬年船	0205	四　畫	
大種乞兒	B030	小鬼唔見得大神	0206		
大難友	B031	小財唔出，大財唔入	0207	〔一起〕	
大癲大廢	B032	小氣〈器〉	0208		
大炮友	0177	小家種	0209	不了了之	0232
大限難逃	0178	小意思	0210	不打不相識	0233
大家心照	0179	山人自有妙計	0211	不打自招	0234
大陣仗	0180	山大斬埋有柴	0212	不是冤家不聚頭	0235
大海撈針	0181	山水有相逢	B034	不到黃河心不死	0236
大隻騾騾	0182	山高水低	0213	不理三七二十一	0237
大粒佬	0183	山窮水盡	0214	不至於……	B037
大喊十	0184	口不對心	0215	不留	B038
大番薯	0185	口水多過茶	0216	比上不足比下有餘	B039
大喉腩	0186	口多多	0217	天下烏鴉一樣黑	0238
大諗頭	0187	口垃濕	0218	天無絕人之路	0239
大模屍樣	0188	口花花	0219	天堂有路你不走，地獄無門闖進來	0240
大禍臨頭	0189	口是心非	0220		
大搖大擺	0190	口甜舌滑	0221	天跌落嚟當被冚	0241
大話夾好彩	0191	口爽荷包垃	0222	天網恢恢，疏而不漏	0242
太覺瞓	0192	口窒窒	0223	木口木面	0243
大雞唔食細米	0193				

木匠擔枷	0244	冇得斟	0276	手急眼快	0310
木獨	0245	冇得諗	0277	手氣	0311
冇一定	B040	冇幾何	0278	手指拗出唔拗入	0312
冇出息	B041	冇揸拿	0279	手痕痕	0313
冇行	B042	冇腰骨	0280	手搵口食	0314
冇口齒	0246	冇哪更	0281	手緊	0315
冇天裝	0247	冇哪喼	0282	手作仔	B047
冇牙老虎	0248	冇話好講	0283	手尾長	B048
冇癮	0249	冇解	0284	手指罅疏	B049
冇手尾	0250	冇掩雞籠	0285	牛一	B044
冇心肝	0251	冇樣吖	0286	牛皮燈籠	0316
冇心機	0252	冇趟雙	0287	牛死送牛喪	0317
冇收	0253	冇頭烏蠅	0288	牛唔飲水唔搇得牛頭低	0318
冇衣食	0254	冇聲氣	0289	牛高馬大	0319
冇耳性	0255	冇檳榔唔嗒得出汁	0290	牛噍牡丹	0320
冇尾飛鉈	0256	冇廕正經	0291	牛頭唔對馬嘴	0321
冇走盞	0257	冇廕搭霎	0292	公死有肉食婆死有肉食	0322
冇走雞	0258	冇譜	0293	公說公有理，婆說婆有理	0323
冇兩句	0259	冇彎轉	B043		
冇呢枝歌仔唱	0260	牙尖嘴利	0294	今時唔同往日，一個酸梅兩個核	0324
冇咁大隻蛤乸隨街跳	0261	牙烟	0295	反口覆舌	0325
冇咁大隻鴿就唔好喊咁大聲	0262	牙斬斬	0296	反斗	0326
冇咁大個頭就唔好戴咁大頂帽	0263	牙齒痕	0297	反骨	0327
		牙齒當金使	0298	反骨仔	0328
冇咁大鴿就唔會喊咁大聲	0264	牙擦擦	0299	反面	0329
		扎實	0300	反轉豬肚就係屎	0330
冇咁大個頭，就唔會戴咁大頂帽	0265	支質	0301	反口咬一啖	B050
		支整	0302	分甘同味	0331
冇咁衰講到咁衰	0266	五行欠金	0303	欠債還錢	B045
冇料	0267	五時花，六時變	0304	勿歇	B046
冇家教	0268	切肉不離皮	0305	片面之詞	B051
冇晒符	0269				
冇晒符弗（法）	0270	〔丿起〕			
冇相干	0271			〔、起〕	
冇紋路	0272	手瓜硬	0306		
冇根兜	0273	手多多	0307	火上加油	0332
冇眼屎乾淨盲	0274	手忙腳亂	0308	火遮眼	0333
冇眼睇	0275	手板係肉，手背又係肉	0309		

火腿繩	0334	日頭唔好講人，夜晚唔好講神	0366	左手嚟，右手去	0389
火頸	0335			左右做人難	0390
火燒棺材	0336	日慳夜慳，唔够老公一舖攤	0367	本地薑唔辣	0391
火燒旗竿	0337			本事	0392
火燒燈芯	0338	少件膶	0368	甘心咯	0393
火麒麟	0339	少數怕長計	0369	未有來	B056
心大心細	0340	水上扒龍船，岸上人有眼	0370	未見官先打三十大板	0394
心中有屎	0341			未見其利，先見其害	0395
心中有數	0342	水上扒龍船，岸上夾死仔	0371	未知心中事，先聽口中言	0396
心不在焉	0343				
心甘命抵	0344	水瓜打狗	0372	未登天子位，先置殺人刀	0397
心多多	0345	水汪汪	0373		
心安理得	0346	水浸眼眉	0374	未學行，先學走	0398
心灰意冷	0347	水鬼升城隍	0375	未觀其人，先觀其友	0399
心足	0348	水過鴨背	0376	石地堂，鐵掃把	0400
心肝椗	0349	水落石出	0377	石灰籮	0401
心服口服	0350	水溝油	0378	石沉大海	0402
心急	0351	水靜河飛	0379	石罅米	0403
心思思	0352			世界仔	0404
心神恍惚	0353	〔冂起〕		世界輪流轉	0405
心淡	0354			去搵周公	0406
心都涼晒	0355	巴結	0380	古老石山	0407
心嘟嘟	0356	巴結有錢佬好過拜靈菩薩	0381	古老當時興	0408
心煩	0357			古/蠱惑	0409
心照不宣	0358	巴閉	0382	古縮	0410
心嗰句，口嗰句	0359	巴渣	0383	瓦風領	0411
心領	0360	引狼入屋拉雞仔	0384	扒灰	0412
心酸	0361			扒逆水	0413
心亂如麻	0362	五　畫		打理	0414
文雀	B052			打牙祭	0415
心抱	B053	〔一起〕		打牙骹	0416
心都實	B054			打尖	0417
六耳不同謀	0363	正話	B058	打同通	0418
六神無主	0364	正一陳顯南	0385	打赤肋/打大赤肋	0419
六親不認	0365	正斗/正嘢	0386	打死不離親兄弟	0420
		平生不作虧心事半夜敲門也不驚	0387	打死狗講價	0421
〔丨起〕				打如意算盤	0422
				打地舖	0423
日久見人心	B055	左耳入，右耳出	0388	打法功夫還鬼願	0424

打完齋唔要和尚	0425	生人勿近	0456	甩底	0485
打劫紅毛鬼進貢佛蘭西	0426	生人唔生膽	0457	甩繩馬騮	0486
		生人霸死地	0458	甩鬚	0487
打斧頭	0427	生勾勾	0459	包尾大番	0488
打個白鴿轉	0428	生仔都唔知仔心肝	0460	包詏/拗頸	0489
打到褪	0429	生白果	0461	包撞板	0490
打特	0430	生安白做	0462	失失慌	0491
打敗仗	0431	生骨大頭菜	0463	失匙夾萬	0492
打真軍	0432	生雞精	0464	失威	0493
打退堂鼓	0433	生死有定	0465	失魂	B062
打草驚蛇	0434	生蝦咁跳	0466	失魂魚	0494
打荷包	0435	生螆貓入眼	0467	失魂落魄	0495
打得更多夜又長	0436	生蟲拐杖	0468	失驚無神	0496
打蛇隨棍上	0437	生水芋頭	B063	禾桿冚珍珠	0497
打單	0438	生息	B064	皮鞋筋	0498
打單泡	0439	生色	B065		
打腳骨	0440	生步	B066	〔、起〕	
打店	B059	生晒	B067		
打惦	B060	……生晒	B068	立心不良	0499
打底	B061	生猛	B069	立立亂	0450
打橫嚟	0441	生鬼	B070	立實心腸	0501
打輸數	0442	生番晒	B071	立糯	0502
打邊爐同打屎窟	0443	生曬	B072	冚蓆矙石	0503
打頭陣	0444	白手興家	0469	冚到密/實	B073
打鐵趁熱	0445	白食	0470	冚檔	B074
打錯主意	0446	白斬雞	0471	冚唪唥	B075
打錯算盤	0447	白鼻哥	0472	半斤八両	0504
打瀉茶	0448	白撞	0473	半天吊	0505
打齋鶴	0449	白撞雨	0474	半吞半吐	0506
打雜	0450	白霍	0475	半夜三更	0507
打醒十二個精神	0451	白鴿眼	0476	半夜食黃瓜	0508
打爛砂盆問到篤	0452	白蟮上沙灘	0477	半信半疑	0509
打爛齋砵	0453	瓜老襯	0478	半途出家	0510
打響頭炮	0454	瓜直	0479	半桶水	0511
可大可小	B057	瓜柴	0480	市橋蠟燭	0512
		瓜得	0481		
〔丿起〕		他他條條	0482	〔丨起〕	
		甩身	0483		
仔大仔世界	0455	甩拖	0484		

條目筆畫索引 323

田雞東	0513	出爾反爾	B091	有酒有肉多兄弟	0559
田雞過河	0514	出山	B080	有得震有得瞓	0560
四方木	0515	出口成文/章	B081	有得諗	0561
四方辮頂	0516	出年	B083	有景轟	0562
四正	B077			有爺生冇乸教	0563
卡嚟	B076			有意栽花花不發，無	
		六 畫		心插柳柳成蔭	0564
〔冂起〕				有福同享，有禍同當	0565
		〔一起〕		有碗話碗，有碟話碟	0566
加料	B078			有錢使得鬼推磨	0567
加埋	B079	有一利必有一害	0534	有錢佬話事	0568
加鹽加醋	0517	有乜冬瓜豆腐	0535	有錢就身痕	0569
		有人辭官歸故里，有		有頭毛冇人想生鬎鬁	0570
〔乚起〕		人漏夜趕科場	0536	有頭有面	0571
		有口無心	0537	有頭威冇尾陣	0572
奶媽湊/抱仔	0518	有口難言	0538	有麝自然香	0573
出人頭地	0519	有仇不報非君子	0539	有雞仔唔管管牙	
出手低	0520	有分有寸	0540	「麻」鷹	0574
出手	B082	有分數	0541	有人做咗手腳	B093
出名	0521	有心唔怕遲，十月都		有毛有翼	B094
出息	0522	係拜年時	0542	有行	B095
出車	0523	有心無力	0543	有尾學人跳，冇尾又	
出面	0524	有心裝冇心人	0544	學人跳	B096
出風頭	0525	有皮宜唔使使頸	0545	有排	B097
出氣	0526	有奶便是娘	0546	有幾何呀	B098
出術	0527	有自唔在，攞苦嚟辛	0547	有聲氣	B099
出符弗〈法〉	0528	有名無實	0548	有蹺蹊	B100
出處不如聚處	0529	有屁就放	0549	西南二伯父	0575
出頭	0530	有咗	0550	死人尋舊路	0576
出貓	0531	有兩下散手	0551	死人燈籠	0577
出醜	0532	有事鍾無艷，無事夏		死口咬實	0578
出鷯哥	0533	迎春	0552	死心不息	0579
出色	B084	有其父必有其子	0553	死心塌地	0580
出身	B085	有招架之功，無還手		死牛一便頸	0581
出便	B086	之力	0554	死死地氣	0582
出門	B087	有咁啱得咁蹺	0555	死有餘辜	0583
出馬	B088	有風駛盡𠲿	0556	死估估	0584
出嚟搵食	B089	有眼不識泰山	0557	死性不改	0585
出嚟撈	B090	有眼無珠	0558	死咗條心	0586

死唔眼閉	0587	至到……	B102	竹織鴨	0650
死冤	0588	至話	B103	各自爲政	0651
死蛇爛蟮	0589	至無	B104	各花落各眼	0652
死慳死抵	0590	在意	B092	各適其適	0653
死雞撐飯蓋	0591			年三十晚謝竈	0637
死纏爛打	0592	〔丿起〕		年少老成	0638
耳邊風	0593			年晚煎堆	0639
百足咁多爪	0594	丟生晒	0622		
百忍成金	0595	丟架	0623	〔丶起〕	
托大腳	0596	丟疏咗	0624		
托水龍	0597	行行企企	0625	江山易改品性難移	0654
托手踭	0598	行行出狀元	0626	江西佬舞死/打死馬	
托塔都應承	0599	行船好過灣	0627	騮	0655
朽棒	0600	行船爭解纜	0628	忙狼	0656
地膽	0601	行得正，企得正	0629	守得雲開見月明	0657
而依哦哦	0602	行運一條龍，失運一		羊毛出在羊身上	0658
老積	B106	條蟲	B107	羊牯	0659
老行	0603	行路打倒退	B108	充大頭鬼	0660
老人成嫩仔	0604	伊撚七	0630	交帶	0661
老人院都唔收	B015	先入爲主	0631	安份	0662
老人精	0605	先小人後君子	0632	安份守己	0663
老友記	0606	先下手爲強	0633	米已成炊	0664
老行尊	0607	先使未來錢	0634		
老定	0608	先敬羅衣後敬人	0635	〔丨起〕	
老虎唔發威當病貓	0609	先禮後兵	0636		
老虎頭上釘虱〈蝨〉		先排	B109	同人唔同命，同遮唔	
乸	0610	先斬後奏	B110	同柄	0665
老虎乸	0611	企喺城樓睇馬打	B111	同一個鼻哥窿出氣	B113
老契	0612	朱義盛	0640	同……有路	B114
老番睇榜	0613	多個香爐多隻鬼	0641	同……行得好埋	B115
老鼠拉龜	0614	合晒心水	0642	同……行埋咗	B116
老鼠跌落天平	0615	合晒合尺	0643	同行如敵國	0666
老鼠貨	0616	自梳	B112	同撈同煲	0667
老貓燒鬚	0617	自己工	0644	同檯食飯，各自修行	0668
老奸巨猾	0618	自己身有屎	0645	吊吊扚	0669
老糠搾出油	0619	自打嘴巴	0646	吊砂煲	0670
老實/豆都要多	0620	自投羅網	0647	吊起嚟賣	0671
老襯	0621	自斟自酌	0648	吊靴鬼	0672
至多唔係……	B101	竹紗	0649	吊癮	0673

早知今日，何必當初	0674	好戲在後頭	0705	扯皮條	0733
早知今日，悔不當初	0675	好聲好氣	0706	扯風波	0734
早知燈係火，唔使黑摸摸	0676	收山	B117	扯貓尾	0735
光棍佬教仔	0677	收手	0707	扯頭纜	B129
光棍遇着冇皮柴	0678	收檔	0708	扯線	B130
因小失大	0679	收科	0709	扯線公仔	B131
肉刺	0680			拋生藕	0736
肉酸	0681	七　畫		拋浪頭	0737
肉隨砧板上	0682			拋頭露面	0738
肉緊	0683	〔一起〕		扭六壬	0739
				扭屎窟花	0740
〔乚起〕				扭計	0741
		走趯	B121	扭紋柴	0742
奸賴	0684	走馬看花	0711	扭擰	0743
好人事	0685	走唔過……嘅手指罅	0712	扰心口	0744
好人難做	0686	走眼	0713	折墮	0745
好女兩頭瞞	0687	走路	0714	杉木靈牌	0746
好天揾埋落雨米	0688	走雞	0715	杌失	0747
好心地	B118	走歸吒	0716	均真	0748
好心唔怕做	0689	走寶	0717	批中	B132
好心唔得好報	0690	豆腐刀	0718	扽氣	0728
好心着雷殛	0691	車天車地	0719	扽蝦籠	0729
好水冇幾多朝	0692	求人不如求己	0720	抚心抚肺	B127
好市	0693	求求其其	0721	找晦氣	B122
好見飯	B119	求先	B128		
好話唔好聽	B120	夾手夾脚	B123	〔丿起〕	
好事不出門壞事傳千里	0694	夾計	B124	含冤莫白	0749
好物沉歸底	0695	夾份	0722	含血噴人	0750
好馬不食回頭草	0696	弄巧反拙	0723	秀才遇着兵	0751
好佬怕爛佬	0697	弄假成真	0724	秀才遇老虎	0752
好眉好貌生沙蝨	0698	奀嫋鬼命	0725	秀才手巾	0753
好喎偈	0699	把屁	0726	佛口蛇心	B139
好喎橋	0700	把鬼	0727	佛都有火	0754
好食懶飛	0701	把火	B125	低頭切肉，把眼看人	0755
好唱口	0702	把幾火	B126	低庄/莊	0756
好腳頭	0703	扮豬食老虎	0730	低低地躝鋪	0757
好漢不吃眼前虧	0704	扮嘢	0731	低聲下氣	0758
		扮傻	0732	作嘔	0759

作怪	0760	坐定粒六	0789				
作狀	0761	坐穩釣魚船	0790	〔丨起〕			
作賤自己	0762	坐食山崩	0791				
作死	0763	成日	B137	忍唔住	0816		
作威作福	0764	成數	B138	忍無可忍	0817		
作賊心虛	0765	私己	B140				
佔上風	0766			## 八　畫			
佔皮宜	0767	〔、起〕					
告枕頭狀	B133			〔一起〕			
你有半斤，我有八兩	0768	沙哩弄銃	0792				
你有張良計，我有過牆梯	0769	沙沙滾	0793	亞斗官	0818		
		沙煲刁眼角	0794	亞昆洗鑊	0819		
你有乾坤，我有日月	0770	沙煲兄弟	0795	亞茂整餅	0820		
你/佢有寶呀	B134	沙塵	0796	亞單睇榜	0821		
你/佢真開胃	B135	沙灣燈籠	0797	亞超着褲	0822		
你/佢想點就點	B136	沐恩弟子	0798	亞崩叫狗	0823		
你唔嫌我籮疏，我唔嫌你米碎	0771	諗鬼食豆腐	0799	亞崩養狗	0824		
		冷手執個熱煎堆	0800	亞崩劏羊	0825		
你做初一，我做十五	0772	初哥	0801	亞駝〈馱〉行路	0826		
		初歸心抱（新婦）落地孩兒	0802	亞駝〈馱〉賣蝦米	0827		
你敬我一尺，我敬你一丈	0773			亞蘭嫁亞瑞	0828		
		〔丨起〕		亞蘭賣豬	B149		
你嗰槓嘢我都有得出賣	0774			亞聾送殯	0829		
		快刀斬亂麻	0710	亞聾燒炮	0830		
你走你嘅陽關路，我過我嘅獨木橋	0775	見人講人話，見鬼講鬼話	0803	亞保亞勝	B150		
		見山就拜	0804	直腸直肚	0831		
吞吞吐吐	0776	見地不平擔鋼鏟	0805	直程	0832		
吞口水養命	0777	見步行步	0806	直頭	0833		
谷住度氣	0778	見屎窟郁唔見米白	0807	兩公婆扒艇	0834		
谷起泡腮/顋	0779	見高就拜，見低就踩	0808	兩公婆見鬼	0835		
利口便辭	0780	見過鬼就怕黑	0809	兩個和尚擔水食，三個和尚冇水食	0836		
利口唔利腹	0781	步步為營	0810				
兵來將擋，水來土掩	0782	吟詩都吟唔甩	0811	兩睇	0837		
身在福中不知福	0783	吼	0812	兩頭唔到岸	0838		
身當命抵	0784	吼斗	0813	兩頭唔受中間受	0839		
我都冇你咁好氣	0785	別緻	0814	兩頭蛇	B145		
肚皮打鼓	0786	吹鬚轆眼	0815	兩騎牛	0840		
肚裏蟲	0787	足水	B141	來者不善，善者不來	0841		
坐一望二	0788						

來說是非者便是是非		抵死	0876	爭住……	B162
人	0842	抵到爛	0877	爭住先	B163
到家	0843	抵得諗	0878	和尚食狗肉	B159
到埗	B151	抵賴	0879	和味	0900
到處楊梅一樣花	0844	拖泥帶水	0880	和諧	0901
到喉唔到肺	0845	扴/砍頭埋牆	0881	使銅銀夾大聲	0902
青磚沙梨	0846	拘執	0882	使頸	0903
青頭仔	0847	拐帶	0883	刮龍	0904
事頭	B143	抬棺材甩褲	0884	物以罕爲貴	0905
事頭婆	B144	扚手瓜	0885	物以類聚	0906
事不關己，己不勞心	0850	扚頸	0886	物輕情義重	0907
事在人爲	0851	枉作小人	0887	物離鄉貴，人離鄉賤	0908
事後孔明	0852	枕住	B152	知人口面不知心	0909
拍心口	0853	枕長	B153	知子莫若父	0910
拍成佢	0854	林沈	B154	知己知彼	0911
拍烏蠅	0855	長腳蟶	B146	知其一不知其二	0912
拍硬檔	0856	長痛不如短痛	0955	知無不言，言無不盡	0913
拍膊頭	0857	奉旨「子」成婚	B147	知情識趣	0914
拍薑咁拍	0858	東莞佬賣蓆	B148	肥缺	0915
拍檔	0859	東家唔打打西家	0849	肥肥白白	0916
拆穿西洋鏡	0860	幸災樂禍	0848	返去舊時嗰度	0917
拃亂戈柄	0861			近山不可燒枉柴，近	
抷頭	B142	〔丿起〕		河不可洗枉水	0918
拚死無大害	0862			近水樓臺先得月	0919
拚啤	0863	制唔過	B157	近住城隍廟求炷好香	0920
拚爛	0864	制得過	0888	近官得力	0921
抽水	0865	狗上瓦桁	0889	近廚得食	0922
抽佣	0866	狗咬呂洞賓	0890	金盆洗手	0923
抽後腳	0867	狗咬狗骨	0891	金睛火眼	0924
抽秤/挭	0868	狗眼看人低	0892	命根	0925
抽絲剝繭	0869	受人二分四	0893	的起心肝	0926
招搖過市	0870	受人錢財，替人消災	0894	依挮/依依挮挮	0927
招搖撞騙	0871	受硬唔受軟	0895	依時依候	B158
拉人裙冚自己腳	0872	受軟唔受硬	0896		
拉牛上樹	0873	受落	0897	〔丶起〕	
拉柴	0874	受唔住	0898		
拉埋天窗	0875	受氣	0899	波羅雞	0928
拉埋……落水	B155	爭	B160	盲公布袋	0929
拉頭纜	B156	爭交	B161		

盲佬貼符	0930	花心蘿蔔	0962	耐唔中	0985
盲拳打死老師傅	0931	花紅	B169	查家宅	0986
盲眼	0932	花弗〈扶〉	0963	耍太極	0987
盲婆餵奶	0933	花多眼亂	0964	耍花槍	0988
盲摸摸	0934	花言巧語	0965	要風得風，要雨得雨	0989
盲頭烏蠅	0935	花花公子	0966	面左左	0990
放下心頭大石	0936	花花綠綠	0967	面皮厚	0991
放水	B167	花門	0968	面紅	0992
放白鴿	0937	花靚仔	0969	面紅面綠	0993
放屁	0938	呷醋	0970	面懵心精	0994
放虎歸山	0939	叔姪縮室	0971	相見好，同住難	0995
放路溪錢	0940	忠忠直直，終須乞食	0972	相睇	B175
放聲氣	0941	虎父無犬子	0973	柑咁大個鼻	0996
定晒形	0942	虎落平陽被犬欺	0974	挑蟲入屎窟	0997
定過抬油	0943	虎頭蛇尾	0975	指天篤地	0998
夜長夢多	B164			指手劃腳	0999
夜遊神	B165	〔㇇起〕		指住禿奴罵和尚	1000
河水不犯井水	0944			指擬	1001
空口講白話	0945	門當戶對	0976	指冬瓜話葫蘆	B178
空心老倌	0946	陀衰家	0977	捌埋	B173
官仔骨骨	0947	阿茴	B170	捌鼓邊	B174
官字兩個口	0948	屈尾十	B171	契家佬	1002
官官相衛	0949	屈質	0978	契家婆	1003
泥水佬開門口	0950			毒鬥毒	1004
泥菩薩過江	0951	〔㇄起〕		奀尾	1005
沫水舂牆	0952			奀頭佬	1006
油瓶	B166	牀下底破柴	0979	奀頭奀腦	1007
炒冷飯	0953	姐	0980	南嘸佬遇鬼迷	1008
炕沙	B168	姐手姐腳	0981	胡帝胡天/胡天胡帝	B176
		妹仔大過主人婆	0982	胡胡混混	B177
〔丨起〕		姑勿論	B173	甚至無……	B178
易過借火	0954				
明人不做暗事	0956	# 九　畫		〔丿起〕	
明刀明槍	0957			食七咁食	1009
明火打劫	0958	〔一起〕		食人唔䚺骨	1010
明槍易擋，暗箭難防	0959			食少啖多覺瞓	1011
花天酒地	0960	耐不耐	0983	食生菜咁食	1012
花心	0961	耐中	0984	食西北風	1013

食夾棍	1014	缸瓦船打老虎	1046	客家佔地主	1071
食死貓	1015	急時抱佛腳	1047	客氣	1072
食咗人隻車	1016	急驚風遇着慢郎中	1048	施恩莫望報	1073
食咗人隻豬	B182	皇天不負有/苦心人	1049	前人種果後人收	1074
食咗火藥	1017	皇帝唔急太監急	1050	前世唔修	1075
食柱米	1018	皇帝女	B188	前世撈亂骨頭	1076
食拖鞋飯	1019	拜神唔見雞	1051	前言不對後語	B192
食屎食着豆	1020	俗骨	1052	前嗰排	B193
食砒霜杜狗	1021	係咁意	1053	洒手擰頭	B189
食得禾米多	1022	係威係勢	1054	派	1077
食得鹹就要抵得渴	B183	香爐墩	B185	派行水/片	1078
食鹽多過食飯行橋多過行路	1023	信邪	B186	穿煲/穿崩	B195
		重係……	B187	穿櫃桶底	B196
食塞米	1024			計正	B197
食過夜粥	1025	〔丶起〕			
食過翻尋味	1026			〔丨起〕	
食碗面,反碗底	1027				
食葱送飯	1028	神主牌都會郁	B234	眈天望地	1079
食飽無憂米	1029	神主牌都會擰轉面	B235	是必要	B199
食飽飯等屎疴	1030	神前桔	B236	是非只爲多問口	1080
食豬血疴黑屎	1031	神不知鬼不覺	1055	是非皆因强出頭	1081
食穀種	1032	神推鬼擁	1056	是非鬼/啄	1082
食軟飯	1033	神臺貓屎	1057	是是但但	1083
食貓麵	1034	神魂顛倒	1058	苦口婆心	1084
食君之祿擔君之憂	B181	神憎鬼厭	1059	苦瓜乾噉嘅面口	B198
食齋不如講正話	B184	神神化化	1060	苦過弟弟	1085
風水佬呃你十年八年,唔呃得一世	1035	神神地	1061	若要人不知除非己莫爲	1086
		恃老賣老	1062		
風水輪流轉	1036	恃熟賣熟	B194	思思縮縮	B200
風生水起	B180	洗碗有相砍	1063	英雄重英雄	1087
風吹芫荽	1037	洗腳唔抹腳	1064	英雄莫問出處	1088
風吹雞蛋殼	1038	洗濕個頭	1065	咬耳仔	1089
風流	1039	恨死隔籬	1066	咬實牙齦	1090
風頭火勢	1040	姜太公釣魚	1067	唓唓西西	1091
風頭躉	1041	姜太公封神	B191	唓契爺咁唓	1092
風擺柳	1042	度住屎窟裁褲	1068	咧啡	1093
看牛不及打馬草	1043	度水	B190	咪拘	1094
看風駛𠪨	1044	扁鼻佬戴眼鏡	1069	柴哇哇	1095
怨命	1045	炮仗頸	1070	柴臺	1096

條目筆畫索引 329

省鏡	1097	桐油埕	1114	借咗聾陳隻耳	1142
		桃榔樹	1115	借花敬佛	1143
〔冂起〕		核突	1116	借艇割禾	1144
		捉用神	1117	借題發揮	1145
屎氹關刀	1098	捉字虱/蝨	1118	倒吊冇滴墨水	1146
屎急開坑	1099	捉到鹿都唔會脱角	1119	倒吊荷包	1147
屎橋	1100	捉豬問地腳	1120	倒米	1148
屎窟生瘡	1101	捉黃腳雞	1121	倒米壽星	1149
屋漏更兼逢夜雨	1102	捉蟲入屎窟	B208	倒掛臘鴨	1150
眉頭一皺，計上心來	1103	捉錯用神	B209	倒瀉籮蟹	1151
眉精眼企	1104	挹坭	1122	倒瓤冬瓜	1152
飛擒大咬	1105	埋牙	1123	個蜆個肉	1153
飛	B201	埋堆	1124	俾人揸住痛腳	1154
門後門	B202	埋櫃	B210	俾心機	1155
架步	B203	班馬	B211	俾個心你食當狗肺	1156
架勢	B204	索油	1125	俾個頭你	1157
架樑	B205	真金不怕洪爐火，石獅不怕雨滂沱	1126	俾人賣豬仔	1323
				俾蕉皮/西瓜皮人踩	B216
〔乚起〕				偏情	B215
		〔丿起〕		修游	1158
姣屍扽篤	1106			修游淡定	1159
姣婆遇着脂粉客	1107	胭脂馬	1127	氣羅氣喘	1160
紅光滿面	B206	特登	1128	笑到肚刺	1161
紅鬚軍師	B207	鬼五馬六	1129	笋嘢	1162
		鬼打鬼	1130	狠過華秀隻狗	1163
十　畫		鬼打都冇咁醒	1131	狠	B223
		鬼拍後尾枕	1132	狠忙	B224
〔一起〕		鬼馬	1133	狠胎	B225
		鬼鬼鼠鼠〈祟祟〉	1134	拿手好戲	1164
原封不動	1108	鬼㨴/揞眼	1135	拿拿聲	B221
起尾注	1109	鬼畫符	1136	針冇兩頭利	1165
起眼	1110	鬼聲鬼氣	1137	針唔拮到肉唔知痛	1166
起痰	1111	鬼食泥噉聲	B218	針鼻削鐵	1167
起快（起筷）	B213	鬼打你	B219	師姑	1168
起飛腳	B214	鬼㨆	B220	留得青山在，哪怕冇柴燒	1169
馬仔	B212	隻[眼]開，隻[眼]閉	1138		
馬死落地行	1112	倀/撐雞	1139	留番唥氣暖吓肚	1170
馬屎憑官勢	1113	倀/撐雞妹	1140	留番嚟攝灶罅	1171
		借刀殺人	1141	幫理不幫親	1172

烏卒卒	1173	差遲	B233	唔忿氣	1231
烏狗得食，白狗當災	1174	疴屎遞草紙	1205	唔使問亞貴	1232
烏哩馬扠	1175	疴屎唔出賴地硬，疴		唔使指擬	1233
烏哩單刀	1176	屎唔出賴風猛	1206	唔使畫公仔畫出腸	1234
烏啄啄	1177	海上無魚蝦自大	1207	唔使擒擒青	1235
烏蛇蛇	1178	海水冲倒龍王廟	B226	唔使慌	B245
烏煙瘴氣	1179	烟〈薦〉韌	1208	唔使恨	B246
烏龍	1180	淨係	B228	唔敢當	1236
烏蠅摟馬尾	1181	流口水	1209	唔信命都信吓塊鏡	1237
臭檔	B217	流馬尿	1210	唔係路	1238
冗神惡煞	B222	流嘢	B229	唔係猛龍唔過江，唔	
		粉板/牌字	B230	係毒蛇唔打霧	1239
〔丶起〕		逆次次	B231	唔係是必要	B256
				唔係講玩	B257
迷頭迷腦	1182	〔丨起〕		唔咬絃	1240
送羊入虎口	1183			唔要斧頭唔得柄甩	1241
送佛送到西	1184	戥起牀板	B262	唔食羊肉一身臊	1242
害人終害己	1185	戥起幡竿有鬼到	1211	唔埋得個鼻	1243
害死亞堅	1186	財不可露眼	1212	唔理三七二十一	1244
家有一老如有一寶	B227	財可通神	1213	唔理得咁多	1245
家和萬事興	1187	財到光棍手	1214	唔做中，唔做保，唔	
家家有本難唸的經	1188	唔……罷就	B237	做媒人三代好	1246
家醜不可外傳	1189	唔一定	B238	唔湯唔水	1247
酒後吐真言	1190	唔三唔四	1215	唔睇白鴿，都睇吓堆	
酒醉三分醒	1191	唔化	1216	屎	1248
冤有頭，債有主	1192	唔在行	1217	唔睇僧面，都睇吓佛	
冤屈	1193	唔打唔相識	1218	面	1249
冤柱嚟，瘟疫去	1194	唔同床唔知被爛	1219	唔喀耕	1250
冤家	1195	唔自在	1220	唔經大腦	1251
冤家宜解不宜結	1196	唔自量	1221	唔該借一借	1252
冤家路窄	1197	唔見得光	1222	唔該借歪啲	1253
冤豬頭都有盟鼻菩薩	1198	唔見棺材唔流眼淚	1223	唔嗅米氣	1254
冤孽	1199	唔見過鬼都唔怕黑	1224	唔算數	1255
剃眼眉	1200	唔志在	1225	唔認賬/數	1256
高不成，低不就	1201	唔知個"醜"字點寫	1226	唔嗲唔吊	1257
高寶	1202	唔怕官，至怕管	1227	唔黐家	1258
消/宵夜	1203	唔怪之得/唔怪得之	1228	唔覺眼	1259
差一皮	B232	唔抵得瘵	1229	唔覺意	1260
差唔多	1204	唔抵得頸	1230	唔止……重兼……	B239

唔中用	B240	啟油撈飯	1270	捩橫折曲	1298
唔爭在……	B241	現眼報	1271	掛羊頭賣狗肉	1299
唔爭氣	B242	帶花	1272	掛臘鴨	B280
唔好手腳	B243	帶挈	1273	推三推四	1301
唔淨只	B244	曹操都有知心友，關		推莊	1302
唔似樣	B247	公亦有對頭人	1274	推心置腹	B278
唔食得豬	B248	爽手	1275	推波助瀾	B279
唔通……	B249	專登	1276	掟煲	1303
唔通氣	B250	執人口水溦	1277	捱世界	1304
唔計帶	B251	執二攤	1278	捱更抵夜	1305
唔話得	B252	執手尾	1279	捱夜	1306
唔制得過	B253	執死雞	1280	捱騾仔	1307
唔恨	B254	執到襪帶累身家	1281	掉忘	1300
唔啱蕎	B255	執番條命	B277	梗板	1308
剒	B258	執笠	1282	乾手淨腳	1309
剒住度氣	B259	執輸	1283	乾時繁月	B275
跂路	B260	執輸行頭慘過敗家	1284	乾塘	B276
骨子	1265	執頭執尾	1285	匿埋	B264
骨痹	B261	頂尖	1286	梳起	B265
蚊髀同牛髀	1261	頂包	1287	牽腸掛肚	B266
蚊都瞓	1262	頂頭上司	1288		
恩將仇報	1263	頂檔	1289	〔丿起〕	
茶瓜送飯	1264	頂肚	B267		
		頂唔住	B268	偏心	B282
〔門起〕		頂唔順	B269	偷偷摸摸	1310
		頂硬上	B270	偷龍轉鳳	1311
除笨有精	1266	頂頭陣	B271	偷雞	1312
除褲疴屁	1267	頂頸	B272	偷雞唔到蝕揸米	1313
		頂撞	B273	做日和尚唸日經	1314
〔乚起〕		頂籠	B274	做世界	1315
		勒時間	1290	做好做醜	1316
紙紮下扒	1269	勒實褲頭帶	1291	做咗鬼會迷人	1317
紗紙	B263	斬腳趾避沙蟲	1292	做鬼都唔靈	1318
		斬纜	B281	做磨心	1319
十一畫		紮炮	1293	做慣乞兒懶做官	1320
		紮紮跳	1294	做薑唔辣，做醋唔酸	1321
〔一起〕		掘尾龍	1295	做醜人	1322
		控拃	1296	做咗人豬仔/俾人賣	
		捩咁嚟	1297	豬仔	1323

得上床掀被冚	1324	混水摸魚	1355	眼掘掘	1387
得寸進尺	1325	混吉	1356	眼矋矋	1388
得米	1326	混混/渾渾噩噩	1357	眼濕濕	1389
得把聲	1327	添食	B288	㗳	1390
得些好意須回手	1328	清官難審家庭事	B289	啞仔食雲吞	1391
得咗	1329	淘古井	1358	啞仔食黃連	1392
得敕/戚	1330	粗人	1359	啪咁多	B291
得啖笑	1331	粗口爛舌	1360	唱心水[緒]	1393
得棚牙	1332	粗心大意	1361	唱唱	B292
得個吉	B283	粗手粗腳	1362	唱唱好	1394
得過且過	1333	粗枝大葉	1363	唱衰人	1395
剝光豬	1334	粗重工夫	1364	荳丁	B293
剝花生	1335	粗茶淡飯	1365	崩口人忌崩口碗	1396
笨手笨腳	1336	粗製濫造	1366	患得患失	1397
笨頭笨腦	1337	粗魯	1367	患難見真情	1398
船到江心補漏遲	1338	羞家	B287	蛇有蛇路，鼠有鼠路	1399
船到橋頭自然直	1339	情人眼裏出西施	1368	蛇見硫磺	1400
船頭慌鬼，船尾慌賊	1340	惦過碌蔗	1369	蛇無頭不行	1401
"貪"字變個"貧"	1341	麻麻地	1370	蛇鼠一窩	1402
貪得無厭	1342	麻雀雖小，五臟俱全	1371	蛇頭鼠眼	1403
貧不與富敵，富不與官爭	1343				
移礵就船	1344	〔丨起〕		〔冂起〕	
兜住	B284	晦氣	B290	陪太子讀書	1404
兜踎	1345	眼大睇過籠/界	1372	陰濕	1405
兜篤將軍	1346	眼火爆	1373	陳皮	1406
夠皮	B285	眼中釘	1374	陳村種	1407
逢場作興	B286	眼坦坦	1375	陸雲庭睇相	1408
		眼金金	1376	通天	B294
〔丶起〕		眼紅	1377	通水	1409
		眼眉毛長過辮	1378	通氣	1410
湊啱	1347	眼眉毛雕通瓏	1379	蛋家婆打仔	1411
寅食卯糧	1348	眼唔見爲伶俐	1380	蛋家婆打醮	1412
密底算盤	1349	眼斬斬	1381	蛋家婆摸蜆	1413
密斟	1350	眼淺	1382	蛋家雞	1414
密實姑娘假正經	1351	眼冤	1383	問師姑攞梳	1415
密鑼緊鼓	1352	眼瞓瞓	1384		
望天打卦	1353	眼闊肚窄	1385	〔乚起〕	
望長條頸	1354	眼噬噬	1386		

終須有日龍穿鳳	1416	散水	B305	腌尖	1478
細心	1417	散更鑼	1446	腌悶	1479
細水長流	1418	散檔	1447	腌尖腥悶	1480
細時偷雞，大時偷牛	1419	搵……（人）過橋	1452	無孔不入	1481
細佬哥剃頭	1420	搵老襯	1453	無功不受祿	1482
將……一軍	1421	搵丁	1454	無名小卒	1483
將/攞……教飛	1422	搵笨	1455	無私顯見私	1484
將心比己	1423	搵得嚟，使得去	1456	無官一身輕	1485
將佢拳頭抌佢嘴	1424	揦手唔成勢	1457	無事不登三寶殿	1486
將計就計	1425	揦西	1458	無事生非	1487
將就	1426	揦起塊面	1459	無事忙	1488
將錯將錯	1427	揦屎上身	1460	無事獻慇勤，非奸即盜	1489
		揦高肚皮	1461	無風三尺浪	1490
十二畫		揦㾗	1462	無風不起浪	1491
		揭盅	1463	無情白事	1492
〔一起〕		提心吊膽	1464	無聊賴	1493
		揞/撐住良心	1465	無債一身輕	1494
惡人自有惡人磨	1428	揞/撐住嘴嚟笑	1466	無嘩嘩	1495
惡人先告狀	1429	揸大葵扇	1467	無端白事	1496
惡有惡報	1430	揸住雞毛當令箭	1468	無端端	1497
惡到凸堆	1431	揸頸就命	1469	無端端發達	1498
惡恐人知，便是大惡	1432	揸鐵筆	B300	無聲狗咬死人	1499
惡死能登	B296	揸鑊鏟	B301	無氈無扇，神仙難變	1500
惡搢搢	B297	揞	B298	週身刀	1501
朝上有人好做官	1433	揞牛黃	1470	週身唔聚財	1502
朝種樹，晚剒板	1434	揞到……鑞鑞脧	B299	爲口奔馳	1503
替死鬼	1435	揞金龜	1471	爲食鬼	1504
黃皮樹鷯哥	1436	揼堆	1472	爲食貓	B306
黃泡髧熟	1437	揼爛塊面	1473	爲意	B307
黃馬褂	1438	棚尾拉箱	1474	傍友	B308
黃綠醫生	1439	棋差一着	1475	衆事莫理，衆定莫企	1505
黃腫腳	1440	棋高一着	1476	猴急	1506
黃面婆	B304	棋逢敵手	1477	猴擒	1507
趁手	1445	掉忌	1300	順口	1508
報效	1442	韌皮	B295	順水人情	1509
越搷越出屎	1443	硬晒舦	1441	順水推舟	1510
越窮越見鬼，肚餓打瀉米	1444	喪家狗	B302	順手	1511
		〔／起〕		順手牽羊	1512

順風駛𢃇	1513	喉門角落頭燒炮仗	1541	發市	1568
順得哥情失嫂意	1514	睇人口面	1542	發吽哣	1569
順得「德」人	1515	睇小	B314	發啷厲	1570
順眼	1516	睇化	1543	發盟憎	1571
順喉	1517	睇水	1544	發噏風	1572
順攤	1518	睇白……/睇死……	1545	發窮惡	1573
		睇穿	1546	發錢寒	1574
〔丶起〕		睇唔過眼	1547	發爛渣	1575
		睇差一皮	1548	發吟發話	B321
着起龍袍唔似太子	1519	睇開啲嘑	1549	發夢冇咁早	B322
着數	1520	睇起	1550	開刀	B323
着緊	1521	睇嚟湊	1551	開口埋口都話……	B324
詐型	1522	睇衰	B315	開古	B325
詐假意	1523	睇餸食飯睇蜀南嚤		開埋井俾人食水	B326
詐[詐]諦[諦]	1524	〈謨〉	1552	開夜車	B327
詐嬌	1525	買水咁嘅頭	1553	開通	B328
勞氣	1526	買生不如買熟	B318	開荒牛	B329
勞嘈	1527	跌咗個橙，執番個桔	1554	開齋	B330
瓷器棺材	1528	跌倒捵番揸沙	1555	開大價	1576
補鑊唔見枳	1529	跌眼鏡	1556	開口及着脷	1577
善財難捨，冤枉甘心	1530	跛腳鷯哥自有飛來蜢	1557	開心見誠	1578
善靜	B310	量地官	1558	開天索價，落地還錢	1579
舂瘟雞	1531	單刀直入	1559	開門見山	1580
惗善	B309	單手獨拳	1560	開明車馬	1581
渣嘢	B311	單身寡仔	1561	開嗙……嗰槓	1582
就嚟	B312	單料銅煲	1562	開籠雀	1583
就嚟……	B313	單單打打	1563	間間地	B331
		單筷箸批豆腐	1564	強中自有強中手	1584
〔丨起〕		單丁	1565		
		單係	B319	〔乚起〕	
唪沉	1532	單眼仔睇榜	B320		
喝咗	1533	異相	B316	幾乎	B332
喱啦	1534	黑口黑面	B317	幾係幾係，五郎救弟	B333
貼錯門神	1535			幾係㗎	B334
貼錢買難受	1536	〔丿起〕		幾難先至……	B335
虛浮	1537			幾難至得……	B336
喺口唇邊	1538	發木獨	1566	幾大就幾大	1585
喺乞兒兜捵飯食	1539	發蟲	1567	媽媽聲	1586
喺孔夫子面前賣文章	1540				

條目筆畫索引　335

十三畫

〔一起〕

斟盤	1587
電燈膽	1588
塘水滾塘魚	B337
塘底特	B338
塘邊鶴	1589
鼓氣袋	1590
煮到嚟就食	1591
煮鬼	1592
煮重米	1593
搗亂	1594
搶手	1595
搶眼	1596
搬弄是非	1597
損手爛腳	1598
搽／揿地游水	1599
搽／揿鷓鴣	1600
搭沉船	1601
搭單	1602
搭錯賊船	1603
搭錯綫	1604
搓得圓，搣得扁	1605
搏一搏	1448
搏命	1449
搏亂	1450
搏懵	1451
搏唔過	B303
碰啱	1606
靳度	1607
想話……	B339
零舍……	B340
勢利	B341
遊車河	B342

〔／起〕

鼠入嚟	1608
鼠嘢	1609
傾唔埋	1610
傾唔埋欄	1611
僅僅夠（一）	1612
僅僅夠……（二）	1613
煲冇米粥	1614
煲老藕	B343
飲咗門官茶	1616
飲頭啖湯	1617
鈴鈴鎈鎈都丟埋	1618
筲箕打水	1619
筲箕冚鬼一窩神	1620
亂晒坑	1621
亂籠	1622
腦囟／顖未生埋	1623
會錯意	1615

〔、起〕

滑頭	B346
滾水淥腳	1624
滾水淥豬腸	1625
滾友	B344
滾紅滾綠	B345
話唔埋	1626
話晒事	1627
話名係……	B348
話唔定……	B349
話落	B350
……（某人）話事偈	B351
話極都係	B352
話實	B353
……（某人）話齋	B354
該死	B347
該釘就釘該鐵就鐵	1628
該煨咯	1629
滋油	1630
滋油淡定	1631

滋陰	1632
煱起／着個火頭	1633
新屎坑三日香	1634
辣撻人有辣撻福	1635
道高一尺，魔高一丈	1636
禀神都冇句真	1637
慌失失	1638
塞古盟憎	1639
塞竇窿	1640

〔｜起〕

過口癮	1641
過水濕腳	1642
過夾吊頸	1643
過咗海就神仙	1644
過骨	1645
過氣老倌	1646
過得去	1647
過橋抽板	1648
過水	B355
過火	B356
過分	B357
過身	B358
蒸生瓜	1268
落……棚牙	1649
落力	1650
落手打三更	1651
落住屎窟吊頸	1652
落……（某人）嘅面	B364
落手	B365
落手落腳	B366
落形	B367
落井下石	B368
落面	B369
落嘴頭	B370
落定	1653
落雨賣風爐	1654
落雨擔遮	1655

落狗屎	1656	隔牆有耳	1684	〔丿起〕	
落膈	1657	叠埋心水/緒	1685		
萬事俱備，只欠東風	1658			鳳凰無寶不落	1708
萬事起頭難	1659	〔乚起〕		算死草	1709
萬無一失	1660			領嘢	1710
萬變不離宗	1661	裝假狗	1686	銅銀買病豬	1711
賊公計，狀元才	1662	裝彈弓	1687	飽死	1712
賊亞爸	1663	嫌棄	1688	飽唔死餓唔親	B380
賊佬試沙煲	1664	嫁雞隨雞，嫁狗隨狗	B374	飽死荷蘭豆	B381
賊眉賊眼	1665			鼻屎好食鼻囊挖穿	B379
賊過興兵	1666				
照單執藥	1667	十四畫		〔丶起〕	
照板煮碗	1668				
督背脊	1669	〔一起〕		認低威	1713
督眼督鼻	1670			認數	B382
暈得一陣	1671			認賬	B383
暗啞抵	1672	壽仔	1689	滿肚密圈	1714
盟塞	1673	壽星公吊頸	1690	漏氣	1715
嗰頭近	1674	壽頭	1691	漏睜	1716
嗰單嘢	1675	壽頭壽腦	1692	漏口風	B384
嗌通街	1676	趕到……絕	1693	滲氣	1717
嗲吊	B359	趕狗入窮巷	B375	敲鼓邊	B385
嘥氣	B360	趕工	B376	煽風點火	B386
跣人	B361	趕唔切	1377	寡母婆死仔	1718
路數	B362	趕住投胎	B378	寡母婆咁多心	1719
跳皮（調皮）	B363	魂不守舍	1694	寧犯天條，莫犯眾憎	1720
跪地餼/餵豬乸	1678	魂不附體	1695	寧食開眉粥，莫食愁眉飯	1721
當時得令	1677	誓神劈願	1696		
當堂	B371	誓願當食生菜	1697	寧欺白鬚公，莫欺鼻涕蟲	1722
當黑	B372	駁嘴	1698	實牙實齒	1723
		輕枷重罪	1699	實食冇黐牙	1724
〔冂起〕		輕佻	1700	實鼓實鑿	1725
		輕浮	1701	瘟瘟沌沌	1726
隔籬飯香	B373	摸門釘	1702	對牛彈琴	1727
隔山買牛	1679	摟蓆	1703	端端度度	1728
隔夜油炸鬼	1680	摟錯人皮	1704	精人出口，笨人出手	1729
隔夜素馨釐戥秤	1681	監人食死貓	1705	精打細算	1730
隔岸觀火	1682	監人賴厚	1706	精到出骨	1731
隔靴捎痕/癢	1683	疑心生暗鬼	1707		

精埋一邊	1732	撞手神	1757	〔、起〕			
精歸左	1733	撞死馬	1758				
塵埃落定	1734	撞[到]正	1759	潤	B402		
塵氣	B387	撞彩	1760	潮州音樂	1781		
慢工出細貨	1735	撞啱	1761	潑冷水	1782		
肇慶荷包	1736	撞鬼	1762	潑辣	1783		
		撚化	1763	論盡	1784		
〔丨起〕		撩是鬥非	1764	謚縮數	1785		
		撒脫/撒撒脫脫	1765	謚爛心肝	1786		
嘥	1737	撐/蹭枱腳	1766	誰不知	B403		
嘥心機	1738	撈臍水	1767	窮到燶	1787		
嘥鬼氣罅	1739	撈過界	1768	窮寇莫追	1788		
嘥燈賣油	1740	撈	B391	熠熟狗頭	1789		
嘥聲壞氣	1741	撈女	B392	熟人買破鑊	1790		
嘥攞	1742	撈家	B393	熟能生巧	B404		
踏墩	1743	撈家仔	B394	熟讀唐詩三百首,唔			
踉踉腳	B388	撈家婆	B395	會吟詩也會偷	B405		
		撈起	B396	熟客仔	B406		
〔冂起〕		撲水	B397	熟檔	B407		
		撒賴	B398	熟行	B408		
聞見棺材香	1744	撒/殺手鐧	B399	熟性	B409		
		擒青/擒擒青	1769	熟落	B410		
十五畫		撬牆腳	1770	摩囉差拜神	1791		
		標青	1771	瘦田冇人耕,耕親有			
〔一起〕		標參	1772	人爭	1792		
		標松柴	1773				
賣大包	1745	磅水	B400	〔丨起〕			
賣口乖	1746						
賣仔莫摸頭	1747	〔丿起〕		數還數,路還路	1793		
賣花姑娘插竹葉	1748			踩着/倒芊荄都當蛇	1794		
賣花讚花香	1749	靠呃	1774	踩親……條尾	1795		
賣面光	1750	靠害	1775	踩死蟻	1796		
賣剩蔗	1751	靠諦	1776	踢竇	B414		
賣鹹酸菜	1752	劉備借荊州	1777	劏死牛	1797		
熱氣飯	1753	㩒嚟都要擔枷	1778	劏光豬	1798		
熱煮不能熱食	1754	蝕底	1779	暴富難睇	1799		
墟冚	1755	膝頭哥揗眼淚	1780	幡竿燈籠	1800		
撞火	1756	嘷礫㬹嘞	B401	踏兩頭船	1801		
				墨七	B411		

弊家伙	B412	擺/搖衫尾	1822	諸事	1849
賤格	B413	擇使	1823	諸事理	1850
嘰嘰咭咭	B390	樹大有枯枝，族大有乞兒	1824	親自出馬	B426
嘩鬼	B389			親力親為	1851
		樹大招風	1825	親身仔不如近身錢	1852
〔丨起〕		樹倒猢猻散	1826	糖黏豆	1853
		樹高千丈，落葉歸根	1827	龍床唔似狗竇	1854
劈炮	1802	橫九惦十	1828	龍游淺水遭蝦戲	1855
劈〈砜〉撚鑿	1803	橫手	1829	褪肽	1856
墮角	B415	橫行霸道	1830	辦蟹	B427
駕步	B416	橫呢	1831		
		橫呢都係一樣	1832	〔丨起〕	
十六畫		橫衝直撞	1833		
		橫蠻無理	1834	撕吓眼	1857
〔一起〕		醒水	1835	踩蹄踩爪	1858
		醒	B417	頻倫	1859
融洽	1804	醒目	B418	頻倫唔得入城	1860
豬頭骨	1805	醒定啲	B419	頻撲	1861
豬欄報數	1806	賴貓	B420	蕩失路	B428
豬籠入水	1807			賭氣	B429
豬朋狗友	B423	〔丿起〕			
豬噱	B424			〔丁起〕	
整古做怪	1808	貓衣/兒毛	1836		
整色整水	1809	貓哭老鼠	1837	險過剃頭	1862
整定	1810	錯有錯着	1838	遲到好過冇到	1863
整蠱	1811	錯蕩	1839	遲嚟先上岸	1864
頭痛醫頭腳痛醫腳	1812	錫住	B425	閻羅王揸攤	1865
頭頭碰着黑	1813	獨家村	1840	閻羅王嫁女	1866
頭髮尾浸浸凉	1814	餓死老婆燻臭屋	1841	隨便	B430
頭先	B421	餓狗搶屎	1842	隨便你/佢	B431
頭路	B422	餓鬼投胎	1843	隨得……	B432
靜靜雞/靜雞雞	1815				
雯眼嬌	1816	〔、起〕		**十七畫**	
雯戀	1817				
輸蝕	1818	燒冷竈	1844	〔凵起〕	
軟皮蛇	1819	燒到……嗰叠	1845		
擔屎都唔偷食	1820	燒枱炮	1846	聰明一世蠢鈍一時	1867
擔戴	1821	燒壞瓦	1847	聲大夾冇準	1868
		燈芯擰成鐵	1848		

聲大夾惡	1869	窿窿罅罅	1894	擺到明	1909
擦鞋	B444			擺烏龍	1910
擦錯鞋	1870	〔丨起〕		擺欵	1911
擤到骨罅都刺埋	1871			櫃桶底穿	B447
擤到樹葉都落埋	1872	臨天光瀨尿	1895	鬆毛鬆翼	B448
擤笨	1873	臨老學吹打	1896		
翳	B434	臨時臨急	B433	〔丿起〕	
戴綠帽	B435	薄皮	B439		
韓信點兵	B436	薄削	B440	雞手鴨腳	1912
		嚟到彈起	1897	雞仔媒人	1913
〔丿起〕		嚟爆爆	1898	雞咁腳	1914
		點算好	1899	雞春咁密都櫼出仔	1915
膽大心細	1874			雞春摸過都輕四両	1916
膽正命平	1875	〔冂起〕		雞疴尿	1917
臊臊都係羊肉爛爛都係絲綢	1876	磡仔拉心肝磡女拉內臟	1900	雞食放光蟲	1918
簕竇	1877	擘網巾	1901	雞啄唔斷	1919
簍休	1878	虿	B441	雞髀打人牙骹軟	1920
				歸根到底	1921
〔丶起〕		〔乚起〕		翻渣茶葉	1922
				翻抄	B449
濕水棉胎	1879	縮沙	1902	翻炒	B450
濕水欖核	1880	縮數	1903	翻閹	B451
濕星	1881	縮骨	B442	獵狗終須山上喪	1923
濕滯	1882	縮頭龜	B443		
濟軍	1883			〔丶起〕	
講心啫	1884				
講多錯多	1885	# 十八畫		雜崩唥	1924
講咗／過就算〔數〕	1886				
講明就陳顯南	1887	〔一起〕		〔丨起〕	
講來／嚟講去都係三幅被	1888	騎牛搵馬	1904	蹟直	1925
講起嚟一匹布咁長	1889	騎硫磺馬	1905	藉／借啲意／藉／借頭藉／借路	1926
講得出就講	1890	轉舦	1906	蟻多摟死象	1927
講開又講	1891	轉膊	1907	舊底	B452
講就易，做就難	1892	轉吓眼	B445	舊時	B453
講到話……	B437	轉死性	B446		
講倒話	B438	擺明車馬	1908	〔乚起〕	
糟質	1893				

斷市	1928			〔、起〕	
斷估	1929				
斷尾	1930	二十畫		顧/因住	B457
斷窮根	B454			顧得頭來/嚟腳反筋	1962
繡花枕頭	1931	〔一起〕		爛口	1963
繞起	1932			爛市	1964
		露出馬腳	1947	爛尾	1965
				爛泥扶唔上壁	1966
十九畫		〔、起〕		爛笪笪	1967
				爛鬥爛	1968
〔一起〕		糯米屎窟	1948	爛船拆埋都有三斤釘	1969
		竈君上天	1949	爛頭蟀	1970
難兄難弟	1933				
顛倒是非	1934	〔丨起〕		二十二畫	
		蘇州屎	1950		
〔丿起〕		蘇州過後冇艇搭	1951	〔一起〕	
		鹹魚	1952		
穩打穩紮	1935	鹹魚番生	1953	攤直	1971
穩如鐵塔	1936	鹹濕	1954	攤凍至嚟食	1972
穩陣	1937	鹹龍	B456	攤攤腰	1973
臘起	1938	獻世	1955	擢皮宜	1974
		獻醜不如藏拙	1956	擢豆	1975
〔、起〕				擢命	1976
				擢朝唔得晚	1977
懶人多屎尿	1939	二十一畫		擢景	1978
懶佬工夫	1940			擢景定贈興/慶	1979
懵盛盛	1941	〔一起〕		擢嚟衰	1980
懵懵閉/懵閉閉	1942			擢嚟賤	1981
瀟湘	1943	趯更	1957	擢膽	1982
識人眉頭眼額	B455	霸槓	B458	聽價唔聽斗	1983
				聽話	B459
〔丨起〕		〔丿起〕		聽講話……	B460
				聽落有骨	B461
藤扔瓜，瓜扔藤	1944	鐵沙梨	1958		
羅通掃北	1945	鐵杵磨成針	1959	〔丿起〕	
		鐵嘴雞	1960		
〔冖起〕		鐸叔	1961	鑑硬	1984
				鑑粗	1985
關人	1946				

	〔、起〕		靈神不用多致燭,好鼓不用多槌	B466
讀壞詩書包壞腳	B462		蠱蟲師爺	B467
	〔丨起〕		〔丨起〕	
囉唆	1986		鹽倉土地	1997
囉囉攣	1987		躝屍趷路	1998
			躝屍	B468

二十三畫

二十五畫

攪手	1988			
攪出個大頭鬼/佛	1989		〔一起〕	
攪屎棍	1990			
攪風攪雨	B463		鬬	B469
			鬬氣	B470
	〔丨起〕		鬬嘥	B471
			鬬踩	B472
籠裏雞作反	1911			
			〔丿起〕	
	〔、起〕			
			籮底橙	1999
變掛	1992			

二十八畫

	〔丨起〕			
			〔一起〕	
齪牙嗻爪	1993			
囖命	1994		攮攮緊	2000
驚住會……	B464		攮唔番	2001
驚青	B465			
			〔、起〕	

二十四畫

		鑿大	2002
〔一起〕		
攬住一齊死	1995	
攬頭攬頸	1996	

條目首字拼音索引

A

a 啞 (a²) 亞 (a³)

啞仔食雲吞	1391
啞仔食黃連	1392
亞斗官	0818
亞昆洗鑊	0819
亞茂整餅	0820
亞單睇榜	0821
亞超着褲	0822
亞崩叫狗	0823
亞崩養狗	0824
亞崩劏羊	0825
亞駝〈馱〉行路	0826
亞駝〈馱〉賣蝦米	0827
亞蘭嫁亞瑞	0828
亞蘭賣豬	B149
亞聾送殯	0829
亞聾燒炮	0830
亞保亞勝	B150

ai 噯 (ai³) 鷖 (ɐi³)

噯通街	1676
鷖	B434

B

ba 巴 (ba¹) 把 (ba²) 霸

巴結	0380
巴結有錢佬好過拜靈菩薩	0381
巴閉	0382
巴渣	0383
把屁	0726
把鬼	0727
把火	B125
把幾火	B126
霸掕	B458

bai 擺 (bai²) 拜 (bai³) 跛 (bɐi¹) 弊 (bɐi⁶)

擺明車馬	1908
擺到明	1909
擺烏龍	1910
擺欵	1911
拜神唔見雞	1051
跛腳鷯哥自有飛來蜢	1557
弊家伙	B412

bark 百 (bak⁸) 白 (bak⁹)

百足咁多爪	0594
百忍成金	0595
白手興家	0469
白食	0470
白斬雞	0471
白鼻哥	0472
白撞	0473
白撞雨	0474
白霍	0475
白鴿眼	0476
白蟮上沙灘	0477

barn 班 (ban¹) 扮 (ban⁶) 辦 (ban⁶)

班馬	B211
扮豬食老虎	0730
扮嘢	0731
扮傻	0732
辦蟹	B427

bart 八 (bat⁸)

八十歲番頭嫁	0125
八掛	0126
八婆	0127
八仙過海	B022

bei 俾，比 (bei²) 鼻 (bei⁶)

俾人揸住痛腳	1154
俾心機	1155
俾個心你食都當狗肺	1156
俾個頭你	1157
俾人賣豬仔	1323
俾蕉皮/西瓜皮人踩	B216
比上不足比下有餘	B039
鼻屎好食鼻囊挖穿	B379

bin 扁 (bin²) 變 (bin³)

扁鼻佬戴眼鏡	1069

變掛		1992	本地薑唔辣	0391			
			本事	0392	bunk 崩 (bɐŋ¹)		
bing 兵 (biŋ¹)			半斤八両	0504			
			半天吊	0505	崩口人忌崩口碗		1396
兵來將擋水來土掩		0782	半吞半吐	0506			
			半夜三更	0507	**but 不 (bɐt⁷)**		
bit 別 (bit⁹)			半夜食黃瓜	0508			
			半信半疑	0509	不了了之		0232
別緻		0814	半途出家	0510	不打不相識		0233
			半桶水	0511	不打自招		0234
biu 標 (biu¹)					不是冤家不聚頭		0235
			bor 波 (bɔ¹)		不到黃河心不死		0236
標青		1771			不理三七二十一		0237
標參		1772	波羅雞	0928	不至於……		B037
標松柴		1773			不留		B038
			bou 煲 (bou¹) 補 (bou²)				
bock 駁,博 (bɔk³)			**報 (bou³) 步,暴 (bou⁶)**		**C**		
薄 (bɔk⁶)							
			煲冇米粥	1614			
駁嘴		1698	煲老藕	B343	**cha 差 (tsa¹) 查,茶 (tsa⁴)**		
搏一搏		1448	補鑊唔見枳	1529			
搏命		1449	報效	1442	差一皮		B232
搏亂		1450	步步為營	0810	差遲		B233
搏懵		1451	暴富難睇	1779	差唔多		1204
搏唔過		B303			查家宅		0986
薄皮		B439	**bow 包 (bau¹) 飽 (bau²)**		茶瓜送飯		1264
薄削		B440					
			包尾大番	0488	**chai 踩 (tsai²) 柴 (tsai⁴)**		
bong 幫 (bɔŋ¹)			包詏/拗頸	0489			
傍,磅 (bɔŋ⁶)			包撞板	0490	踩着芋莢都當蛇		1794
			飽死	1712	踩親……條尾		1795
幫理不幫親		1172	飽死荷蘭豆	B381	踩死蟻		1796
傍友		B308	飽唔死餓唔親	B380	柴哇哇		1095
磅水		B309			柴臺		1096
			bun 笨 (bɐn²) 笨 (bɐn⁶)				
boon 搬 (bun¹)					**chark 拆 (tsak⁸) 賊 (tsak⁹)**		
本 (bun²) 半 (bun³)			笨神都冇句真	1637			
			笨手笨腳	1336	拆穿西洋鏡		0860
搬弄是非		1597	笨頭笨腦	1337	賊公計狀元才		1662

條目拼音索引　　345

賊亞爸	1663	青磚沙梨	0846		
賊佬試砂煲	1664	青頭仔	0847	chit 切 (tsit³)	
賊眉賊眼	1665				
賊過興兵	1666	cheong 搶 (tsœŋ²)		切肉不離皮	0305
		唱 (tsœŋ³) 長 (tsœŋ⁴)			
charm 杉 (tsam³)		搶手	1595	chiu 朝，潮 (tsiu⁴)	
蠶 (tsam⁴)		搶眼	1596	另見 jiu 音	
杉木靈牌	0746	唱衰人	1395	朝上有人好到官	1433
蠶蟲師爺	B467	長痛不如短痛	0955	潮州音樂	1781
		長腳蜢	B146		
chart 擦 (tsat)				chock 斲 (tsɔk³)	
擦鞋	B444	chi 瓷，遲 (tsi⁴) 恃 (tsi⁵)		斲	B258
擦錯鞋	1870	瓷器棺材	1528	斲住度氣	B259
		遲到好過冇到	1863		
chau 抽 (tsɐu¹)		遲嚟先上岸	1864	choi 啋 (tsɔi¹) 財 (tsɔi⁴)	
臭，湊 (tsɐu³)		恃老賣老	1062	啋	1390
抽水	0865	恃熟賣熟	B194	財不可露眼	1212
抽佣	0866			財可通神	1213
抽後腳	0867	chin 千 (tsin¹) 前 (tsin⁴)		財到光棍手	1214
抽秤/挦	0868	千年道行一朝喪	0200		
抽絲剝繭	0869	千里送鵝毛物輕情義		chong 牀 (tsɔŋ⁴)	
臭檔	B217	重	0201		
湊啱	1347	千金小姐當作丫鬟賣	0202	牀下底破柴	0979
		千真萬確	0203		
che 車 (tsɛ¹) 扯 (tsɛ²)		千揀萬揀，揀着個爛		chor 初，搓 (tsɛ¹) 錯 (tsɔ³)	
		燈盞	0204	坐 (tsɔ⁵) 另見 jor 音	
車天車地	0719	前人種果後人收	1074		
扯皮條	0733	前世唔修	1075	初哥	0801
扯風波	0734	前世撈亂骨頭	1076	初歸心抱落地孩兒	0802
扯貓尾	0735	前言不對後語	B192	搓得圓㩒得扁	1605
扯頭纜	B129	前嗰排	B193	錯有錯着	1838
扯線	B130			錯蕩	1839
扯線公仔	B131	ching 清 (tsiŋ¹) 情 (tsiŋ⁴)		坐穩釣魚船	0790
		清官難審家庭事	B289		
cheng 青 (tsɛŋ¹)		情人眼裏出西施	1368	chou 粗 (tsou¹) 曹 (tsou⁴)	

粗人	1359	出術	0527	趁手	1445
粗口爛舌	1360	出符弗〈法〉	0528	陳皮	1406
粗心大意	1361	出處不如聚處	0529	陳村種	1407
粗手粗腳	1362	出頭	0530	塵埃落定	1734
粗枝大葉	1363	出貓	0531	塵氣	B387
粗重功夫	1364	出醜	0532		
粗茶淡飯	1365	出鵰哥	0533	chung 充,聰 (tsuŋ¹)	
粗製濫造	1366	出色	B084		
粗魯	1367	出身	B085	充大頭鬼	0660
曹操都有知心友,關公亦有對頭人	1274	出便	B086	聰明一世蠢鈍一時	1867
		出門	B087		
		出馬	B088	chut 七 (tsɐt⁷)	
chound 撐/蹭 (tsaŋ³) 倀 (tsaŋ⁴)		出嚟搵食	B089		
		出嚟撈	B090	七七八八	0086
		出爾反爾	B091	七老八十	0087
撐/蹭柏腳	1766	出山	B080	七國咁亂	0088
倀/撐雞	1139	出口成文/章	B081	七零八落	0089
倀/撐雞妹	1140	出年	B083	七嘴八舌	0090
				七竅生烟	0091
chow 炒 (tsau²)		chui 吹 (tsœy¹) 除,隨 (tsœy⁴)			
炒冷飯	0953			D	
		吹鬚轆眼	0815		
chuen 穿 (tsyn)		除笨有精	1266	da 打 (da²)	
		除褲放屁	1267		
穿煲/穿崩	B195	隨便	B430	打理	0414
穿櫃桶底	B196	隨便你/佢	B431	打牙祭	0415
		隨得……	B432	打牙骹	0416
chuet 出 (tsœt⁷)				打尖	0417
		chum 滲 (tsɐm³)		打同通	0418
出人頭地	0519			打赤肋/打大赤肋	0419
出手低	0520	滲氣	1717	打死不離親兄弟	0420
出手	B082			打死狗講價	0421
出名	0521	chun 親 (tsɐn¹) 趁 (tsɐn³) 陳,塵 (tsɐn⁴)		打如意算盤	0422
出息	0522			打地鋪	0423
出車	0523			打法功夫還鬼願	0424
出面	0524	親力親為	1851	打完齋唔要和尚	0425
出風頭	0525	親生仔不如近身錢	1852	打劫紅毛鬼,進貢佛蘭西	0426
出氣	0526	親自出馬	B426		

條目拼音索引　347

打斧頭	0427	大一歲長一智	0158	大模屍樣	0188
打個白鴿轉	0428	大人物	0159	大禍臨頭	0189
打倒褪	0429	大人大姐	B024	大搖大擺	0190
打特	0430	大小通吃	0160	大話夾好彩	0191
打敗仗	0431	大大話話	0161	大覺瞓	0192
打真軍	0432	大方	0162	大雞唔食細米	0193
打退堂鼓	0433	大王眼	0163	大碌藕	0194
打草驚蛇	0434	大石責死蟹	0164	大槽	0195
打荷包	0435	大好沉香當爛柴	0165	大驚小怪	0196
打得更多夜又長	0436	大好鮮花插在牛屎裏	0166	大纜絞唔埋	0197
打蛇隨棍上	0437	大行其道	0167	低頭切肉把眼看人	0755
打單	0438	大光燈	0168	低庄/莊	0756
打單泡	0439	大耳窿	0169	低低地躓舖	0757
打腳骨	0440	大泡和	0170	低聲下氣	0758
打店	B059	大枝嘢	0171	抵死	0876
打怗	B060	大事化小，小事化無	0172	抵到爛	0877
打底	B061	大花面搊眼淚	0173	抵得諗	0878
打橫嚟	0441	大花筒	0174	抵賴	0879
打輸數	0442	大食唔窮倒算窮	0175		
打邊爐同打屎窟	0443	大食細	0176	darm 眈，擔 (dam¹)	
打頭陣	0444	大食有指擬	B028	膽 (dam²)	
打鐵趁熱	0445	大丈夫能屈能伸	B025		
打錯主意	0446	大把	B026	眈天望地	1079
打錯算盤	0447	大命	B027	擔屎都唔偷食	1820
打瀉茶	0448	大拿拿	B029	擔戴	1821
打齋鶴	0449	大種乞兒	B030	膽大心細	1874
打雜	0450	大難友	B031	膽正命平	1875
打醒十二個精神	0451	大癲大廢	B032		
打爛砂盆問到篤	0452	大炮友	0177	darn 單 (dan¹) 蛋 (dan⁶)	
打爛齋砵	0453	大限難逃	0178		
打響頭炮	0454	大家心照	0179	單刀直入	1559
		大陣仗	0180	單手獨拳	1560
dai 帶，戴 (dai³)		大海撈針	0181	單身寡仔	1561
大 (dai⁶) 低 (dɐi¹)		大隻騾騾	0182	單料銅煲	1562
抵 (dɐi²)		大粒佬	0183	單單打打	1563
		大喊十	0184	單筷箸批豆腐	1564
帶花	1272	大番薯	0185	單丁	1565
帶挈	1273	大喉欖	0186	單係	B319
戴綠帽	B435	大諗頭	0187		

單眼仔睇榜	B320			定晒形	0942
蛋家婆打仔	1411	deng 掟 (dɛŋ³)		定過抬油	0943
蛋家婆打醮	1412				
蛋家婆摸蜆	1413	掟煲	1303	dip 疊 (dip⁹)	
蛋家雞	1414				
		di 啲 (di¹)		疊埋心水/緒	1685
darp 搭 (dap⁸) 踏 (dap⁹)					
		啲咁多	B291	dit 跌 (dit⁸)	
搭沉船	1601				
搭單	1602	dick 的 (dik⁷)		跌咗個橙執番個桔	1554
搭錯賊船	1603			跌倒揦番揸沙	1555
搭錯綫	1604	的起心肝	0926	跌眼鏡	1556
踏兩頭船	1801				
		dim 點 (dim²) 惦 (dim⁶)		diu 刁，丟 (diu¹)	
dau 兜 (dɐu¹) 鬭 (dɐu³)				吊 (diu³/⁶)	
豆，逗，荳 (dɐu⁶)		點算好	1899		
		惦過碌蔗	1369	刁/丟蠻	0130
兜住	B284			刁/丟眼角	0128
兜踭	1345	din 顛 (din¹) 電 (din⁶)		刁/丟喬扭擰	0129
兜篤將軍	1346			丟生晒	0622
鬭	B469	顛倒是非	1934	丟架	0623
鬭氣	B470	電燈膽	1588	丟疏咗	0624
鬭唯	B471			吊砂煲	0670
鬭踩	B472	ding 丁 (diŋ¹) 頂 (diŋ²)		吊起嚟賣	0671
豆腐刀	0718	定 (diŋ⁶)		吊靴鬼	0672
逗坭	1122			吊癮	0673
荳丁	B293	丁文食件	0085	吊吊扒	0669
		頂尖	1286		
de 嗲 (dɛ²)		頂包	1287	dock 度，鐸 (dɔk⁶)	
		頂頭上司	1288		
嗲吊	B359	頂檔	1289	度住屎窟裁褲	1068
		頂肚	B267	度水	B190
deck 趯 (dɛk³)		頂唔住	B268	鐸叔	1961
		頂唔順	B269		
趯更	1957	頂硬上	B270	dong 當 (dɔŋ¹) 蕩 (dɔŋ⁶)	
		頂頭陣	B271		
dei 地 (dei⁶)		頂頸	B272	當時得令	1677
		頂撞	B273	當堂	B371
地膽/地頭蟲	0601	頂籠	B274	當黑	B372

條目拼音索引 349

蕩失路　　　　　　　B428

dor 多 (dɔ¹) 墮 (dɔ⁶)

多個香爐多隻鬼　　　0641
墮角　　　　　　　　B415

**dou 倒, 賭, 搗 (dou²)
到 (dou³) 道 (dou⁶)**

倒吊冇滴墨水　　　　1146
倒吊荷包　　　　　　1147
倒米　　　　　　　　1148
倒米壽星　　　　　　1149
倒掛臘鴨　　　　　　1150
倒瀉籮蟹　　　　　　1151
倒瓢冬瓜　　　　　　1152
賭氣　　　　　　　　B429
搗亂　　　　　　　　1594
到家　　　　　　　　0843
到埗　　　　　　　　B151
到處楊梅一樣花　　　0844
到喉唔到肺　　　　　0845
道高一尺魔高一丈　　1636

duck 得 (dɐk⁷) 特 (dɐk⁹)

得上牀掀被冚　　　　1324
得寸進尺　　　　　　1325
得米　　　　　　　　1326
得把聲　　　　　　　1327
得些好意須回手　　　1328
得咗　　　　　　　　1329
得戚　　　　　　　　1330
得啖笑　　　　　　　1331
得棚牙　　　　　　　1332
得個吉　　　　　　　B283
得過且過　　　　　　1333
特登　　　　　　　　1128

**duen 斷 (dyn³) 另見
tuen 音端 (dyn¹)**

斷估　　　　　　　　1929
端端度度　　　　　　1728

dui 對 (dœy)

對牛彈琴　　　　　　1727

**duk 督 (duk⁷)
獨, 毒, 讀 (duk⁹)**

督背脊　　　　　　　1669
督眼督鼻　　　　　　1670
獨家村　　　　　　　1840
毒門毒　　　　　　　1004
讀壞詩書包壞腳　　　B462

**dum 扰 (dɐm²) 揼 (dɐm³)
踩 (dɐm⁶)**

扰心口　　　　　　　0744
揼堆　　　　　　　　1472
揼蹄踩爪　　　　　　1858

dun 拖 (dɐn³)

拖氣　　　　　　　　0728
拖蝦籠　　　　　　　0729

dung 東 (duŋ¹) 戙 (duŋ³)

東家唔打打西家　　　0849
東莞佬賣蓆　　　　　B148
戙起幡竿有鬼到　　　1211
戙起牀板　　　　　　B262

dunk 燈 (dɐŋ¹)

燈芯擰成鐵　　　　　1848

dup 耷 (dɐp⁷) 捧 (dɐp⁶)

耷尾　　　　　　　　1005
耷頭佬　　　　　　　1006
耷頭耷腦　　　　　　1007
掊金龜　　　　　　　1471

F

fa

花天酒地　　　　　　0960
花心　　　　　　　　0961
花心蘿蔔　　　　　　0962
花紅　　　　　　　　B169
花弗〈扶〉　　　　　0963
花多眼亂　　　　　　0964
花言巧語　　　　　　0965
花花公子　　　　　　0966
花花綠綠　　　　　　0967
花門　　　　　　　　0968
花靚仔　　　　　　　0969

fai 快 (fai³)

快刀斬亂麻　　　　　0710

**farn 幡, 翻, 返 (fan¹)
反 (fan²)**

幡竿燈籠　　　　　　1800
翻渣茶葉　　　　　　1922
翻抄　　　　　　　　B449
翻炒　　　　　　　　B450
翻閹　　　　　　　　B451
返去舊時嗰度　　　　0917

反口覆舌	0325	放下心頭大石	0936	風水佬呃你十年八年	
反斗	0326	放水	B167	唔呃得一世	1035
反骨	0327	放白鴿	0937	風水輪流轉	1036
反骨仔	0328	放屁	0938	風生水起	B180
反面	0329	放虎歸山	0939	風吹芫荽	1037
反轉豬肚就係屎	0330	放路溪錢	0940	風吹雞蛋殼	1038
反咬一啖	B050	放聲氣	0941	風流	1039
				風頭火勢	1040
				風頭躉	1041
				風擺柳	1042

fart 發 (fat⁸)

		for 火 (fɔ²)		奉旨「子」成婚	B147
發木獨	1566			鳳凰無寶不落	1708
發蟲	1567	火上加油	0332	逢場作興	B286
發市	1568	火遮眼	0333		
發吽哣	1569	火腿繩	0334		
發啷厲	1570	火頸	0335	fut 佛 (fɐt⁹)	
發盟憎	1571	火燒棺材	0336		
發噏風	1572	火燒旗竿	0337	佛口蛇心	B139
發窮惡	1573	火燒燈芯	0338	佛都有火	0754
發錢寒	1574	火麒麟	0339		
發爛渣	1575				
發吟發話	B321	fu 虎，苦 (fu²)		**G**	
發夢冇咁早	B322				
		虎父無犬子	0973	ga 加，家 (ga¹)	
		虎落平陽被犬欺	0974	架，嫁，駕 (ga³)	
fei 飛 (fei¹) 肥 (fei⁴)		虎頭蛇尾	0975		
		苦口婆心	1084	加料	B078
飛	B201	苦瓜乾噉嘅面口	B198	加埋	B079
飛擒大咬	1105	苦過弟弟	1085	加鹽加醋	0517
肥缺	0915			家有一老如有一寶	B227
肥肥白白	0916	fui 晦 (fui³)		家和萬事興	1187
				家家有本難唸的經	1188
fing 拎 (fiŋ⁶)		晦氣	B290	家醜不可外傳	1189
				架步	B203
拎頭	B142	fun 分 (fɐn¹) 粉 (fɐn²)		架勢	B204
				架樑	B205
fong 慌 (fɔŋ¹)		分甘同味	0331	嫁雞隨雞，嫁狗隨狗	B374
炕 (fɔŋ²) 放 (fɔŋ³)		粉板/牌字	B230	駕步	B416
慌失失	1638	fung 風 (fuŋ¹)			
桄榔樹	1115	奉，鳳(fuŋ⁶) 逢 (fuŋ⁴)			

gai 雞 (gɐi¹) 計 (gɐi³)

雞手鴨腳	1912
雞仔媒人	1913
雞咁腳	1914
雞春咁密都裸出仔	1915
雞春摸過都輕四両	1916
雞疴尿	1917
雞食放光蟲	1918
雞啄唔斷	1919
雞髀打人牙骹軟	1920
計正	B197

gark 隔 (gak⁸)

隔山買牛	1679
隔夜油炸鬼	1680
隔夜素馨釐戥秤	1681
隔岸觀火	1682
隔靴搯痕/癢	1683
隔牆有耳	1684
隔籬飯香	B373

garm 監 (gam¹) 鑑 (gam³)

監人食死貓	1705
監人賴厚	1706
鑑硬	1984
鑑粗	1985

garn 奸 (gan¹)

奸賴	0684

garp 夾 (gɐp³ / gap³)

夾手夾腳	B123
夾計	B124

夾份	0722

gau 狗 (gɐu²) 夠 (gɐu³) 舊 (gɐu⁶)

狗上瓦桁	0889
狗咬呂洞賓	0890
狗咬狗骨	0891
狗眼看人低	0892
夠皮	B285
舊底	B452
舊時	B453

gei 幾 (gei¹ / gei²)

幾乎	B332
幾係幾係，五郎救弟	B333
幾係㗎	B334
幾難先至……	B335
幾難至得……	B336
幾大就幾大	1585

geng 驚 (gɛŋ¹)

驚住會……	B464
驚青	B465

geong 姜 (gœŋ¹)

姜太公釣魚	1067
姜太公封神	B191

gi 嘰 (gi¹)

嘰嘰趷趷	B390

gin 見 (gin³)

見人講人話見鬼講鬼	

話	0803
見山就拜	0804
見地不平擔鎯鏟	0805
見步行步	0806
見屎窟郁唔見米白	0807
見高就拜見低就踩	0808
見過鬼就怕黑	0809

giu 撬 (giu⁶)

撬牆腳	1770

gock 各 (gɔk³)

各自為政	0651
各花落各眼	0652
各適其適	0653

goi 該 (gɔi¹)

該釘就釘該鐵就鐵	1628
該煨咯	1629
該死	B347

gon 乾 (gɔn¹) 趕 (gɔn²)

乾手淨腳	1309
乾時緊目	B275
乾塘	B276
趕到……絕	1693
趕狗入窮巷	B375
趕工	B376
趕唔切	B377
趕住投胎	B378

gong 江，缸 (gɔŋ¹) 講 (gɔŋ²)

江山易改品性難移	0654

江西佬舞死/打死馬騮	0655	姑勿論	B172	gung 工，公 (guŋ¹)	
缸瓦船打老虎	1046	古老石山	0407	工多藝熟	0154
講心啫	1884	古老當時興	0408	公死有肉食婆死有肉食	0322
講多錯多	1885	古/蠱惑	0409	公說公有理婆說婆有理	0323
講咗/過就算[數]	1886	古縮	0410		
講明就陳顯南	1887	鼓氣袋	1590	gunk 梗 (gɐŋ²)	
講來/嚟講去都係三幅被	1888	顧得頭來/嚟腳反筋	1962	梗板	1308
講起嚟一匹布咁長	1889	顧/因住	B457		
講得出就講	1890			gup 急 (gɐp⁷)	
講開又講	1891	guk 谷 (guk⁷)		急時抱佛腳	1047
講就易做就難	1892	谷住度氣	0778	急驚風遇着慢郎中	1048
講到話……	B437	谷起泡腮/顋	0779		
講倒話	B438			gut 趷	
		gum 今，金，甘，柑 (gɐm¹) 揿/撳 (gɐm⁶)		趷路	B260
gor 嗰 (gɔ²) 個 (gɔ³)		今時唔同往日一個酸梅兩個核	0324	H	
嗰頭近	1674	金盆洗手	0923		
嗰單嘢	1675	金睛火眼	0924	ha 下 (ha³)	
個蜆個肉	1153	甘心咯	0393		
		柑咁大個鼻	0996		
gou 高 (gou¹) 告 (gou³)		揿/撳地游水	1599	下扒輕輕	0155
高不成低不就	1201	揿/撳鵪鶉	1600	下馬威	0156
高竇	1202			下欄	0157
告枕頭狀	B133	gun 僅 (gɐn²) 靳 (gɐn³) 近 (gɐn⁶)		下氣	B033
gow 交 (gau¹) 攪 (gau²)		僅僅够（一）	1612	hai 喺 (hɐi²) 係 (hɐi⁶)	
交帶	0661	僅僅够……（二）	1613		
攪手	1988	靳度	1607	喺口唇邊	1538
攪出個大頭佛	1989	近山不可燒枉柴近河不可洗枉水	0918	喺乞兒兜掬飯食	1539
攪屎棍	1990	近水樓臺先得月	0919	喺孔夫子面前賣文章	1540
攪風攪雨	B363	近住城隍廟求炷好香	0920	喺門角落頭燒炮仗	1541
gu 姑 (gu¹) 古，鼓 (gu²) 顧 (gu³)		近官得力	0921	係咁意	1053
		近廚得食	0922	係威係勢	1054

hark 黑 (hak⁷) 客 (hak⁶)

黑口黑面	B317
客家佔地主	1071
客氣	1072

harm 鹹 (ham⁴)

鹹魚	1952
鹹魚番生	1953
鹹濕	1954
鹹龍	B456

harn 閒 (han⁴)

閒閒地	B331

harp 呷 (hap⁸)

呷醋	0970

hau 吼 (hɐu¹) 口 (hɐu²) 猴 (bɐu⁴)

吼	0812
吼斗	0813
口不對心	0215
口水多過茶	0216
口多多	0217
口垃濕	0218
口花花	0219
口是心非	0220
口甜舌滑	0221
口爽荷包垃	0222
口窒窒	0223
口疏疏	0224
口輕輕	0225
猴急	1506
猴擒	1507

hei 起 (hei²) 氣 (hei³)

起尾注	1109
起眼	1110
起痰	1111
起快（起筷）	B213
起飛腳	B214
氣羅氣喘	1160

heng 輕 (hɛŋ¹) 另見 hiŋ¹ 音

輕枷重罪	1699

heong 香 (bœŋ¹)

香爐墩	B185

him 險 (him²) 欠 (him³)

險過剃頭	1862
欠債還錢	B045

hin 牽 (hin¹) 獻 (hin³)

牽腸掛肚	B266
獻世	1955
獻醜不如藏拙	1956

hing 輕 (hiŋ¹) 另見 heng 音

輕枷重罪	1699
輕佻	1700
輕浮	1701

hoi 開 (hɔi¹) 海 (hɔi²) 害 (hɔi⁶)

開大價	1576
開口及着脷	1577
開心見誠	1578
開天索價落地還錢	1579
開門見山	1580
開明車馬	1581
開嗒……嗎槓	1582
開籠雀	1583
開刀	B323
開口埋口都話……	B324
開古	B325
開埋井俾人食水	B326
開夜車	B327
開通	B328
開荒牛	B329
開齋	B330
海上無魚蝦自大	1207
海水冲倒龍王廟	B226
害人終害己	1185
害死亞堅	1186

hon 看 (hɔn¹/³) 韓 (hɔn⁴)

看牛不及打馬草	1043
看風駛𥈭	1044
韓信點兵	B436

hong 炕 (hɔŋ³) 行 (hɔŋ⁴) 另見 hound 音

炕沙	B164
行行出狀元	0626

hor 可 (bɔ²) 河 (bɔ⁴)

可大可小	B057
河水不犯井水	0944

hou 好 (hou²/³)

好人事	0685
好人難做	0686
好女兩頭瞞	0687
好天搵埋落雨米	0688
好心地	B118
好心唔怕做	0689
好心唔得好報	0690
好心着雷殛	0691
好水有幾多朝	0692
好市	0693
好見飯	B119
好話唔好聽	B120
好事不出門壞事傳千里	0694
好物沉歸底	0695
好馬不食回頭草	0696
好佬怕爛佬	0697
好眉好貌生沙蝨	0698
好唱偈	0699
好唱橋	0700
好唱口	0702
好腳頭	0703
好漢不吃眼前虧	0704
好戲在後頭	0705
好聲好氣	0706
好食懶飛	0701

hound 行 (hɐŋ⁴)

行行企企	0625
行船好過灣	0627
行船爭解纜	0628
行得正企得正	0629
行運一條龍失運一條蟲	B107
行路打倒退	B108

how 敲 (hau¹) 姣 (hau⁴)

敲鼓邊	B385
姣屍扽篤	1106
姣婆遇着脂粉客	1107

hue 虛,墟 (hœy¹) 去 (hœy³)

虛浮	1537
墟冚	1755
去搵周公	0406

hum 扻/砍 (hɐm²) 含 (hɐm⁴) 冚 (hɐm⁶) 另見 kum 音

扻/砍頭埋牆	0881
含冤莫白	0749
含血噴人	0750
冚唪唥	B075

hun 恨 (hɐn⁶)

恨死隔籬	1066

hung 空,兇 (hʊŋ¹) 紅 (hʊŋ⁴)

空口講白話	0945
空心老倌	0946
兇神惡煞	B222
紅光滿面	B206
紅鬚軍師	B207

hunk 幸 (hɐŋ⁶) 行 (hɐŋ⁴) 見 hound 音

幸災樂禍	0848

hup 合 (hɐp⁶)

合晒心水	0642
合晒合尺	0643

J

ja 揸 (dʒa¹) 渣 (dʒa²) 詐 (dʒa³) 拃 (dʒa⁶)

揸大葵扇	1467
揸住雞毛當令箭	1468
揸頸就命	1469
揸鐵筆	B300
揸鑊鏟	B301
渣嘢	B311
詐型	1522
詐家〈假〉意	1523
詐[詐]諦[諦]	1524
詐嬌	1525
拃亂戈柄	0861

jai 仔 (dʒɐi²) 制,濟 (dʒɐi³)

仔大仔世界	0455
制得過	0888
制唔過	B157
濟軍	1883

jark 擇 (dʒak²)

擇使	1823

jarm 斬,嶄 (dʒam²)		借咗聾陳隻耳	1142	知其一不知其二	0912
		借花敬佛	1143	知無不言言無不盡	0913
斬腳趾避沙蟲	1292	借艇割禾	1144	知情識趣	0914
斬纜	B281	借題發揮	1145	滋油	1630
嶄吓眼	1857	藉/借啲意/藉/借頭		滋油淡定	1631
		藉/借路	1926	滋陰/滋微	1632
				指天篤地	0998
jarp 雜 (dʒap⁹)		jeck 隻 (dʒɛk⁸)		指手劃腳	0999
雜崩唥	1924			指住禿奴罵和尚	1000
		隻[眼]開隻[眼]閉	1138	指擬	1001
jart 札,紮 (dʒat⁸)				指冬瓜話葫蘆	B178
		jeng 精 (dʒɛŋ¹) 另見 jing 音		紙紮下扒	1269
札實	0300	正 (dʒɛŋ³) 另見 jing 音		至多唔係……	B101
紮炮	1293			至到……	B102
紮紮跳	1294	精人出口笨人出手	1729	至話	B103
		精到出骨	1731	至無	B104
jau 週 (dʒɐu¹)		精理一便	1732	自己工	0644
走,酒 (dʒou²) 就 (dʒɐu⁶)		精歸左	1733	自己身有屎	0645
		正斗/正嘢	0386	自打嘴巴	0646
週身刀	1501			自投羅網	0647
週身唔聚財	1502	jeong 將 (dʒœŋ¹)		自斟自酌	0648
走馬看花	0711			自梳	B112
走唔過……嘅手指罅	0712	將……一軍	1421		
走眼	0713	將/攞……教飛	1422	jick 直 (dʒik⁹)	
走路	0714	將心此己	1423		
走雞	0715	將佢拳頭抆佢嘴	1424	直腸直肚	0831
走歸左	0716	將計就計	1425	直程	0832
走寶	0717	將就	1426	直頭	0833
走趲	B121	將錯就錯	1427		
酒後吐真言	1190			jim 佔 (dʒim³)	
酒醉三分醒	1191	ji 支,知,滋 (dʒi¹)			
就嚟	B312	指,紙 (dʒi²) 至 (dʒi³)		佔上風	0766
就嚟……	B313	自 (dʒi⁶)		佔皮宜	0767
		支質	0301		
je 姐 (dʒɛ²) 借,藉 (dʒɛ³)		支整	0302	jin (dʒin⁶)	
姐	0980	知人口面不知心	0909		
姐手姐腳	0981	知子莫若父	0910	賤格	B413
借刀殺人	1141	知己知彼	0911		

jing 精，蒸 (dʒiŋ¹) 整 (dʒiŋ²) 正 (dʒiŋ³) 净，靜 (dʒiŋ⁶)

精打細算	1730
蒸生瓜	1268
整古做怪	1808
整色整水	1809
整定	1810
整蠱	1811
正話	B058
正一陳顯南	0385
正斗/正嘢	0386
淨係	B228
靜靜雞/靜雞雞	1815

jit 折 (dʒit⁸)

折墮	0745

jiu 招，朝 (dʒiu¹) 照 (dʒiu³)

招搖過市	0870
招搖撞騙	0871
朝種樹晚剝板	1434
照單執藥	1667
照板煮碗	1668

jock 作 (dʒɔk⁸) 鑿 (dʒɔk⁹)

作嘔	0759
作怪	0760
作狀	0761
作賤自己	0762
作死	0763
作威作福	0764
作賊心虛	0765
鑿大	2002

joi 在 (dʒɔi⁶)

在意	B092

jong 裝 (dʒɔŋ¹) 撞 (dʒɔŋ⁶)

裝假狗	1686
裝彈弓	1687
撞火	1756
撞手神	1757
撞死馬	1758
撞[到]正	1759
撞彩	1760
撞唔	1761
撞鬼	1762

jor 左 (dʒɔ²) 坐 (dʒɔ⁶)

左耳入右耳出	0388
左手嚟右手去	0389
左右做人難	0390
坐一望二	0788
坐定粒六	0789
坐食山崩	0791

jou 糟 (dʒou¹) 早 (dʒou²) 竈 (dʒou³) 做 (dʒou⁶)

糟質	1893
早知今日何必當初	0674
早知今日悔不當初	0675
早知燈係火唔使黑摸摸	0676
竈君上天	1949
做日和尚唸日經	1314
做世界	1315
做好做醜	1316
做咗鬼會迷人	1317
做鬼都唔靈	1318
做磨心	1319
做慣乞兒懶做官	1320
做薑唔辣做醋唔酸	1321
做醜人	1322
做咗人豬仔/俾人賣豬仔	1323

jound 爭 (dʒaŋ¹)

爭	B160
爭交	B161
爭住……	B162
爭住先	B163

jow 掉 (dʒau⁶) 找 (dʒau²)

掉忌	1300
找晦氣	B122

jue 朱，諸，豬 (dʒy¹) 煮 (dʒy²)

朱義盛	0640
諸事	1849
諸事理	1850
豬頭骨	1805
豬欄報數	1806
豬籠入水	1807
豬朋狗友	B423
豬嚟	B424
煮到嚟就食	1591
煮鬼	1592
煮重米	1593

juen 專 (dʒyn¹) 轉 (dʒyn²/³)

專登	1276
轉吓眼	B445

條目拼音索引　357

轉舦	1906
轉膊	1907
轉死性	B446

juk 足，竹 (dʒuk⁷)
捉 (dʒuk⁷/³) 俗 (dʒuk⁹)

足水	1314
竹紗	0649
竹織鴨	0650
捉到鹿都唔會脫角	1119
捉豬問地腳	1120
捉黃腳雞	1121
捉蟲入屎窟	B208
捉錯用神	B209
捉用神	1117
捉字蝨/虱	1118
俗骨	1052

jum 針，斟 (dʒɐm¹)
枕 (dʒɐm²)

針冇兩頭利	1165
針唔拮到肉唔知痛	1166
針鼻削鐵	1167
斟盤	1587
枕住	B152
枕長	B153

jun 真 (dʒɐn¹)

| 真金不怕洪爐火石獅 | |
| 　不怕雨滂沱 | 1126 |

jung 忠，終，舂 (dʒuŋ¹)
粽 (dʒuŋ³) 重 (dʒuŋ⁶)

忠忠直直終須乞食	0972
終須有日龍穿鳳	1416
舂瘟雞	1531
衆事莫理衆定莫企	1505
重係……	B187

jup 執 (dʒɐp⁷)

執人口水漪	1277
執二攤	1278
執手尾	1279
執死雞	1280
執到襪帶累身家	1281
執番條命	B277
執笠	1282
執輸	1283
執輸行頭慘過敗家	1284
執頭執尾	1285

jurk 着 (dʒœk⁸/⁹)

着起龍袍唔似太子	1519
着	1522
着數	1520
着緊	1521

K

ka 卡 (ka³)

| 卡罅 | B076 |

kai 契 (kɐi³)

| 契家佬 | 1002 |
| 契家婆 | 1003 |

kau 求 (kɐu⁴)

求人不如求己	0720
求求其其	0721
求先	B128

ke 騎 (kɛ⁴)

| 騎牛搵馬 | 1904 |
| 騎硫磺馬 | 1905 |

kei 棋 (kei⁴) 企 (kei⁵)

棋差一着	1475
棋高一着	1476
棋逢敵手	1477
企喺城樓睇馬打	B111

keong 強 (kœŋ⁴)

| 強中自有強中手 | 1584 |

king 傾 (kiŋ¹)

| 傾唔埋 | 1610 |
| 傾唔埋欄 | 1611 |

kit (kit⁸) 揭

| 揭盅 | 1463 |

kiu 繞 (kiu⁵)

| 繞起 | 1932 |

kow 靠 (kau³)

靠呃	1774
靠害	1775
靠諦	1776

kue 拘 (kœy¹)

拘執	0882

kum 冚 (kɐm²) 擒 (kɐm⁴)

冚席瞓石	0503
冚到密/實	B073
冚檔	B074
擒青/擒擒青	1769

kung 窮 (kuŋ⁴)

窮到燶	1787
窮寇莫追	1788

kwa 瓜 (gwa¹) 寡 (gwa²) 掛 (gwa³)

瓜老襯	0478
瓜直	0479
瓜柴	0480
瓜得	0481
寡母婆死仔	1718
寡母婆咁多心	1719
掛羊頭賣狗肉	1299
掛臘鴨	B280

kwai 歸 (gwɐi¹) 鬼 (gwɐi¹) 跪,櫃 (kwɐi⁶) 枴 (gwai²)

歸根到底	1921
鬼五馬六	1129
鬼打鬼	1130
鬼打都冇咁醒	1131
鬼拍後尾枕	1132
鬼馬	1133
鬼鬼鼠鼠〈祟祟〉	1134
鬼揞/搇眼	1135
鬼畫符	1136
鬼聲鬼氣	1137
鬼食泥噉聲	B218
鬼打你	B219
鬼猾	B220
跪地餵/餧豬乸	1678
櫃桶底穿	B447
拐帶	0883

kwarn 關 (gwan¹) 躓 (gwan³)

關人	1946
躓直	1925

kwart 刮 (gwat³)

刮龍	0904

kwick 虢 (gwik⁷)

虢礫嘩嘞	B401

kwong 光 (gwɔŋ¹)

光棍佬教仔	0677
光棍佬遇着冇皮柴	0678

kwoon 官 (gun¹)

官仔骨骨	0947
官字兩個口	0948
官官相衞	0949

kwor 過 (gwɔ³)

過口癮	1641
過水濕腳	1642
過夾吊頸	1643
過咗海就神仙	1644
過骨	1645
過氣老倌	1646
過得去	1647
過橋抽板	1648
過水	B355
過火	B356
過分	B357
過身	B358

kwun 均 (gwɐn¹) 滾 (gwɐn²)

均真	0748
滾水淥腳	1624
滾水淥豬腸	1625
滾友	B344
滾紅滾綠	B345

kwut 骨 (gwɐt⁷) 倔,掘 (gwɐt⁹)

骨子	1265
骨痹	B261
倔情	B215
掘尾龍	1295

L

La 抐 (la²) 另見 na 音

抐手唔成勢	1457
抐西	1458
抐起塊面	1459
抐屎上身	1460
抐高肚皮	1461
抐脷	1462

lai 拉，瓎 (lai¹) 賴 (lai³) 捩 (lɐi²)

拉人裙冚自己腳	0872
拉牛上樹	0873
拉柴	0874
拉埋天窗	0875
拉埋……落水	B155
拉頭纜	B156
瓎仔拉心肝瓎女拉內臟	1900
賴貓	B420
捩咁㶶	1297
捩橫折曲	1298

lark 勒，簕 (lak⁹)

勒時間	1290
勒實褲頭帶	1291
簕竇	1877

larm 攬 (lam²)

攬住一齊死	1995
攬頭攬頸	1996

larn 斕 (lan¹) 懶 (lan⁵) 爛 (lan⁶)

躝屍趷路	1998
躝屍	B468
懶人多屎尿	1939
懶佬工夫	1940
爛口	1963
爛市	1964
爛尾	1965
爛泥扶唔上壁	1966
爛笪笪	1967
爛鬥爛	1968
爛船拆埋都有三斤釘	1969
爛頭蟀	1970

larp 立，臘 (lap⁹)

立心不良	0499
立立亂	0500
立實心腸	0501
臘起	1938

lart 辣 (lat⁹) 捌，燩 (lat³)

辣撻人有辣撻福	1635
捌埋	B173
捌鼓邊	B174
燩起/着個火頭	1633

lau 摟，簍 (lɐu¹) 留 (lɐu⁴) 流 (lɐu⁴/⁶) 漏 (lɐu⁶) 劉 (lɐu⁴)

摟篩	1703
摟錯人皮	1704
簍休	1878
留得青山在哪怕冇柴燒	1169
留番啖氣暖吓肚	1170
留番嚟攝灶罅	1171
流口水	1209
流馬尿	1210
流嘢	B229
劉備借荊州	1777
漏氣	1715
漏罅	1716
漏口風	B384

le 咧 (lɛ⁵)

咧啡	1093

lei 匿 (lei¹) 利 (lei⁶)

匿埋	B264
利口便辭	0780
利口唔利腹	0781

leng 領 (lɛŋ⁵)

領嘢	1710

leong 量 (lœŋ⁴) 兩 (lœŋ⁵)

量地官	1558
兩公婆扒艇	0834
兩公婆見鬼	0835
兩個和尚擔水食，三個和尚冇水食	0836
兩睇	0837
兩頭唔到岸	0838
兩頭唔受中間受	0839
兩頭蛇	B145
兩騎牛	0840

li 喱 (li¹)

喱啦	1534

ling 鈴 (liŋ¹) 靈 (liŋ⁴)

鈴鈴鎈鎈都丟埋	1618
靈神不用多致燭，好鼓不用多槌	B446

lip 獵 (lip⁹)

獵狗終須山上喪	1923

liu 撩 (liu⁴)

撩是鬥非	1764	攞皮宜	1974	老鼠拉龜	0614
		攞豆	1975	老鼠跌落天秤	0615
lock 落 (lɔk⁷/⁸)		攞命	1976	老鼠貨	0616
		攞朝唔得晚	1977	老貓燒鬚	0617
落……棚牙	1649	攞景	1978	老奸巨猾	0618
落力	1650	攞景定贈興/慶	1979	老糠搾出油	0619
落手打三更	1651	攞嚟衰	1980	老竇都要多	0620
落住屎窟吊頸	1652	攞嚟賤	1981	老襯	0621
落……嘅面	B364	攞膽	1982	路數	B362
落手	B365	羅通掃北	1945	露出馬腳	1947
落手落腳	B366	籮底橙	1999		
落形	B367			**lound 冷 (laŋ⁵)**	
落井下石	B368	**lou 撈 (lou¹) 勞 (lou⁴)**			
落面	B369	**老 (lou⁵) 路，露 (lou⁶)**		冷手執個熱煎堆	0800
落嘴頭	B370				
落定	1653	撈膥水	1767	**low 朽 (lau²)**	
落雨賣風爐	1654	撈過界	1768		
落雨擔遮	1655	撈	B391	朽桍	0600
落狗屎	1656	撈女	B392		
落膈	1657	撈家	B393	**luen 亂 (lyn⁶)**	
		撈家仔	B394		
loi 來 (lɔi⁴)		撈家婆	B395	亂晒坑	1621
		撈起	B396	亂籠	1622
來者不善善者不來	0841	勞氣	1526		
來說是非者便是是非人	0842	勞嘈		**luk 六，陸 (luk⁹)**	
		老積	B106		
		老行	0603	六耳不同謀	0363
long 狼 (lɔŋ⁴)		老人成嫩仔	0604	六神無主	0364
		老人院都唔收	B105	六親不認	0365
狼過華秀隻狗	1163	老人精	0605	陸雲庭睇相	1408
狼	B223	老友記	0606		
狼忙	B224	老行尊	0607	**lum 臨 (lɐm⁴) 林 (lɐm⁶)**	
狼胎	B225	老定	0608		
		老虎唔發威當病貓	0609	臨天光瀨尿	1895
lor 囉 (lɔ¹) 攞 (lɔ²)		老虎頭上釘虱〈蝨〉		臨老學吹打	1896
羅，羅 (lɔ⁴)		乸	0610	臨時臨急	B433
		老虎乸	0611	林沈	B154
囉唆	1986	老契	0612		
囉囉攣	1987	老番睇榜	0613	**lun 論 (lœn⁶)**	

論盡		1784	唔怕官至怕管	1227	唔覺意		1260
			唔怪之得/唔怪得之	1228	唔止……重兼……		B239
lung 窿 (luŋ¹) 龍，籠			唔抵得瘝	1229	唔中用		B240
(luŋ⁴) 弄 (luŋ⁶)			唔抵得頸	1230	唔爭在……		B241
			唔忿氣	1231	唔爭氣		B242
隆隆嘩嘩		1894	唔使問亞貴	1232	唔好手腳		B243
龍牀唔似狗竇		1854	唔使指擬	1233	唔淨只		B244
龍游淺水遭蝦戲		1855	唔使畫公仔畫出腸	1234	唔似樣		B247
籠裏雞作反		1991	唔使擒擒青	1235	唔食得豬		B248
弄巧反拙		0723	唔使慌	B245	唔通……		B249
弄假成真		0724	唔使恨	B246	唔通氣		B250
			唔敢當	1236	唔計帶		B251
lut 甩 (lɐt⁷)			唔信命都信吓塊鏡	1237	唔話得		B252
			唔係路	1238	唔制得過		B253
甩身		0483	唔係猛龍唔過江，唔		唔恨		B254
甩拖		0484	係毒蛇唔打霧	1239	唔啱蕎		B255
甩底		0485	唔係是必要	B256			
甩繩馬騮		0486	唔係講玩	B257	ma 媽 (ma¹) 麻 (ma⁴)		
甩鬚		0487	唔咬弦	1240	馬 (ma⁵)		
			唔要斧頭唔得柄甩	1241			
M			唔食羊肉一身臊	1242	媽媽聲		1586
			唔埋得個鼻	1243	麻麻地		1370
m 唔 (m⁴)			唔理三七二十一	1244	麻雀雖小五臟俱全		1371
			唔理得咁多	1245	馬仔		B212
唔……罷就		B237	唔做中唔做保，唔做		馬死落地行		1112
唔一定		B238	媒人三代好	1246	馬屎憑官勢		1113
唔三唔四		1215	唔湯唔水	1247			
唔化		1216	唔睇白鴿都睇吓堆屎	1248	mai 埋 (mai⁴) 買 (mai⁵)		
唔在行		1217	唔睇僧面都睇吓佛面	1249	賣 (mai⁴) 迷 (mɐi⁴)		
唔打唔相識		1218	唔掅耕	1250	米，咪 (mɐi⁵)		
唔同牀唔知被爛		1219	唔經大腦	1251			
唔自在		1220	唔該借一借	1252	埋牙		1123
唔自量		1221	唔該借歪啲	1253	埋堆		1124
唔見得光		1222	唔嗅米氣	1254	埋櫃		B120
唔見棺材唔流眼淚		1223	唔算數	1255	買水咁嘅頭		1553
唔見鬼唔怕黑		1224	唔認賬/數	1256	買生不如買熟		B318
唔志在		1225	唔嗲唔吊	1257	賣大飽		1745
唔知個醜字點寫		1226	唔黏家	1258	賣口乖		1746
			唔覺眼	1259	賣仔莫摸頭		1747

條目拼音索引 *361*

賣花姑娘插竹葉	1748	未登天子位先置殺人刀	0397	門當户對	0976
賣花讚花香	1749			滿肚密圈	1714
賣面光	1750	未學行先學走	0398		
賣剩蔗	1751	未觀其人先觀其友	0399	mor 摩 (mɔ¹) 摸 (mɔ²)	
賣鹹酸菜	1752	沫水舂牆	0952		
迷頭迷腦	1182			摩囉差拜神	1791
米已成炊	0664	meng 命 (mɛŋ⁶)		摸門釘	1702
咪拘	1094				
		命根	0925	mou 無 (mou⁴) 冇 (mou⁵)	
mark 擘 (mak³) 墨 (mak⁶)					
		min 面 (min⁶)		無孔不入	1481
擘網巾	1901			無功不受祿	1482
墨七	B441	面左左	0990	無名小卒	1483
		面皮厚	0991	無私顯見私	1484
marn 攔 (man¹)		面紅	0992	無官一身輕	1485
另見 mound 音萬, 慢 (man⁶)		面紅面綠	0993	無事不登三寶殿	1486
		面憎心精	0994	無事生非	1487
				無事忙	1488
攔唔番	2001	ming 明 (miŋ⁴)		無事獻慇懃非奸即盜	1489
萬事俱備只欠東風	1658			無風三尺浪	1490
萬事起頭難	1659	明人不做暗事	0956	無風不起浪	1491
萬無一失	1660	明刀明槍	0957	無情白事	1492
萬變不離宗	1661	明火打劫	0958	無聊賴	1493
慢工出細貨	1735	明槍易擋暗箭難防	0959	無債一身輕	1494
				無嘩嘩	1495
mau 踎 (mɐu¹)		mock 剝 (mɔk⁷)		無端白事	1496
				無端端	1497
踎墩	1743	剝光豬	1334	無端端發達	1498
		剝花生	1335	無聲狗咬死人	1499
mei 眉 (mei⁴)				無氈無扇神仙難變	1500
未, 沬 (mei⁶)		mong 忙 (mɔŋ⁴)		冇一定	B040
		望 (mɔŋ⁶)		冇出息	B041
眉頭一皺計上心來	1103			冇行	B042
眉精眼企	1104	忙狼	0656	冇口齒	0246
未有來	B056	望天打掛	1353	冇天裝	0247
未見官先打三十大板	0394	望長條頸	1354	冇牙老虎	0248
未見其利先見其害	0395			冇癮	0249
未知心中事先聽口中言	0396	moon 門 (mun⁴) 滿 (mun⁵)		冇手尾	0250
				冇心肝	0251

條目拼音索引　363

冇心機	0252	冇趙雙	0287	文，聞(mɐn⁴)問(mɐn⁶)	
冇收	0253	冇頭烏蠅	0288	mun 蚊(mɐn¹)	
冇衣食	0254	冇聲氣	0289		
冇耳性	0255	冇檳榔唔噍得出汁	0290	蚊脾同牛脾	1261
冇尾飛鉈	0256	冇釐正經	0291	蚊都瞓	1262
冇走盞	0257	冇釐搭霎	0292	文雀	B052
冇走雞	0258	冇譜	0293	聞見棺材香	1744
冇兩句	0259	冇彎轉	B043	問師姑攞梳	1415
冇呢枝歌仔唱	0260				
冇咁大隻蛤乸隨街跳	0261	mound 掹(mɐŋ¹)		mung 懵(muŋ²)	
冇咁大隻鴿就唔好喊		盲(maŋ⁴)			
咁大聲	0262			懵盛盛	1941
冇咁大個頭就唔好戴		掹掹緊	2000	懵懵閉／懵閉閉	1942
咁大頂帽	0263	盲公布袋	0929		
冇咁大隻鴿就唔會喊		盲佬貼符	0930	munk 揈(mɐŋ¹)盟(mɐŋ⁴)	
咁大聲	0264	盲拳打死老師傅	0931		
冇咁大個頭就唔會戴		盲眼	0932	揈／搖衫尾	1822
咁大頂帽	0265	盲婆餵奶	0933	盟塞	1673
冇咁衰講到咁衰	0266	盲摸摸	0934		
冇料	0267	盲頭烏蠅	0935	mut 乜(mɐt⁷)	
冇家教	0268			勿，物，密(mɐt⁹)	
冇晒符	0269	mou 貓(mau¹)孟(mau⁴)			
冇晒符弗〈法〉	0270			乜都［係］假	0131
冇相干	0271	貓衣／兒毛	1836	勿歇	B046
冇紋路	0272	貓哭老鼠	1837	物以罕爲貴	0905
冇根兜	0273	孟	B441	物以類聚	0906
冇眼屎乾淨盲	0274			物輕情義重	0907
冇眼睇	0275	mui 妹(mui¹)		物離鄉貴人離鄉賤	0908
冇得斟	0276			密底算盤	1349
冇得諗	0277	妹仔大過主人婆	0982	密斟	1350
冇幾何	0278			密實姑娘假正經	1351
冇揸拿	0279	muk 木，沐(muk⁹)		密鑼緊鼓	1352
冇腰骨	0280				
冇哪更	0281	木口木面	0243	N	
冇哪嗱	0282	木匠擔枷	0244		
冇話好講	0283	木獨	0245	na 捹(na²)另見	
冇解	0284	沐恩弟子	0798	la 音拿(nɑ⁴)	
冇掩雞籠	0285				
冇樣叻	0286			捹起塊面	1459

nai 奶 (nai⁵) 泥 (nɐi⁴)

奶媽湊/抱仔	0518
泥水佬開門口	0950
泥菩薩過江	0951

narm 南 (nam⁴)

南嘸佬遇鬼迷	1008

narn 難 (nan⁴)

難兄難弟	1933

nau 嬲 (nɐu¹) 扭 (nɐu²)

嬲到彈起	1897
嬲爆爆	1898
扭六壬	0739
扭屎窟花	0740
扭計	0741
扭紋柴	0742
扭擰	0743

nei 你 (nei⁵)

你有半斤我有八両	0768
你有張良計我有過牆梯	0769
你有乾坤我有日月	0770
你/佢有寶呀	B134
你/佢真開胃	B135
你/佢想點就點	B136
你唔嫌我籮疏我唔嫌你米碎	0771
你做初一我做十五	0772
你敬我一尺我敬你一丈	0773
你嘅槓嘢我都有得出賣	0774
你走你嘅陽關路我過我嘅獨木橋	0775

ng 五 (ŋ⁵)

五行欠金	0303
五時花六時變	0304

nga 牙 (ŋa⁴) 瓦 (ŋa⁵) 椏 (ŋa⁶)

牙尖嘴利	0294
牙烟	0295
牙斬斬	0296
牙齒痕	0297
牙齒當金使	0298
牙擦擦	0299
瓦風領	0411
椏拃	1296

ngai 捱 (ŋai⁴) 呢 (ŋɐi¹) 蟻 (ŋɐi⁵)

捱世界	1304
捱更抵夜	1305
捱夜	1306
捱騾仔	1307
呢呢西西	1091
呢契爺咁呢	1092
蟻多摟死象	1927

ngark 逆 (ŋak⁹)

逆次次	B231

ngarm 啱 (ŋam¹)

啱心水「緒」	1393
啱啱	B292
啱啱好	1394

ngarn 眼 (ŋan⁵)

眼大睇過籠/界	1372
眼火爆	1373
眼中釘	1374
眼坦坦	1375
眼金金	1376
眼紅	1377
眼眉毛長過辮	1378
眼眉毛雕通瓏	1379
眼唔見爲伶俐	1380
眼斬斬	1381
眼淺	1382
眼冤	1383
眼睩睩	1384
眼闊肚窄	1385
眼噬噬	1386
眼掘掘	1387
眼矑矑	1388
眼濕濕	1389

ngau 牛 (ŋɐu⁴)

牛一	B044
牛皮燈籠	0316
牛死送牛喪	0317
牛唔飲水唔撳得牛頭低	0318
牛高馬大	0319
牛嚼牡丹	0320
牛頭唔對馬嘴	0321

(拿手好戲 1164; 拿拿聲 B221)

ngor 我 (ŋɔ⁵) 餓 (ŋɔ⁶)		寧犯天條莫犯衆憎	1720	O	
我都冇你咁好氣	0785	寧食開眉粥莫食愁眉飯	1721	ock 惡 (ɔk⁸)	
餓死老婆燻臭屋	1841	寧欺白鬚公莫欺鼻涕蟲	1722	惡人自有惡人磨	1428
餓狗搶屎	1842	零舍……	B340	惡人先告狀	1429
餓鬼投胎	1843			惡有惡報	1430
		noi 耐 (nɔi⁶)		惡到凸堆	1431
ngound 硬 (ŋaŋ⁶)				惡恐人知便是大惡	1432
硬晒舦	1441	耐不耐	0983	惡死能登	B296
		耐中	0984	惡揞揞	B297
ngow 咬 (ŋau⁵)		耐唔中	0985		
咬耳仔	1089	nor 糯 (nɔ⁶)		on 安 (ɔn¹)	
咬實牙齦	1090	糯米屎窟	1948	安份	0662
				安份守己	0663
ngum 唫 (ŋɐm⁴)		nou 腦 (nou⁵)			
唫沉	1532	腦囟/顖未生理	1623	or 疴，阿 (ɔ¹)	
				疴屎遞草紙	1205
ngun 奀 (ŋɐn¹) 踭 (ŋaŋ³) 韌 (ŋɐn⁶)		nui 女 (nœy⁵)		疴屎唔出賴地硬疴屎唔出賴風猛	1206
奀嫋鬼命	0725	女人纏腳佈	B036	阿箇	B170
踭踭腳	B388				
韌皮	B295	num 諗 (nɐm²) 燶 (nɐm⁴)		ow 拗 (au²/³)	
		諗縮數	1785	拗手瓜	0885
ngut 杌 (gɐt⁷)		諗爛心肝	1786	拗頸	0886
杌失	0747	燶善	B309		
				P	
nin 年 (nin⁴)		nun 撚 (nɐn²)		pa 扒 (pa⁴)	
年三十晚謝竈	0637	撚化	1763	扒灰	0412
年少老成	0638			扒逆水	0413
年晚煎堆	0639	nup 立 (nɐp⁶)			
ning 寧，零 (ŋiŋ⁴)		立糯	0502	pai 派 (pai¹/³) 批 (pɐi¹)	

派	1077	揼水	B397		**S**	
派行水/片	1078					
批中	B132	poon 拚 (pun²)		sa 沙,紗 (sa¹/⁶)		
		拚死無大害	0862	洒,耍 (sa²)		
park 拍 (pak⁸)		拚啤	0863			
拍心口	0853	拚爛	0864	沙煲刁眼角	0794	
拍成佢	0854			沙煲兄弟	0795	
拍烏蠅	0855	poot 潑 (put³)		沙塵	0796	
拍硬檔	0856			沙灣燈籠	0797	
拍膞頭	0857	潑冷水	1782	沙哩弄銃	0792	
拍薑咁拍	0858	潑辣	1783	沙沙滾	0793	
拍檔	0859			紗紙	B263	
		pound 棚 (paŋ⁴)		洒手擰頭	B189	
peck 劈/殛 (pɛk⁸)		棚尾拉箱	1474	耍太極	0987	
劈炮	1802			耍花槍	0988	
劈〈殛〉撚鑿	1803	pow 拋 (pau¹) 炮 (pau³)				
		拋生藕	0736	sai 曬 (sai¹) 曬 (sai³)		
pei 皮 (pei⁴)		拋浪頭	0737	西 (sɐi¹) 洗,使 (sɐi²)		
皮鞋筋	0498	拋頭露面	0738	世,細,勢 (sɐi³)		
		炮仗頸	1070	誓 (sɐi⁶)		
pin 偏 (pin¹) 片 (pin³)				曬	1737	
偏心	B282	pui 陪 (pui⁴)		曬心機	1738	
片面之詞	B051	陪太子讀書		曬鬼氣罅	1739	
				曬燈賣油	1740	
ping 平 (piŋ⁴)		pun 貧,頻 (pɐn⁴)		曬聲壞氣	1741	
平生不作虧心事半夜		貧不與富敵富不與官		曬撻	1742	
敲門也不驚	0387	爭	1343	曬命	1994	
		頻倫	1859	西南二伯父	0575	
pit 撇 (pit³)		頻倫唔得入城	1860	洗碗有相砍	1063	
撇脫/撇撇脫脫	1765	頻撲	1861	洗腳唔抹腳	1064	
				洗濕個頭	1065	
pock 撲 (pɔk³)		pung 碰 (puŋ³)		使銅銀夾大聲	0902	
		碰啱	1606	使頸	0903	
				世界仔	0404	
				世界輪流轉	0405	
				細心	1417	

細水長流	1418	閂後門	B202	手尾長	B048
細時偷雞大時偷牛	1419	散水	B305	手指罅疏	B049
細佬哥剃頭	1420	散更鑼	1446	守得雲開見月明	0657
勢利	B341	散檔	1447	秀才遇着兵	0751
誓神劈願	1696			秀才遇老虎	0752
誓願當食生菜	1697	sarp 霎 (sap³) 熠 (sap⁶)		秀才手巾	0753
				繡花枕頭	1931
sarm 三 (sam¹)		霎眼嬌	1816	瘦田冇人耕耕親有人爭	1792
		霎戀	1817	受人二分四	0893
三十六度板斧都出齊/埋	0134	熠熟狗頭	1789	受人錢財替人消災	0894
三十六着走爲上着	0135	sart 撒,殺 (sat⁸)		受硬唔受軟	0895
三九兩丁七	0136			受軟唔受硬	0896
三[九]唔識七	0137	撒賴	B398	受落	0897
三口兩脷	0138	撒/殺手鐧	B399	受唔住	0898
三心兩意	0139			受氣	0899
三不管	0140	sau 收,修,羞 (sɐu¹)		壽仔	1689
三水佬睇走馬燈	0141	手,守 (sɐu²)		壽星公吊頸	1690
三分顏色當大紅	0142	秀,繡,瘦 (sɐu³)		壽頭	1691
三句不離本行	0143	受,壽 (sɐu⁶)		壽頭壽腦	1692
三扒兩撥	0144				
三更窮,四更富	0145	收山	B117	se 蛇 (sɛ⁴)	
三長兩短	0146	收手	0707		
三枝櫃	0147	收檔	0708	蛇有蛇路鼠有鼠路	1399
三姑六婆	0148	收科	0709	蛇見硫磺	1400
三隻手	0149	修游	1158	蛇無頭不行	1401
三羣五隊	0150	修游淡定	1159	蛇鼠一窩	1402
三腳櫈	0151	羞家	B287	蛇頭鼠眼	1403
三歲定八十	0152	手瓜硬	0306		
三頭六臂	0153	手多多	0307	seck 錫 (sɛk³) 石 (sɛk⁶)	
		手忙腳亂	0308		
sarn 山,閂 (san¹)		手板係肉手背又係肉	0309	錫住	B425
散 (san³)		手急眼快	0310	石地堂鐵掃把	0400
		手氣	0311	石灰籮	0401
山人自有妙計	0211	手指拗出唔拗入	0312	石沉大海	0402
山大斬埋有柴	0212	手痕痕	0313	石罅米	0403
山水有相逢	B034	手搵口食	0314		
山高水低	0213	手緊	0315	sei 死 (sei²) 四 (sei³)	
山窮水盡	0214	手作仔	B047	另見 si 音	

死人尋舊路	0576	上樑唔正下樑歪	0230	食西北風	1013
死人燈籠	0577			食夾棍	1014
死口咬實	0578	si 思,私,師,施 (si¹)		食死貓	1015
死心不息	0579	屎 (si²) 四 (si³)		食咗人隻車	1016
死心塌地	0580	(參閱 sei 音) 市 (si⁵)		食咗人隻豬	B182
死牛一便頸	0581	士,是,事,豉 (si⁶)		食咗火藥	1017
死死地氣	0582			食枉米	1018
死有餘幸	0583	思思縮縮	B200	食拖鞋飯	1019
死估估	0584	私己	B140	食屎食着豆	1020
死性不改	0585	師姑	1168	食砒霜杜狗	1021
死咗條心	0586	施恩莫望報	1073	食得禾米多	1022
死唔眼閉	0587	屎氹關刀	1098	食得鹹就要抵得渴	B183
死冤	0588	屎急開坑	1099	食鹽多過食飯行橋多	
死蛇爛鱔	0589	屎橋	1100	過行路	1023
死慳死抵	0590	屎窟生瘡	1101	食塞米	1024
死難撐飯蓋	0591			食過夜粥	1025
死纏爛打	0592	四 (參閱 sei 音)		食過番尋味	1026
四方木	0515			食碗面反碗底	1027
四方辮頂	0516	市橋蠟燭	0512	食葱送飯	1028
四正	B077	士「事」急馬行田	0198	食飽無憂米	1029
		是必要	B199	食飽飯等屎疴	1030
seng 聲 (sɛŋ¹) 成 (sɛŋ⁴)		是非只爲多開口	1080	食豬血疴黑屎	1031
另見 sing 音		是非皆因强出頭	1081	食穀種	1032
		是非鬼/啄	1082	食軟飯	1033
聲大夾冇準	1868	是是但但	1083	食貓麵	1034
聲大夾惡	1869	事頭	B143	食君之祿擔君之憂	B181
成日	B137	事頭婆	B144	食齋不如講正話	B184
		事不關己不勞心	0850		
seong 相 (sœŋ¹)		事在人爲	0851	sin 先 (sin¹)	
想 (sœŋ²) 上 (sœŋ⁵ᐟ⁶)		事後孔明	0852	跣,煽 (sin³) 善 (sin⁶)	
		豉油撈飯	1270		
相見好同住難	0995			先入爲主	0631
相睇	B175	sick 識 (sik⁷) 食 (sik⁹)		先小人後君子	0632
想話……	B339			先下手爲强	0633
上天無路入地無門	0226	識人眉頭眼額	B455	先使未來錢	0634
上得山多終遇虎	0228	食七咁食	1009	先敬羅衣後敬人	0635
上當	0229	食人唔瞓骨	1010	先禮後兵	0636
上咗岸	B035	食少啖多覺瞓	1011	先排	B109
上氣唔接下氣	0227	食生菜咁食	1012	先斬後奏	B110

跌人	B361
煽風點火	B386
善財難捨冤枉甘心	1530
善靜	B310

sing 聲 (siŋ¹) 醒 (siŋ²) 成 (siŋ⁴) 另見 sing 音聲 (參閱 seng 音)

醒水	1835
醒	B417
醒目	B418
醒定啲	B419
成數	B138
成日	B137

sit 蝕 (sit⁹)

蝕底	1779

siu 消，燒，瀟 (siu¹) 小，少 (siu²) 笑 (siu³) 肇 (siu⁶)

消/宵夜	1203
燒冷竈	1844
燒到……嘓叠	1845
燒枱炮	1846
燒壞瓦	1847
瀟湘	1943
小心駛/使得萬年船	0205
小鬼唔見得大神	0206
小財唔出大財唔入	0207
小氣〈器〉	0208
小家種	0209
小意思	0210
少件膶	0368
少數怕長計	0369
笑到肚刺	1161

肇慶荷包	1736

sock 索，嗍 (sɔk³)

索油	1125
嗍氣	B360

song 爽 (sɔŋ²) 喪 (sɔŋ³)

爽手	1275
喪家狗	B302

sor 梳 (sɔ¹)

梳起	B265

sou 臊，蘇 (sou¹) 數 (sou³)

臊臊都係羊肉爛爛都係絲綢	1876
蘇州屎	1950
蘇州過後冇艇搭	1951
數還數路還路	1793

sound 生 (saŋ¹) 省，揎 (saŋ²)

生人勿近	0456
生人唔生膽	0457
生人霸死定	0458
生勾勾	0459
生仔都唔知仔心肝	0460
生白果	0461
生安白做	0462
生骨大頭菜	0463
生雞精	0464
生死有定	0465
生蝦咁跳	0466

生蟚貓入眼	0467
生蟲拐杖	0468
生水芋頭	B063
生息	B064
生色	B065
生步	B066
生晒	B067
……生晒	B068
生猛	B069
生鬼	B070
生番晒	B071
生曬	B072
省鏡	1097
揎	B298
揎牛黃	1470
揎到……鑠鑠睩	B299

sow 筲 (sau¹)

筲箕打水	1619
筲箕冚鬼一窩神	1620

suck 塞 (sɐk⁷)

塞古盟憎	1639
塞竇窿	1640

sue 輸 (sy¹) 鼠 (sy²) 樹 (sy⁶)

輸蝕	1818
鼠入嚟	1608
鼠嘢	1609
樹大有枯枝族大有乞兒	1824
樹大招風	1825
樹倒猢猻散	1826
樹高千丈落葉歸根	1827

suen 損 (syn²) 算 (syn³) 船 (syn⁴)		熟行	B408	神主牌都會郁	B234
		熟性	B409	神主牌都會擰轉面	B235
		熟落	B410	神前桔	B236
損手爛腳	1598			神不知鬼不覺	1055
算死草	1709	sum 心 (sɐm¹) 甚 (sɐm⁶)		神推鬼擰	1056
船到江心補漏遲	1338			神臺貓屎	1057
船到橋頭自然直	1339	心大心細	0340	神魂顛倒	1058
船頭慌鬼船尾慌賊	1340	心中有屎	0341	神憎鬼厭	1059
		心中有數	0342	神神化化	1060
sui 水 (sœy²) 誰 (sœy⁴)		心不在焉	0343	神神地	1061
		心甘命抵	0344		
水上扒龍船岸上人有眼	0370	心多多	0345	sung 鬆 (suŋ¹) 送 (suŋ³)	
		心安理得	0346		
水上扒龍船岸上夾死仔	0371	心灰意冷	0347	鬆毛鬆翼	B448
		心足	0348	送羊入虎口	1183
水瓜打狗	0372	心肝椗	0349	送佛送到西	1184
水汪汪	0373	心服口服	0350		
水浸眼眉	0374	心急	0351	sunk 生 (sɐŋ¹) 擤 (sɐŋ³) 生（見 sound 音）	
水鬼升城隍	0375	心思思	0352		
水過鴨背	0376	心神恍惚	0353		
水落石出	0377	心淡	0354	擤到骨罅都刺埋	1871
水溝油	0378	心都涼晒	0355	擤到樹葉都落埋	1872
水靜河飛	0379	心嘟嘟	0356	擤笨	1873
誰不知	B403	心煩	0357		
		心照不宣	0358	sup 濕 (sɐp¹) 十 (sɐp⁶)	
suk 叔，縮 (suk⁷) 熟 (suk⁹)		心嗰句口嗰句	0359		
		心領	0360	濕水棉胎	1879
		心酸	0361	濕水欖核	1880
叔姪縮室	0971	心亂如麻	0362	濕星	1881
縮沙	1902	心抱	B053	濕滯	1882
縮數	1903	心都實	B054	十人生九品	0074
縮骨	B442	甚至無……	B178	十三點	0075
縮頭龜	B443			十月芥菜	0076
熟人買破鑊	1790	sun 新，身 (sɐn¹) 神 (sɐn⁴/⁵)		十五個銅錢分兩份	0077
熟能生巧	B404			十五十六	B018
熟讀唐詩三百首唔會吟詩也會偷	B405			十年逢一閏	0078
		新屎坑三日香	1634	十年唔耕九年唔種	0079
熟客仔	B406	身在福中不知福	0783	十指孖埋	0080
熟檔	B407	身當命抵	0784	十拿九穩	0081

十隻手指有長短	0082	ta 他 (ta¹)		偷龍轉鳳	1311
十個甕缸九個蓋	0083			偷雞	1312
十割都未有一撇	0084	他他條條	0482	偷雞唔到蝕揸米	1313
				頭痛醫頭腳痛醫腳	1812
surn 笋 (sœn²) 信 (sœn³)		tai 睇 (tei²) 剃,替 (tei³)		頭頭碰着黑	1813
順 (sœn⁶)		提 (tei⁴)		頭髮尾浸浸涼	1814
				頭先	B421
笋嘢	1162	睇人口面	1542	頭路	B422
信邪	B186	睇小	B314		
順口	1508	睇化	1543	teck 踢 (tɛk³)	
順水人情	1509	睇水	1544		
順水推舟	1510	睇白……/睇死……	1545	踢寶	B414
順手	1511	睇穿	1546		
順手牽羊	1512	睇唔過眼	1547	teng 聽 (tɛŋ¹)	
順風駛哩	1513	睇差一皮	1548		
順得哥情失嫂意	1514	睇開啲嚹	1549	聽價唔聽斗	1983
順得「德」人	1515	睇起	1550	聽話	B459
順眼	1516	睇嚟湊	1551	聽講話……	B460
順喉	1517	睇衰	B315	聽落有骨	B461
順攤	1518	睇餸食飯睇蟲南無			
		〈謨〉	1552	tim 添 (tim¹)	
sut 失,膝,虱 (sɐt⁷)		剃眼眉	1200		
實 (sɐt⁹)		替死鬼	1435	添食	B288
		提心吊膽	1464		
失失慌	0491			tin 天 (tin¹) 田 (tin⁴)	
失匙夾萬	0492	tarm 貪 (tam¹)			
失威	0493			天下烏鴉一樣黑	0238
失魂	B062	"貪"字變個"貧"	1341	天無絕人之路	0239
失魂魚	0494	貪得無厭	1342	天堂有路你不走地獄	
失魂落魄	0495			無門闖進來	0240
失驚無神	0496	tarn 攤 (tan¹)		天跌落嚟當被冚	0241
膝頭哥擤眼淚	1780			天網恢恢疏而不漏	0242
虱乸都要擔枷	1778	攤直	1971	田雞東	0513
實牙實齒	1723	攤凍至嚟食	1972	田雞過河	0514
實食冇黐牙	1724	攤攤腰	1973		
實鼓實鑿	1725			tip 貼 (tip⁸)	
		tau 偷 (tɐu¹) 頭 (tɐu⁴)			
				貼錯門神	1535
T		偷偷摸摸	1310	貼錢買難受	1536

tit 鐵 (tit⁸)

鐵沙梨	1958
鐵杵磨成針	1959
鐵嘴雞	1960

tiu 挑 (tiu¹) 跳 (tiu³)

挑蟲入屎窟	0997
跳皮（調皮）	B363

tock 托 (tɔk³)

托大腳	0596
托水龍	0597
托手踭	0598
托塔都應承	0599

toi 抬 (tɔi⁴)

抬棺材甩褲	0884

tong 劏 (tɔŋ¹) 塘，糖 (tɔŋ⁴)

劏死牛	1797
劏光豬	1798
塘水滾塘魚	B337
塘底特	B338
塘邊鶴	1589
糖黏豆	1853

tor 拖 (tɔ¹) 陀 (tɔ⁴)

拖泥帶水	0880
陀衰家	0977

tou 土 (tou²) 淘 (tou³) 肚 (tou⁵)

土鯪魚	0199
淘古井	1358
肚皮打鼓	0786
肚裏蟲	0787

tuem 斷 (tyn⁵)

斷市	1928
斷尾	1930
斷窮根	B454

tui 推 (tœy¹)

推三推四	1301
推莊	1302
推心置腹	B278
推波助瀾	B279

tum 諗 (tɐm³)

諗鬼食豆腐	0799

tun 吞 (tɐn¹) 褪 (tɐn³)

吞吞吐吐	0776
吞口水養命	0777
褪舦	1856

tung 通 (tɐŋ¹) 同，桐，銅 (tɐŋ⁴)

通天	B294
通水	1409
通氣	1410
同人唔同命同遮唔同柄	0665
同一個鼻哥窿出氣	B113
同……有路	B114
同……行得好埋	B115
同……行埋咗	B116
同行如敵國	0666
同撈同煲	0667
同檯食飯各自修行	0668
桐油埕	1114
銅銀買病豬	1711

tunk 藤 (tɐŋ⁴)

藤扔瓜瓜扔藤	1944

U

uk 屋 (uk⁷)

屋漏更兼逢夜雨	1102

um 揞/掩 (ɐm²) 暗 (ɐm³) mu

揞/掩住良心	1465
揞/掩住嘴嚛笑	1466
暗啞抵	1672

W

wa 嘩 (wa¹) 挖 (wa²) 話 (wa⁶)

嘩鬼	B389
挖爛塊面	1473
話咁埋	1626
話晒事	1627
話名係……	B348
話唔定……	B349
話落	B350
……（某人）話事偈	B351

……（某人）話齋 B354
話極都係…… B352
話實 B353

wai 爲 (wɐi⁴/⁶)

爲意 B307
爲口奔馳 1503
爲食鬼 1504
爲食貓 B306

warn 患 (wan⁶)

患得患失 1397
患難見真情 1398

wart 滑 (wat⁹)

滑頭 B346

wong 枉 (wɔŋ²) 黃，皇 (wɔŋ⁴)

枉作小人 0887
黃皮樹鷯哥 1436
黃泡髧熟 1437
黃馬褂 1438
黃綠醫生 1439
黃腫腳 1440
黃面婆 B304
皇天不負有/苦心人 1049
皇帝唔急太監急 1050
皇帝女 B188

wor 禾，和 (wɔ⁴) 喎 (wɔ⁵)

禾稈冚珍珠 0497
和尚食狗肉 B159

和咪 0900
和邁 0901
喝咗 1533

wound 橫 (waŋ⁴)

橫九怗十 1828
橫手 1829
橫行霸道 1830
橫唔 1831
橫唔都係一樣 1832
橫衝直撞 1833
橫蠻無理 1834

wu 烏 (wu¹) 胡 (wu⁴)

烏卒卒 1173
烏狗得食白狗當災 1174
烏哩馬扠 1175
烏哩單刀 1176
烏啄啄 1177
烏蛇蛇 1178
烏煙瘴氣 1179
烏龍 1180
烏蠅搜馬尾 1181
胡帝胡天/胡天胡帝 B176
胡胡混混 B177

wui 會 (wui⁶)

會錯意 1615

wun 瘟 (wɐn¹) 穩，搵 (wɐn²) 暈 (wɐn⁴) 混 (wɐn⁶)

瘟瘟沌沌 1726
穩打穩紮 1935
穩如鐵塔 1936

穩陣 1937
搵……（人）過橋 1452
搵老襯 1453
搵丁 1454
搵笨 1455
搵得嚟使得去 1456
暈得一陣 1671
魂不守舍 1694
魂不附體 1695
混水摸魚 1355
混吉 1356
混混/渾渾噩噩 1357

wut 屈 (wɐt⁷) 核 (wɐt⁹)

屈質 0978
屈尾十 B171
核突 1116

Y

ya 也 (ja⁶)

也文也武 0231

yau 油，遊 (jɐu⁴) 有 (jɐu⁵) 又 (jɐu⁶)

油瓶 B166
遊車河 B342
有一利必有一害 0534
有乜冬瓜豆腐 0535
有人辭官歸故里有人
　漏夜趕科場 0536
有口無心 0537
有口難言 0538
有仇不報非君子 0539
有分有寸 0540

有分數	0541	有毛有翼	B094	二四六八單	B020
有心唔怕遲十月都係		有行	B095	二叔公割禾	0073
拜年時	0542	有尾學人跳冇毛又學		易過借火	0954
有心無力	0543	人跳	B096	異相	B316
有心裝冇心人	0544	有排	B097		
有皮宜唔使使頸	0545	有幾何呀	B098	yim 腌 (jim¹)	
有奶便是娘	0546	有聲氣	B099	悶，鹽，嫌 (jim⁴)	
有自唔在揾苦嚟辛	0547	有蹺蹊	B100		
有名無實	0548	又姣又怕痛見人生仔		腌尖	1478
有屁就放	0549	又眼紅	0132	腌悶	1479
有咗	0550	又試	0133	腌尖腥悶	1480
有兩吓散手	0551			閻羅王揸攤	1865
有事鍾無艷無事夏迎		ye 夜 (jɛ⁶)		閻羅王嫁女	1866
春	0552			鹽倉土地	1997
有其父必有其子	0553	夜長夢多	B164	嫌棄	1688
招架之功無還手之力	0554	夜遊神	B165		
有咁啱得咁蹺	0555			yin 烟，胭 (jin¹)	
有風駛盡𢃇	0556	yeong 羊 (jœŋ⁴)		現 (jin⁶)	
有眼不識泰山	0557				
有眼無珠	0558	羊毛出在羊身上	0658	烟〈鷰〉靭	1208
有酒有肉多兄弟	0559	羊牯	0659	胭脂馬	1127
有得震有得瞓	0560			現眼報	1271
有得諗	0561	yi 依，伊，𪘓 (ji¹)			
有景轟	0562	而，移，疑 (ji⁴)		ying 英 (jiŋ¹) 認 (jiŋ⁶)	
有爺生冇乸教	0563	耳 (ji⁵) 二，易，異 (ji⁶)			
有意栽花花不發，無				英雄重英雄	1087
心插柳柳成蔭	0564	依挹/依依挹挹	0927	英雄莫問出處	1088
有福同享有禍同當	0565	依時依候	B158	認低威	1713
有碗話碗有碟話碟	0566	伊撈七	0630	認數	B382
有錢使得鬼推磨	0567	𪘓牙崍爪	1993	認賬	B383
有錢佬話事	0568	而依哦哦	0602		
有錢就身痕	0569	移磉就船	1344	yit 熱 (jit⁹)	
有頭毛冇人想生鬎鬁	0570	疑心生暗鬼	1707		
有頭有面	0571	耳邊風	0593	熱氣飯	1753
有頭威冇尾陣	0572	二一添作五	0069	熱煮不能熱食	1754
有麝自然香	0573	二口六面	0070		
有難仔唔管管牙		二仔底	0071	yiu 抁 (jiu¹) 要 (jiu³)	
「麻」鷹	0574	二世祖	0072		
有人做咗手腳	B093	二打六	B019	抁心抁肺	B127

要風得風要雨得雨	0989	yun 因，恩 (jɐn¹) 忍 (jɐn²) 寅，人 (jɐn⁴) 引 (jɐn⁵)		人窮志不窮	0120
				人窮志短	0121
yuen 冤 (jyn¹) 怨 (jyn³) 原 (jyn⁴) 轅 (jyn⁵)				人講你又講	0122
				寅食卯糧	1348
		因小失大	0679	引狼入屋拉雞仔	0384
冤有頭債有主	1192	因/顧住	B457		
冤屈	1193	恩將仇報	1263	yung 融 (juŋ⁴)	
冤枉嚟瘟疫去	1194	忍唔住	0816		
冤家	1195	忍無可忍	0817	融洽	1804
冤家宜解不宜結	1196	人一世物一世	0092		
冤家路窄	1197	人山人海	0093	yup 入 (jɐp⁹)	
冤豬頭都有盟鼻菩薩	1198	人比人比死人	0094		
冤孽	1199	人心不足蛇吞象	0095	入境問禁	0123
怨命	1045	人心肉做	0096	入埋……嘅數	B023
原封不動	1108	人心隔肚皮	0097	入鄉隨俗出水隨灣	0124
軟皮蛇	1819	人生路不熟	0098		
		人在人情在	0099	yurk 若 (jœk⁹)	
yuet 越 (jyt⁹)		人有三衰六旺	0100		
		人有三急	0101	若要人不知除非己莫 為	1086
越揀越出屎	1443	人有失手馬有失蹄	0102		
越窮越見鬼肚餓打瀉 米	1444	人同此心心同此理	0103	yurn 潤 (jœn⁶)	
		人多手腳亂	0104		
		人多熠狗唔炝	B021	潤	B402
yuk 肉 (juk⁹)		人多好做作	0105		
		人老心不老	0106	yut 一 (jɐt⁷) 日 (jɐt⁹)	
肉刺	0680	人老精鬼老靈	0107		
肉酸	0681	人爭一口氣佛爭一爐 香	0108	一人計短二人計長	0001
肉隨砧板上	0682			一人做事一人當	0002
肉緊	0683	人怕出名豬怕壯	0109	一人得道雞犬升天	0003
		人要衣裝佛要金裝	0110	一了百了	0004
yum 陰 (jɐm¹) 飲 (jɐm²) 吟 (jɐm⁴)		人急智生	0111	一刀兩斷	0005
		人面獸心	0112	一山不能藏二虎	0006
		人情世故	0113	一口咬定/實	0007
		人情物理	0114	一子錯滿盤皆落索	0008
陰濕	1405	人細鬼大	0115	一弓射兩箭	0009
飲咗門官茶	1616	人望高處水往低流	0116	一不做二不休	0010
飲頭啖湯	1617	人渣	0117	一手一腳	0011
吟詩都吟唔甩	0811	人無千日好	0118	一天光晒	0012
		人算不如天算	0119	一生兒女債半世老婆 奴	0013

一件還一件	0014	一時唔偷雞做父老/		日慳夜慳唔够老公一	
一死了之	0015	保長	B010	舖攤	0367
一次生兩次熟	0016	一家皮宜兩家着數	0038		
一字咁淺	0017	一家唔知一家事	0039		
一竹篙打死一船人	0018	一個做好一個做醜	0040		
一言爲定	0019	一個够本兩個有利	0041		
一言難盡	0020	一個餅印噉	0042		
一言驚醒夢中人	B007	一唊沙糖一唊屎	0043		
一五一十	B001	一部通書睇到老	0044		
一本萬利	B002	一條鎖匙唔聞聲兩條			
一向	B003	鎖匙冷冷聲	0045		
一次過	B004	一眼關七	0046		
一把火	B005	一場歡喜一場空	0047		
一身蟻	0021	一朝天子一朝臣	0048		
一沉百踩	0022	一筆勾銷	0049		
一波三折	0023	一筆還一筆	0050		
一波未平一波又起	0024	一傳十十傳百	0051		
一物治一物糯米治木		一網打盡	0052		
蝨	0025	一腳牛屎	0053		
一息間	B008	一腳踢	0054		
一枝公	0026	一腳踏兩船	0055		
一面屁	0027	一模一樣	0056		
一面之詞	B006	一碌木噉	0057		
一哥	0028	一樣米養百樣人	0058		
一隻乙噉	0029	一輪嘴	0059		
一隻手掌拍唔響	0030	一磚豆腐想升仙	0060		
一隻屐噉	0031	一擔擔	0061		
一陣間	0032	一龍去二龍追	B016		
一陣陣	B103	一雞死一雞鳴	B017		
一理通百理明	0033	一頭霧水	0062		
一氣	B011	一講曹操曹操就到	0063		
一就一二就二	B012	一蟹不如一蟹	0064		
一坺迾	B014	一嚿飯噉	0065		
一箸夾中	B015	一鑊泡	0066		
一動不如一靜	0034	一鑊撟起	0067		
一餇都冇	0035	一鑊熟	0068		
一清二楚	0036	日久見人心	B055		
一時一樣	0037	日頭唔好講人夜晚唔			
一時時	B009	好講神	0366		

編 後 記

　　這本書的收錄範圍，只限於廣東口頭俚語及歇後語，連同補遺共收錄條目二仟四佰多條。

　　用英文對應詞翻譯廣東口語，確是不容易的工作。有些廣東俚語，根本沒法子在英文詞彙中找出有關連意義的對應詞。同時，不少俚語常因上下文及語氣不同，而意義亦隨之變化。有些俚語更經常有同一俚語，意義大異；又或同一意義，而俚語不同的現象，處理十分困難。廣州人有句話說 "小功夫，大行器"（siu² guŋ¹ fú, dai⁶ hɐŋ⁴ hei⁴ — Do a small job with the Herculean labours. — ）。對於編譯這本書而言，真是一點也沒錯，不善不盡的地方，希望前輩及讀者原諒及指正。

　　本書之所以附有補遺，實在是無可奈何。在脫稿後不久，前澳門嶺英中學及蔡高中學校長羅作祥先生知我着手編譯本書，他老人家不惜以杖朝之年，竟遠道枉顧，憑他多年教授英文的經驗，給我指點，並贈我一叠剪報及一份他從記憶中列出的俚語，不少是我所未收錄的。由於不忍捨割，我又參考有關書籍增添了一些，為避免重新編號的麻煩，這樣便成了補遺了。

　　編寫過程中，曾參攷下列各書，這裏衷心地向各有關出版社及作者致以謝意。

1. 漢英詞典　　　北京外國語學院英語系編寫組編　　　商務印書館
2. 漢英對照成語詞典　　陳永禎、陳善慈編著　　　商務印書館
3. 廣州話方言詞典　　　饒秉才、歐陽覺亞、周無忌編著　商務印書館
4. 普通話、粵音中華新字典　　　　　　　　　　　　中華書局
5. 粵音韻彙　　　　黃錫凌　　　　　　　　　　　　中華書局
6. 新英漢詞典　　　新英漢詞典編寫組　　　　　　　三聯書店

7. 廣州話、普通話口詞對譯手冊　　曾子凡　　　　　　　三聯書店
8. 麥氏漢英大辭典　　R. H. Mathews　　Harvard University Press
9. 英語動詞成語詞典　　〔英〕弗雷德里 T. 伍德　　北京出版社
10. 英漢習語文學大辭典　　　　　　　　　　　　　　建文書局
11. American Slang Dictionary　　（手頭存書殘缺不完，無從知編者及出版社）

　　最後要提的，便是承蒙商務印書館羅志雄先生花了近半年時間審閱本書，並且在定稿後，更不厭其煩地加以訂正，俾益本書不少，謹此向他表示謝忱。

　　　　　　　　　　　　　　　　編譯者謹記於一九八七年四月廿日